Women And Health:

THE POLITICS OF SEX
IN MEDICINE

Edited by Elizabeth Fee

POLICY,
POLITICS,
HEALTH AND
MEDICINE
Series

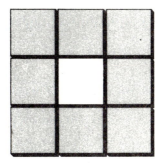

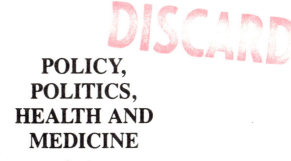

Baywood Publishing Company, Inc.

Farmingdale, N.Y.   11735

Library of Congress Catalog Card Number: 82-6726

ISBN: 0-89503-034-9

© 1983, Baywood Publishing Company, Inc.

Library of Congress Cataloging in Publication Data
Main entry under title:
Women and health.
(Policy, politics, health, and medicine series ; 4) Includes
bibliographical references.
1. Women's health services. 2. Women in medicine. I. Fee,
Elizabeth. II. Series. [DNLM: 1. Women – Collected works. 2. Health
manpower – Collected works. 3. Women's rights – Collected works.
4. Family planning – Collected works. 5. Iatrogenic disease – Collected
works. HQ 1233 W872]
RA564.85.W655   362.1'088042   82-6726
ISBN 0-89503-034-9   AACR2

Women And Health:
THE POLITICS OF SEX IN MEDICINE
Edited by Elizabeth Fee

PREFACE

The broadly defined topic of "women and health" covers a great diversity of issues and methods of analysis. The essays in this volume represent that diversity; several of the papers seek to apply Marxist methods of analysis to the issues of the women's health movement, while others approach the issues from the more familiar framework of social science research. All the papers are reprinted from the *International Journal of Health Services* with the intention of making them more readily available to scholars, activists and all those concerned with the relationship of sexual politics to health and the medical care system.

This collection, of course, does not cover all dimensions of the topic. It does, however, provide discussions of a number of important specific issues of the women's health movement, including childbirth, birth control, iatrogenic disease, and wife battering. In addition, there are more general analyses of the place of women within the health labor force and the relationship between health and women's employment. Finally, there are discussions of the ways in which medical and scientific knowledge reproduce and reinforce sexual inequality.

This inclusion of a variety of issues and methods of analysis is deliberate; the volume is intended to stimulate debate and dialogue within the different currents of the women's movement. In the first essay, I have tried to outline the main positions within the feminist analysis of health and medicine, showing the differences between the liberal, radical and Marxist approaches. This article can be read as an introduction to feminist theory and as an implicit critique of the liberal and radical positions; it argues that the theoretical development of both Marxism and radical feminism will be aided to the extent that each can benefit from the insights of the other. Subsequent essays suggest that progress is being made in this direction and that the theoretical explorations now underway increasingly will help us understand the politics of gender in the realm of medical science and practice.

How does medicine deal with the female body? The physiology of the female body is known and managed by a predominantly male medical profession; women are alienated from their bodies through the current structure of medical knowledge and practice. Despite our cultural obsession with the female body as a sexual object, the female sexual organs are mysterious to most women. When the radical women's health movement began self-examinations in self-help groups and women's clinics, many women saw the interior of the vagina and the cervix for the first time. Women were encouraged to learn more about their bodies; they began to invade the professional territory of the gynecologist. Women were arrested for practicing medicine without a

7

license as they openly questioned professional control and sought to recover the knowledge of their own bodies.

Childbirth is an obvious example of the way a woman can become alienated from her body as a result of professional control. The control of the physician who "delivers" the baby and the use of complex technology to monitor the birth process make women the passive objects of their labor. Women are further removed from conscious participation as the subjects of the birthing process by the widespread use of drugs and Cesarean sections. Women have struggled to regain a measure of control over childbirth through the movement for natural births. In this volume, Rindfuss, Ladinsky, Coppock, Marshall and Macpherson show that human birth—a preeminently natural process—is often and perhaps routinely managed for the convenience of physicians. They warn that this management of the birth process poses health risks for both mother and child.

The feminist analysis of patriarchy is easily extended to the doctor-patient relationship. In a patriarchal relationship, a woman gives up her independence in return for the promise of protection. Physicians, the patriarchs of the body, appear to promise protection against disease, decay and death. The dependent patient accepts this promise with gratitude. Increasingly, however, women have come to view the patriarchal doctor-patient relationship more as threat than protection.

The process of becoming conscious of the politics of the body involves a demystification of the power of the physician and a critical view of medical practice and technology. In her article on vaginal cancer, Kay Weiss raises questions about the often casual prescribing of estrogens to women. One synthetic estrogen, diethylstilbestrol (DES), given to women in labor, has produced an epidemic of vaginal cancer in the next generations of daughters. Weiss documents the reluctance of government and medical institutions to locate and test DES daughters, and contrasts the loose controls on prescription drugs with the significantly tighter controls on other consumer goods.

The essays by Rindfuss et al. and Weiss are examples of a broad range of recent studies suggesting that an increasingly critical attitude on the part of patients towards medical technology and decision-making is well justified. This lesson is especially addressed to women because male dominance and professional dominance often reinforce each other in the medical setting. The women's health movement has argued that women should control the major decisions affecting their health. "Control" in this sense is the power to decide and is a radical demand, to be clearly differentiated from the victim-blaming that professionals call "taking responsibility for one's health."

For women, "control over one's own body" means, most obviously, the ability to decide when, whether, and how to give birth. In her essay on birth control, Linda Gordon provides a history of the movement for reproductive rights. She shows how and why the early birth control movement lost its popular base and became dominated by professionals—physicians and eugenicists—and how it lost its early intimate connection with socialist and feminist politics. In part, the professionalization of this movement resulted from the refusal of the left to see birth control as a fundamental issue, and from the willingness of feminists to ally with any group able to promote the birth control cause. Gordon's analysis, which is extremely useful in understanding the complexities of contemporary struggles around abortion rights, is more fully presented in her book, *Woman's Body, Woman's Right.*[1]

The issues of reproductive rights, abortion, and sexuality have now moved towards the center of national consciousness and have been an emotional focus of the New Right's popular appeal. Here, the feminist demand for control over our own reproductive capacity is seen as a threat to traditional "Christian" and patriarchal forms of family stability. The New Right opposes the movement of women into the paid labor force and the demand for equal rights between the sexes. Economic demands for equal pay and equal opportunity (involved in such proposed legislation as the Equal Rights Amendment) are intimately linked to the question of reproductive rights; both offer women an alternative to economic and physical dependence on the patriarchal family. The family thus becomes a freely entered social and emotional unit rather than the necessary definition of woman's place.

In their essay on family violence, Stark, Flitcraft and Frazier suggest that wife battering may be understood as an attempt to reassert patriarchal domination over women. Here, to use a medical analogy, the "disease" is the conflict between capitalist social relations, the promises of corporate advertising, the often unfulfilled desires of patriarchal power and the realities of the marketplace. The "symptom" is women's resistance, refusal to do women's work, or inability to perform contradictory social demands; the "cure" is an attempt to reimpose women's work and reconstitute the family, either through violence exerted by the individual male or through the social control exerted by medical, social and welfare services.

This essay illustrates the extent to which the issues of the women's health movement have gone far beyond the traditional health/disease model of biomedical science. When we pose the question of women's health not as the absence of disease, but as the control over our own bodies, and as the maintenance of physical and psychic integrity, then we are led to a new and expanded conception of health. Once we redefine the issues of rape, wife battering and violence against women as health issues, we find that they are of epidemic proportions. The article by Stark *et al.* suggests, for example, that half of all injuries suffered by women may be the result of family violence. Medical services are, however, unable to deal with problems that do not fit easily into the individualistic and pathophysiological assumptions of the biomedical model. Since, in the case of a battered woman, no internal physiological cause can be found to link the episodes of injury, the injuries tend to be reaggregated as symptoms of the woman's psychopathology—as connected, for example, to alcoholism or depression—and she then becomes a legitimate object of medical concern. This refocusing of medical attention on the individual victim of social pathology, with the implication that she, herself, is the problem, will be familiar to those who have worked on the issue of rape; it may also prove useful to understanding the medical response to depression, alcoholism and drug addiction.

In studying the pathology of the family, we find that the medical system often acts as an "extended patriarchy" that reinforces patterns of male domination. If we

---

[1] Linda Gordon, *Woman's Body, Woman's Right: A Social History of Birth Control in America*, New York: Grossman Publishers, 1976.

examine the medical system itself, we find the power relations of the traditional family writ large in the health care hierarchy. Those with power, members of boards of trustees, administrators and physicians, are usually white upper class and upper-middle class men, while the vast majority of health workers are lower-middle class and working class women. Control over decision-making, finances and the technical apparatus of the "cure" are in the hands of men, while women are in helping and serving roles: they have the responsibility for the "care" of patients. They are also responsible for managing the housekeeping functions of the hospital, although much of the manual labor of the laundry, cleaning and kitchen services may be relegated to minority men. The hospital thus becomes an institutional parody of the wealthy white family, with father, mother, and non-white servants: the patients are the children.

The sexual and racial divisions of labor and the split between mental and manual labor in the health care system have not yet been sufficiently addressed; much more discussion is needed of their implications for the quality of patient care. In this volume, the article by Weaver and Garrett provides an introduction to the issues of racism and sexism as reflected in the health labor force, and argues for the need to make political connections between these two forms of discrimination. Although they focus mainly on medical school training and specialization, the authors also begin to discuss the composition of nursing and other health care occupations and argue that affirmative action programs have done little to address the root causes of inequality.

Carol Brown then looks at the division of labor within the health labor force in somewhat greater detail; she traces the ways in which occupational and sexual status serve to reinforce the health care hierarchy. As some of the lines of sex segregation begin to blur, the struggle for power and control among different health occupations becomes more sharply drawn. Brown ends by discussing the alternative ideologies of professionalism and unionism presented to mid-level skilled hospital workers who are placed between the upper level of physicians and administrators and the lower levels of semi-skilled hospital workers. This paper offers a brief review of the conflicts within the health labor force; further discussions may be found in another volume in this series, *Organization of Health Workers and Labor Conflict*, edited by Samuel Wolfe.[2]

The existence within the health care system of sexually segregated and stereotyped occupations is, of course, only one prominent example of the sexual segregation that pervades the larger economy. Service jobs, such as nursing, teaching, and waitressing, are supposed to be particularly suited to women's capacities and abilities. This sexual division of labor has given rise to endless debate about the differences between the sexes, and whether such differences are "social" or "biological." While it would be difficult to claim that women carry a special gene for social service, the assumption persists that women are "naturally" suited for these kinds of occupations. Karen Messing addresses the larger question: "Do men and women have different jobs because of their biological differences?" Messing finds that many "women's jobs" *do* have something in common: they offer a low level of pay relative to the level of

[2]Samuel Wolfe (editor), *Organization of Health Workers and Labor Conflict*, Farmingdale, N.Y.: Baywood Publishing Company, 1978.

skill required—jobs, in other words, that only women are willing to do. We may conclude that sexual segregation serves the economic interests of employers rather than the requirements of "nature."

The question of women's occupational health was dramatically posed several years ago when four women at American Cyanamid Company stated that they had voluntarily undergone sterilization in order to keep their jobs at a lead pigment plant. Such companies have excluded women of child-bearing age from working with toxic substances on the grounds that children with birth defects might later sue for damages. At the same time, studies of office workers have increasingly shown that many supposedly safe jobs pose occupational health hazards. Just how dangerous is the work that women do? Ingrid Waldron provides a guide to the extensive, but often contradictory, literature on employment and women's health. She compares morbidity data for working women and housewives and finds that, in general, working women report better health, though this difference may simply mean that healthy women are more likely to seek and find jobs. Waldron also reviews the occupational hazards and stresses to which many working women are exposed and finds that the effects of employment on health vary according to the type of job; there is no meaningful overall effect of employment on health. While this conclusion might appear obvious, it contradicts the frequent assumption that as women enter the paid labor force they will necessarily face new and increased health hazards, with consequent increased morbidity and mortality. In fact, the home may be as unhealthy as the workplace. Clearly, it is not a question of whether women work, but where, and under what conditions.

The last two essays in this volume deal with the social construction of medical and scientific knowledge. Since social relations are so often reinforced and legitimized by appeal to scientific and medical knowledge, critiques of these forms of knowledge are of special importance. Too often, statements and pronouncements claiming to be "scientific" may be simply accepted as true, without examination of their ideological content. Both Figlio and Lewontin understand all our forms of knowledge as historically contingent, constituted in the context of a particular set of class and sex relations. In this view, we cannot separate a pure scientific "concept" from the society that produces it.

Figlio begins his analysis with the concept of "chlorosis," also known as the "green sickness" and the "virgin's disease." Chlorosis was clearly described in the 18th century, became common in the 19th century, and vanished in the 20th. Its history is the history of a newly invented female adolescence; like hysteria, the disease summarized and symbolized the social experience of a group of women defined by their sexual and class positions. Chlorosis was a disease of idleness, refinement and sexual suppression. Here, Figlio discusses the medical conception of this disease as a reflection of the class relationships of 19th century England, and he suggests ways in which this kind of analysis can be extended to other forms of medical knowledge. His article also provides a useful introduction to recent work in the social history of medicine, much of it dealing with sexuality and women's health.

As we know from the work of many feminist historians, medicine in the late 19th century generated many theories of female inferiority; physiology was said to determine the feminine character, making women weak, emotional, and subject to a wide variety of afflictions. Medicine, we may say, took a class-bound idea of "the feminine" and reified it as a natural object: the Physiology of Woman. In the 20th century, the need to create "male" and "female" as clearly distinct entities has persisted, but has taken different theoretical forms, including, for example, endocrinology and psychoanalytic theory. Many previously "biological" facts however have been redefined as "social," the "biological" residue being open for debate.

For some years, the feminist position that male and female differences were a result of socialization gained ground, and biological determinism became distinctly unfashionable. However, the dominant theoretical frame again is shifting towards a conservative position: the newest theories seeking to define male and female differences as "natural" come from sociobiology. Richard Lewontin's critique of sociobiology is included in this volume in part because of the immediate political importance of this debate, and in part because it so clearly articulates the general problems involved in any form of biological determinism. The feminist position, that any differences between male and female should be regarded as "social," has been open to criticism because it appears entirely to discount biology and nature. However, the point is not to retreat to the determinist position, which sees all social relationships as "natural." Instead, we need a more critical view of the ways in which our perceptions of nature are filtered through particular class and sex interests. We tend to reproduce our own social organization in our conception of the "natural," and then, in turn, to justify our social arrangements as being in accordance with this "natural" order. Instead of using biological investigation to increasingly liberate human potential, we may thus create in "nature" externally imposed limits to social and human progress.

The essays in this volume are part of a collective effort to examine the politics of health, disease and medicine and to understand the specific ways in which sexual divisions are reinforced in medical institutions, knowledge and practice. A better understanding of the politics of sex in medicine will be one contribution to the larger struggle for a society that can promote the health and well being of all its members.

Elizabeth Fee
School of Hygiene
and Public Health
The Johns Hopkins University

TABLE OF CONTENTS

PART 1

The Women's Movement

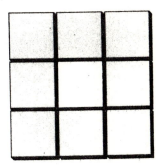

CHAPTER 1

Women and Health Care:
A Comparison of Theories

Elizabeth Fee

What do feminists have to say about the health care system in relation to women? A great deal, and most of what they have to say is highly critical.

Women are recipients of health care, and, increasingly, they have been critical of the form and content of this care. Particularly in those areas of medical care that most directly impinge on women's lives as women—gynecologic examinations, birth control and abortions, sexuality, childbirth, and psychotherapy—feminists have been articulate critics of the nature and quality of medical treatment.

Women are also dispensers of health care. For millennia, mothers traditionally assumed responsibility for the health of their families. Many of these traditional women's tasks have now been socialized, professionalized, and organized in giant medical institutions, but the overwhelming majority of the workers are still female. They occupy the lowest rungs of the medical hierarchy, are poorly paid, and have little power or voice in the organizations in which they work. Clearly, women experience their oppression not only as patients but also within the delivery system itself.

Has a systematic analysis of the relationship of women to health care emerged from the feminist writings of the last decade? Specific complaints are widely shared and generally recognized by feminists, and indeed by women in general, but although they may agree as to the existence and symptoms of a diseased state of health care, the diagnosis of the problem takes several distinct forms. Consequently, different groups may be led to prescribe various cures.

All recognize that women's problems with the organization and delivery of health care cannot be solved within the context of the medical system alone; since this is only one aspect of their social oppression as women, the solutions required must involve more radical social change. One's diagnosis of what is wrong with medical care must be related

17

to one's diagnosis of what is wrong with society in general. Here, not all feminists agree. A feminist consciousness grows from the surfacing of anger at being constantly manipulated, harrassed, limited, and repressed into the social role of "woman"; but the answers to the obvious questions of why this thing happens and how to best struggle against it are not self-evident.

There are at least three forms of social criticism which the women's movement has taken; these may be labeled as liberal feminism, radical feminism, and Marxist-feminism. As these three branches of the feminist movement have differing approaches to the analysis of women's situation, their prescriptions for the ailing American health care system are also different. This discussion of feminism and medicine will therefore be presented in three parts. Each section will briefly describe the general political framework adopted by one branch of the movement and then proceed to a consideration of that group's analysis of medical care. This general and perhaps overly schematic approach is intended for purposes of clarification and also to stimulate discussion; it should be noted that it presents as static positions ones which are in fact highly dynamic and in process of development. Also, although the categories used do describe distinct approaches to the analysis of "the woman question," this is a classification of modes of analysis and not of individuals. Particular women and/or organizations may, and do, adopt elements of each analysis; they may, and do, change their perspective over time, as a result of both external conditions and internal discussion and development. Any attempted description of a dynamic political movement should be out-of-date as soon as it is printed.

LIBERAL FEMINISM

Liberal feminism is the most widely diffused and generally acceptable version of feminism. Even many of those antagonistic to "women's lib" can accept, at least in principle, the goals of equal pay and equal opportunity for women. The liberal feminist position was crystallized by Betty Friedan's now classic text, *The Feminine Mystique,* and given organizational form in the National Organization of Women (NOW); the movement demanded equal opportunity for women to enter the upper reaches of the job market and equal treatment once they got there (1). Liberal feminists do not seriously challenge the hierarchical structure of American society; they simply want access to the same choices as are available to men. NOW fought to "bring women into full participation in the mainstream of American society *now,* exercising all the privileges and responsibilities thereof in truly equal partnership with men" (2).

One of the tasks of this movement was to prove that women were as capable as men, that their exclusion from all the centers of power had no rational or biologic basis. They therefore attacked the nexus of ideas and attitudes, "male chauvinism," that held women to be inferior beings. If women were not *really* inferior, then they were victims of a sexist ideology, supported and reinforced by a system of socialization which trained women to accept and adapt to a limited social role. If the women's problem was not real but ideological, it could be effectively countered by a program that combined persuasion, reeducation, the provision of "role models," and the development of pressure groups which would change both people's ideas of women and the legal and economic discrimination which reflected these ideas.

An underlying assumption was that the chauvinist complex of derogatory feminine stereotypes served no essential social function; chauvinism was either a male psychologic peculiarity or a species of bigotry. It ill served the ideals of equal rights to which democratic societies were supposed to be committed; indeed, it assured the waste of valuable human resources and human talent. It was clearly outmoded, counterproductive, and a vestige of earlier unenlightened eras. The movement would carry on the banners first raised by feminists a hundred years earlier and finally banish the historical hangover of sexual discrimination. The tempo of the sixties favored the belief that equality, or at least the more cautious "equality of opportunity" could be won without the necessity of transforming the economic and social infrastructures of the United States. This considered optimism gained support from a review of their numbers: women were the majority of the population. Unaided if needs be, in alliance with progressive males if they were willing, women could enforce the changes they wanted and needed. In those heady early days few believed that all women did not share the same essential interests or that historical cleavages of class or race might disturb female unanimity. The movement launched a campaign for all the equalities: equal rights in the eyes of the law, equal job opportunity, equal pay, equal access to education, equal promotion and professional advancement, equal credit. Child care and housework—the tangible requirements of the existing order—could be equally shared with men within the family or socially organized in day-care centers and communal living arrangements (3). Future socialization of children into sex-specific roles would be combatted by pressure on the educational system, on publishers of children's books, and on toy manufacturers.

During the flush economic times of the sixties, the liberal feminist movement made considerable headway. The case for equality gained widespread publicity and seemed compelling to many women and men; concrete legislative victories reinforced the belief that gains toward equality were possible "within the system"; they moved on toward a constitutional amendment that would embody their central demand in the fundamental law of the land as their predecessors had done with the women's suffrage amendment fifty years before. The resistance to apparently reasonable demands has proved stronger and more stubborn than the theory would seem to predict, particularly on the part of other women, some of whom cling to women's roles as housewife and mother in preference to the free labor market. Liberals counter with the explanation that women are to have a free choice whether to stay at home or go out to work, but the ideal of free choice seems increasingly implausible in the face of growing unemployment and inflation. Indeed, as the state of the economy has begun to restrict and erode some of the hard won gains of the last decade, many have begun to search for a more penetrating analysis of the roots of their oppression. For many more, however, the direction already marked out seems sufficiently correct and they continue with the struggle to win women's rights and equality within the established system.

Liberal Feminism and the Health Care System

Liberal feminists see the social subordination of women reflected in the sexual structure of the organization of medicine, i.e. in a field where women are the majority of health workers, the upper reaches of the medical hierarchy constitute a virtual male monopoly. The imbalance of the sexes here is more extreme than in most other areas of employment, a situation which seems particularly ironic since the practice of medicine requires personal characteristics compatible with those traditionally ascribed to women. The case of the Soviet Union, where the majority of physicians are female, has been frequently cited to show that no social or biologic necessity enforces the rule that men become doctors and women, nurses. The demand for sexual equality in education and employment should rather result in approximately equal numbers of men and women in each occupational category.

Another area of criticism concerns the nature of the patient-doctor interaction. Physicians heal (or do not heal) from a position of power; they relate in either a paternal or an authoritarian manner to their patients. They may withhold information about a diagnosis, be deliberately vague and obfuscatory, or be simply incapable of explaining the problem in nontechnical terms; they seem to doubt that patients have a right to an explanation of their illness. Aware that these attitudes are also directed at men, liberal feminists correctly argue that they are exaggerated when the patient is female: well or ill, women are accorded less respect. Many women feel that their symptoms are treated less seriously than those of men because doctors harbor the secret suspicion that most of the medical problems presented are psychosomatic.

The "specialist" is a more accurate term than "doctor" to describe the focus of the liberal feminist critique of medical attitudes. Middle-class women usually do not see a general practitioner, but rather a series of specialists: a gynecologist for birth control and pap smears, a pediatrician for the kids' fevers and a psychiatrist for depression and anxiety. The disaffection with medical care, already directed at the upper strata of the profession, tends to concentrate on two specialties: gynecology and psychiatry (4-7). These are the medical areas in which contempt for women is most evident; each has a long history of explicating the disadvantages of a female body and a female mind. A survey of gynecologic or psychiatric textbooks reveals the contribution of medical education to the reproduction of these attitudes in new generations of medical students.

The criticism of the sex-typing of health occupations and that of the sexist attitudes of physicians intersect in the call for more women to be admitted to medical schools. Women physicians should be more capable of treating the health problems presented by women patients with respect, if only because the female body would be less alien and the female mind less mysterious. The overwhelmingly male bias of gynecology and psychiatry would be difficult to maintain if even half of their practitioners were female. Medical research might become less male biased if the research teams were composed of equal numbers of each sex. Rigid distinctions between medical skills and "caring" functions would weaken if they were not reinforced by sexual differentiation; the widespread desire for such an integration is attested to by the popularity of the Marcus Welby image, fictional though it be. Then, too, a feminization of the medical profession and a corresponding invasion of nursing by men would erode the artificial income and status distinctions between doctors and nurses; this relation is maintained as a traditional male-dominant, female-subordinate one.

This liberal critique thus approaches the problems of medical care at the point most visible to the middle- and upper-middle-class consumer, the private office of the physician or specialist. From this vantage point, the giant medical institutions, clinics, and hospital emergency rooms tend to fade from view, although it is here that the health needs of most women are met—or, more frequently, not met. In speaking to the attitudes of male doctors, this critique centers on the tip of the medical iceberg and tends not to deal with the majority of health workers—medical technicians, orderlies, household workers, and practical nurses, over 70 per cent of whom are women (8, 9). In emphasizing the need to equalize the upper ranks of the medical profession by sex, it implicitly acquiesces in a hierarchical structure which rests on a base of exploited, largely female labor. The liberal position offers most to those who can afford a view from the top, to women who might have gone to medical school had admissions been equal to both sexes, to women who would be able to pay for feminist therapy if it were available. It offers less to the woman who cleans the floors of the hospital or is sick because medical care is unavailable or too expensive.

RADICAL FEMINISM

Radical feminist goals are not to achieve equality with men under the existing social and economic structures, but to entirely transform existing social institutions. Liberal feminist solutions seem weakly reformist and inadequate to serve the needs of women; radical feminists do not want to perpetuate a society which is perceived as fundamentally inhuman.

Many of the women oriented toward radical feminism had participated in civil rights, student, and anti-war movements. With radical men they shared certain characteristic ideas and attitudes: a profound alienation from American culture, a distaste for formal hierarchical systems, a contempt for traditional political forms, and a commitment to the radical restructuring of both values and institutions.

It became apparent, however, that existing Left organizations, for all their disaffection from the dominant culture, yet shared one important characteristic with it: sexism. The SDS (Students for a Democratic Society) proved male biased and male dominated; radical women were either invisible or clearly subordinate (10). Most Left women did not object to the idealistic and utopian nature of the New Left but they did want a utopian vision that satisfied *them* as well as their male counterparts.

Even those branches of the Left more firmly based on a Marxist perspective exhibited similar characteristics, some simply grounded in personal sexist attitudes of many radical males, some more deeply rooted in socialist theory and practice. Many Marxists viewed feminism as a bourgeois protest which had nothing to offer a working-class movement except divisiveness. Women's issues, the men would say, should be subordinated to the larger struggle. In any case women would only be able to win their liberation *after* socialism was attained (11). Movement women who looked at the socialist models held up to support this claim—China, Cuba, and the Soviet Union—found at best a mixed record on women's rights. On a theoretical level, too, Marxist analyses seemed inadequate to explain the particular oppressions of women; Marxist emphasis on the production of commodities in the workplace seemed to slight women's work, e.g. raising children, keeping house. Left intellectuals did not provide a satisfactory theoretical account of love, marriage, the family, reproduction, sexuality, the socialization of children. The canon's basic text, Engels' *The Origin of the Family, Private Property and the State* (12), seemed insufficient (13).

Some of these women abandoned Left organizations, formed independent movements, and developed alternate theoretical perspectives; they attacked those who remained behind as "politicos" who subordinated their own interests as women to male-defined politics (14).

Radical feminists then began producing studies of specific aspects of women's oppression in the United States (2, 14). They analyzed and attacked the patriarchal family. Not only did it directly oppress women, but it socialized children into an artificial and destructive sexual polarization (15). They attacked Freudian psychoanalysis, calling it the ideological basis of patriarchal control, and a justification of the patriarchal family (16). They undermined the conventional model of female sexual passivity, another prop to patriarchalism (17, 18). They dismantled prevailing assumptions about the naturalness and universality of the patriarchal family via historical examinations and anthropologic investigations of matriarchal mythology, rediscovering images of women that contrasted sharply with the vapid feminity of social and media acculturation (19, 20).

These approaches shared an implicit or explicit theoretical assumption—that the central oppressive agent of society was the patriarchal family and the set of psychic and cultural structures it created. Kate Millett (16) wrote that "a referent scarcely exists with which it might be contrasted or by which it might be confuted. While the same might be said of class, patriarchy has a still more tenacious and powerful hold through its successful habit of passing itself off as nature." Class and economic revolutions might succeed and still leave "the socializing processes of temperament and role differentiation intact." Feminists planned to attack the psychic structure itself: "the arena of sexual revolution is within the human consciousness even more pre-eminently than it is within human institutions. So deeply embedded is patriarchy that the character structure it creates in both sexes is perhaps even more a habit of mind and a way of life than a political system" (16).

For radical feminists the central struggle of history was the battle between the sexes, not the class struggle of which the Marxists spoke. This theoretical tendency was given full expression in Shulamith Firestone's *The Dialectic of Sex* (21). Firestone claimed that the biologic division of the sexes was the first and most fundamental class division of history; it provided the basis for the later division into socioeconomic classes. Feminist revolution should thus overthrow not only a specific form of social organization (capitalism) but Nature itself. The revolutionary means of annihilation of sex differences would be the transcendence of normal human reproduction through technology; artificial fertilization and test tube babies would relieve the women of the future of the burdens of natural reproduction, thus ending the biologic underpinning of their oppression. Firestone's brilliant analysis of the structures of women's oppression collapsed at the point where she tried to speculate how the contradictions between the sexes were to be overcome. The difficulty with posing sex as the primary contradiction is that it becomes almost impossible to pose any final solution to the problem; one may suggest the abolition of men but usually without much conviction that such a step would be possible or practicable. Firestone's idea of the abolition of natural human reproduction was an original and even plausible solution to the question, if still not a convincing blueprint for feminist revolution.

The emphasis on sexual oppression as the primary contradiction has served several essential functions. It has directed women's attention to their oppression as women and thus focused attention on precisely those areas where women's experience is different from that of men; it was a necessary precondition for exploring that half of human experience which had generally been ignored or passed off as inessential in the literature produced by men.

Nevertheless, the theoretical difficulties of a perspective based on biologic sex as the basis of women's oppression deserve to be emphasized (22). If women are everywhere oppressed by men on the basis of this biologic difference, then how has this situation developed, how is it maintained, and how is it to be overcome? How is a raised consciousness of patriarchal oppression to be translated into a public political movement dedicated to the transformation of concrete reality? Male supremacy can hardly be predicated on physical strength in a society where strength is not a noticeable characteristic of those in positions of power; the ability to have babies is woman's most obvious biologic trait but not one which can carry the weight of women's oppression. Must women give up having babies to be free? Firestone believed so; she represents one tendency within radical feminism, which views women's biology as the enemy of her human freedom. A different, even opposite position is the glorification of women's reproductive ability as the central and most significant aspect of human life. The *Proceedings of the First International Childbirth Conference* (23) provides a range of views and experience supporting this perspective which has been further popularized in the movement for natural childbirth and breast-feeding as women's most sensual experiences (24, 25).

If the Firestone view seems to slight women's special human contribution in reproduction, the resurrection of childbirth as an essential female experience offers no way out of the impasse. Rather, it seems to return women's attention to the same social roles which can only be experienced as imprisonment within the structures of present social reality.

If the theoretical work of the radical feminists has been uneven, it has been productive in actual struggles against an oppressive reality, and inventive in developing new forms of resistance. In addition to their demystification of paternalist ideology, women have created special organizational structures to combat specific symptoms of their oppression. Among these are the consciousness-raising group, the women's center, the rape crisis center, the women's commune, and the self-help group.

Within these structures women have experimented with different organizational forms, with or without formal authority or recognized leadership; they have sought to break down barriers between women and base their relationships on collective responsibility and mutual support rather than on competition and individual isolation. The thrust has been not so much to demand equality of opportunity in a system known to be structurally oppressive, but rather to organize women collectively, and arm them with ideological tools, so that they may resist their oppression politically. Their general solution is organized, knowledgeable self-defense, backed by a newfound pride in their sex, its history, and its culture. A possible drawback to the small-group strategy may be that it restricts the struggle to the margins of the established order, or leads to the development of alternative enclaves within it. As a political form, the small group may not allow development of sufficient power to confront or overthrow the dominant structures but it aids the development of a collective consciousness and helps to break down the dominant ideology. Thus the ideas of radical feminism have spread from a strong base in the United States and have influenced the development of feminism throughout all Western capitalist countries where the special oppression of women is being explored and rejected. The separate organization of women and the development of both consciousness and theory are a precondition—necessary but not sufficient—for the liberation of women.

Radical Feminists and Health Care

Radical feminists see the medical profession as yet another system which conforms to the patriarchal pattern established in the family. The doctor-father runs a family composed of the nurse (wife and mother) and the patient (the child). The doctor possesses the scientific and technical skills and the nurse performs the caring and comforting duties; these roles, of course, replicate relations within the patriarchal family.

This perspective helps both patients and medical workers make sense of the attitudes they encounter and the feelings they experience when they confront physicians. Visiting a doctor *is* indeed an infantilizing experience; nurses *are* often treated as wives.

What then is the radical feminist solution to health care problems? It is not simply to increase the percentage of female doctors. Radical feminists would agree that it is difficult for a woman to be as authoritarian as a male doctor (if for no other reason than that patients will expect her to be more sympathetic and understanding). But they also realize that women doctors are likely to be socialized into the "physician role" as long as the role itself remains unaltered. Paternalism and authoritarianism are not genitally but structurally and culturally determined. Nor do radicals recommend the construction of health "teams" as an antidote. That solution might simply produce a polygamous rather than a monogamous family; if the patriarchal structure stays intact, then each new health worker would be socialized into the submissive female role. Studies of the roles played by members of existing health teams bear out this suspicion (26). In addition to their criticism of the power of physicians and hospital administrators, radical feminists work to increase the knowledge and thus the ability of patients to resist their infantilization at the hands of those who possess that knowledge. Rather in the manner of the Naderites, they seek to inform and organize those who receive health care and thus indirectly bring pressure on the patriarchs of the system (27).

Radicals argue that women should understand their bodies and know what reasonably to expect from physicians. Only then can they judge for themselves the competence of the care they receive. When dealing with physicians (as when dealing with auto mechanics) knowledge is power. Women are encouraged to press their doctors for information about the results of tests, to draw up lists of questions to ask gynecologists, to acquire their own medical records, to get names of drugs being given, to sit in on medical conferences. Aware that this path is a difficult one—the disparity in specialized knowledge is enormous—feminists call for the formation of medical consciousness-raising groups. The self-help groups of women meet regularly to explore health problems, to share knowledge and experiences about the health system, to become familiar with their own and each other's bodies, to aid one another in following their own cycles by self-examination, to generate an understanding of the normal variations among healthy women in order to facilitate the recognition of symptoms of illness, and to break through the body-alienation imposed on females by patriarchal culture.

The self-help movement started with women's sexual and reproductive functions, the areas of maximum alienation between women and the health system. Members learned to view their own and one another's cervixes, using a simple and inexpensive (50 cents) technologic device, the plastic speculum. This simple self- and mutual examination proved a revelation for many women who had assumed that the impersonality of the routine gynecologic exam—being draped with white sheets, probed by cold metal instruments, surrounded by secrecy and embarrassment—was somehow inherent in the process. The self-help group atmosphere of gentleness, warmth, and mutual support made clear that this too was just another by-product of the existing order. Self-help groups in fact allow the potential patient to make great progress in understanding her own body, and she becomes immeasurably strengthened in future dealings with professional physicians (28).

Another aspect of the radical Women's Health Movement was the development of protest against the American way of childbirth. Normal hospital procedures for expectant mothers are among the most inhumane of medical practices. The prone position, the impersonality, the shaving and probing, the enemas and the drugging, the isolation and the labor inducement, the expense, the enforced passivity—all these lead to misery for the mother and often physical impairment for the infant. Feminists have been articulate critics of this system and have called for the legalization of midwifery, and many have argued that the best way to give birth is at home with husbands and relatives present (23, 29).

As the feminists confronted the intransigence of the health care system, they turned increasingly from consumer resistance to the construction of alternate modes of health care—the women's health centers. These institutions, set up and controlled by women, seek to help women with their health problems *outside* the established institutions. In the women's clinics patients learn about their bodies; they are not turned into passive recipients of treatment. Information is shared and the patient retains control over essential decisions concerning her own health. Education, moreover, is reciprocal: the "providers" seek to learn from the "consumers." Patients may sometimes keep their own records. Care is free whenever possible, or a sliding scale of fees is arranged. Some clinics choose to give free health care by charging for abortions; the income so obtained pays for the running of the entire clinic (30). The Feminist Women's Health Center in Los Angeles is the model for many others. It offers self-help clinics, gynecologic exams and treatment, pregnancy screening and counseling, and paramedical training programs, and it has its own abortion clinic. All staff members participate to some extent in decision making; "directorship" depends on degree of commitment to the health center and the length of time worked (31). In line with the ideal of sharing rather than restricting medical knowledge and skills, there is a summer session to train women to staff other women's health facilities (32).

As radical feminists moved to develop the women's centers as a widespread alternative to the established medical order, they ran into roadblocks imposed by that very system. Increasingly they began to confront the same sorts of problems that confronted the communes, problems inherent in any attempt to organize real alternatives while the old order remains intact, powerful, and in command of the wealth, resources, and political and legal mechanisms of society.

For one thing, there are not enough women doctors to fill the demand. Many clinics have had to rely on male physicians to perform abortions while seeking to retain control and policy-making power in the hands of women. There is a real tension, however, between the power that comes from the possession of knowledge (in this case, medical expertise) and the desire to keep power in non-expert hands. More generally, the radical dictum that knowledge is power itself points to the difficulties inherent in a virtual monopoly of specialized knowledge by the established order. Lack of credentials and shortage of funds make it difficult to obtain access to sophisticated technology and difficult to obtain necessary drugs.

The profession, too, is not loath to defend itself from what it correctly perceives to be a threat to its power and prerogatives. Legal charges of practicing medicine without a license are an available weapon; three women midwives were arrested in March 1974 for their work at the Santa Cruz Home Birth Center on such charges (33). The use of legal restraints to prevent women from carrying on self-help activities has generally failed if only because of the difficulty of deciding the exact point at which an individual's control over her own body is superseded by the restriction of medical practice to licensed professionals. Nevertheless, economic pressures can be brought to bear. The Women's Health Clinic in Portland, Oregon was to have been partially supported by the Office of

Economic Opportunity, but funds were cut because the women refused to set up the proper hierarchy, and had decided to operate the clinic without a doctor (30).

The most important limitation of the radical feminist program for remaking health care is that it deals only with those areas where women's health needs are different from those of men. But a woman's health needs are greater than the care of her reproductive system. The very advances of the women's clinics have only pointed up the obvious shortcomings of the rest of the health care system. Some clinics have attempted to move ahead, and have begun counseling in nutrition and drug problems, but it is manifestly impossible—without a nationwide reordering of health priorities for men and women—for these clinics, operating on the margin of a powerful (though ineffective) health establishment, to cope with all health problems. Women are thus forced back into reliance on the established and unsatisfactory order.

The various feminist alternatives have therefore demonstrated the depth of the difficulties; they have become—in addition to forms of self-help—arenas of political development. Thus Ellen Frankfort complained (in *Vaginal Politics*) that the self-help group was medically dangerous. The flood of congratulatory mail she received from doctors demonstrated to her that they were in fact much more upset at the potential independence the groups afforded women, than over any potential medical dangers. On that score she realized that the doctors themselves had conflicting opinions—profound disagreements—about the medical "facts" in question. This forced her to question her earlier uncritical appreciation of medical expertise (4, pp. 202-204).

The potential of the Women's Health Movement depends not only on the extent to which it is able to provide a more human and less alienating context in which women may learn about their bodies, but also on its role as a model for general health care (34). Thus, its success may increase the awareness among health consumers of the deficiencies in other areas of health care and increase the pressures for a more human and humane reordering of medical priorities. The demand for more consumer knowledge and control over the health delivery system develops as that system becomes increasingly alienated from the needs of the people whom in theory it exists to serve.

MARXIST-FEMINISM

Marxist-feminists have tried to understand the position of women by utilizing the method of analysis developed by Marx and Engels, believing that this is the most effective tool available for understanding all social contradictions, including the oppression of women. They see the essential task of theoretical development within the Women's Movement as that of bringing together feminist consciousness with the historical and dialectical method of analysis.

According to Engels: "We make our history ourselves, but in the first place, under very definite assumptions and conditions. Among these the economic ones are ultimately decisive" (35). Thus, for example, even that most biologic function, reproduction, is ultimately governed by the existing economic structure, as is evident when one looks at the research, distribution, and control of contraception on a national or international level. This is not, however, to say that there is a simple cause and effect relationship between economic structures and human experience and action; in a dialectical relationship, women (and men) both form and are formed by the conditions of their existence. This interaction is a dynamic and evolutionary one. Thus, the development of the mode of production erodes old patterns of social organization which must be gradually, and perhaps painfully, destroyed, and replaced by new patterns adapted to and made possible by the changed economic organization.

Engels (36, p. 618) emphasized that the dialectical mode of thought was not simple determinism:

> Cause and effect are conceptions which hold good only in their application to individual cases; but as soon as we consider the individual cases in their general connection with the universe as a whole, they run into each other, and they become confounded when we contemplate that universal action and reaction in which causes and effects are eternally changing places, so that what is effect here and now will be cause there and then, and vice versa.

Marxist-feminists believe this conception to be of use in exploring and explaining the changes in women's status and consciousness in relation to the development and organization of capitalism.

Sexism has historically been useful to capitalists. Patriarchal assumptions about women's special social role as wife and mother support and reinforce the system whereby women are almost invariably paid lower wages than men for the same work. This system has other functions: it has the effect of depressing wages in general, of increasing profit margins, and of dividing the labor force along sex lines. Yet the very fact that women's labor can be bought more cheaply frequently leads to an employer's preference for female over male labor, especially in the newer areas of mass employment such as clerical and service work. Women are then increasingly drawn into the work force, a fact which in turn undermines the structure of the patriarchal family. Whether the woman has entered the labor force in search of a career and personal fulfillment, or whether she has been unwillingly compelled to do so by the pressures of inflation and male unemployment, the result in either case will be a weakening of the patriarchal family bonds. The wife who is no longer completely economically dependent on her husband can afford to challenge his authority when it runs counter to her own interest. Nancy Seifer (37) has recently provided a sympathetic description of some of the changes in women's consciousness which are occurring in white working-class communities and the increased community activism which is one of the consequences. Other consequences of the increased employment of women outside the home include the increased consumption of prepared foods, the growing demand for day-care centers, and a rising divorce rate as marriages prove unable to adapt to the new social reality.

A division of labor which once appeared natural or inevitable no longer appears reasonable to many women (36, p. 623):

> The growing perception that existing social institutions are unreasonable and unjust, that reason has become unreason and right wrong, is only proof that in the modes of production and exchange changes have silently taken place with which the social order, adapted to earlier economic conditions, is no longer in keeping. From this it also follows that the means of getting rid of the incongruities that have been brought to light must also be present, in a more or less developed condition, within the changed modes of production themselves.

The women who are abandoning their earlier social definitions as protected and dependent wives and mothers are in turn led to demand equal pay and employment as the patriarchal ideology loses its force and social content. Whether the wage differential between men's and women's work will tend to increase or decrease is important for the relationship of feminism to socialism because it will determine the extent to which the labor force will be split along sex lines. Braverman's analysis (38) suggests that while the trend is toward an equalization of labor force participation rates between men and women, the polarization of income will increase as women are concentrated in the lowest paid sectors of employment. The rejection of the sex-typing of occupations by an organized feminist movement and the campaigns against sexual discrimination in employment may, however, impede this development. The support of the Equal Rights Amendment by organized labor is also significant.

What are the historical sources of women's oppression and which structures are responsible for maintaining the ideology of sexism? While Marxists tend to agree in identifying the family as the immediate source of sexual oppression, they see the form of the family as ultimately determined by the nature of economic development and the "social relations of production." Thus Engels in *The Origin of the Family, Private Property and the State* correlates the beginning of women's oppression with the rise of private property and class exploitation. He argues that in primitive cultures males and females divided the tasks, the women gathering and preparing the food, the men hunting; this division of labor was initially reciprocal and not exploitative. With the use of tools, the domestication of animals, and the development of property rights in herds and land (both in the man's domain), the male sphere expanded rapidly in power and importance. Men who now owned the sources of wealth required monogamous marriage to guarantee an orderly inheritance of private property. With the rise of capitalism and class divisions, the oppression of women received further economic underpinning. Almost all males and females came to work for some males, not because the latter group was male, but because it owned the means of production. The working-class family, which still exhibited the sexual division of labor, was always in a precarious financial position. The male laborer was responsible, as Eleanor Leacock (39) writes, "not only for his own maintenance but also that of his wife and children. This to a large measure insured not only his labor, but also his docility; it rendered him—as he is to this day—fearful of fighting against the extremities of exploitation as endangering not only himself but also his wife and his dependent children." To the male fears that stem from responsibilities as breadwinner in a class society are added the fears of increased competition from "liberated" women for scarce jobs. This economic insecurity which Guettel (40, p. 14) terms "the heart of male chauvinism" serves the interests of the owners of capital.

But as capitalist development shifts more and more areas of women's labor outside the family, it undermines the basis of home production. It therefore provides the material conditions for a future abolition of the distinctions between women's and men's work: the cooking of food and the making of clothes are functions which are increasingly absorbed by factory production while the state conducts the unprofitable business of the socialization of children. The development of the technology of contraception holds the potential for women to control their own reproduction (41):

> As long as reproduction remained a natural phenomenon, of course women were effectively doomed to social exploitation. In any sense they were not "masters" of a large part of their lives. They had no choice as to whether or how often they gave birth to children (apart from precarious methods of contraception or repeated dangerous abortions); their existence was essentially subject to biological processes outside their control.

The potential for the eradication of sexual inequality is, however, realized only to the extent that serves the development of capital, and women are the victims of the contradictory requirements which result. Domestic labor within the family serves the production, maintenance, and reproduction of labor power; this essential labor is unpaid yet socially necessary and the arrangement serves the stabilization of capitalism (42-44). Yet women also serve as a convenient reserve labor force. The family burden puts a woman at a disadvantage when she enters the work force (which, if she is a member of the working class, she must frequently do if her family is to survive economically); she is "unprepared, untrained, limited by the children's schedules, etc., [so she] tends to have to settle for what job she can get, and capitalists have always taken advantage of this" (40, p. 54). Women receive lower pay for the same work or are shuttled into low-paid service jobs, particularly those which are motherlike in character (social services, education, health care). Women's wage labor is widely utilized during periods of economic necessity (e.g. wartime) and the women are then pushed back into the family when no longer required. Thus day-care centers may be provided when an influx of women into the labor force is deemed necessary, only to disappear again when economic conditions change. Marxist-feminists conclude that although capitalism has developed a material base for the dissolution of the patriarchal family and the liberation of women, the final steps cannot be taken toward that goal as long as the production and property relations of capitalism remain intact. It is not, therefore, a set of ideas that stands between women and freedom, but an actual concrete set of institutions and relations.

Guettel (40, pp. 25-26) can agree with Millett that male chauvinism is a deeply rooted psychic structure. But from whence do those structures come, she asks?

> For a Marxist, consciousness is not transmitted autonomously from the minds of one generation to those of the next. Psychic realities are always bound to the social and production relations of a society, through social institutions, including the family, that are created out of very real material needs . . . True, masculine-feminine character patterns are far-reaching and will take generations to eliminate, but that is because they are based on a male-female division of labor, the elimination of which requires the transformation of not only the forces and relations of production but also the vast superstructure of social institutions.

To summarize, the relationship of capitalism and sexism has been a contradictory one. On the one hand, capitalism has supported and drawn support from the subordination of women. On the other hand, capitalism has eroded the material base on which the subordination rests.

Feminists have sought to strengthen and hasten along the development of the liberatory side of this dialectic. Marxist-feminists support this effort, believing with Marx that while history affords the possibilities, it is up to people to realize them in practice. But Marxist-feminists argue that although feminism may heighten the contradictions inherent in capitalist society, liberation cannot be attained within the framework of this system. Women's gains will remain contingent, dependent, and limited by the repressive side of the dialectic, by the fact that sexism remains useful for capitalism. Gains won, moreover, will often be hollow ones; equal treatment by a profoundly unequal society is not a satisfactory solution. Finally, any significant gains extorted from the system, and there have been many, are vulnerable to capitalism's repeated convulsions and collapses. During depressions, women and blacks are the first to be fired, day-care centers are swiftly shut down, and programs and policies which are not directly system supportive are cut back or eliminated.

Capitalism, many Marxists argue, cannot free itself from dependence on sexism any more than it can transcend class oppression or the pursuit of private profit at the expense of the satisfaction of real human needs. These drawbacks are built-in components. So a necessary condition of the complete liberation of women, Marxist-feminists would say, is the rejection of capitalism and its replacement by a humane, democratic socialism. The example of China, even after all the difficulties are noted, remains instructive. From a history steeped in the most extreme forms of patriarchalism and the most debilitating poverty, China has taken immense strides forward toward equality and prosperity. Chinese women, in particular, have made extraordinary gains in a mere 25 years (45, 46).

In the United States, a new social order would certainly not automatically eliminate sexism. But with full employment, no inflation, socialized medicine, expanded education, free transportation, cheap food and public services, and the elimination of consumerism and the cult of the home, women would be in a far better position to carry on the struggle. Once the constant nourishment and support that sexism received from the warped priorities and material conditions characteristic of capitalism were removed, once sexism's sustenance was withdrawn, women's liberation would finally be capable of attainment.

Marxist-Feminism and Health Care

Marxist-feminists believe that the specific structures of the American health system which are oppressive to women—as workers and as patients—cannot be understood without an analysis of that system as a whole. That system, in turn, becomes fully comprehensible only when it is recognized as one component of a capitalist economic and social structure. Many of the deficiencies of the modern American health system, like those of the education, transportation, and communications industries, flow from its commitment to the imperative of production for profit, rather than the fulfilment of people's needs.

The health system mirrors the priorities and organization of the larger system which supports it, and which it in turn supports, in a variety of ways: in its intense concentration of financial and political power at the top, in its thoroughgoing stratification of its work force by class, sex, and race, in its division of labor and specialization, in its very definitions of health and illness, and in its lack of accountability to the American population whom it theoretically serves. Let us consider these characteristics in turn.

As in other sectors of the American society, power is concentrated at the top, in a handful of monopolistic institutions. One of them, the American Medical Association, was once the undisputed dominant force in the health field. Times have changed, however. As the standard 19th-century capitalist enterprise—the small competitive firm—gave way to the giant monopoly corporation, so too has the undisputed power of the small fee-for-service solo practitioner been overtaken and largely surpassed by new forms of medical organization. As in other areas of the economy, the increasing reliance on large-scale, expensive technology gave the competitive edge to those who could muster the capital resources to obtain the new equipment. Also complementing the pattern in other sectors, the enlightened wing of the rising corporate class in the early 1900s, the Rockefellers and the Carnegies, strove to nationalize, organize, and centralize the medical system; the Flexner Report (1910) was an important milestone in the process (47).

Power now rests with a coalition that includes, in addition to the American Medical Association, the commercial insurance companies, the research and teaching hospitals, and the voluntary and public community hospitals. These institutions are themselves dominated by members of the corporate class, or of the upper-middle class (middle management and professionals), who occupy commanding positions in almost all major American institutions. At the top are the ten largest commercial health insurers (Aetna, Travellers, Metropolitan Life, Prudential, CNA, Equitable, Mutual of Omaha, Connecticut General, John Hancock, and Provident); among them they control nearly 60 per cent of the multi-billion-dollar industry. Their leadership is tightly interlocked with the corporate and banking sectors, and they exert decisive influence on state policy in matters of health care. In the current debate over how to deal with the financial crisis of the health delivery system, they have (with lavish expenditure of funds) managed to so dominate the discussion that nearly all the proposals for action are simply varieties of publicly supported insurance programs. Most would enhance the profit-making capacity of the commercials and further shift the fiscal burden of the health system to working- and middle-class citizens via regressive tax structures (48, 49).

The great teaching and research institutions are also dominated by representatives of the corporate class. In 1970, for example, Columbia Presbyterian Medical Center had a director of Texaco presiding over a major teaching hospital, the president of United States Steel chairing its finance committee, and the president of American Telephone & Telegraph running its planning and real estate committee (50). These institutions train and socialize the people who staff the upper and middle echelons of the health system. They encourage the development of and reliance upon sophisticated medical technology, an extreme specialization and division of labor, and the flow of funds to esoteric research projects (often involving experimentation on poor, minority, or working-class women) (51).

The voluntary community hospitals are controlled by boards composed of upper-middle-class professionals, rather than representatives of corporate capital; doctors, lawyers, and smaller businessmen predominate. Women, members of minority groups, and representatives of organized or unorganized labor are virtually excluded from access to any of these decision-making bodies (52, 53).

Far below the capitalists and the professionals are the lower-middle and working classes of the health industry. The former comprise the nurses and paraprofessional auxiliary and service personnel, representing 54.2 per cent of the total labor force (48). Both groups are predominantly female; the working class includes an overrepresentation of minority groups. These classes are often played off against one another. Middle-ranking groups are given a degree of control over those below them (though they are excluded from the real decision-making bodies above them). The employment of lower-level workers may be used to undercut the bargaining position of the mid-level groups, as, for example, in the mass employment of licensed practical nurses and nurses aides over the opposition of registered nurses (54).

The non-physician workers are divided into over 375 independent occupations, most of them narrow, specific, and rigidly defined, most representing one aspect of the work once done by a doctor or a nurse, most dead-end, low-wage positions, boring, repetitious, and firmly under someone else's control and direction (55). This process of breaking up labor into little bits, each of which may be parceled out to a single worker, is a general tendency of modern capitalism. The fragmentation, as Braverman (38) shows, is not to increase efficiency, but to maximize management control over labor, and to replace highly paid workers with less skilled and thus less costly ones.

Seventy-five per cent of these health workers are women, doing modern forms of traditional women's work. The old female roles of nurturing, caring, cooking, educating, and cleaning have become, under corporate medicine, such occupations as nurse, housekeeper, dietitian, clerk, or technician. Ninety-eight per cent of nutritionists and dietitians are women (55).

If capitalist medicine fragments the organization of work, it also fragments the delivery of health care. First it provides multi-level services based on a patient's ability to pay. It affords very high quality service to the wealthy; shoddy, assembly-line care for the poor. Specialization makes it difficult, at almost any level, to find comprehensive care.

Medical fragmentation rests on the premise that the body is rather like a machine, and can, like any mechanical system, be broken down into interlocking parts for purposes of repair (56). The patient (the whole) —becomes invisible while parts of her or his anatomy engross the attention of different (and highly paid) specialists. Where the patient has no power over the forms of medical care, his or her experiences of pain or illness become much less relevant to the "case" than the pathologist's report. Where there are class, race, and/or sex differences between the physician and patient, the situation becomes still more acute, personal communication still further hindered.

Capitalist medicine reinforces the capitalist order in still other, subtle ways, in its very definitions of health and sickness. Health is defined in terms of the system rather than the individual. The central concern of medical institutions, Dreitzel (57) finds, is whether or not the patient is well enough to go to work. (This orientation suggests why women's illnesses are taken less seriously than those of men; they are not as crucial to the production process. Their ills rarely interfere with their ability to do housework.)

Capitalist medicine, moreover, prefers to concentrate (in research and treatment) upon the "scientific," "objective," organic basis of illness. Thus it evades the social causes of much ill-health, causes rooted in the structure of the capitalist system itself. Vast quantities are spent seeking the organic basis of cancer, but it proves extraordinarily difficult to wipe out known causes of the disease such as cigarette smoking, asbestos dust in factories, or coal soot in mines. Improving health in those areas would require confronting the powerful interests of tobacco companies, asbestos manufacturers, and coal mine operators.

The process of ignoring the social causes of disease becomes self-legitimating. Disease which cannot be given a specific biomedical correlate is defined out of existence. The physician draws his own distinction between a "real" disease—one whose organic basis can be identified by the available technology—and functional or psychosomatic illness in which the patient's experience cannot be legitimated by a laboratory report. Complaints stemming from such environmental factors as poverty, sexism and racism, the nature of work outside and inside the home, crises in housing and education, problems in personal relationships, and the like, can be "treated" only by tranquillizers or placebos. American women consume large quantities of both. (If the patient has enough money, she, or he, may be able to obtain sympathy from a psychoanalyst, but this option is not generally available.)

In addition to defining many forms of disease as "not real," some forms of health are defined as medical problems. Pregnancy and childbirth are, or should be, considered natural and healthy aspects of human life. American medicine treats them as forms of illness, to be removed from the "patient's" control, a development which the radical Women's Health Movement is struggling to reverse.

In medicine, then, as in the condition of women generally, Marxists find crucial contradictions. On the one hand, the possibility of extending superb health care to the entire population exists; we have the knowledge, the resources, and the need. But the social relations of health care, the way in which it is controlled and organized, act as fetters. The needs of the giant insurance companies, the industrial corporations, and the professional organizations predominate.

Marxists believe that a thoroughgoing reordering of priorities is not possible within the present system. Capitalist medicine's internal dynamics point toward still greater concentration of control, still greater subordination of workers, yet more scientific medicine, and ever-increasing specialization and dehumanizing division of labor—a poor prognosis for workers and consumers alike. Marxists believe that the only way to liberate the potential for improved care and better preventive measures is to retire and replace the capitalist order with a democratic socialist one.

A final note: many who are developing a Marxist analysis of health care are male. It is imperative that the specific concerns of women be further integrated into this developing analysis. Contributions to the advancement of Marxist theory must come from women, whether they define themselves as feminists or socialists. Men sensitive to the achievements and concerns of the women's liberation movements can also help oppose the systematic bias toward the male sex evident in much of the existing Left literature, a bias that has operated as a barrier between Marxists and feminists. (A case in point is the book *Sexuality and Class Struggle,* which, despite its title, demonstrates no awareness of understanding of the women's movement, a point made nicely by David Fernbach in his review (58).)

Radical feminists are now increasingly confronting the issues of class and race. *Class and Feminism*, a collection of essays by the Furies, a lesbian-feminist collective, is an excellent discussion of class attitudes and behavior within the feminist movement (59). The theoretical development of both Marxism and radical feminism is aided to the extent to which each can benefit from the insights of the other. In the aim to create a healthy system, indeed a society, which exists to fulfil people's human needs, there is, after all, no contradiction between them.

REFERENCES

1. Friedan, B. *The Feminine Mystique.* Dell, New York, 1963.
2. National Organization of Women's Bill of Rights. Adopted at NOW's First National Conference. In *Sisterhood is Powerful: An Anthology of Writings from the Women's Liberation Movement.* edited by R. Morgan, p. 512. Vintage, New York, 1970.
3. Bernard, J. *Women and the Public Interest*. Aldine, Atherton, Chicago, 1972.
4. Frankfort, E. *Vaginal Politics*. Bantam, New York, 1973.
5. Seaman, B. *The Doctor's Case Against the Pill*. Avon, New York, 1971.
6. Chesler, P. *Women and Madness,* Doubleday, New York, 1972.
7. Miller, J. B., editor. *Psychoanalysis and Women.* Penguin, Baltimore, 1973.
8. Ehrenreich, B., and English, D. *Witches, Midwives and Nurses: A History of Women Healers,* p. 1. Feminist Press, Old Westbury, N. Y., 1973.
9. Rossi, A. S. Barriers to the career choice of engineering, medicine or science among American women. In *Readings on the Psychology of Women,* edited by J. Bardwick, pp. 72-82. Harper & Row, New York, 1972.
10. Dunbar, R. *Female Liberation as the Basis for Social Revolution.* New England Free Press, Boston, undated.
11. Waters, M. A. *Feminism and the Marxist Movement.* Pathfinder Press, New York, 1972.
12. Engels, F. *The Origin of the Family, Private Property and the State,* edited by E. B. Leacock. International Publishers, New York, 1973.
13. Schein, M., and Lopate, C. On Engels and the liberation of women. *Liberation* 16: 409, 1972.
14. Firestone, S. On American feminism. In *Woman in Sexist Society,* edited by V. Gornick and B. K. Moran, pp. 665-686. New American Library, New York, 1972.
15. Figes, E. *Patriarchal Attitudes.* Fawcett Publications, Greenwich, Conn., 1970.
16. Millett, K. *Sexual Politics.* Doubleday, New York, 1970.
17. Masters, W. H., and Johnson, V. E. *Human Sexual Response.* Little, Brown and Company, New York, 1966.
18. Sherfey, M. J. *The Nature and Evolution of Female Sexuality*. Random House, New York, 1972.
19. Davis, E. G. *The First Sex.* Penguin, Baltimore, 1972.
20. Dinar, H. *Mothers and Amazons: The First Feminine History of Culture.* Anchor, Doubleday, New York, 1973.
21. Firestone, S. *The Dialectic of Sex: The Case for Feminist Revolution.* Bantam Books, New York, 1971.

22. Magas, B. Sex politics: Class politics. *New Left Review* 66: 69-96, 1971.
23. Tennov, D., and Hirsch, L., editors. *Proceedings of the First International Childbirth Conference.* New Moon Communications, Stamford, Conn., 1973.
24. Niles, N. Trebly sensuous woman. In *The Female Experience,* by the editors of *Psychology Today,* pp. 22-25. Communications/Research/Machines, Inc., Del Mar, Cal., 1973.
25. Tanzer, D. Natural childbirth: Pain or peak experience? In *The Female Experience,* by the editors of *Psychology Today,* pp. 26-32. Communications/Research/Machines, Inc., Del Mar, Cal., 1973.
26. Fry, R. E., Alech, B., and Rubin, I. Working with the primary care team: The first intervention. In *Making Health Teams Work,* edited by H. Wise, R. Beckhard, I. Rubin, and A. Kyte, pp. 27-67. Ballinger Publishing Company, Cambridge, Mass., 1974.
27. Boston Women's Health Book Collective. *Our Bodies, Ourselves.* Simon and Schuster, New York, 1973.
28. Hirsch, L., and Hirsch, J. *The Witch's Os.* New Moon Publications, Stamford, Conn., 1973.
29. Lang, R. *Birth Book.* Genesis Press, Ben Lomond, Cal., undated.
30. Grimstad, K., and Rennie, S., editors. *The New Woman's Survival Catalog,* pp. 71-73. Coward, McCann and Geoghegan Berkeley Publishing Company, New York, 1973.
31. Downer, C. What makes the Feminist Women's Health Center "feminist"? *The Monthly Extract, An Irregular Periodical* 2: 10-11, Feb/March, 1974.
32. Hornstein, F. An interview on women's health politics. *Quest* 1: 27-36, 1974.
33. Hirsch, L. Police bust. Midwives arrested. *The Monthly Extract, An Irregular Periodical* 3:7, March/April, 1974.
34. Reynard, M. J. *Gynecological Self-Help. An Analysis of Its Impact on the Delivery and Use of Medical Care for Women.* Thesis presented to School of Allied Health Professions, State University of New York, Stonybrook, 1973.
35. Engels, F. Letter to Joseph Bloch, Sept. 21-22, 1890. In *The Marx-Engels Reader,* edited by R. C. Tucker, p. 641. W.W. Norton, New York, 1972.
36. Engels, F. Socialism: Utopian and scientific. In *The Marx-Engels Reader,* edited by R. C. Tucker, pp. 605-639, W.W. Norton, New York, 1972.
37. Seifer, N. *Absent from the Majority: Working Class Women in America.* National Project on Ethnic America, New York, 1973.
38. Braverman, H. *Labor and Monopoly Capital: The Degradation of Work in the Twentieth Century,* pp. 392-397. Monthly Review Press, New York, 1974.
39. Leacock, E. B. Introduction to F. Engels, *The Origin of the Family, Private Property and the State,* p. 42. International Publishers, New York, 1973.
40. Guettel, C. *Marxism and Feminism.* Women's Press, Toronto, 1974.
41. Mitchell, J. *Woman's Estate,* p. 108. Vintage, New York, 1971.
42. Benston, M. The political economy of women's liberation. *Monthly Review* 21: 13-27, 1969.
43. Vogel, L. The earthly family. *Radical America* 7: 9-50, 1973.
44. Gerstein, I. Domestic work and capitalism. *Radical America* 7: 101-128, 1973.
45. Rowbotham, S. *Women, Resistance and Revolution.* Vintage, New York, 1974.
46. Feeley, D. Women and the Russian Revolution. In *Feminism and Socialism,* edited by L. Jenness, pp. 113-118. Pathfinder Press, New York, 1972.
47. Kelman, S. Toward the political economy of medical care. *Inquiry* 8: 30-38, 1971.
48. Navarro, V. Social policy issues: An explanation of the composition, nature and function of the present health sector of the United States. *Bull. N.Y. Acad. Med.* 51: 199-234, 1975.
49. Bodenheimer, T. S. Health care in the United States: Who pays? *Int. J. Health Serv.* 3(3): 427-434, 1973.
50. Ehrenreich, B., and Ehrenreich, J. *The American Health Empire: Power, Profits and Politics,* p. 52. Vintage, New York, 1971.
51. Ehrenreich, B., and English, D. *Complaints and Disorders: The Sexual Politics of Sickness,* pp. 76-78. Feminist Press, Old Westbury, N.Y., 1973.
52. Navarro, V. Women in Health Care. Testimony presented before the Hearings on Women and Health Care of the Governor's Commission on the Status of Women, Pennsylvania, 1974.
53. Robson, J. The NHS Company, Inc.? The social consequence of the professional dominance in the National Health Service. *Int. J. Health Serv.* 3(3): 413-426, 1973.
54. Brown, C. A. The division of laborers: Allied health professions. *Int. J. Health Serv.* 3(3): 435-444, 1973.
55. Reverby, S. Health: Women's work. *Health/Pac Bulletin* 40: 15-16, 1972.
56. Rossdale, M. Health in a sick society. *New Left Review* 34: 82-91, 1965.
57. Dreitzel, H. P., editor. *The Social Organization of Health,* introduction, p. xi. Macmillan Company, New York, 1972.
58. Fernbach, D. Sexual oppression and political practice. *New Left Review* 64: 87-96, 1970.
59. Bunch, C., and Myron, N. *Class and Feminism.* Diana Press, Baltimore, 1974.

PART 2

Case Studies
In Women's Health

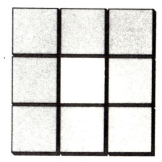

CHAPTER 2

Convenience and the Occurrence of Births: Induction of Labor in the United States and Canada

Ronald R. Rindfuss, Judith L. Ladinsky, Elizabeth Coppock, Victor W. Marshall, and A.S. Macpherson

Since the early 1960s, England has been changing from home-based, midwife-delivered births to hospital-based, physician-delivered births. This has prompted considerable critical examination within Great Britain of various interventionist obstetrical practices which are sometimes used in hospital-based deliveries, but are not used in home-based deliveries (1-5). Within North America, there has been less examination of these aspects of the routine practice of hospital-based obstetrics—perhaps because hospital-based, physician-delivered births have been the rule for decades. In fact, for North America, basic incidence estimates are unavailable for many of the practices considered controversial by the British. In this article, we present indirect evidence that one such controversial obstetrical practice—the elective induction of labor—is in widespread use in both the United States and Canada.

By "induction of labor" we mean the practice of starting labor prior to its spontaneous occurrence by using a drug, or by mechanical means, or both. Labor may be induced for medical reasons, such as pre-eclampsia, diabetes, or RH disease (6-9), *or* it may be induced for the convenience of the physician, the patient, or both. We define this latter type as elective induction of labor. The justification of elective induction exists at the personal and scheduling-preference levels, rather than at the

The analysis reported here was supported in part by Center for Population Research Grant No. HD05876 to the Center for Demography and Ecology, University of Wisconsin, from the Center for Population Research of the National Institute of Child Health and Human Development; by funds granted to the Institute for Research on Poverty of the University of Wisconsin by the Department of Health, Education, and Welfare; and by a grant from the Canada Council through McMaster University.

medical level. The practice has appeal for patient and physician because it introduces predictability (10-12).

The use of elective induction of labor is controversial primarily because its safety has never been conclusively established. Indeed, there is evidence that it might introduce risk to mother and child (13-22), and recent work suggests that the risk introduced is small, but nonetheless significant. For example, Schaffer and Kaern (23), in a series of 5986 cases with 57 perinatal deaths, considered 2 deaths directly related to induction, 14 deaths possibly related, and 41 deaths unrelated (see also 24). Moreover, recent obstetrics textbooks almost unanimously discourage the use of elective induction (25-32). Some are more vehement than others, but no textbook examined encouraged the practice.

Given the concerns about the safety of induction of labor, and given that there is no medical need to *electively* induce labor, it might be expected that the procedure would be sparingly used. Direct estimates of the use of induction are not routinely collected. Previous estimates of the incidence of the induction of labor have been limited to one physician or one hospital (33, 34), and previous indirect estimates of the incidence of elective induction of labor have been limited to one state (35). The indirect evidence presented here indicates that the use of induction is widespread in both the United States and Canada. To the extent that such induction is not medically indicated but is truly elective, its widespread use introduces unnecessary risk to mother and child for the sake of convenience.

BIRTH REGISTRATION DATA

The data for this article consist of birth registration data for the United States and Canada for 1971. Although the birth certificates in neither country include information regarding the use of elective induction, by using the day on which the birth occurred, along with other information available on the birth certificate, it is possible to obtain evidence about the use of induction. For Canada, all registered births for all provinces except Newfoundland are included in the sample. For the United States, a 50 percent sample is used, and the numbers reported have been multiplied by 2 to reflect the actual number of births. Whenever comparable data are available from both countries, they will be included in the analysis. Often, however, data will be available from only one country, and in these cases only one country will be included in the analysis. While the range of data obtainable from birth registration systems is limited, such registration systems provide the largest population base available for examining the prevalence of elective induction.

RESULTS

National Patterns

The average number of births occurring on each day of the week in 1971 is shown in Table 1 for the United States and Canada. Also shown is the average percent deviation from the number of births expected if the occurrence of a birth were random with respect to day of the week. In both the United States and Canada, there were

Table 1

Average percent deviation from the expected number of births and average number of births by day of the week,
United States and Canada, 1971

Country	Mon.	Tues.	Wed.	Thurs.	Fri.	Sat.	Sun.	Ave. of All Days
				Percent Deviation[a]				
United States	2.6	7.3	3.8	1.8	4.0	-7.0	-12.6	
Canada	-0.3	6.3	5.6	3.2	2.1	-5.4	-11.9	
				Average Number of Births				
United States	10,017.2	10,472.6	10,130.6	9,939.0	10,157.2	9,079.4	8,530.4	9,762.0
Canada	955.2	1,018.0	1,014.7	989.2	978.0	906.8	844.3	958.1
				Number of Births				
United States	520,890	544,574	526,792	516,824	538,334	472,130	443,582	3,563,126
Canada	49,669	52,937	52,765	51,439	51,885	47,152	43,906	349,723

[a]Defined as: $\dfrac{\bar{X}_i - \bar{X}_T}{\bar{X}_T}$ where $\bar{X}_i$ is the average for the day of the week, and $\bar{X}_T$ is the expected average number of births, that is, the average irrespective of day of the week.

fewer births on weekends than would be expected. On Sundays, this deficit is approximately 12 percent. The largest number of births occurred on Tuesdays and Wednesdays.

This pattern is not the result of a few Sundays having a small number of births.

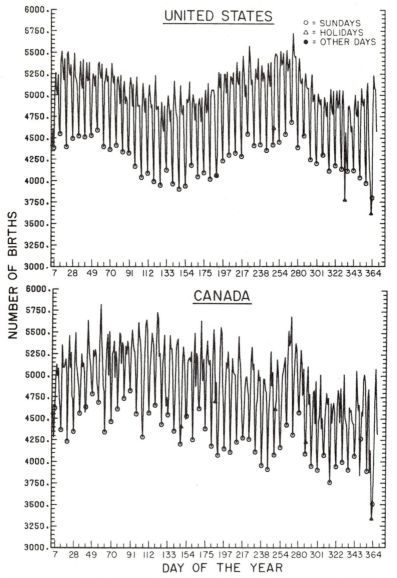

Figure 1. Number of births by day, January 1 through December 31, 1971, United States and Canada. The number of births for Canada has been inflated to the United States total so that the graphs for both countries are at the same scale. This inflating factor affects only the scale and not the patterns.

The weekend deficit is evident for each of the 52 weeks in the year. This can be seen in Figure 1, which shows the number of births occurring on each of the 365 days in 1971 for both the United States and Canada. (The number of births for Canada has been inflated to the United States total so that the graphs for both countries are at the same scale. This inflating factor affects only the scale and not the patterns.) For the United States, for every week, the smallest number of births occurring during the week occur on Sundays or on a holiday such as Thanksgiving or Christmas. For Canada, the smallest number of births occur on a Sunday or a holiday in almost every week; and for the weeks that are exceptions, Saturday has the smallest number of births.

As we will argue in the remainder of this article, the probable explanation for this persistent weekend deficit is the use of elective induction in conjunction with a preference to induce or be induced during the normal Monday through Friday work week. The number of births peaks on Tuesdays or Wednesdays, rather than on Mondays, perhaps because a scheduled induction would be preceded by an office visit to determine whether the patient is ready for the elective induction of her labor and such office visits probably occur on Mondays and Tuesdays.

An alternative explanation for this patterning of births might be that it is the result of scheduled Caesarean sections. Unfortunately, these national data do not allow a partialing out of Caesarean sections, nor are direct estimates of the number of elective inductions available. However, in an earlier study for the State of Wisconsin (35), it is possible to examine this patterning by type of delivery. Nine types of delivery are recorded on Wisconsin birth certificates: spontaneous; manipulation without instruments; forceps, low; forceps, mid and high; other surgical or instrumental; Caesarean, low cervical; Caesarean, classical; Caesarean, other; and other types of delivery. Approximately two-thirds of the deliveries were classified as spontaneous. The term "spontaneous" here refers to the delivery, and thus an induced labor could be a spontaneous delivery. Thus, if the pattern persists among spontaneous deliveries, then presumably one can rule out the possibility that the pattern is caused by Caesarean sections or other types of deliveries. Exclusion of all births except spontaneous reduces the Sunday deficit for that state from 14.5 to 13.1. Caesarean sections therefore do not greatly affect the weekend deficit of births in that state; and, unless Wisconsin is very atypical, Caesarean sections are unlikely to greatly affect the weekend deficit of births in the United States or Canada.

The similarity between Canada and the U.S. in patterns of births by day of week is noteworthy. Such similarity might not be expected, given the range of social, cultural, and historical differences between the two countries. Yet the import of these differences diminishes, given the similarity between the two countries in the organization of the delivery of obstetrical services. In both countries, obstetrical service is organized on a fee-for-service basis, all but a fraction of the deliveries occur in hospitals, and a large share of the births are delivered by obstetricians rather than by general practitioners.

Variation in "Preferred" Day

Because birth certificates do not routinely include information regarding the onset of labor, it is not possible to directly determine the extent to which induction is responsible for this weekly variation in births. Neither is it possible from these birth registration data to determine the extent of the incidence of elective induction; we can only say that it is probably of sufficient magnitude to affect the pattern of the number of births delivered on each day of the week. The reason is that different patients and different physicians might have preferences for scheduling inductions on days other than Tuesdays and Wednesdays. Some might prefer to have the induction occur on weekends. To the extent that this is occurring, the data shown in Figure 1 and Table 1 would understate the extent to which labor is induced.

In order to see whether there are indeed physicians[1] who prefer to schedule inductions on weekends, rather than during the week, we examined data from the 1975 maternity room log of a midwestern United States hospital. Although these maternity room log data are sufficient to suit our limited purposes, it should be noted that they are less than ideal for the general study of elective induction. In the first place, when it is recorded that labor was induced, the reason for the induction is not indicated. So it is not possible to distinguish between elective inductions and medically indicated inductions. Secondly, the maternity room log is not kept for the explicit purpose of providing information on inductions. We expect that inductions, particularly amniotomies, would be underreported. Finally, the data relate only to one hospital, and we know that there is variation across hospitals (33, 34). Given these reservations, the data are nevertheless sufficient to establish the fact that some physicians prefer to induce on weekends.

In this hospital, there were several thousand deliveries in 1975; approximately one-fifth of these births were induced. As might be expected, there was considerable variation across physicians in the proportion of deliveries that were induced. One physician induced almost half of the births he delivered, and another induced fewer than 10 percent.

The principal utility of these data from the maternity room log is that they establish the fact that some physicians do indeed prefer to induce on weekends rather than during the week. One physician performed more than one-third of his inductions on Sundays, and another physician performed one-fifth of his inductions on Saturdays. The motivation to prefer to induce on weekends may involve the desirability of having less competition for hospital facilities or the preference for having free time during the week when stores are open. Whatever the motivation, it is clear from these data that some physicians perform elective inductions on weekends; therefore, the indirect evidence on elective induction from examination of patterns of births by day of the week underestimates the incidence of elective induction. The remainder of this paper presents circumstantial evidence from birth registration data that the weekly pattern of births is an indication of the widespread incidence of elective induction.

Prenatal Care and Elective Induction

A critical factor in the decision about inducing a patient is knowledge of whether the patient is at term, because it is difficult to safely induce unless she is at term. One

---

[1] In order to infer physicians' preferences, attitudinal data would be necessary. In fact, to conclusively determine patients' preferences, attitudinal data would also be necessary from them.

of the most serious risks associated with the elective induction procedure is prematurity (9, 13, 14, 21, 36). The principal way of knowing whether a patient is at term, and thus a potential candidate for elective induction, is to have had her under prenatal care for the duration of the pregnancy. Thus, among those women who received prenatal care early in their pregnancy, we would expect a comparatively high incidence of elective induction, and among women who began care later in their pregnancy, we would expect a very low incidence of elective induction.

The average number of births each day of the week in 1971 and the percent deviation from the expected number are shown in Table 2 for five categories of prenatal care for reporting states[2] in the United States. As expected, the weekend deficit is greatest for those who began their prenatal care in the first or second month of pregnancy. The size of this weekend deficit diminishes steadily as patients begin their prenatal care later and later in their pregnancy. For those who receive no prenatal care, there is essentially no weekend deficit. The contrast between the two extreme groups is particularly dramatic.

Socioeconomic Variation

Since, we noted previously, the use of elective induction generally requires that the patient has had adequate prenatal care, we would expect the incidence of elective induction to be lowest among those groups that generally do not receive proper medical care. By adequate prenatal care is meant not only initiating prenatal care early in the pregnancy, but also receiving it on a regular basis throughout the pregnancy. To the extent that elective induction is responsible for the weekend birth deficit, we would expect the deficit to be smallest among those groups that generally do not receive proper medical care.

One group that receives poorer prenatal care than the general population is women who have children out of wedlock (38, 39). Part of the reason for the lower level of prenatal care involves the racial, ethnic, educational, and age composition of women bearing illegitimate children. Over and above compositional differences, there probably is some reluctance on the part of unmarried pregnant women to visit an obstetrician unless or until it is absolutely necessary. As can be seen in Table 3, for both the United States and Canada, the weekend birth deficit is substantially less among illegitimate births than among legitimate births. The contrast is particularly striking for the United States; the reason, as will be seen below, involves the racial composition of illegitimate births in the United States.

Within the United States, there are large racial and socioeconomic differences with respect to health care.[3] Numerous studies have concluded that blacks obtain more

[2] In the United States, birth registration data are collected by state departments of health which then release records to the National Center for Health Statistics. Not all states collect all the information recommended on the U.S. Standard Certificate of Live Birth. The states collecting information on prenatal care and on other characteristics used in this paper are listed in reference 37, Ch. 4, Table 8.

[3] A similar statement probably applies to Canada. Unfortunately, the Canadian birth certificate does not contain information on socioeconomic characteristics that would allow examination of the effects of differential access to health care on the pattern of births by day of the week. On the Canadian situation, especially as affected by the introduction of universal health insurance, see reference 40.

Table 2

Percent deviation from the expected number of births and average number of births by day of the week, by month of pregnancy when prenatal care began, United States, 1971[a]

Month of Pregnancy when Prenatal Care Began	Mon.	Tues.	Wed.	Thurs.	Fri.	Sat.	Sun.	Ave. of All Days
Percent Deviation[b]								
1st or 2nd	2.8	8.6	4.8	2.3	4.5	− 8.0	−15.1	
3rd or 4th	2.4	7.4	3.7	2.0	3.9	− 6.7	−12.9	
5th or 6th	2.7	5.7	0.9	0.6	2.6	− 5.1	− 8.2	
7th, 8th, or 9th	2.3	2.9	1.7	−0.4	2.6	− 4.2	− 4.9	
No prenatal care	6.7	0.4	0.2	−4.5	−1.5	− 4.0	2.7	
Average Number of Births								
1st or 2nd	3,257.9	3,443.8	3,323.2	3,244.0	3,314.0	2,918.0	2,690.8	3,170.4
3rd or 4th	3,094.1	3,243.8	3,133.1	3,081.4	3,139.1	2,816.9	2,631.0	3,020.2
5th or 6th	941.8	969.2	925.1	922.3	940.9	869.7	842.0	916.9
7th, 8th, or 9th	449.3	451.5	446.2	437.0	450.0	429.4	417.3	438.8
No prenatal care	135.4	127.4	127.2	121.2	125.0	122.0	130.4	127.0
Number of Births								
1st or 2nd	169,412	179,076	172,802	168,688	175,644	151,738	139,926	1,157,286
3rd or 4th	160,894	168,676	162,922	160,234	166,370	146,478	136,812	1,102,386
5th or 6th	48,972	50,400	48,106	48,014	49,870	45,226	43,786	334,374
7th, 8th or 9th	23,362	23,478	23,204	22,722	23,848	21,860	21,698	160,172
No prenatal care	7,050	6,628	6,616	6,308	6,630	6,342	6,784	46,358

[a] For reporting states only.
[b] See Table 1 for definition.

Table 3

Average percent deviation from the expected number of births and average number of births by day of the week, by legitimacy status, United States and Canada, 1971[a]

Country and Legitimacy Status	Mon.	Tues.	Wed.	Thurs.	Fri.	Sat.	Sun.	Ave. of All Days
Percent Deviation [b]								
United States								
Legitimate	2.8	8.2	4.0	1.9	4.2	−7.8	−13.4	
Illegitimate	2.3	3.7	1.4	0.3	0.9	−3.7	−5.0	
Canada								
Legitimate	−0.6	6.5	6.2	3.5	2.4	−5.7	−12.3	
Illegitimate	2.8	3.3	2.9	0.6	−0.7	−1.7	−7.8	
Average Number of Births								
United States								
Legitimate	5,967.0	6,281.4	6,035.2	5,917.4	6,049.6	5,351.6	5,030.2	5,805.2
Illegitimate	773.4	784.0	766.6	758.2	762.8	727.6	718.4	756.0
Canada								
Legitimate	866.7	929.2	926.2	902.7	893.0	822.3	764.5	872.1
Illegitimate	88.4	88.8	88.5	86.5	85.4	84.5	79.8	86.0
Number of Births								
United States								
Legitimate	310,284	326,632	313,830	307,704	320,624	278,280	261,566	2,118,920
Illegitimate	40,212	40,772	39,862	39,426	40,438	37,840	37,360	275,910
Canada								
Legitimate	45,070	48,320	48,164	46,940	47,328	42,758	39,754	318,334
Illegitimate	4,599	4,617	4,601	4,499	4,527	4,394	4,152	31,389

[a] Only births in reporting states are included for the United States.
[b] See Table 1 for definition.

45

erratic health care than whites (41-47). Given this circumstance, we would expect that blacks would have fewer elective inductions than whites, and that blacks would thus have a less pronounced patterning of births by day of the week. Table 4 shows that this is indeed the case. Although both blacks and whites have fewer births on weekend days than on weekdays, the weekend deficit is substantially less pronounced for blacks than for whites.

Table 5 shows the distribution of births by day of the week for legitimate and illegitimate births within the white and black populations. Two points are evident from this table. First, for both legitimate and illegitimate births, the weekend birth deficit is less among the black population than among the white population. Secondly, within both the black and white populations, the weekend deficit is less for illegitimate births than for legitimate births. The contrast, however, is much less in the black population than in the white population, probably reflecting the lower level of prenatal care received by both segments of the black population.

The only indicator of socioeconomic status available from United States birth registration data is education. Education is expected to be correlated with access to and utilization of medical services because better educated people would probably demand proper medical care and because better educated people would be able to communicate more effectively with trained medical personnel (48-51). Education is also correlated with medical care because it is correlated with income, and income is correlated with the nature of medical care received (52-54). Table 6 shows the distribution of births by day of the week by education of mother within the white and black population. As expected, within both the white and black populations, the patterning of births by day of the week increases as education increases. Furthermore, this table again points out the differences between the black and white populations: the weekend deficit of births is greater for grade school education whites than for blacks who attended college.

The fact that the patterning of births decreases among groups least likely to receive adequate prenatal care further suggests that the elective induction of labor is a principal factor in this patterning. Furthermore, if the elective induction of labor is considered a questionable medical practice, then we have the somewhat paradoxical finding that those who receive the best medical care with respect to prenatal care receive questionable medical care with respect to elective induction. (This argument should not be construed as suggesting that the level of prenatal care should be reduced. Quite the contrary, all members of the population should have access to adequate prenatal care.)

Birth Weight

To the extent that elective induction is a major factor in the patterning of births by day of the week, then we would expect that the extent of the patterning would vary with weight at birth. The lowest level of elective inductions would be expected for low-birth-weight infants. Low birth weight is typically the result of prematurity, and elective induction would not knowingly be used unless the patient were at term. A comparatively high level of inductions would be expected among high-birth-weight infants. These, however, would be medically indicated inductions rather than elective

Table 4

Percent deviation from the expected number of births and average number of births by day of the week, by race of mother, United States, 1971

Race[a]	Mon.	Tues.	Wed.	Thurs.	Fri.	Sat.	Sun.	Ave. of All Days
Percent Deviation[b]								
White	2.5	8.2	4.4	2.2	4.5	-7.6	-14.3	
Black	3.4	2.7	0.8	0.0	1.4	-3.7	- 4.5	
Average Number of Births								
White	8,259.6	8,720.8	8,413.2	8,240.6	8,426.6	7,448.4	6,911.8	8,061.2
Black	1,567.4	1,556.8	1,527.6	1,515.2	1,536.6	1,459.4	1,447.0	1,515.8
Number of Births								
White	429,506	453,482	437,488	428,506	446,612	387,314	359,410	2,942,318
Black	81,504	80,950	79,438	78,790	81,438	75,886	75,242	553,248

[a] Other nonwhite are not included.
[b] See Table 1 for definition.

47

Table 5

Percent deviation from the expected number of births and average number of births by day of the week, by race and legitimacy status of child, United States, 1971[a]

Race and Legitimacy Status	Mon.	Tues.	Wed.	Thurs.	Fri.	Sat.	Sun.	Ave. of All Days
			Percent Deviation[b]					
White								
Legitimate	2.8	8.9	4.3	2.2	4.6	-8.3	-14.6	
Illegitimate	0.4	5.5	3.0	1.2	1.4	-4.7	-6.9	
Black								
Legitimate	3.1	2.8	1.7	0.4	1.1	-4.3	-4.9	
Illegitimate	3.4	2.3	0.2	-0.2	0.8	-2.9	-3.5	
			Average Number of Births					
White								
Legitimate	5,192.8	5,504.6	5,268.4	5,163.2	5,285.4	4,635.8	4,315.4	5,052.8
Illegitimate	297.8	312.8	305.6	300.4	301.0	282.8	276.2	296.6
Black								
Legitimate	660.8	658.8	651.4	643.2	648.0	613.4	609.2	640.8
Illegitimate	457.4	452.8	443.2	441.6	446.2	429.8	427.0	442.6
			Number of Births					
White								
Legitimate	270,024	286,234	273,952	268,490	280,124	241,066	224,396	1,844,286
Illegitimate	15,484	16,270	15,890	15,616	15,948	14,702	14,362	108,272
Black								
Legitimate	34,360	34,262	33,876	33,448	34,346	31,900	31,682	233,874
Illegitimate	23,786	23,550	23,050	22,958	23,650	22,348	22,200	161,542

[a] For reporting states only.
[b] See Table 1 for definition.

Table 6

Percent deviation from the expected number of births and average number of births by day of the week, by race and education of mother, United States, 1971[a]

Race and Education of Mother	Mon.	Tues.	Wed.	Thurs.	Fri.	Sat.	Sun.	Ave. of All Days
			Percent Deviation[b]					
White								
0-8 yrs	4.4	5.6	1.2	0.1	3.7	– 5.7	– 9.3	
9-11 yrs	3.3	6.8	3.0	0.0	2.5	– 5.6	–10.0	
12 yrs	1.4	9.4	4.1	2.5	4.9	– 7.7	–14.8	
13+ yrs	3.0	7.8	5.9	2.7	5.4	– 8.3	–16.6	
Black								
0-8 yrs	6.0	0.1	-1.6	0.6	3.2	– 5.3	– 3.1	
9-11 yrs	4.5	3.7	-1.4	-0.6	-0.1	– 3.7	– 2.4	
12 yrs	2.8	2.9	1.3	-0.3	2.5	– 4.0	– 5.3	
13+ yrs	1.1	3.5	6.2	-0.5	2.5	– 5.4	– 7.2	
			Average Number of Births					
White								
0-8 yrs	357.0	361.2	346.2	342.4	354.6	322.6	310.2	342.0
9-11 yrs	1,132.0	1,170.4	1,127.8	1,095.6	1,122.8	1,033.8	985.4	1,095.4
12 yrs	2,603.8	2,808.0	2,672.4	2,631.6	2,691.6	2,369.4	2,188.0	2,566.6
13+ yrs	1,314.1	1,375.2	1,350.8	1,309.8	1,344.2	1,169.5	1,064.3	1,275.6
Black								
0-8 yrs	111.2	105.0	103.2	105.4	108.2	99.4	101.6	104.8
9-11 yrs	406.0	402.8	383.2	386.0	388.0	374.2	379.0	388.4
12 yrs	390.6	390.8	385.0	378.6	389.4	364.6	360.0	379.8
13+ yrs	115.1	117.8	120.8	113.2	116.7	107.6	105.6	113.8

Table 6 (continued)

Race and Education of Mother	Mon.	Tues.	Wed.	Thurs.	Fri.	Sat.	Sun.	Ave. of All Days
			Number of Births					
White								
0-8 yrs	18,562	18,780	18,000	17,802	18,792	16,778	16,132	124,846
9-11 yrs	58,860	60,860	58,646	56,974	59,508	53,760	51,244	399,852
12 yrs	135,394	146,014	138,906	136,844	142,652	123,204	113,776	936,844
13+ yrs	68,332	71,512	70,240	68,110	71,240	60,812	55,344	465,590
Black								
0-8 yrs	5,780	5,456	5,366	5,484	5,732	5,164	5,284	38,266
9-11 yrs	21,112	20,946	19,926	20,068	20,562	19,454	19,708	141,776
12 yrs	20,308	20,320	20,018	19,692	20,638	18,958	18,716	138,650
13+ yrs	5,986	6,126	6,284	5,886	6,184	5,594	5,492	41,552

[a] For reporting states only.
[b] See Table 1 for definition.

50

inductions. A higher proportion of high-birth-weight infants are born past term than is the case for infants in other weight groups, and, if the patient is significantly past term, this is a medical indication for induction of labor (3, 7-9, 55).

Table 7 shows that the weekend deficit varies with birth weight as expected. The smallest deficits are found for the low-birth-weight group, and the largest deficits are found for the high-birth-weight group. This is the case in both the United States and Canada. Furthermore, if we combine data from Canada and the United States and look at the small group of infants weighing less than 1000 grams at birth, we find no weekend deficit. Thus, this variation by birth weight further suggests that elective induction is at least partly responsible for the weekend birth deficit.

Trends

The fact that the weekend deficit has increased dramatically over time is the final piece of indirect evidence that this patterning of births by day of the week is the result of the use of elective induction in conjunction with a preference to schedule deliveries during the week. Even though induction of labor has been practiced at least since 1609 and elective induction advocated at least since 1871 (3, 15, 36), it was not until the mid-1950s that the problem of chemical synthesis of oxytocin was solved and it was demonstrated that the native and the synthetic hormone acted identically (56-58). In short, the drug routinely used in elective inductions was not widely available until the mid-1950s. Thus, we would expect that the use of elective induction, and the patterning of births by day of the week, would have increased from the early 1950s to the present.

Table 8 shows, for Canada, the average number of births by day of the week for selected years from 1951 through 1971. The increase in the weekend birth deficit over time is clearly evident. In 1951, the pattern of births by day of the week was almost random; by 1971, there were large differences in the number of births occurring on weekdays and weekends. The extent of this transformation can be seen in Figure 2, which contrasts the first and final years in the time series. (The number of births in 1951 has been inflated to the total for 1971 to insure that both graphs are on the same scale.) There can be no doubt that there has been a dramatic change in the proportion of births occurring on weekends,[4] and we argue that the most probable cause is the use of elective induction, coupled with the preference to have deliveries scheduled during the week. Unfortunately, a similar time series is not available for the United States.

DISCUSSION AND CONCLUSION

To summarize, we find, for both the United States and Canada, a persistent pattern of births by day of the week. There are far fewer births on weekends and holidays than would be expected if day of birth were a random event, and the circumstantial

---

[4] The over-time contrasts would be even more striking if we were able to control for birth order. The incidence of elective induction is greater among second and higher-order births than among first births. Since 1951, there has been a decline in higher-order births, and a corresponding increase in the proportion of first births (see reference 35).

Table 7

Average percent deviation from the expected number of births and average number of births by day of the week, by birth weight (in grams), United States and Canada, 1971[a]

Country and Birth Weight	Mon.	Tues.	Wed.	Thurs.	Fri.	Sat.	Sun.	Ave. of All Days
Percent Deviation[b]								
United States								
≤2500 gr	4.1	3.7	1.6	-0.8	1.7	-3.9	- 6.5	
2501-4000	2.5	7.4	3.8	2.1	4.4	-7.2	-13.1	
4001+	1.8	9.0	5.9	1.4	3.0	-7.6	-15.7	
Canada								
≤2500 gr	2.5	2.2	2.4	-0.7	0.6	-1.7	- 5.5	
2501-4000	-0.4	6.4	6.2	3.1	2.3	-5.5	-12.3	
4001+	-2.3	8.3	5.7	8.0	1.5	-7.5	-13.8	
Average Number of Births								
United States								
≤2500 gr	776.4	773.4	757.8	739.6	758.6	716.6	697.0	745.6
2501-4000	8,351.1	8,747.9	8,451.4	8,314.4	8,498.7	7,556.4	7,078.7	8,143.6
4001+	863.3	924.0	897.6	859.7	873.4	783.2	732.4	847.7
Canada								
≤2500 gr	74.1	73.9	74.0	71.8	72.7	71.1	68.3	72.3
2501-4000	803.0	857.4	856.0	831.1	824.7	761.7	707.1	805.9
4001+	77.8	86.2	84.1	86.0	80.8	73.6	68.6	79.6

Number of Births

United States								
≤ 2500 gr	40,376	40,214	39,402	38,462	40,210	37,264	36,248	272,176
2501–4000	434,258	454,890	439,472	432,348	450,432	392,932	368,094	2,972,426
4001 +	44,892	48,048	46,674	44,702	46,290	40,728	38,086	309,420
Canada								
≤ 2500 gr	3,852	3,843	3,850	3,733	3,851	3,698	3,554	26,381
2501–4000	41,755	44,587	44,513	43,219	43,709	39,606	36,768	294,157
4001 +	4,040	4,483	4,375	4,470	4,283	3,825	3,568	29,044

[a] Births with missing data on birth weight are not included.
[b] See Table 1 for definition.

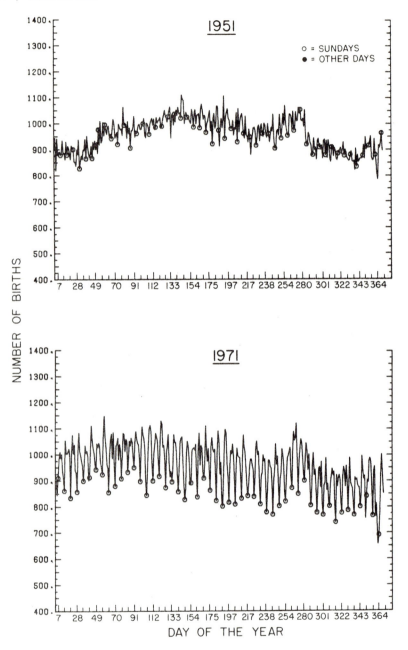

Figure 2. Number of births by day, January 1 through December 31, 1951 and 1971, Canada. The number of births for 1951 has been inflated to the 1971 total so that the graphs for both years are at the same scale. This inflating factor affects only the scale and not the patterns.

Table 8

Average percent deviation from the expected number of births and average number of births by day of the week, for selected years, Canada, 1951-1971

Year	Mon.	Tues.	Wed.	Thurs.	Fri.	Sat.	Sun.	Ave. of All Days
			Percent Deviation[a]					
1951	0.0	0.7	0.1	-0.1	0.4	1.0	- 2.0	
1956	-0.9	2.3	0.8	-0.5	1.4	0.9	- 3.8	
1961	-1.6	3.1	2.5	0.3	2.4	-0.5	- 6.0	
1966	-1.4	5.6	3.1	1.7	2.2	-2.7	- 8.4	
1971	-0.3	6.3	5.6	3.2	2.1	-5.4	-11.9	
			Average Number of Births					
1951	1,081.2	1,089.1	1,082.3	1,079.8	1,085.5	1,092.0	1,059.4	1,081.3
1956	1,227.8	1,267.4	1,249.0	1,232.7	1,256.8	1,250.8	1,192.8	1,239.5
1961	1,303.5	1,366.7	1,357.7	1,328.9	1,357.4	1,318.1	1,245.2	1,325.1
1966	1,061.9	1,136.9	1,109.9	1,095.0	1,100.8	1,047.9	986.5	1,076.9
1971	955.2	1,018.0	1,014.7	989.2	978.0	906.8	844.3	958.1
			Number of Births					
1951	57,302	56,631	56,280	56,148	56,447	56,783	55,088	394,679
1956	65,072	65,906	64,949	64,102	65,355	65,044	63,216	453,644
1961	67,784	71,069	70,598	69,105	70,585	68,539	65,994	483,674
1966	55,221	59,117	57,715	56,939	57,242	55,539	51,300	393,073
1971	49,669	52,937	52,765	51,439	51,885	47,152	43,906	349,723

[a]See Table 1 for definition.

evidence presented here suggests that elective induction of labor is the main factor responsible for this patterning. Furthermore, the evidence from the midwestern hospital that some physicians may prefer to schedule births on weekends, rather than during the week, suggests that the practice of elective induction is even more widespread than these birth registration data suggest.

The importance of our findings pointing to the widespread practice of induction stems from the facts that (a) the procedure *is* often elective, and (b) the procedure may introduce risk. It is impossible to determine from these data whose convenience is being served—the patient's or the physician's. But no matter whose convenience is being served, the fact remains that a medical procedure is being justified on the ground of convenience. Furthermore, as noted in the introduction, the use of elective induction introduces risk to mother and child. The risk is very small, but can this risk be justified for the sake of convenience?

The bases on which to evaluate a practice such as the elective induction of labor have to be different from those used to evaluate typical medical procedures. In the usual case, a medical procedure is employed if it is judged that the medical benefits to the patient outweigh the risk introduced by employing the procedure—even if the risk is quite severe. That is not the case here because, by definition, there are no medical benefits to be obtained by the patient or the infant because of the utilization of elective induction.

It is also possible that the widespread use of elective induction may impart some risk to women and infants who are not induced. The connection is indirect. If a large proportion of deliveries become concentrated during the weekdays, then one response a hospital may make is to reduce the staff on weekends. Thus, nonscheduled deliveries on weekends would be handled by a reduced staff, which may not be equipped to deal with serious complications. However, others might argue the reverse: that increasing planning for deliveries makes it possible to tailor resources to needs. From the data available to us it is not possible to sort out the cost-benefit trade-offs of reducing or increasing the scheduling of labor. What we have done is present evidence that the scheduling of labor is a common practice, and, as a result, questions such as the cost-benefit trade-offs of the practice deserve serious consideration from future researchers and policy makers.

In conclusion, we recommend, at a minimum, the routine collection of data on the onset and management of labor. At present, it is impossible to determine exactly how many elective inductions occur or precisely what effect their occurrence has. Such information would be extremely valuable in assessing the implications of the procedure. We also recommend that the medical profession and consumers alike consider whether it is wise and justifiable to introduce risk solely for the sake of convenience.

Acknowledgments—We appreciate the assistance of Statistics Canada, and note that the views expressed in this paper do not necessarily represent the views of that organization. The assistance of the Carolina Population Center in the final stages of preparation of this manuscript is also appreciated. The research assistance of Debra Julian, Cheryl Knobeloch, and Margaret Knoll is gratefully acknowledged.

REFERENCES

1. Dunn, P. M. Obstetric delivery today. For better or for worse? *Lancet* 1(7963): 790-793, April 1976.
2. Editorial. A time to be born. *Lancet* 2(7890): 1183-1184, November 1974.
3. MacVicar, J. Acceleration and augmentation of labour. *Scott Med. J.* 18: 201-214, November 1973.
4. Richards, M. P. Innovation in medical practice: Obstetricians and the induction of labour in Britain. *Soc. Sci. Med.* 9(11-12): 595-602, 1975.
5. Theobald, G. W. Letter: Dangers of oxytocin-induced labour to fetuses. *Br. Med. J.* 4(5936): 102, October 1974.
6. Keettel, W. C. Elective induction of labor. In *Controversy in Obstetrics and Gynecology*, edited by D. E. Reid and T. C. Barton, pp. 109-114. W. B. Saunders Company, Philadelphia, 1969.
7. MacDonald, D. Surgical induction of labor. *Am. J. Obstet. Gynecol.* 107:908-911, July 1970.
8. Pinkerton, J. H. Induction of labour on behalf of the fetus. *Journal of the Irish Medical Association* 66: 592-596, November 1973.
9. Zuspan, F. P., coordinator. Induction of labor—Part II, an invitational symposium. *J. Reprod. Med.* 6(2): 17-32, February 1971.
10. Cole, R. A., Howie, P. W., and Macnaughton, M. C. Elective induction of labour. A randomised prospective trial. *Lancet* 1(7910): 767-770, April 1975.
11. Hall, R. E. Standard practices at Sloane Hospital. The management of the induction of labor. *Bulletin of the Sloane Hospital of Women* 7: 55-58, summer 1961.
12. Pinkerton, J. H. M., Martin, D. H., and Thompson, W. Selective planned induction in conditions of civil strife. *Lancet* 1(7900): 197-198, January 1975.
13. Blacow, M., et al. Letter: Induction of labor. *Lancet* 1(7900): 217, January 1975.
14. Campbell, N., Harvey, D., and Norman, A. P. Increased frequency of neonatal jaundice in a maternity hospital. *Br. Med. J.* 2(5970): 548-552, June 1975.
15. Fields, H., Greene, J., and Smith, K. *Induction of Labor.* Macmillan Company, New York, 1965.
16. Frost, A. C. Death following intrauterine injection of hypertonic saline solution with hydatidiform mole. *Am. J. Obstet. Gynecol.* 101: 343-344, June 1968.
17. Keettel, W. C., Randall, J. H., and Donnelly, M. M. The hazards of elective induction of labor. *Am. J. Obstet. Gynecol.* 75(3): 496-510, 1968.
18. Liston, W. A., and Campbell, A. J. Dangers of oxytocin-induced labour to fetuses. *Br. Med. J.* 3(5931): 606-607, September 1974.
19. Niswander, K. R., and Patterson, R. J. Hazards of elective induction of labor. *Obstet. Gynecol.* 22: 228-233, August 1963.
20. Rubin, L., and Baskett, T. F. "Silent" uterine rupture during labour. *Can. Med. Assoc. J.* 104: 612, April 1971.
21. Schwarcz, R. L., et al. Fetal and maternal monitoring in spontaneous labors and in elective inductions. A comparative study. *Am. J. Obstet. Gynecol.* 120(3): 356-362, October 1974.
22. Smith, A. M. Letter: Rupture of uterus during prostaglandin-induced abortion. *Br. Med. J.* 1(5951): 205, January 1975.
23. Schaffer, B., and Kaern, T. Risks of induction of labor by intravenous oxytocin. *Acta Obstet. Gynecol. Scand.* [Suppl] 9: 69, 1971.
24. Rindfuss, R. R., Gortmaker, S. L., and Ladinsky, J. L. Elective induction of labor and the health of the infant: Evidence from New York City. *Am. J. Public Health* 68(9): 872, 1978.
25. Hawkins, D. F., editor. *Obstetric Therapeutics: Clinical Pharmacology and Therapeutics in Obstetric Practice.* Williams and Wilkins Company, Baltimore, 1974.
26. Wilson, J. R., Beecham, C. T., and Carrington, E. R. *Obstetrics and Gynecology*, 5th edition. C. V. Mosby Company, St. Louis, 1975.
27. Romney, S. L., et al. *Gynecology and Obstetrics: The Health Care of Women.* McGraw-Hill, New York, 1975.
28. Benson, R. C. *Handbook of Obstetrics and Gynecology*, 5th edition. Lange Medical Publications, Los Altos, Cal., 1974.
29. Greenhill, J. P., and Friedman, E. A. *Biological Principles and Modern Practice of Obstetrics.* W. B. Saunders Company, Philadelphia, 1974.
30. Hellman, L. M., and Pritchard, J. A. *Williams Obstetrics*, 14th edition. Appleton-Century-Crofts, New York, 1971.

31. Page, E. W., Villee, C. A., and Villee, D. B. *Human Reproduction.* W. B. Saunders Company, Philadelphia, 1972.
32. Garrey, M. M., et al. *Obstetrics Illustrated.* Churchill Livingstone, Edinburg, 1974.
33. Alvarez, H. Editorial. In Induction of labor—Part II, an invitational symposium, coordinated by F. P. Zuspan. *J. Reprod. Med.* 6(2): 18, February 1971.
34. Barber, H. R., Graber, E. A., and Orlando, A. Augmented labor. *Obstet. Gynecol.* 39: 933-941, June 1972.
35. Rindfuss, R. R., and Ladinsky, J. L. Patterns of births: Implications for the incidence of elective induction. *Med. Care* 14(8): 685-693, August 1976.
36. Fields, H. Induction of labor: Its past, its present and its place. *Postgrad. Med.* 44: 226-231, September 1968.
37. National Center for Health Statistics. *Vital Statistics of the United States, 1971.* 1 (Natality). Public Health Service, Rockville, Md., 1975.
38. Kessner, D. M., et al. *Infant Death: An Analysis by Maternal Risk and Health Care.* National Academy of Sciences, Washington, D.C., 1973.
39. Watkins, E. L. Low-income Negro mothers—Their decision to seek prenatal care. *Am. J. Public Health* 58: 655-667, April 1968.
40. Wolfe, S. Primary health care for the poor in the United States and Canada. *Int. J. Health Serv.* 2(2): 217-228, 1972.
41. Alpert, J. J., Kosa, J., and Haggerty, R. J. A month of illness and health care among low-income families. *Public Health Rep.* 82: 705-713, August 1967.
42. Brooks, C. H. The changing relationship between socioeconomic status and infant mortality: An analysis of state characteristics. *J. Health Soc. Behav.* 16(3): 291-303, September 1975.
43. Herman, M. W. The poor: Their medical needs and the health services available to them. *The Annals of the American Academy of Political and Social Science* 399: 12-21, January 1972.
44. Lerner, M. Social differences in physical health. In *Poverty and Health,* edited by J. Kosa and I. K. Zola. Harvard University Press, Cambridge, 1969.
45. Weinerman, E. R., et al. Yale studies in ambulatory medical care. V. Determinants of use of hospital emergency services. *Am. J. Public Health* 56: 1037-1056, July 1966.
46. Roth, J. A. The treatment of the sick. In *Poverty and Health,* edited by J. Kosa and I. K. Zola. Harvard University Press, Cambridge, 1969.
47. Taylor, D. G., Aday, L. A., and Andersen, R. A social indicator of access to medical care. *J. Health Soc. Behav.* 16(1): 39-49, March 1975.
48. Bullough, B. Poverty, ethnic identity and preventive health care. *J. Health Soc. Behav.* 13: 347-359, December 1972.
49. Cartwright, A. *Human Relations and Hospital Care.* Routledge and Kegan Paul, London, 1973.
50. Pratt, L., Seligmann, A., and Reader, G. Physicians' views on the level of medical information among patients. *Am. J. Public Health* 47(10): 1277-1283, October 1957.
51. Waitzkin, H., and Stoeckle, J. D. The communication of information about illness; clinical, sociological and methodological considerations. *Adv. Psychosom. Med.* 8: 180-215, 1972.
52. Mechanic, D. *Public Expectations and Health Care.* Wiley-Interscience, New York, 1972.
53. Monteiro, L. A. Expense is no object: Income and physician visits reconsidered. *J. Health Soc. Behav.* 14: 99-115, June 1973.
54. Ward, R. A. *The Economics of Health Resources.* Addison-Wesley, Reading, Mass., 1975.
55. Barter, R. H. Induction of labor: Helpful or harmful? *Postgrad. Med.* 43: 141-144, June 1968.
56. Boissonnas, R. A., et al. Une nouville synthese de l'oxytocine. *Helvetica Chimica Acta* 38: 1491-1501, 1955.
57. DuVigneaud, V., Ressler, C., and Trippett, S. The sequence of amino acids in oxytocin, with a proposal for the structure of oxytocin. *J. Biol. Chem.* 205(2): 949-957, December 1953.
58. DuVigneaud, V., et al. The synthesis of an octapeptide amide with the hormonal acitivity of oxytocin. *J. Am. Chem. Soc.* 75: 4879-4880, 1953.

CHAPTER 3

Vaginal Cancer: An Iatrogenic Disease?

Kay Weiss

Between 1943 and 1970, diethylstilbestrol (DES), a synthetic nonsteroidal estrogen, was widely prescribed in this country to prevent threatened miscarriage in spite of the fact that as early as 1953 reports appeared in the medical literature disproving its effectiveness (1, 2).[1] It is estimated that estrogens were prescribed for nearly 6 million pregnant women between 1943-1959, resulting in the births of 2.8 million females exposed in utero to estrogens (1.9 million to synthetic estrogens).[2] Research of pharmacy records for the period 1960-1970 shows that between 10,000 and 50,000 females were born of DES pregnancies each year (3). These figures result in a total estimate that between 2.1 and 3.5 million females were exposed to estrogens in utero before the practice was discontinued in 1971.

In 1971 a cluster of eight cases of a rare type of vaginal adenocarcinoma appeared in women under the age of 20 whose mothers had been treated with DES in pregnancy (4). Prior to 1971, clear-cell adenocarcinoma of the vagina in women of that age was almost unreported in the world literature. Between 1971 and 1974, 220 cases[3]

---

[1] A review of the epidemiology of vaginal adenocarcinoma and adenosis by K. Weiss is presented in the *Journal of the American Medical Women's Association* 30(2): 59-63, 1975. A discussion of those results is presented here.

[2] National Cancer Institute Research Contracts Branch RFP No. NIH-NCI-CN-74-23, December 1, 1973.

[3] Personal communication, Registry of Clear-cell Adenocarcinoma of the Genital Tract in Young Females, Boston.

of histologically identical vaginal and cervical adenocarcinoma[4] in women between the ages of 7 and 29 were reported to the Registry of Clear-cell Adenocarcinoma of the Genital Tract in Young Females in Boston (5). About 85 per cent of these women were exposed to DES or one of its congeners prior to the fourth month in utero (6). Twenty-four deaths have occurred to date. In addition to the 220 known cases of adenocarcinoma, benign vaginal adenosis has been noted in about 90 per cent of DES daughters examined (7, 8).

The pattern of this epidemic, and the etiologic relationship between DES administration in pregnancy and genital adenocarcinoma in offspring, will not be confirmed until more DES-exposed offspring reach puberty and adequate epidemiologic studies can be conducted. Some prominent epidemiologists stated after the first eight cases were reported that the cause had been demonstrated to their satisfaction to be DES (9, 10). Nevertheless, the theory of DES causality has been subjected to much scrutiny and this skepticism has delayed the implementation of definitive public health action on behalf of the DES-exposed.

THEORY OF DES CAUSALITY

Hypotheses have been projected to explain why male offspring of DES pregnancies, the mothers themselves, and the vast majority of DES daughters who have reached puberty have not developed the disease. An understanding of the mechanism of action of DES in the production of clear-cell adenocarcinoma can best answer these questions. Folkman (9) has conjectured that during a critical stage of fetal vaginal development,

> a single fetal cell in the future vaginal tissue undergoes malignant transformation because of stilbestrol ... this genetic defect might not be disclosed during the prepubertal years, when cellular renewal is sluggish and only a rare cell is undergoing mitosis. At puberty the vaginal epithelium responds to surges of hormonal stimulation and depletion. Millions of cells are swept into the mitotic cycle . . . this provides the opportunity for a lurking defective cell to display its malignant nature.

The fact that mothers exposed to stilbestrol did not develop adenocarcinoma when it appeared in their daughters may be explained by the exquisite sensitivity of fetal tissues to carcinogens (9). That these cancers have not appeared in male offspring of DES pregnancies can be related to the embryology of sexual development (11). The vagina is formed from pregenital Müllerian tissue; during formation of male genitalia this tissue becomes vestigial and is represented by the appendix of the testis. This may explain the absence of tumors of Müllerian origin in male offspring of DES pregnancies.

The embryology of sexual development may also explain the absence of adenocarcinoma in the majority of DES daughters. Exposure to estrogens had to occur during genital organogenesis for genital anomalies to develop (11). DES was typically prescribed when the pregnant woman first reported "spotting" to her physician. For many women who see their obstetricians in scheduled monthly appointments this may have been after the fourth month of pregnancy when the vagina of the fetus was already formed. The low known incidence of adenocarcinoma in the population at risk might also be explained by underreporting of the disease to the Boston Registry as well as by individual endogenous factors. During congressional hearings on the

---

[4]Although about 40 per cent of the 220 clear-cell adenocarcinomas are cervical, it is thought that these may be vaginal tumors which had already spread to the cervix by the time of diagnosis.

regulation of DES (12), Saffiotti explained how the carcinogenic qualities of any compound vary from person to person in reference to endogenous factors:

> The induction of cancer, as the biological response leading to the appearance of a tumor, is a process that is controlled at different levels, not only by the initial triggering off of a carcinogenic change in the cell by the original chemical, but also by cell population growth control systems, by endocrinological factors and others.

Dose, duration, and specific time of exposure to carcinogens are all determinants of disease. The dosage of DES as an "anti-miscarriage" drug was widely varied and often arbitrarily decided by the obstetrician. A common administration began at 2 milligrams daily and was increased to 200 milligrams daily at term. Critical time of exposure, i.e. the 6th to 20th week of gestation, was of greater importance than dosage or duration of exposure in production of vaginal adenocarcinoma in offspring; dosages as little as 1.5 milligrams and for as short an interval as 12 days during the first trimester have both been associated with development of the tumor in female offspring (4, 13).

Other factors may be associated with the development of these cancers, but retrospective studies have so far established an association only between maternal estrogen and adenocarcinoma in offspring (4, 14). These have not studied a large number of mothers with the tendency to miscarry who did not receive estrogen, but according to Folkman "this omission is irrelevant, because of the extreme rarity of adenocarcinoma of the vagina in young women" and because, if the tendency to miscarry conferred some hidden genetic factor which operated to produce adenocarcinoma, we would have seen many more cases throughout the past and many more at present, for the tendency to miscarry is exceedingly common. Folkman continues that "if stilbestrol acted only to salvage fetuses with high susceptibility to cancer, it is unlikely that all the tumors would be of the same cell type" (9).

Histologic similarity of the tumors, or specificity of tissue response to a carcinogen, is an important consideration in the determination of cause and effect, i.e. whether DES is associated with tumors other than clear-cell adenocarcinoma, and conversely whether vaginal adenocarcinoma occurs in association with drugs other than DES. Reviews of cancer cases reported to the New York State Cancer Registry between 1950–1971 and to the California Tumor Registry between 1963–1969 showed no association between maternal estrogen use and cancer in sites other than the vagina (15, 16). The absence of synthetic estrogen exposure in utero was documented in cancers of 12 endocrine-dependent urogenital sites in males and females other than the vagina.

The New York State Cancer Registry data also support the thesis that clear-cell vaginal adenocarcinoma is in fact a new disease, not simply one which has been unrecognized, unreported, or misdiagnosed in the past. If it had been prevalent in New York State during that period it would likely have been reported to the Registry along with cancers of the uterus, urethra, fallopian tube, uterine corpus, male urethra and breast, prostate, epididymis, and spermatic cord.

RELATIONSHIP OF ADENOSIS TO ADENOCARCINOMA

The presence of glandular structures (adenosis) in the vagina or cervix is considered to be an indication of the adenosis-carcinoma syndrome (13, 17). Adenosis may be accompanied by irregular bleeding. In utero exposure to stilbestrol is thought to result in the persistence of Müllerian-type glandular epithelium which is further stimulated by estrogen at puberty to form glandular cells from normal epithelium. Two laboratory animal experiments have duplicated this effect (18, 19).

Adenosis was previously a rare condition, but is now found to coexist with clear-cell adenocarcinoma in the majority of cases. Its high incidence in DES daughters who do not have adenocarcinoma also suggests that adenosis may be an anomaly of vaginal development in response to DES. Herbst and Scully (20) were first to report adenosis in about 30 per cent of a small group of DES daughters, and none in 285 non-exposed controls. But with the aid of a colposcope, Stafl and colleagues (7) found adenosis in 91 per cent of 63 DES daughters, and none in the controls. In the largest study of DES daughters to date, Sherman and colleagues (8) examined 528 daughters and found 90 per cent of those with a documented history of DES exposure in utero to have adenosis. If we extrapolate from the results of these studies to the larger population at risk, we may expect a high percentage of DES daughters to develop adenosis. While it is established that adenosis coexists with adenocarcinoma, it is not known whether it is a stage in the transformation of benign to malignant lesions, although this has been suspected in a few cases (21-23).

DETERMINATION OF RISK

The risk of developing adenocarcinoma for a daughter who has been exposed to DES in utero cannot be computed in the absence of an adequate data base to study incidence and prevalence rates for the disease. Determination of these rates cannot be made until the first cohort of exposed daughters has undergone the endocrine stimulation of puberty, menstruation, and pregnancy. These rates would reflect demographic patterns and changing DES usage rates by age structure, mortality by age, latency-time distribution, and co-carcinogenic relationships. Epidemiologic studies enabling projection of future incidence and prevalence rates are a public health mandate in view of the fact that thousands of women have been exposed to DES but have not been told their risk of developing vaginal cancer.

In an attempt to estimate risk, the Mayo Clinic conducted a follow-up of 1719 persons born at the Mayo Clinic between 1943 and 1959 who were exposed to estrogens in utero, and published the findings that no cases of adenocarcinoma of the vagina or cervix were found (24). However, this study had several limitations. Of the 818 females in this group, only 279 had a gynecologic examination at time of follow-up, and of these only 246 had a special colposcopic examination. Furthermore, four in situ squamous-cell carcinomas of the cervix were found, three of these among women who had the colposcopic examination. Adenocarcinoma is often asymptomatic and occult, and routine pelvic examinations have been shown to be insufficient in detecting disease (7, 25). In lieu of testing DES offspring, the Mayo Clinic mailed questionnaires to physicians who had most currently seen DES-exposed individuals and inquired whether any cases of adenocarcinoma had come to their attention. It is unlikely that asymptomatic or occult carcinoma would have been found in this way, particularly since only 279 women received a recent pelvic examination.

DETECTION, TREATMENT, AND PROGNOSIS

Verification of a history of maternal stilbestrol should be made by consulting obstetric or pharmacy records and by asking the mother whether estrogens were administered during pregnancy. When there is suspicion of exposure, daughters of the age group 8–30 should be examined for abnormal cellular changes in the vagina every 6 months throughout their lives. Most of the women who have developed adenocarcinoma had advanced disease at the time of diagnosis; some have died within 18 months of diagnosis. Adenocarcinoma, unlike squamous-cell carcinoma, is associated with an extremely poor prognosis because of its high metastatic potential. Twenty-six per cent of the first 65 patients treated either have died or had recurrence of disease within 5 years of therapy (5).

Although adenocarcinoma is asymptomatic in about 16 per cent of cases (5) and adenosis is asymptomatic in the majority of cases, they may be accompanied by vaginal bleeding or "spotting" that is often assumed by the gynecologist to be due to anovulation, and which is often treated by hormone therapy (17). Vaginal bleeding in children may be mistaken for early onset of menarche. The poor prognosis associated with adenosis might well be related to the delay in correct diagnosis caused by hormone therapy. Such therapy is unwise in view of the fact that estrogen is generally contraindicated for women with breast or genital cancers. "One can no longer assume that irregular vaginal bleeding in adolescent girls is related to anovulatory cycles and proceed with treatment on this assumption," states Hill (17).

Schiller iodine staining is valuable in detecting clear-cell adenocarcinoma, but the colposcope can augment the physician's ability to detect precancerous adenosis, localizing hidden lesions and eliminating the need for blind biopsies (26). With colposcopic detection, Stafl and coworkers (7) reported an incidence of 91 per cent adenosis in a group of DES daughters along with the disturbing finding that most had been assured by other gynecologists that they were free of disease:

> Exfoliative cytology, visual examination, pelvic examination and the use of the Schiller's test have proven to be inaccurate methods for defining and localizing the extent of vaginal adenosis. In the present series, routine cytology completely failed to detect vaginal adenosis. Gross examination was completely normal in 71% of the girls with histologically proven vaginal adenosis. Pelvic examination was also inconclusive in diagnosing adenosis. Thirty-one girls had had previous gynecologic examinations by other gynecologists, with clinical suspicion of vaginal adenosis in only 7 (23%) of the cases. Twenty-four girls (77%) who had a negative gynecologic examination, were erroneously reassured of the absence of this condition which was later detected by colposcopic examination (7).

Other investigators (25) have confirmed Stafl and coworkers' finding that "vaginal adenosis is clinically unrecognizable in most cases by conventional diagnostic methods." Unfortunately, in young patients in whom the hymen is intact, hymenotomy and examination under anesthesia are often necessary to permit intensive colposcopy. Young women who show no evidence of cellular abnormalities cannot be safely considered to be free of latent adenocarcinoma, because as endocrinologist Hertz stated at congressional hearings on the regulation of DES (12), "tissues exposed to known carcinogens frequently have an essentially normal microscopic appearance during the decade of latency. . . ."

There is no definitive medical prophylaxis to prevent benign adenosis from becoming malignant and medical therapy for adenocarcinoma is equally noncommittal. Treatment of adenosis has so far involved surgical excision, cauterization, and cryotherapy (13) although, since adenosis lesions may be multifocal, these cannot guarantee its eradication. Local progesterone vaginal suppositories may aid regression of adenosis and avoid the onset of adenocarcinoma (27). Progesterone has aided in regression of endometrial adenocarcinoma and may have application in treatment of vaginal adenocarcinoma (28). At present, treatment of vaginal and cervical adenocarcinoma has been limited to surgical therapy ranging from excision of small lesions to removal of the uterus, vagina and pelvic lymph nodes, or external radiation therapy, implantation of radium needles in the tumor, or some combination of these.

Although it was not known at the time that DES was used as an anti-miscarriage drug that it was a teratogen, existing knowledge of physiology, i.e. the dependence of fetal formation on a specific predetermined intrauterine hormonal milieu, should have caused more obstetricians to hesitate to introduce exogenous hormones into the balanced fetal environment to prevent the naturally occurring phenomenon of early pregnancy loss. In addition, even before the peak years of DES use, the association of estrogen with cancer in women and in laboratory animals was established in the medical literature (18, 29-31). Many obstetricians routinely prescribed DES to women who had no history of miscarriage because they felt it insured a strong pregnancy.

To assume that our health care system will provide optimum treatment for vaginal cancer victims embraces an inherent contradiction. It implies that the shortcomings in the medical care system that allowed the event to occur will not be operating when the event is being remedied. Many DES daughters with adenocarcinoma or adenosis will have to choose among surgery, radiotherapy, or chemotherapy. To assume that they will make their choice with informed consent would be to ignore the fact that their present condition is in part a result of a lack of informed consent in the past.

Since treatment of this previously unknown disease necessarily involves some degree of experimentation, use of these therapies requires a warning of their suspected side effects. Radiation directed at the vagina for treatment of adenosis might cause mutation of ova, making future childbearing unwise. In addition, it could result in uterine cancer (32). Local progesterone therapy, while successful in regression of disease in some cases, has also been reported to exacerbate the growth of tumors (33). Use of such prophylaxes on hundreds of thousands of DES daughters with adenosis would certainly involve liability exposure to physicians if unaccompanied by an explanation of suspected adverse effects.

FAILURE OF PUBLIC HEALTH AGENCIES TO RECALL AND TEST DES-EXPOSED WOMEN

For most young women with adenocarcinoma medical therapy comes too late, and for many with precancerous lesions medical prophylaxis may come too late as well. Nevertheless, it is the right of unwitting victims of the unwarranted use of a drug (1, 2) to be informed of their risk of disease. The "no need to worry" doctrine and warnings of the "scare tactics" of press reports offered by many physicians in response to inquiry by DES daughters (34) too often means that the physicians do not have access to Schiller staining or colposcopic equipment, do not want to admit liability, or would feel an obligation to provide similar testing for all of their patients. DES daughters are too often given routine pelvic examinations and cervical "pap smears" which do not test for vaginal adenocarcinoma. This is illustrated by the fact that the American Cancer Society recently advised that DES daughters increase their cervical smears to two per year. Even when colposcopic tests are performed, DES daughters are sometimes told that the results of their tests were negative when they were actually negative for cancer, but positive for adenosis. These occurrences mirror the fact that our health care system is not equipped to handle the results of mass experimentation with unproven drugs.

The failure of governmental health agencies to notify the DES generation of the risk and to institute comprehensive testing programs, and the failure of most prescribing physicians to recall patients to whom they prescribed DES (35), illustrate a head-in-the-sand approach to an iatrogenic epidemic. The lack of urgency or organized concern of medical institutions is evident. In response to a query as to whether an effort would be made to trace the women who were prescribed DES in the 1950–1952 clinical trials, the American Medical Association Department of Drugs stated (36):

> An organized effort by the medical profession to inform all women who were given estrogen therapy . . . of the possible tragic consequences for the female offspring is of questionable advisability. . . . a determination of risk must await the results of a further compilation of statistics from reports of hospitals, physicians and tumor registries.

In November 1971 during congressional hearings on the regulation of DES, Representative L. H. Fountain asked Charles Edwards, then Commissioner of the Food and Drug Administration (FDA) why he did not use the news media to advise young women to have immediate medical examinations if their mothers had taken DES during pregnancy or if they had irregular vaginal bleeding. Edwards responded (35),

> I think that we have to be careful, in our activities and overpronouncements, not to create an emotional crisis on the part of American women. The average woman does not probably know, if she threatened to abort, what her doctor may have given her. I think this is one of the responsibilities that has to be laid directly at the doorstep of the American doctor. I think he has to come up with the answer.

But in July 1974 D. H. Mills of the editorial board of the *Journal of the American Medical Association* advised physicians, "since the risk of these lesions seems small, it may not be wise to stir a national alarm. . . ." Mills continued that where records are available, preprinted notices informing DES daughters to seek testing could be mailed to mothers' last known addresses, i.e. addresses of 10–20 years previous, and although "many mothers . . . will never receive these notices, further attempts to locate them should not be the responsibility of individual physicians, but rather the task of some governmental agency, if any" (37).

Minimal effort has been made by any governmental agency to recall and test a substantial percentage of the present generation of DES daughters. The etiologic relationship between prenatal DES and delayed genital neoplasia became established in 1971, yet by early 1975 definitive public health action had yet to be instituted to manage the welfare of the victims. The National Cancer Institute Cancer Control Project recently contracted with five university medical facilities to test 1000 DES daughters in each facility for the purpose of studying the incidence and natural history of the disease.[5] However, in practice, the centers at Baylor University, Harvard University, the University of Southern California, and the Mayo Clinic will probably test many referral patients and therefore may neglect the lower socioeconomic classes which were amply represented in prenatal DES clinics. Moreover, the testing of 5000

[5] National Cancer Institute Research Contracts Branch RFP No. NIH-NCI-CN-74-23, December 1, 1973.

daughters leaves a remainder of hundreds of thousands who have to date been uninformed that they need seek testing themselves.

At present it is up to the majority of DES-exposed individuals to learn from the media of the disease and the controversy surrounding the drug, attempt to obtain prescribing information from their mothers' obstetricians even though many will not release records without legal intervention, locate a physician who is aware of the stilbestrol problem and who will order a colposcopic examination, and pay about $45 every six months for the rest of their lives for the test. This expenditure represents an annual public health bill of approximately $180 million to be absorbed by the DES-exposed individuals.

CARCINOGENICITY OF SYNTHETIC ESTROGENS

The evidence of the transplacental carcinogenicity of estrogens provided by the vaginal cancer epidemic raises the question of the carcinogenicity of other synthetic or natural estrogens in women who take them, i.e. *in the recipients of the drug,* as opposed to their offspring. The ubiquitousness of estrogen prescriptions for women in the form of the oral contraceptive and hormone replacement at menopause (notably estradiol and premarin) and numerous other gynecologic uses makes a review of the carcinogenicity of estrogens in order.

Roy Hertz, former Chief of Endocrinology of the National Cancer Institute, stated at congressional hearings on the regulation of DES that the best available information suggests that all estrogens given at comparable doses and for comparable periods of time as DES would cause the same carcinogenic effects as DES (12). Mortimer Lipsett, Associate Scientific Director of Reproductive Biology at the National Institute of Child Health and Human Development, concurred that all estrogens "have the same effect on biochemical systems, on biological responses, and probably on carcinogenesis" (12). Hertz continued that,

> our inadequate knowledge concerning the relationship of estrogens to cancer in women is comparable with what was known about the association between lung cancer and cigarette smoking before extensive epidemiologic study delineated this overwhelmingly significant relationship (12).

Numerous experimental studies have established the carcinogenicity of estrogens, both exogenous and endogenous, nonsteroidal and steroidal, in experimental animals. Estrogens are carcinogenic in mice, rats, rabbits, hamsters and dogs, and produce tumors in all estrogen-dependent sites: the breast, uterus, vagina, kidney, ovary, testicle, pituitary gland, and bone marrow (18, 29-31, 38-43). In some cases extremely low levels of DES in the daily diet of mice (approximately 1 microgram) have induced breast tumors (40). Endometrial hyperplasia and adenocarcinoma similar to that observed in women have developed in rabbits following estrogen administration (29), and clear-cell adenocarcinoma of the vagina pathogenically identical to that occurring in DES daughters has followed the injection of rats with DES and estradiol (19).

While the carcinogenic effects of estrogen in animals are established, clinical evidence of carcinogenicity in humans is conflicting. Numerous case reports demonstrate an association between the administration of estrogens and the development of cancer in estrogen-dependent organs, although epidemiologic evidence of an increased incidence of cancer in women who take estrogens is inconclusive. Although some studies show a negative association between estrogen and cancer (44, 45), it is worthwhile in light of the current evidence of the (transplacental) carcinogenicity of synthetic estrogens to reexamine data which have shown a positive association.

It is known that the development of breast and endometrial cancer is influenced by endogenous estrogen metabolism (46, 47), and numerous studies indicate that there has been a high incidence of artificial estrogen ingestion sometime during the reproductive life of women with endometrial cancer (48, 49). Jensen and Ostergaard (50) indicate from their controlled study that "a continuous estrogen stimulation constitutes an important factor in the etiology of endometrial cancer." Gusberg and Hall (51) commented on the histology of endometrial adenocarcinomas which developed in women who received moderate doses of estrogen (estradiol, estrone, or stilbestrol) for moderate periods of time for menopausal hormone replacement:

> The resemblance of these lesions to adenomatous hyperplasia that can be produced by estrogens and their resemblance to lesions seen in the endometrium of patients with estrogen-producing ovarian tumors, forces one to the conclusion that this growth hormone plays some role in the development of these tumors. In the past 20 years when estrogen therapy has been widely used for therapeutic purposes on our ageing female population, there has been a relative increase in the incidence of [endometrial] cancer.

The prevalence of adenocarcinoma of the endometrium has increased from 2 to 14 per cent among all endometrial cancers between 1950–1965 (52), although in some areas of the country it has remained stable (53).

Oral contraceptives are known to produce distinct qualitative changes in the lining of the cervix, but the prognosis of these changes is unknown (54, 55). In a report on cervical "erosions" in pill users Taylor and colleagues (55) stated, "Thus far, this variety of hyperplasia has been found only in women taking oral progestins, usually for purposes of contraception. Such lesions have been observed by us with increasing frequency during the past two years and are important because they are sufficiently disturbing histologically to raise the question of carcinoma." Hertz (12) warns that,

> [Cancer of the endometrium] arises in a tissue which is delicately controlled by the hormonal balance in women. That the oral contraceptives disturb this balance is readily observable on microscopic examination of samples of this tissue. . . . It is important to appreciate that the renewed uterine lining is generated from the persistent remnants of the same lining which has previously undergone these profound changes [of estrogen stimulation]. Hence the impact of these earlier cellular changes is transmitted to the subsequently developed tissues for the remainder of the patient's life. . . . Addition of any artificial estrogen beyond the natural estrogen produced in the body disturbs a natural balance which, even under ideal conditions is precarious, demonstrated by the fact that one of each 16 women will develop breast cancer during her lifetime.

In a study of the association of oral contraceptives with cervical carcinoma in situ, Melamed and coworkers (56) observed 40,000 women who attended Planned Parenthood clinics. They noted a small but statistically significant increase in the prevalence rate of cervical carcinoma in situ in the group that chose and used steroid contraceptives, compared to the group that chose and used the diaphragm. This difference was consistently present when these groups were matched for age, ethnic origin, age at first pregnancy, parity, and economic level. They conclude that the difference in prevalence could be due either to a decrease in the rate of cervical carcinoma among those using the diaphragm or to an increase among those using the oral contraceptive.

Other studies report a negative association between the oral contraceptive and cancer (44, 45) and some report a lower than normal incidence of cancer in women who receive estrogen for hormone replacement at menopause. Such studies often lack necessary length of observation, however: the carcinogenicity of estrogens is usually expressed after a latency period of 10–20 years (12). Although epidemiologic studies are inconclusive, the lack of definitive data regarding the effect of estrogens on cancer of the breast, cervix, and endometrium may be comparable to the lack of data concerning the pill's effect on thromboembolism just a few years ago.

Where the administration of estrogens and the unknown risk of cancer is concerned, Saffiotti (12) comments:

> We should have a cautious attitude and when there is a potential hazard, recommend any measure that could reduce or eliminate that hazard, even if it is not clearly demonstrated by the direct observation in man. This is because a demonstration in man is such a difficult thing to obtain that we cannot wait for hazardous exposure to continue for decades before evidence in man is obtained.

THE MORNING-AFTER PILL:
A LACK OF INFORMED CONSENT

Current widespread misuse of the morning-after pill postcoital contraceptive, a 250-milligram dosage of DES taken over five days, was a subject of the February 1973 subcommittee hearings on human experimentation (35). The hearings concluded that new legislation governing unapproved uses of drugs and informed consent of patients is sorely needed, that FDA and Department of Health, Education, and Welfare reliance on institutional peer review committees to monitor experimentation is inadequate, and that experimentation on humans is not limited to clinical trials but is sometimes part of the routine practice of medicine. In spite of the carcinogenicity of lower doses of DES and the FDA-unapproved status of DES as a morning-after pill, about 50 per cent of university health services and an unknown number of private physicians were prescribing the morning-after pill to some 2 million women without explicit disclosure of its experimental status. Of a sample of 15 university health services investigated in the hearings, not one had filed with the FDA for an Investigational New Drug Permit before prescribing DES as a postcoital contraceptive in accordance with FDA guidelines. Clinical trials with DES at one university led to a publication in the October 1971 *Journal of the American Medical Association* (57) stating that DES had proved 100 per cent effective as a postcoital contraceptive in 1000 women exposed to unprotected intercourse. Subsequent investigations of those data by a National Institutes of Health committee revealed that adequate follow-up to determine the pill's effectiveness had not taken place, and further that some pregnancies had occurred in the series but had been excluded from the official study. Estimates are that DES is less than 90 per cent effective as a postcoital contraceptive (34) and that only 4 per cent of women who have unprotected intercourse have need of a morning-after pill (58).

The hearings examined the nationwide lack of informed consent among women receiving DES at university health services. A survey (34) of women conducted by the author at the university where the pilot study of the morning-after pill's effectiveness took place showed that of 69 women who received the morning-after pill at that institution in 1972, two were informed that the drug was experimental; none were informed of a possible cancer hazard to themselves; five were informed of a cancer hazard to their offspring should the pill fail; four were questioned about or tested for preexisting pregnancy from a previous intercourse even though DES could not terminate such a pregnancy and could cause cancer in the fetus; only three were asked of their family medical history in spite of the fact that a family history of breast or uterine cancer is a known contraindication for DES; only 17 were followed up to determine short-term adverse effects or the pill's effectiveness; none were asked if they were DES daughters.

Contraindications for the morning-after pill include a family history of breast, cervical or uterine cancer, thromboembolism, hypertension, hypoglycemia, diabetes, sickle-cell trait, or any of the contraindications of the oral contraceptive (59).

In 1973 the Center for Population Research of the National Institutes of Health awarded contracts to university health services and family planning agencies to test the effectiveness of natural estrogens as morning-after pills (34) in spite of the testimony of National Cancer Institute endocrinologists Lipsett and Hertz at congressional hearings on the regulation of DES (12) that all estrogens are potentially as carcinogenic as DES. One university health service accepted the National Institutes of Health proposal for morning-after pill experimentation without even consulting its own Institutional Peer Review Committee (35).

The testing of the morning-after pill on thousands of college women places the present generation of DES daughters at particular risk. As previously mentioned, little information has been made available to health professionals or to the daughters themselves about their risk of developing adenocarcinoma, specialized testing for adenocarcinoma has been available to few, and most of these daughters may be unaware that they were exposed to DES in utero. Sampling studies indicate that 90 per cent of DES daughters may be expected to develop adenosis (7, 8). Further stimulation of target organs with estrogen in the morning-after pill may increase their risk of developing adenocarcinoma by causing precancerous lesions to become malignant. Many DES daughters may already have latent or occult adenocarcinoma; additional estrogen may produce an exacerbation of their disease (59-62).

BANNED FOR CATTLE, APPROVED FOR WOMEN

For 12 years scientists have been lobbying to secure an FDA ban on DES as an additive to cattle feed because small residues of DES remain in beef liver marketed for human consumption. Not until the first cases of vaginal cancer in women exposed to DES in utero were reported in 1971 did they have clinical evidence that DES could cause cancer in humans. Consequently, in August 1972 the FDA banned DES as a cattle feed, even though residues of only 0.3 microgram were remaining in marketed beef (63, 64). Although cancer in women provided the clinical evidence against DES, in February 1973 the FDA approved for manufacture a new 250-milligram dosage of DES for use as a morning-after pill even though this amount represents 833,000 times the amount of DES banned for human consumption. Although approval of the morning-after pill is for "emergency uses only, such as rape and incest" (65), there are no legal limitations on a physician's judgment of what constitutes an emergency. It is interesting to note that the alleged state of panic of women after unprotected intercourse was cited by researchers as the reason for administering DES in morning-after pill trials (34), and prevention of a crisis in women was cited by FDA Commissioner Edwards as the reason for not recalling DES daughters for testing.

The unwillingness of many public health authorities to admit DES causality in the vaginal cancer epidemic and to take definitive action in behalf of the DES-exposed is an example of the aura of secrecy that often surrounds health information when profit or reputation of an industry is involved. To recall thousands of people and create a cancer scare surrounding a drug which is still in wide use in many forms (3) and whose manufacture is yielding increasing annual profits (34) would require that federal regulatory agencies infringe, perhaps prematurely, on the rights of private corporate interests with whom they seem to share a symbiotic relationship (66). An example of the FDA's reluctance to curb the free enterprise of the pharmaceutical industry before absolute proof of damage by a drug has been secured in a significant number of people was clearly spelled out by congressional investigations of the FDA regulation of DES as an additive to cattle feed (64). FDA Chief Counsel Hutt explains: "Industry is likely to challenge in the courts any FDA action where the net adverse economic impact exceeds the legal fees involved" (67).

Ideally, legislation should be introduced which would make it the responsibility of the manufacturer that marketed a drug later proved dangerous to recall people to whom it was prescribed. Automobile manufacturers are obliged to recall millions of vehicles when a defect is found which might put the consumer at risk before the defect is proven by cause and effect to result in a substantial number of injuries. If this standard of health protection were applied to the medical-research industry, pharmaceutical firms and research institutions would be obliged to recall, through pharmacy records, medical facilities, and prescribing physicians, all individuals exposed to unsafe products and provide compensation for testing and treatment. In a health care system based on private entrepreneurship, such legal sanctions would insure the respect of the medical-research industry for the potency of drugs, and responsibility for the effects of drug use would be shared by both consumer and manufacturer.

That the health industry is exempt from some legal requirements which apply to other providers of consumer products can be explained by the aura of deific authority which surrounds the practice of medicine and pharmacology: the population has traditionally been asked to put unquestioning trust in the beneficence of these scientific institutions which care for their health. A culture which rewards consumers of medical services for assuming a posture of inferiority and gratitude is one in which consumer check on the quality of those services is unlikely.

SOCIAL, POLITICAL, AND ECONOMIC INFLUENCES ON SCIENTIFIC JUDGMENTS MADE BY GOVERNMENTAL REGULATORY AGENCIES

Both industrial pressures and population control interests appear to have influenced FDA approval of the oral contraceptive, the anti-miscarriage drug, and the morning-after pill prior to the accomplishment of sufficient testing to prove their safety. The anti-miscarriage drug was developed during a period of social and economic pressure for population growth (1945-1955). Spontaneous abortion was seen as a condition to be avoided albeit at unknown risks. In present times of population expansion, the same drug is being used to achieve the opposite effect: DES is being tested as an abortifacient or postcoital contraceptive. With the development of both uses of DES as a fertility regulator, social and economic determinants appear to take precedence over concern for long-term effects on women. The encouragement from pharmaceutical advertising to doctors to prescribe the anti-miscarriage drug may have far outweighed any encouragement from pregnant women to give a hormone of which they knew nothing. Major drug companies spend approximately $3,000 per physician annually to reach the nearly 200,000 physicians who choose drugs for their patients (66).

The example of DES is an illustration of scientific and political ambivalence toward public health protection from a dangerous drug. Congressional investigation of the FDA (64) showed that,

> Despite urgent recommendation [in March 1971] and although DES had not been shown to be effective in preventing spontaneous abortion, FDA took no action to inform physicians of the danger of DES use during pregnancy until November 10, 1971.... FDA's failure to act promptly in this instance delayed public health protection for 5 months, and this delay might well have been substantially longer in the absence of the subcommittee's investigation of this matter.

FDA approval of new drugs hinges on a determination of their benefit versus risk to the consumer. However, congressional investigations have enumerated instances where definitions of benefit-risk ratio were made using drug industry rather than consumer criteria, i.e. where the risks to the consumer were not properly weighed against the benefits to the drug industry (35, 64, 68). Approval also hinges on scientific judgment in the evaluation of data on safety and effectiveness. However, when conflicting results are obtained, the assessment of safety and effectiveness is in the final analysis a subjective one not free of sensitivity to the benefits of the assessor. What is seen as best for the consumer's welfare (such as DES in cattle feed, the anti-miscarriage drug, or the morning-after pill) is determined in part by an industry which profits from the manufacture and sale of the drug. The major manufacturer of DES, Eli Lilly Company, increased profits from the manufacture of DES by 4 per cent in the nine months after the FDA warning to physicians that its use be discontinued in pregnancy (34). The FDA has no jurisdiction to prohibit pharmaceutical firms from marketing DES for other uses or to prohibit physicians from prescribing DES for unapproved uses. Use of DES in pregnancy is not banned by the FDA. Instead, an *FDA Drug Bulletin* (69) informed physicians in November 1971 that its use is contraindicated in pregnancy.

The 1962 Harris-Kefauver Drug Amendments sought to insure the safety of new drugs (such as DES as a postcoital contraceptive) by requiring that human clinical trials be conducted before the FDA allowed the drug to be marketed. A shortcoming of this law is that it assumes that the safety of a drug can be demonstrated during clinical trials. The carcinogenic effects of DES and other estrogens may not be expressed until 10 to 20 years after use (12).

Hertz (12) cites the inadequacy of tests of oral contraceptive safety on laboratory animals over a 7-year period:

> Thus far, two such preparations, Ethynerone and Neonovum, previously on clinical trial in women, have been withdrawn from further study because of breast tumors arising in animals. The estrogenic component of these two mixtures is identical with that contained in most of the preparations currently marketed .... concomitant testing and clinical use continues on the presumption that because of the relatively shorter lifespan of dogs and monkeys, tumors may become detectable sooner in the test animals than in women. The ultimate outcome of this race between dogs, monkeys and women can be anticipated by informed observers only with great apprehension and concern .... Breast cancer exists [in the population at large] in

some cases for years before it can be clinically detected. However, since one woman in 20 will at some time in her life develop a breast cancer, it is obvious that in using the pill we are exposing at least this portion of women to a substance known to stimulate preexisting breast cancer in women.

That the pharmaceutical industry earns $120 million annually from the manufacture of oral contraceptives may make an objective assessment of their risks more difficult to reach (70, 71). Since the manufacture of estrogens became established 25 years ago, pharmaceutical firms have devised numerous other uses for them (treatment of acne, thinning hair, excess facial hair, menstrual tension, depression, menopausal symptoms, to dry up breast milk following birth, and others) and advertised them to physicians in medical journals. In this way, the scientific direction of medical care is in part determined by the economic motives of a profit-making industry. Estrogens are currently offered to virtually every American woman from puberty throughout life for any of dozens of uses. According to a Senate subcommittee on competition in the drug industry (71),

> There exists little convincing scientific evidence to support many of the cited indications for the use of drugs that are currently in good standing in medical practice.

Holsten (72) of the California Bureau of Food and Drug concurs:

> I cannot find reported in the medical literature any well controlled, scientific studies conducted to prove the safe and effective use of DES in any dose or duration for treatment of even the generally recognized medical conditions, although there is ample literature of endorsement.

Public regulatory agency tolerance of the profusion of new, often inadequately tested prescription drugs on the market is a major contributing cause of the vaginal cancer epidemic. Congressional subcommittees (12, 35, 64, 66, 68, 70, 71) have examined potential conflicts of financial interest between the medical-research industry and governmental regulatory agencies which permit the indiscriminate use of drugs, including the fact that some doctors receive gifts from industry detail men for purchasing drugs, the fact that half of the American Medical Association's revenue has come from advertisements drug companies place in its journal, and the close relationships between FDA and pharmaceutical industry board officials. It should be pointed out that the $5 billion drug industry averages an 8 per cent higher profit margin than other major industries (66). "The Drug Establishment is a close-knit, self-perpetuating power structure consisting of drug manufacturers, government agencies and select members of the medical profession," states James Goddard, former FDA Commissioner (35, p. 319).

CONCLUSION

We have examined the etiologic relationship between DES and vaginal cancer in an attempt to stimulate the implementation of testing and treatment for DES daughters. There is evidence that the majority of these women may be expected to develop adenosis with an uncertain prognosis. Further, there are preliminary data pointing to an association between other estrogens and cancer. We have discussed the influence of economic and political interests in scientific judgments made by federal health regulatory agencies. By improving testing procedures for new drugs to insure their safety and efficacy prior to marketing and by the more judicious use of drugs in medical practice, the occurrences of such man-made epidemics may be prevented in the future. The public health response to DES-induced diseases must now be a political as well as a medical one, stressing public health information about the effects of DES and more effective controls of its use.

REFERENCES

1. Dieckman, W. J., Davis, M. E., Rijnkiewica, I. M., and Pottinger, R. E. Does the administration of diethylstilbestrol during pregnancy have therapeutic value? *Am. J. Obstet. Gynecol.* 66: 1062-1081, 1953.
2. Goldzieher, J. W., and Benigno, B. B. The treatment of threatened and recurrent abortion: A critical review. *Am. J. Obstet. Gynecol.* 75: 1202-1214, 1958.
3. Heinonen, O. Diethylstilbestrol in pregnancy. *Cancer* 31: 573-577, 1973.
4. Herbst, A. L., Ulfelder, H., and Poskanzer, D. C. Adenocarcinoma of the vagina: Association of maternal stilbestrol therapy with tumor appearance in young women. *New Engl. J. Med.* 284: 878-881, 1971.
5. Herbst, A. L., Robboy, S. J., Scully, R. E., and Poskanzer, D. C. Clear-cell adenocarcinoma of the vagina and cervix in girls: Analysis of 170 registry cases. *Am. J. Obstet. Gynecol.* 119: 713-724, 1974.
6. Ulfelder, H. Stilbestrol, adenosis and adenocarcinoma. *Am. J. Obstet. Gynecol.* 117: 794-800, 1973.
7. Stafl, D., Mattingly, R. F., Foley, D. V., and Fetherson, W. C. Clinical diagnosis of vaginal adenosis. *Obstet. Gynecol.* 43: 118-128, 1974.
8. Sherman, A., Goldrath, M., Berlin, A., Vakariya, V., Banooni, F., Michaels, W., Goodman, P., and Brown, S. Cervical-vaginal dystrophy (adenosis) following in utero exposure to synthetic estrogens. In press.
9. Folkman, J. Transplacental carcinogenesis by stilbestrol. *New Engl. J. Med.* 285: 404-405, 1971.
10. Langmuir, A. D. New environmental factor in congenital disease. *New Engl. J. Med.* 284: 912-913, 1971.
11. Herbst, A. L. Exogenous hormones in pregnancy. *Clin. Obstet. Gynecol.* 16: 37-50, 1973.
12. U.S. Congress, House of Representatives, Government Operations Committee. *Regulation of Diethylstilbestrol: Its Use as a Drug in Humans and in Animal Feeds,* pp. 37-73, 1st Session, 92nd Congress, Part I, November 11, 1971. U.S. Government Printing Office, Washington, D.C. 1972.
13. Herbst, A. L., Kurman, R. J., and Scully, R. E. Vaginal and cervical abnormalities after exposure to stilbestrol in utero. *Obstet. Gynecol.* 40: 287-290, 1972.
14. Greenwald, P., Barlow, J. J., Nasca, P. C., and Burnett, W. S. Vaginal cancer after maternal treatment with synthetic estrogens. *New Engl. J. Med.* 285: 390-391, 1971.
15. Henderson, B. E., Benton, B. D. A., Weaver, P. T., Linden, G., and Nolan, J. F. Stilbestrol and urogenital tract cancer in adolescents and young adults. *New Engl. J. Med.* 288: 354, 1973.
16. Greenwald, P., Nasca, P. C., Burnett, W. S., and Polan, A. Prenatal stilbestrol experience of mothers of young cancer patients. *Cancer* 31: 568-572, 1973.
17. Hill, E. C. Clear-cell carcinoma of the cervix and vagina in young women. *Am. J. Obstet. Gynecol.* 116: 470-481, 1973.
18. Greene, R. R., Burrill, M. W., and Ivy, A. C. Experimental intersexuality. The paradoxical effects of estrogens on the sexual development of the female rat. *Anat. Rec.* 74: 429-438, 1939.
19. Forsberg, J. G. Effect of sex hormones on the development of the rat vagina. *Acta Endocrinol. (Kbh.)* 33: 520-531, 1960.
20. Herbst, A. L., and Scully, R. E. Maternal stilbestrol–genital adenocarcinoma and follow-up of exposed young women. *American College of Obstetricians and Gynecologists Technical Bulletin* No. 22, May 1973.
21. Ruffolo, E. H., Foxworthy, D., and Fletcher, J. C. Vaginal adenocarcinoma arising in vaginal adenosis. *Am. J. Obstet. Gynecol.* 111: 167-172, 1971.
22. Barber, H. R. K., and Somers, S. C. Vaginal adenosis, dysplasia, and clear-cell adenocarcinoma after diethylstilbestrol treatment in pregnancy. *Obstet. Gynecol.* 43: 645-652, 1974.

23. Plaut, A. and Dreyfuss, M. L. Adenosis of vagina and its relation to primary adenocarcinoma of vagina. *Surg. Gynecol. Obstet.* 71: 756, 1940.
24. Lanier, A. P., Noller, K. L., Decker, D. G., Elveback, L. R., and Kurland, L. T. Cancer and stilbestrol: A follow-up of 1,719 persons exposed to estrogens in utero and born 1943-1959. *Mayo Clin. Proc.* 48: 793-799, 1973.
25. Scott, J. W., Seckinger, D., and Puente-Duany, W. Colposcopic aspects of management of vaginal adenosis in DES children. *J. Reprod. Med.* 12: 187-193, 1974.
26. Aldrich, J. O., Henderson, B. E., and Townsend, D. E. Diagnostic procedures for the stilbestrol-adenosis-carcinoma syndrome. *N. Engl. J. Med.* 287: 934, 1972.
27. Herbst, A. L., Robboy, J. S., MacDonald, G. J., and Scully, R. E. The effects of local progesterone on stilbestrol-associated vaginal adenosis. *Am. J. Obstet. Gynecol.* 118: 607-615, 1974.
28. Rozier, J. C., and Underwood, P. B. Use of progestational agents in endometrial adenocarcinoma. *Obstet. Gynecol.* 44: 60-64, 1974.
29. Meissner, W. A., Sommers, S. C., and Sherman, G. Endometrial hyperplasia, endometrial carcinoma and endometriosis produced experimentally by estrogen. *Cancer* 10: 500-509, 1957.
30. Gardner, W. U. The effect of estrogenic hormones on the incidence of mammary and pituitary tumors in hybrid mice of strains with varying susceptibilities to mammary tumors. *Cancer Res.* 1: 345-358, 1951.
31. Allen, E., and Gardner, W. U. Cancer of the cervix of the uterus in hybrid mice following long-continued administration of estrogen. *Cancer Res.* 1: 359-365, 1941.
32. Fehr, P. E., and Prem, K. A. Malignancy of the uterine corpus following irradiation therapy for squamous-cell carcinoma of the cervix. *Am. J. Obstet. Gynecol.* 119: 685-692, 1974.
33. Sekiya, S., Yano, A., and Takamizawa, H. Enhancement of tumor growth and metastases by medroxyprogesterone acetate in transplanted uterine adenocarcinoma cells of the rat. *J. Natl. Cancer Inst.* 52: 297-298, 1974.
34. Weiss, K. Health Research Group Report on the Morning-After Pill and Fact Sheet. In U.S. Congress, Senate Committee on Labor and Public Welfare, *Quality of Health Care—Human Experimentation,* 93rd Congress, Part I, February 21 and 22, 1973 pp. 193-212 and 300-315. U.S. Government Printing Office, Washington, D. C.
35. U.S. Congress, Senate Committee on Labor and Public Welfare, *Quality of Health Care—Human Experimentation,* 93rd Congress, Part I, February 21 and 22, 1973. U.S. Government Printing Office, Washington, D. C., 1973.
36. Huss, K. S. Editorial. *JAMA* 218: 1564, 1971.
37. Mills, D. H. Prenatal diethylstilbestrol and vaginal cancer in offspring. *JAMA* 229: 471-472, 1974.
38. Jabara, A. G. Induction of canine ovarian tumors by diethylstilbestrol and progesterone. *Aust. J. Exp. Biol. Med. Sci.* 49: 139, 1962.
39. Dunn, T. B. Cancer of the uterine cervix in mice fed a liquid diet containing an antifertility drug. *J. Natl. Cancer Inst.* 43: 671-679, 1969.
40. Gass, G. H., Coags, D., and Graham, N. Carcinogenic dose-response curve to oral diethylstilbestrol. *J. Natl. Cancer Inst.* 33: 971-977, 1964.
41. Hooker, C. W., Gardner, W. U., and Pfeiffer, C. A. Testicular tumors in mice receiving estrogens. *JAMA* 115: 443-445, 1940.
42. Gardner, W. U. Carcinoma of the uterine cervix and upper vagina: Induction under experimental conditions in mice. *Ann. N.Y. Acad. Sci.* 75: 543-564, 1959.
43. Murphy, E. D. Carcinogenesis of the uterine cervix in mice; effect of diethylstilbestrol after limited application of 3-methylcholanthrene. *J. Natl. Cancer Inst.* 27: 611-653, 1961.
44. Pincus, G., and Garcia, C. R. Preliminary Findings on Hormonal Steroids and Vaginal, Cervical and Endometrial Histology. Paper presented at International Union Against Cancers, Mexico City, February 5, 1964.
45. Garcia, C. R., Rocamora, H., and Pincus, G. Advances in planned parenthood. *Excerpta Medica* 138: 53, 1967.
46. Cole, P., and MacMahon, B. Oestrogen fractions during early reproductive life in the etiology of breast cancer. *Lancet* 1: 604, 1969.
47. Hausknecht, R. U., and Gusberg, S. B. Estrogen metabolism in patients at high risk for endometrial carcinoma. *Am. J. Obstet. Gynecol.* 105: 1161-1167, 1969.
48. Sherman, A. I., and Woolf, R. B. Endocrine basis for endometrial carcinoma. *Am. J. Obstet. Gynecol.* 77: 233, 1959.
49. Cutler, B. S., Forbes, A. P., Ingersoll, F. M., and Scully, R. E. Endometrial carcinoma after stilbestrol therapy in gonadal dysgenesis. *New Engl. J. Med.* 287: 628-630, 1972.
50. Jensen, E. I., and Ostergaard, E. Clinical studies concerning the relationships of estrogens to the development of cancer of the corpus uteri. *Am. J. Obstet. Gynecol.* 67: 1094-1102, 1954.

51. Gusberg, S. B., and Hall, R. E. Precursors of corpus cancer. *Obstet. Gynecol.* 17: 397-412, 1961.
52. Ng, A. B. P. Mixed carcinoma of the endometrium. *Am. J. Obstet. Gynecol.* 102: 506-515, 1968.
53. Christopherson, W. M., Mendez, W. M., Lundin, F. E., Jr., and Parker, J. E. A 10-year study of endometrial carcinoma in Louisville, Ky. *Cancer* 18: 554-558, 1965.
54. Candy, M., and Abel, M. R. Progesterone-induced adenomatous hyperplasia of the uterine cervix. *JAMA* 203: 323, 1968.
55. Taylor, H. B., Irey, N. S., and Morris, H. J. Atypical endocervical hyperplasia in women taking oral contraceptives. *JAMA* 202: 637, 1967.
56. Melamed, M. R., Koss, L. G., Flehinger, B. J., Kelisky, R. P., and Dubrow, H. Prevalence rates of uterine cervical carcinoma in situ for women using the diaphragm or contraceptive oral steroids. *Br. Med. J.* 3: 195-200, 1969.
57. Kuchera, L. K. Postcoital contraception with diethylstilbestrol. *JAMA* 218: 562-563, 1971.
58. Tietze, C. Problems of pregnancy resulting from a single unprotected coitus. *Fertil. Steril.* 11: 485-488, 1960.
59. *AMA Drug Evaluations,* Ed. 2, pp. 415-431. Publishing Sciences Group, Inc., Acton, Mass., 1973.
60. Pearson, O. H., West, C. D., Hollander, V. P., and Treves, N. E. Evaluation of endocrine therapy for advanced breast cancer. *JAMA* 154: 234, 1954.
61. Hall, T. C. Cited in *Biological Activities of Steroids in Relation to Cancer,* edited by G. Pincus and E. P. Vollmer, p. 487. Academic Press, New York, 1960.
62. Kennedy, B. J. Massive estrogen administration in premenopausal women with metastatic breast cancer. *Cancer* 15: 641, 1962.
63. Washington Correspondent. *Nature* 238: 67-68, 1972.
64. *Twelfth Report of the Committee on Government Operations. Regulation of Diethylstilbestrol and Other Drugs Used in Food Producing Animals.* U.S. House of Representatives, 93rd Congress, House Report No. 93-708, December 10, 1973. U.S. Government Printing Office, Washington, D. C., 1974.
65. *FDA Drug Bulletin,* May 1973.
66. *U.S. Senate, Committee on the Judiciary, Kefauver Subcommittee on Antitrust and Monopoly,* Parts 22 and 23, May and June 1960, U.S. Government Printing Office, Washington, D. C., 1960.
67. *How Safe Is Safe? The Design of Policy on Drugs and Food Additives.* Printing and Publishing Office, National Academy of Sciences, Washington, D. C. 1974.
68. *U.S. Senate, Select Committee on Small Business, Task Force on Prescription Drugs.* 90th Congress, 2nd Session, August 30, 1968. U.S. Government Printing Office, Washington, D. C., 1968.
69. *FDA Drug Bulletin,* November 1971.
70. *U.S. House of Representatives, Committee on Government Operations, FDA Regulation of Oral Contraceptives,* 91st Congress, 2nd Session, July 15 and 16, 1970. U.S. Government Printing Office, Washington, D. C., 1970.
71. *U.S. Senate, Select Committee on Small Business, Hearings before a Subcommittee on Monopoly, Competitive Problems in the Drug Industry.* February and March, 1973, U.S. Government Printing Office, Washington, D. C., 1973.
72. Holsten, W. D. Protecting patients from drugs. *New Engl. J. Med.* 285: 1202, 1971.

PART 3

Women In The Health Labor Force

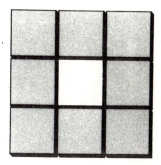

CHAPTER 4

Sexism and Racism in the American Health Care Industry: A Comparative Analysis

Jerry L. Weaver and Sharon D. Garrett

The suppression of the social, economic, and political desires of American women and racial minorities and the exploitation of their labor are two primary characteristics of American society; despite legislation and judicial decisions, women and minorities continue to be discriminated against (1-5). Nowhere is discrimination more prevalent than in the treatment which women and minorities receive at the hands of the health industry. Whether as providers or consumers, they are exploited, abused, and discriminated against.

This situation is widely reported. Review the issues of any major health care periodical over the past 5 years and you will surely encounter one or more accounts of discrimination. Yet for all the notoriety that sexism and racism receive, it remains difficult to obtain a comprehensive picture of these two problems. Nurses write about the exploitation which they experience; readers of the *Journal of the National Medical Association* see accounts of discrimination experienced by blacks; psychiatrists find discussions of sexism and racism in their mental health publications; medical educators confront stories about the problem of recruiting and retaining women and minority students. But we have no detailed comparisons of the manifestations and consequences of sexism and racism (6, 7).

This specialized and episodic treatment obscures the magnitude and scope of discrimination. Moreover, it perpetuates the myth that situational remedies are called for. For instance, when it was "discovered" that women are vastly underrepresented in medical schools, reformers demanded the admission of greater numbers of women.

This paper was written while the senior author was Visiting Professor of Political Science and Public Health at the University of California at Los Angeles.

But, at about the same time, blacks, Native Americans, and Spanish heritage groups also called for more equitable representation for their communities. Not recognizing, or preferring to ignore, that sexism and racism have similar roots as well as consequences, women and minorities strove to advance their own particular claim for greater enrollment rather than joining their considerable individual resources to present a united front. By competing against each other, the disadvantaged denied themselves the combined strength capable of challenging the status quo and perhaps precipitating major reforms in the admission policies, curriculae, value systems, and attitudes found in medical schools. Thus, after a decade of "affirmative action," medical and other health professional schools point to "impressive" increases in the proportional recruitment of women and minorities while their absolute numbers entering the industry remain hugely disproportionate to their share in the overall population.

It is axiomatic that those who enjoy the benefits of a situation will strive to perpetuate it. When threatened, the advantaged will either work to exclude competitors or seek to expand the pool of contested resources and to attenuate the reallocative pressures by offering to their most vocal or talented critics a share of the pool. This latter course is being followed by those who control the health industry. By expanding enrollments, creating new schools, and adding subprofessions (such as "physician extenders"), the health industry is recruiting more individuals but power and prestige are retained by the traditional elite.

The divisive tendency of considering sexism and racism as isolated or "particular" problems must be stopped and a clear understanding of the identity of interests among women and minorities developed if an effective challenge is to be made to the discriminatory practices prevalent in the health industry. As a prerequisite to this consciousness-building, a thorough exploration of the conditions of women and minorities is in order. The present effort takes a short step down this road. Here we shall bring together evidence of sexism and racism from a number of sources. We shall review the conditions facing women and minorities as candidates for professional schools, as health care workers and providers, and as consumers of these services.

ENTRY INTO HEALTH PROFESSIONS

Where enjoyment of greater wealth, social status, or more personally fulfilling employment depends on obtaining a formal certification of competence, the process of selecting candidates for admission to apprenticeship has great social significance. Those who get past this first barrier *may* attain their personal goals; those who fail usually are precluded forever from them. Since criteria for admission are often subjective, the possibility that nontraditional candidates will be discriminated against is always present.

Recruitment and Admission

Traditionally, women and minorities have been segregated into a few professional areas such as nursing and health aide work and are not found in any substantial numbers in medical and dental schools. In recent years, medical schools have announced impressive increases in the proportions of these former undesirables among their student bodies. These numbers are often interpreted to mean that if discrimination in admissions was once the rule, it is so no longer.

It is argued that individual women actually have an easier time gaining admittance than men: the ratio of admissions to applications is 1:17 compared with 1:80, respectively. Moreover, the percentage of women in medical and other health professional schools is increasing dramatically: as Table 1 reveals, the proportion of women to total enrollment has grown by at least 100 percent in all schools except pharmacy (and here the 1969-1970/1973-1974 increase is 89 percent) (8).

A clearer picture of the admission of women to medical schools is presented in Figure 1. Here we see that although the female application and admission rates have climbed during the past decade, neither is anywhere close to those of males. It is striking that although greater attention has been given to recruiting women during the past decade, the number of applications from men has increased much more rapidly

Table 1

Percent of women among total enrollment and graduates of selected
health professional schools, 1969-1975[a]

Schools	1969-70	1970-71	1971-72	1972-73	1973-74	1974-75	Percent Increase in No. of Women over Period
Medical							
Enrollment	9.0	9.6	10.8	12.8	15.4	18.0	184
Graduates	8.4	9.2	9.0	8.9	11.1	NA[b]	80
Dental							
Enrollment	1.1	1.4	1.9	2.8	4.3	6.8	987
Graduates	NA	NA	1.0	1.5	2.0	NA	130
Optometry							
Enrollment	2.9	2.9	3.6	5.1	7.3	9.4	373
Graduates	5.2	2.3	2.6	2.5	4.3	4.4	43
Pharmacy							
Enrollment	20.8	21.9	24.9	26.5	28.3	NA	89
Graduates	18.1	20.1	22.6	24.2	26.1	NA	78
Podiatry							
Enrollment	0.9	1.4	1.3	1.5	2.4	3.2	490
Graduates	1.2	2.0	0.4	0.4	1.3	1.1	33
Veterinary							
Enrollment	8.8	9.3	11.5	13.6	17.3	20.3	183
Graduates	7.5	7.4	8.7	10.1	10.4	14.2	112

[a] Source, American Public Health Association, *Women in Health Careers: Chartbook for International Conference on Women in Health Fields Held in Washington, D.C., on June 16-18, 1975* (available from National Technical Information Services, Springfield, Va., PB-243-111).
[b] NA = not available.

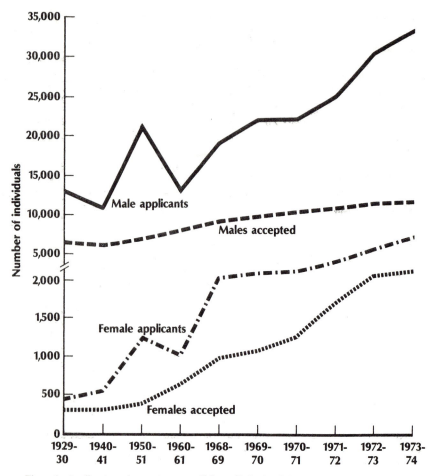

Figure 1. Applicants and acceptances to U.S. medical schools by sex, selected academic years. Source, United States Department of Health, Education, and Welfare, *Minorities and Women in the Health Fields* (HRA 76-22), Government Printing Office, Washington, D.C., 1975.

than the number from women. We shall return below to the problems of recruiting women. Suffice it here to note the continued discrepancy in admission and acceptance rates between the genders.

Similar growth rates are reported for minorities. In medical schools, for instance, in the short period 1972-1973/1975-1976, the number of blacks enrolled climbed 34 percent; Spanish heritage (Chicano, Puerto Rican, Cuban, Latin American, and similar ancestry) jumped 95 percent; and Native Americans leaped by 159 percent (9).

What these statistics gloss over is the continuing tiny *absolute* numbers of women and minorities in school—especially small considering the proportion of the total population which they represent. While the percentage of women graduates of medical

Table 2

Percent and number of women and minority students among total
medical school enrollment and graduates, 1972-1973 to 1975-1976[a]

Year	Black		Native American		Spanish Heritage		Women	
	%	No.	%	No.	%	No.	%	No.
1972-1973								
Enrollment	5.5	2,593	0.1	68	1.0	478	12.8	6,082
Graduates	3.3	341	0.1	8	0.5	48	8.9	860
1975-1976								
Enrollment	6.2	3,488	0.3	176	1.7	931	20.5	11,527
Graduates	5.5	743	0.2	27	0.9	159	16.2	2,200
Increase 1975-1976 over 1972-1973								
Enrollment	34.5	895	158.8	108	94.7	453	89.5	5,445
Graduates	117.8	402	237.5	19	231.2	111	155.8	1,340

[a] Source, reference 9.

Table 3

Percent of minority students among total enrollment of health professions schools[a]

Profession	Black	Native American	Spanish Heritage	Total Minority
Medicine (1974-75)	6.3	0.3	1.5	10.4
Dentistry (1974-75)	4.7	0.2	1.2	9.1
Pharmacy (1974-75)	3.3	0.1	1.3	7.8
Optometry (1972-73)	1.0	0.1	1.0	5.9
Podiatry (1972-73)	2.1	0.1	0.4	3.2
Osteopathic medicine (1972-73)	1.2	0.3	0.8	2.7
Total U.S. population, 1970	11.1	0.39	4.5	16.8

[a] Source, United States Department of Health, Education, and Welfare, *Minorities and Women in the Health Fields,* p. 7, (HRA 76-22). Government Printing Office, Washington, D.C., 1975.

schools increased from 8.9 percent in 1972-1973 to 16.2 percent in 1975-1976 (an increase of 82 percent), only 2200 women were graduated in 1975-1976 (Table 2). Somewhat earlier figures reported in Table 3 illustrate the underrepresentation of minorities in all major health professions' preparatory programs. Nowhere do we find anything like the proportions equivalent to their fraction of the total population.

It is also misleading to assume that the increases in enrollment and graduation are having a positive impact on the provider-to-consumer ratios in the minority communities. While it is dangerously simplistic to assume that *all* black or Native American graduates will return to provide services exclusively to blacks or Native Americans, a brief review of the data dispels any notion that present levels of enrollment of minorities in professional schools will do much to alter the gross disparities in provider-consumer ratios between the Anglo and minority communities. For example, the ratio of black physicians to black consumers was 1:3377 in 1942; 1:3927 in 1967; and 1:4298 in 1972. The swelling enrollment and graduation figures of the 1970s project a 1976 ratio still above 1:4000 (10).

In the two decades since *Brown vs. School Board of Topeka* struck down separate-but-equal education and ostensibly opened all educational doors to minorities, the graduation of black physicians from medical schools has failed to keep pace with the black population's natural increase.

Admission to medical school is governed by many factors. But first and foremost is making an application; you simply don't get a seat if you don't apply. Uncritically accepting that the applicant to admission ratio is more "favorable" for women than men or that the ratio of women and minority students to Anglo male students is "improving" diverts attention from an important issue. Sex and race role stereotyping acts to dissuade prospective female and minority doctors at an early age. Many years before they might apply to medical school, these potential candidates have been inculcated with and deterred by social stereotyping. One can only guess at the number of potential doctors lost to these more subtle forms of gender and racial role stereotyping.

Gender role playing has operated to reduce the number of women who might seek entry into medicine, dentistry, health care administration, and pharmacy. Women are taught from infancy that certain traits are "female," others "male." Little boys play "doctor," little girls "nurse." Similarly, blacks, Native Americans, Spanish heritage individuals, and other minorities find few role models from health professions with which to identify. The Anglo-dominated educational and media industries have systematically excluded minority community members who have succeeded in the health and other professions from the eyes and minds of minority children (11, 12).

Since most health professions require postgraduate training, the extent and quality of student counselling bear heavily on the numbers of women and minorities seeking admission. There is very little acknowledgement in the literature of the potential role of undergraduate (or high school) counselling as a force motivating nontraditional applicants toward careers in health professions. From accounts seen, however, it appears that racial and gender stereotyping and lack of sensitivity are pervasive. Many minority students with outstanding high school records in science have reported that they were told by their counsellors to consider cosmetology, short-order cooking, or dental technology training.

Women who wish to combine a career and a family are given little advice about specialties in medicine which are compatible with child rearing (13). For women and minority students who need financial support to enable them to continue a professional career program, information about such programs may be vital—but it is often overlooked by counsellors, financial aid officers, and others who do not consider women and minorities as appropriate individuals to receive this information (14).

For those women who are not deterred by gender roles or lack of information and counselling, admission procedures offer particular challenges. On the record of their examination scores and other measures of academic and personality characteristics, women medical school applicants differ as a group only slightly from men (15-17). It is not clear on the basis of the limited available information whether women are discriminated against at this stage of admission—that is, to what extent are men with inferior records given preference over women with superior records. But for many women who make it to the oral interviews, special and potentially discriminatory treatment is the standard.

These interviews, usually conducted by medical school faculty and advanced medical students, are crucial because here subjective impressions and judgments may be formally placed on the applicant's balance sheet. Although there is little hard information about the dynamics of this interview procedure, Ortiz (18), Benedek (19), and Campbell (20) independently have reported that interview boards, almost exclusively composed of males, take great interest in the sex life and reproductory attitudes of female candidates. While male medical students do not recall being asked about their plans for families or warned that marriage combined with a medical career is difficult or impossible, women almost uniformly recall such questions. And while male medical students are commonly married, what Campbell calls "motherstudents" are rarely encountered. Campbell speculates that the absence of "motherstudents" may be attributable to a lack of child care facilities and financial support plus an unwillingness to schedule classes and on-call rounds to accommodate pregnancy and child tending. In addition, however, the absence of women with children may reflect the (subconscious) traditional and stereotypic views of a woman's role in the family unit—that mothers take care of children, but fathers do not; that children cannot thrive unless their mothers care for them full time; and that mothers cannot also be competent workers and students (20).

A general discriminatory policy against mother/wifestudents cannot be ascertained unless we know a great deal more about the dynamics of admission procedures. But a 7-year study of women physicians found that women in medical (and presumably other health professional) schools undergo "rites of passage" different in kind and degree from their male colleagues (21).

During oral interviews, prospective students are often asked about their proposed area of specialization. Examiners see this as a means of putting the applicant at ease as well as ascertaining the applicant's motivation for entering the profession, the information the applicant has about the school, and the interviewee's knowledge about the current trends, opportunities, and "hot spots" of the profession. In medical education, family practice and "going out into the medically impoverished areas" have been looked on as "good things to plan a career in" since the late 1960s.

But the interviewers' subjective evaluations triggered by the applicants' answers to these questions may work a special hardship on minority applicants. Haynes (22) points to an assumption widely held, yet little mentioned, by health educators: that minority students will be trained so that they may return to their "people." The discriminatory nature of this assumption may be subtle, yet it is clear enough. "Many institutions are willing to train black students for the ghetto, but other students are expected to enjoy a free choice. It is true that black physicians are providing much of the health care for the black ghetto, but the health of the ghetto residents is everyone's responsibility ... this obligation cannot be met by accepting a few black students and hoping that they will practice only in the ghetto."

There may be many reasons for approving a minority applicant who indicates a firm commitment to general practice in underserved areas—reasons that would not come into play if the minority candidate indicated an equally firm commitment to surgery, radiology, or one of the other "elite" specialties. It is certainly worth considering how traditional attitudes and stereotypical thinking influence the evaluation of minority as well as women applicants.

Women and Minority Students

The most comprehensive review of sexism in the training of health professionals is Campbell's study (20) of the experiences of women medical students. The discrimination which she reports takes three major forms: institutional discrimination, overt discrimination, and subtle discrimination. We have already mentioned the institutional discrimination reflected in recruitment, admissions, and the lack of "motherstudents." Other examples of institutional sexism include: inability to gain financial aid for child care or for dependent husbands; inferior or nonexisting on-call lodging; scarcity of dressing rooms or toilets for women; lack of athletic facilities for women (shower rooms, equipment, lockers, etc.); absence of gynecological services for women medical students; failure to provide *parents* with child care facilities; and a whole range of institutionally sponsored activities which do not reflect a sensitivity to the presence of women.

Overt discrimination reported by women medical students includes "baiting" by instructors designed, apparently, to annoy, anger, or provoke women; belittling of ability, motivation, or competence of women; and overt hostility toward women as colleagues. Notman and Nadelson (23) report, "We have been impressed with the frequent discussion of the hostility that many women students feel is directed at them from peers and instructors ... women students as a visible minority are not infrequently the targets of displaced anxiety. Men students often seem to have difficulty relating directly to women as colleagues and competitors; instead, they may sexualize their relationships" (23). Jokes and "nudie" slides are frequently reported forms of hostility, baiting, and belittling directed at women.[1] Insulting and vulgar behavior that would be seen instantly as inappropriate if directed at Jews, blacks, and other "minorities" is reported as served routinely to women medical students.

Subtle discrimination is seen in the ostracizing of women from membership in the profession by treating them—and expecting them to act—like dependent daughters, pampered sisters, nurturant mothers, help-mate wives, or seductive playmates. This may take the form of condescension, overprotection, reference to women as "honey" or "the gals," and the exclusion from the comeraderie of "the fellows." The reverse may also happen: the presence of women in medical schools is often overlooked or forgotten—for example, failing to provide dressing rooms, sending out letters such as "Attention students: Does your wife have clerical skills?", treating women in

---

[1] Title IX of the 1972 Amendment to the Higher Education Act makes salacious language in the lecture hall and nude slides, among other things, forms of discrimination subject to loss of federal funds (24).

surgical clerkships as scrub nurses, and referring to the class as "gentlemen." A not-too-subtle form of discrimination is "spotlighting": constantly calling attention to the presence of women (25).

In reading Campbell's narrative, one may well wonder about the distinction between "overt" and "subtle" sexism: perhaps a more appropriate distinction might be "conscious" and "subconscious." Are male instructors aware of their own hostilities to women when they spotlight and bait women or pander to the male sexual prurience during lectures, consultations, and other contacts with women students? The implication is that they *are* aware and are venting their hostilities on a group of women who are largely powerless or unwilling to challenge them. Several respondents in Campbell's study said that they were aware of and resented these attacks, but, given the instructor's leverage with them through grading, they chose to remain silent. Does awareness by instructors of this vulnerability whet their misogynous aggression?

The experiences of minority students have been even more widely ignored than those of women. The American Medical Association reports that minorities are more likely to repeat classes and take reduced course loads—proof, according to the AMA, that medical education has retained its standards while making special accommodations to the "less-qualified" minority applicants which "affirmative action" has forced upon medical schools (26). In fact, although minorities do more often repeat classes and take reduced academic loads, findings of a 1970-1972 national survey indicate a dropout rate for all minorities higher than that for Anglos (27).

Women medical students suffer a significantly higher rate of dropouts than men; 88 percent of the former and 91 percent of the latter finish medical school (28). Men drop out mostly for academic reasons, but women mostly for "family" or what are recorded as "nonacademic" reasons.[2] It could be that the various forms of sexism which we have reviewed are taking their toll on women. Perhaps more women could survive these pressures if they had strong role models with which to identify—that is, mothers or sisters with a professional career—or women among their instructors. One of the observations repeated over and over again by Campbell's respondents was the absence of women on admission-interview panels and the scarcity of women instructors. Those women whom they did encounter in medical school were often clearly the objects of contempt and ridicule by their colleagues and students alike or were espousing the "forget you're a woman and compete like a man" philosophy (20).

It would be useful in building the base for expanding the numbers of women and minorities in health professions schools to examine the effects on student success of the presence of strong positive role models. But such an examination should be part of a broader study of the impact of the male-controlled educational system on the attitudes and behavior of women and minorities. We cannot come to an understanding of the situation of women and minorities in the medical school without an understanding of the world of men and the distribution of social, economic, and political power within that world. To understand the situation of those discriminated against, we must move away from the so-called women's question and the minority's question and focus on the social and economic institutions and historical forces which create and perpetuate these "questions" (30).

---

[2]Marriage as such does not seem to contribute to withdrawal, but having children does (29).

WOMEN AND MINORITIES AS PROVIDERS

The discrimination and exploitation visited on women and minorities in professional schools is fitting preparation for their treatment at the hands of their professional colleagues. In the caste-like hierarchy of health care, women and minorities are discriminated against in salaries, occupational mobility, and range of career opportunities. The socioeconomic mechanisms which operate in the broader society to channel women and minorities to low-paying jobs also operate in the health care industry. As Table 4 illustrates, the further one descends the income/status hierarchy, the greater becomes the probability of encountering women and minorities. And as we reach occupational categories which are "reserved" for women (those which require less education and training—and command lower salaries), the proportion of *minority* women in turn increases. From wage scales for the occupational levels in which minorities and women predominate, we see the effects of the double burden of sexism plus racism carried by minority women.

Comparing the salaries of males and females who are relatively low-status health technicians, we see quite clearly that sex differentials for the same occupations are far more significant than race differentials (Table 5). While there are very few men in these strata, they apparently hold the best-paying positions. The finding that blacks outearn Anglos in three of the four comparisons should be read with some

Table 4

Percent of persons employed in selected health professions by ethnicity and sex, April 1970[a]

Occupation	Black	Spanish Heritage	Female
Physicians (M.D. and D.O.)	2.2	3.7	9.4
Dentists	2.3	1.3	3.4
Optometrists	0.6	1.7	4.0
Veterinarians	1.3	1.3	5.1
Pharmacists	2.3	1.9	11.9
Registered nurses	7.5	2.1	97.3
Dieticians	21.0	3.0	92.0
Therapists	7.5	2.5	63.3
Health administrators	4.7	2.0	44.6
Dental assistants	3.4	3.5	97.9
Health aides	18.9	4.2	84.6
Lay midwives	40.4	1.2	79.6
Nursing aides, orderlies, and attendants	25.2	3.8	84.8
Practical nurses	21.9	3.3	96.4
Total U.S. population	11.1	4.5	51.3

[a]Source, United States Department of Health, Education, and Welfare, *Decennial Census Data for Selected Health Occupations: United States, 1970*, pp. 22-23, (HRA 76-1231), Government Printing Office, Washington, D.C., 1975.

Table 5

Comparison of median income of health workers by sex and by race, 1970[a]

Worker and Race	Male	Female	Sex Differentials
Health technologists and technicians			
Anglo	$7368	$5182	-$2186
Black	$6932	$5252	-$1680
Race differentials	-$436	+$70	
Health service workers			
Anglo	$4425	$3265	-$1160
Black	$4595	$3682	-$913
Race differentials	+$170	+$417	

[a] Source, computed from U.S. Bureau of the Census, *Statistical Abstract of the U.S.*, Table 375, Government Printing Office, Washington, D.C., 1973.

caution. After all, these black health workers are disproportionately located in the major urban areas—New York, Los Angeles, Chicago, St. Louis, and the like—where the prevailing wage *and* cost of living are a good deal higher than in the rest of the country. Consequently, Anglos may earn lower median wages but, because a larger proportion live outside the metropolitan regions, Anglos enjoy a higher standard of living than their black counterparts. The caveat about regional distribution affecting the racial comparisons does not detract from the gender comparisons since we are comparing metropolitan black males with metropolitan black females and so forth.

Physicians

Working through the AMA, the Anglo medical establishment effectively shut out blacks from the mainstream of the profession. An Anglo physician has observed: "The treatment accorded the black doctor for more than a century by the American Medical Association and its component societies is a shameful record of social injustice ... the black doctor has been socially and professionally ostracized. He has been barred from the medical seminars without which a physician stagnates, excluded from medical conventions, and denied the right to become a member of a hospital staff" (31). Not until 1964 did the AMA vote to oppose racial exclusionary membership policies. (As recently as 1965 the National Dental Association claimed that in 11 of the southern states the American Dental Association "will only rarely accept Negro members") (32). Faced with overt racism, blacks formed a parallel professional structure complete with medical schools, professional associations, and a national organization (National Medical Association) to promote the interests of black physicians.

The medical establishment eliminated competition from women somewhat differently. Blacks were outlawed by racial exclusionary provisions but were "permitted" to build their own delivery system to serve a caste of patients which most Anglos wished to avoid. Women, however, had traditionally performed much primary patient care among working and middle classes. In the 1910s, they gained a beachhead in the care of "desirable" patients through the willingness of proprietary medical schools to sell them admission (33). Then, too, millions of women were attended at delivery by midwives. These two sources of female competition were closed by a widely successful AMA-sponsored push in the 1920s to outlaw midwifery and by state legislative action in the aftermath of the 1910 Flexner Report which condemned inadequacies in medical education. Women could turn to nursing, or could take their chances with men for the seats in the remaining medical schools. For over half a century only a small number of women have entered mainline medicine, and their career patterns are notably different from those of men (34, 35).

More than half again as many male as female physicians are engaged in office-based, self-employed practice; women, on the other hand, are twice as likely to be found in hospitals and public health departments. Carpenter and Walker (36) speculate that this dualism reflects another facet of gender socialization: the role of the private practitioner involves risk taking and competitive (with males) behavior—traits that women are taught to avoid. Moreover, financial success in private practice is often linked to the charismatic qualities of the practitioner—qualities which in our society are usually ascribed to males, not females (36).

Gender discrimination extends beyond the organization of one's practice to one's medical specialization. Table 6 reveals that women physicians specialize disproportionately in pediatrics, psychiatry, and anesthesiology; few women are seen in surgery, radiology, or internal medicine (37). Lopate (38) points out that in the traditionally male dominated postgraduate hospital departments of neurological surgery, ophthalmology, orthopedic surgery, otolaryngology, and plastic surgery over 90 percent of the residencies are occupied—an indication of popularity and status within the profession. Conversely, in areas in which women are more often encountered, as

Table 6

Income and hours worked by active physicians (M.D.) by specialty and sex, 1972[a]

Specialty	Percent Females	Avg. Hours of Direct Patient Care per Week		Avg. Net Income from Medical Practice	
		Males	Females	Males	Females
Radiology	5.7	41.9	34.9	$58,891	$33,308
Surgery	1.4	48.0	37.8	$56,377	$40,000
Obstetrics/gynecology	7.5	49.2	37.4	$53,940	$32,864
Anesthesiology	14.4	48.3	43.5	$50,898	$35,543
Internal medicine	6.5	47.5	40.7	$45,043	$23,267
General practice	4.5	47.9	39.2	$41,634	$22,339
Pediatrics	21.9	45.8	37.0	$40,529	$23,549
Psychiatry	13.7	40.8	32.1	$40,433	$24,797
All specialties	7.5	46.5	17.4	$47,945	$27,558

[a]Source, American Public Health Association, *Women in Health Careers: Chartbook for International Conference on Women in Health Fields Held in Washington, D.C., on June 16-18, 1975*, p. 44 (available from National Technical Information Services, Springfield, Va., PB-243-111).

many as 25-50 percent of the available residencies go unfilled. Thus, where competition is keen, (male) department heads seem to select disproportionately more male applicants. Women are "allowed" into the less desirable specialties which are "appropriate" expressions of female concerns—child rearing, community service, providing compassion and understanding (38).

Reflecting their exclusion from the "elite" specialties and entrepreneurial forms of care, women physicians report a substantially lower median income than their male counterparts: between a third and a half less income than male peers (39). Table 6 shows that the proportion of women in the medical specialties increases as the median income decreases. But women also report fewer hours than their male colleagues—perhaps reflecting their preference for salaried positions with fixed hours which accommodate their family obligations and needs, or their unwillingness or inability to compete with men in fee-for-service private practice. At any rate, Table 7 demonstrates that the income of women is significantly lower than would be expected, given their fewer hours worked. For example, women physicians work, on the average, about 80 percent as many hours as their male counterparts in the same specialty, but they receive only about 60 percent of the salary. Figure 2 depicts the dollar value per hour worked by male and female physicians and reveals the discrepancy in earning power between the genders.

Just as women are shut out of top income specialties, they are excluded from professional decision making. There is not a single woman in the AMA House of Delegates and only a handful have been alternates. Similarly, women are not found in the power positions of the medical education establishment. While 4000 women serve on teaching staffs nationally (half on a full-time basis), in 1971 only 4 percent of the full professors were women (Figure 3). Women academics suffer the same income inequality as do their sisters in patient care. A 1975 study at the University

Table 7

Comparison of hours worked and net income of male and female physicians, 1972[a]

Specialty	Female Hours as a Percent of Male Hours	Female Income as a Percent of Male Income
Radiology	.83	.56
Surgery	.78	.70
Obstetrics/gynecology	.75	.60
Anesthesiology	.90	.69
Internal medicine	.85	.51
General practice	.81	.53
Pediatrics	.80	.58
Psychiatry	.73	.61
All specialties	.80	.57

[a] Source, American Public Health Association, *Women in Health Careers: Chartbook for International Conference on Women in Health Fields Held in Washington, D.C., on June 16-18, 1975*, p. 44 (available from National Technical Information Services, Springfield, Va., PB-243-111).

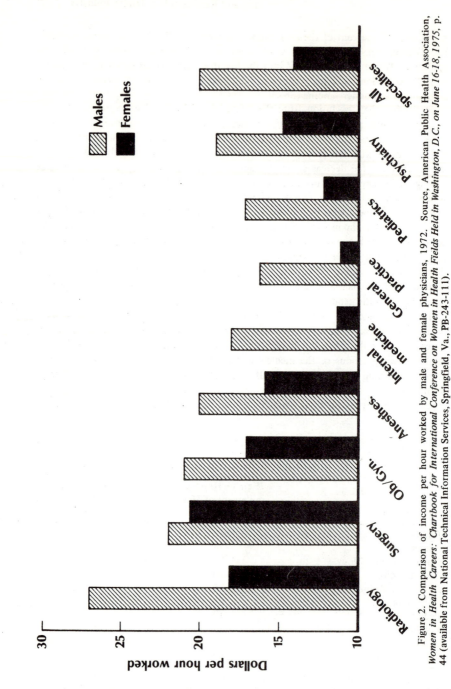

Figure 2. Comparison of income per hour worked by male and female physicians, 1972. Source, American Public Health Association, *Women in Health Careers: Chartbook for International Conference on Women in Health Fields Held in Washington, D.C., on June 16-18, 1975*, p. 44 (available from National Technical Information Services, Springfield, Va., PB-243-111).

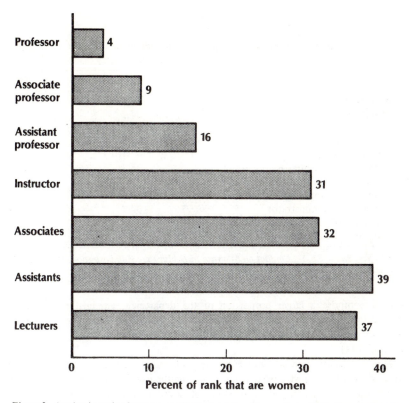

Figure 3. Academic rank of woman medical school faculty members, 1971. Source, American Public Health Association, *Women in Health Careers: Chartbook for International Conference on Women in Health Fields Held in Washington, D.C., on June 16-18, 1975,* p. 46 (available from National Technical Information Services, Springfield, Va., PB-243-111).

of California at San Francisco Medical School shows that male doctors made $7000 a year more than females with the same experience, training, and productivity (40).

Health Care Administrators

Nationally, women hold roughly half of the positions classified as health administration. But this finding is misleading because it fails to reflect the distribution of women within the administrative hierarchy and across the spectrum of types of institutions. A closer look by several scholars found that women are disproportionately administrating in small, rural, proprietary facilities and in lesser-status, lower-paying positions (41-43).

Results of a 1973 survey (44) of 70 health care facilities (acute care short term, convalescent, state mental, Veterans Administration, Health Maintenance Organizations, outpatient clinics) in Southern California show that women amount to only 24 percent of the middle and upper administrative cadre. Table 8 shows that these

Table 8

Distribution of females among Southern Californian administrators
by type of facility and occupational category[a]

	Percent of Category	Number
Type of facility		
Proprietary	27.2	6
Nonprofit	27.7	15
Government	17.1	6
Occupational category		
Convalescent hospital administrator	35.3	6
Chief administrator, short term and extended care hospitals	13.6	3
Department administrator	37.2	16
Administrative assistant	4.3	1
Outpatient clinic administrator	16.6	1

[a] Source, Weaver, J. L., *Conflict and Control in Health Care Administration*, p. 21, Sage Publications, Beverly Hills, 1975.

women comprise a larger proportion of the department administrators, but they are located in such traditional "women's" departments as housekeeping, dietetics, and nursing; only a small fraction are found in institution-wide policy-making positions (44).

Minority health care administrators are even more rarely encountered. Elling and Shepard (45) found just 2 percent blacks among their sample of public health hospital administrators. The comprehensive study of Southern California facilities previously mentioned turned up 4.5 percent minorities in its sample. Nationally, the 1970 Census found about 5 percent of health administrators are black, and 2 percent are of Spanish heritage. In a study of hospital occupational stratification in four cities containing large Chicano populations, D'Antonio and Samora (46) found that Chicanos are vastly underrepresented in the high-status occupations—administrators and policy makers, while equally overrepresented in the lowest-status occupations—aides, porters, and kitchen workers. Applewhite (47) reports that although 7428 Masters of Health Administration had been awarded through 1974, only 53 had gone to blacks. Apart from the difficulties which minorities face in moving up from labor to administrative strata due to lack of educational credentials, it has been claimed that out-and-out discrimination keeps minority individuals out of supervisory and executive positions (48-50).

Nurses

During the early 1970s the American Nurses Association became much more aggressive in negotiations and attempted to improve wages, job security, and control over the working conditions of rank-and-file nurses (51). The California Nurses Association and several other state-level organizations have begun collective bargaining with facility administrators, and these associations seem to be fully committed to traditional labor negotiations procedures, including strikes (52). In many California hospitals the CNA has signed contracts establishing "Professional Performance Committees" which are analogous to shop grievance committees in other industries. These committees not only bring nurses' representatives and management together to discuss firing, promoting, and scheduling; they also deal with matters associated with the quality and procedures of patient care (53).

Demands by nurses and other occupational groups in hospitals for increased pay, better working conditions, and formalization of personnel procedures often have at their root the belief that the facility is victimizing and exploiting its employees (54-56). Writing to this point, Cleland (57) calls sex discrimination the nurse's most pervasive problem (see also reference 58). And Roberts and Group (59) compare the plight of women in the health industry to that of blacks in American society.

Blacks and Spanish heritage individuals are disproportionately overrepresented in the lowest stratum of the nursing profession: nursing aides, orderlies, and attendants. Table 9 shows that over three times as many black women are aides or practical nurses as hold the higher-paying position of registered nurse. Moreover, both black and Spanish heritage women are found among registered nurses well below the frequency suggested by their proportion of the total and health-employed populations (60).

Lack of role models, limited information about careers in nursing, financial pressures, and inferior educational preparation affect the size of the pool from which minority nurses can be drawn just as these factors work to restrict the number of

Table 9

Percent of black and Spanish heritage workers in health occupations by sex, 1970[a]

Occupation	Black		Spanish Heritage	
	Male	Female	Male	Female
Clinical lab technicians	12	9	6	3
Radiologic technicians	9	7	6	3
Dental assistants	8	3	4	4
Dental hygienists	5	2	3	1
Dental lab technicians	5	7	7	5
Dieticians	29	20	7	3
Health aides (except nursing)	20	19	7	4
Nursing aides, orderlies, and attendants	28	25	5	4
Practical nurses	23	22	6	3
Registered nurses	15	7	5	2
Therapists	9	7	3	2
Therapists' assistants	16	15	4	6
Employed in all health occupations	8	14	3	3
Total employed in U.S. labor force	9	11	4	3
Total U.S. population	11	11	5	5

[a] Source, United States Department of Health, Education, and Welfare, *Decennial Census Data for Selected Health Occupations: United States, 1970*, p. 5, (HRA 76-1231), Government Printing Office, Washington, D.C., 1975.

applications to other health professions. In addition, the unwillingness of hospitals to advance individuals upward on the basis of experience, skill, and ability keeps minorities within the lower strata. As long as entry into registered nursing is based on educational preparation alone, minorities will be disproportionately affected. The reliance on formal education presents a double barrier since predominantly minority programs do not offer adequate numbers of positions, while Anglo-dominated schools of nursing allegedly discriminate against blacks (and presumably other minorities) (61).

While nurses have been fighting to upgrade their status, pay, and authority within the delivery systems, an unexpected yet important change has occurred within the profession. Whether because of the increasingly attractive pay scale offered nurses, the possibilities for advancement into nursing administration, or the opportunity provided by equal employment opportunity programs, growing numbers of men are becoming nurses. (Table 9 shows that minority men are twice as likely as minority women to hold the better-paying, higher-prestige position of registered nurse.) While the actual number of men is small, one observer commented: "males are disproportionately found in administrative positions. In addition, males are taking over the administration of nursing at an increasing rate. Given these present trends, nursing could evolve into a sex-segregated profession, with men at the top, much as men have become the principals and administrators in the field of elementary education" (62).

Racism has been prevalent in the nursing profession for a long time; and the entry of males in significant numbers is very recent. It would be useful to study the dynamics which keep minorities at the bottom and allow men to rise to the top of the profession.

HEALTH INDUSTRY REFLECTS DUAL LABOR MARKET

The inequalities between the professional and worker strata of the health industry illustrate a cardinal feature of American capitalism. The low pay and prestige, absence of job security, rapid turnover, and indications of high levels of job alienation among workers reflect the operations of the dual labor market: the labor market is divided into two essentially distinct sectors, termed the *primary* and the *secondary* sectors. The former offers jobs with relatively high wages, good working conditions, chances of advancement, equity and due process in the administration of work rules, and, above all, employment stability. Jobs in the secondary sector, by contrast, tend to be low paying, with poorer working conditions and little chance of advancement; with a highly personalized relationship between workers and supervisors, which leaves wide latitude for favoritism and is conducive to harsh and capricious work discipline; and with considerable instability in jobs and a high turnover among the labor force (63). While this model was designed to explain the problems of urban black workers, it appears to offer powerful analytical advantage in considering the situation of women as well as ethnic minorities.

In the context of the dual labor market hypothesis, the effort by rank and file health workers to unionize takes on a new meaning. On one side, collective bargaining, clarification of the conditions of employment, job security, and other concomitants of union protection offer important new protections to the individual worker. But of equal, perhaps even greater significance, is the attack which collectivization may herald on the secondary labor market. By combining together, individual workers begin to offer an effective challenge to the managers and executives who control the economic, social, and political power of the health industry. The potential historical significance of action at this level is far greater than the admittedly important direct individual benefits derived from organizing bargaining units; yet it remains to be seen if the employee unions and associations attempting to organize health workers will emerge as truly progressive forces in the struggle to overcome sexism and racism.

WOMEN AND MINORITIES AS CONSUMERS

Discrimination against women and minorities by providers of health care services takes a number of forms—unnecessary procedures (sterilization and overprescription of tranquilizers for women); location of practices beyond the reach of people lacking private transportation; disrespectful and insensitive treatment; unwillingness of insurance companies to provide gynecological coverage for single women; and the charging of increased premiums for carriers of the sickle-cell trait (presumed, incorrectly, to reduce life expectancy). Sometimes the discrimination is subtle, such as the practice of Anglo physicians asking black but not Anglo patients questions about drug abuse or sexual behavior. Sometimes it is overt, such as the refusal of nursing homes to accept an elderly minority patient (64).

Much of this discrimination is rooted in the sexism and racism of the American economic and social institutions. But a good deal of it stems directly from the health industry. A full exploration of the forces that sustain sexism and racism in the delivery of care awaits further research. Here we shall simply point to some apparent relationships which invite additional study.

Treatment of Women

It is a mystery why physicians are so willing to cut, drug, and bully women. But they do. A hundred years ago, surgery was often performed with the explicit goal of "taming" a high-strung woman (65). Clitoridectomy and ovariotomy were the methods of preference then. Now, similar results are obtained by telling women that their illnesses are of psychologic origins and then treating them with tranquilizers, psychiatric therapy, shock, or institutionalization (66, 67). Hysterectomies appear to be another favorite treatment, and there is a growing concern that many or most hysterectomies may be performed without proper indications (68). The surgeons' preference for radical mastectomies, in the presence of clear evidence of their emotional trauma and equally unclear evidence of their curative superiority, is also disturbing. Yet while this cutting and drugging is going on, pelvic examinations are not performed routinely, and many physicians do not teach their patients breast self-examination (69, 70).

Part of the explanation for this syndrome of physician behavior rests in what they have been taught about women in medical school. Howell (70) notes that patients in most medical school lectures are referred to exclusively by the male pronoun. There is, however, a notable exception: in discussing a hypothetical patient whose disease is of psychogenic origin, the lecturer often automatically uses "she." It is widely taught, both explicitly and implicitly, that women patients (when they receive notice at all) have uninteresting illnesses, are unreliable historians, and are beset by such emotionality that their symptoms are unlikely to reflect "real" disease (70, p. 304).

Physicians diagnose women as mentally healthy or mentally ill on the basis of a different standard from that of men. The standard is more restrictive in the range of behavior considered normal and has the effect of confirming and reinforcing the subordinate social status of women (71-74). Sexual stereotyping is being recognized, however; but unfortunately psychiatrists and others are only now beginning to recognize that the bored housewife syndrome is not necessarily psychopathology but a healthy response to a career as a chauffeur, maid, and jack-of-all trades. Instead of pinning labels on women, it may be appropriate to examine the reality of women patients' depression, boredom, anxiety, lack of fulfillment in life, and loss of identity (19, p. 1134).

In fostering and sustaining misogyny, psychiatrists are aided and abetted by gynecologists. Scully and Bart (75) conducted a systematic review of the 27 most widely used gynecology texts published since 1943 and found a continued reinforcement of the stereotyped roles for women. It has been said of the male gynecologist: "If, like all human beings, he [the gynecologist] is made in the image of the Almighty, and if he is kind, then his kindness and concern for his patient may provide her with a glimpse of God's image" (62, p. 428). Gynecology textbooks teach that women are fundamentally a reproductory machine with little or no capacity for sexual pleasure. Following from this premise, it is a simple step to conclude that once the baby-making duty is done (or the woman wishes it stopped), hysterectomy is called for. A variation of the same theme may be reflected in the uncritical acceptance of hormone therapy, either as contraceptive or menopausal treatment. It is breathtaking to note how easy it is for the "traditionalists" (women are baby-making machines) and the "humanists" (plan families, prolong female sex appeal) to ignore the social, economic, and emotional consequences which such treatment imposes on their patients.

Ehrenreich and English (65, p. 83) offer a useful point of departure for further investigation of the medical treatment of women in their claim that the medical system is not just a service industry. It is a powerful instrument of social control, replacing organized religion as a prime source of sexist ideology and as an enforcer of sex roles.

Minorities as Consumers

The history of segregated health care is seen in the utilization patterns of millions of minorities (76-78). For instance, Jackson (79) writes that it seems the opinion of most members of the black community that the average black cannot receive fair treatment because of racism on the part of those providing services. Hines (80) argues that because of prejudice throughout the country, ". . . the Negro has been discouraged from approaching agencies and facilities providing health care." Robertson and associates (81) claim that blacks' greater use of public health facilities rather than private providers is not simply a consequence of the inavailability of the latter or of economic constraints; rather, it stems from the blacks' desire to avoid personal relationships with Anglo providers. Here the impersonalism of the public provider is actively sought. Roth (82) suggests that impersonalism and fragmented care form a social distance between providers and consumers and reduce the frequency and extent of racist abuse.

Scattered research has sought to document consumer perceptions of discrimination and abusive treatment. Powell's survey of low-income New Yorkers (83) turned up the following differences in perceptions between Anglo and minority respondents:

	Puerto Ricans %	Blacks %	Anglos %
Doctors are rude			
Sometimes	61.6	70.5	34.9
Doctors are prejudiced against people on welfare			
Yes	73.3	71.6	46.0
Doctors are prejudiced against Puerto Ricans and blacks			
Yes	61.4	66.7	not asked

A study of the reaction of blacks to treatment by Anglo nurses concluded that although the nurses were responsive to their patients, blacks may have perceived prejudice (84). Jonas (49, p. 74) points out that working-class blacks and Latins repeatedly report incidents in the delivery of health care in which they feel that they have been treated rudely, crassly, or poorly simply because the provider was white and they were not.

A detailed examination of the treatment procedures of Anglos and blacks in hospitals concluded that "the data show differences in care"—differences not attributable to variation in condition of the patient (85). And Yamamoto, Dixon, and Bloombaum (86) determined that black and Chicano patients do not receive equal frequency or type of treatment from mental health therapists. They found that the level of the therapist's ethnocentricity was strongly associated with the percent of patients seen six or more times by the provider.

Ethnocentrism makes it difficult for providers to communicate with many minority patients. And lack of awareness of a patient's cultural preferences and style of interaction often generates antagonisms which lead to curtailed or aborted treatment. A classic example is found in a confrontation between an Anglo physician and a traditional South Texas Chicano. After the physician laughed at the Chicano's diagnosis that his wife's complaint resulted from witchcraft, the physician ordered the lady to undress. "This I could not stand, that my wife should be naked with this man. We never returned, of course, and my wife was treated by a [folk healer]. Maybe Anglos let doctors stare at their wives' bodies and fool around with them but not me. And the fool didn't even know about *susto* [magically induced 'fright']. He is lucky I did not reduce his arrogance right there" (87).

Racist ethnocentrism apparently is built into the preparation of psychiatrists and other mental health workers. Predominantly white psychoanalytically oriented residency programs are failing to produce psychiatrists, black or white, who are motivated or prepared to address themselves to the mental health needs of the black community. The ethnocentric white middle-class psychoanalytic orientation of these programs and facilities is held to be responsible—covert in its design and insidious in its practice (88).

As a result of this definition of mental health/illness, many blacks in need of treatment are ignored or misdiagnosed (89). A mental health program studied by Jones and his colleagues (88) selected for treatment far fewer blacks than their proportion of walk-ins; those selected were overwhelmingly assigned to the drug clinic, to a 15-minute clinic, or to programs with a rapid turnover of inexperienced therapists. When the staff was questioned about the biased behavior, their defenses were all couched in language suggesting that these patients did not seem to be able to benefit from our kind of treatment, did not seem to be motivated, were not sufficiently introspective, and so forth.

To the burden of ethnocentrism and institutionalized racism carried by minorities must be added the crushing weight of de facto segregation—separate and unequal health services. The National Advisory Commission on Civil Disorders reported in 1968 that "... some private hospitals still refuse to admit Negro patients or accept doctors with Negro patients. And many individual doctors still discriminate against Negro patients" (90).

The federal government has been a major contributor to this situation. For instance, under the Hospital Survey and Construction Act of 1946 (Hill-Burton), an estimated 1,000,000 hospital beds were constructed and over $1.6 billion were spent in tax revenues on a program which officially sanctioned segregated facilities. By 1963, when "separate-but-equal" hospital services were finally declared unconstitutional, only 13 new hospitals had been specially constructed for blacks, while 76 had been specially designed to exclude blacks (91). Asians, Chicanos, Native Americans, and other minorities also have been turned away from facilities built with their tax monies.

Contemporary programs also sustain racism. A close examination of Medicare and Medicaid reveals a significantly lower rate of benefits payments received by minorities. Hearings on the House Judiciary Committee indicate that this pattern of lower benefits is a reflection of both overt and institutional discriminatory practice. Physicians can refuse to treat minority patients, maintain segregated waiting rooms, or reserve only limited hours for treatment of minority patients without fear of disqualification as Medicare providers. Discriminatory practices by physicians also restrict access of minorities to high-quality hospital and nursing home care. Davis (92) explains that while direct discrimination by hospitals is prohibited in Medicare and Medicaid, considerable disparities continue to exist in the care received by members of different racial groups. Deficiencies in administration of the programs are partly responsible for this failure. Only about 5 percent of medical facilities were site-visited to check for compliance in the 15 months ending March 1973, and fewer than 3 percent in 1971. In addition, the Medicare program has not insisted that hospitals and nursing homes have affirmative action policies to attract minority patients.

The inability or unwillingness of the government to challenge racism and sexism directly and effectively continues. None of the national health insurance plans thus far presented in Congress prohibits racial discrimination; none establishes tough enforcement provisions; and none contains positive programs to offset the negative effects of past discrimination or to stimulate incentives for remedial service to medically disadvantaged communities. Discrimination has been fostered by federal programs past, present, and future: ". . . the pattern of Medicare and Medicaid, in which whites receive average payments for physicians that are 35 to 60% higher than those received by blacks and other minorities, is likely to persist, and the goal of ensuring quality medical care for all Americans will not be fully achieved" (92, p. 157).

CONCLUSION

This brief review of sexism and racism in the health industry has been a stock-taking venture. We have suggested a number of situations or conditions, such as the sexist nature of medical school instruction, which call for further research. Yet we have avoided exploring the "why?" questions, not because it is unimportant to seek origins and motivations, but because we are ill-equipped to evaluate proffered explanations. Although it appears that surgeons as a group are remarkably sexist (of course, the sexist surgeons are the subset most likely to attract attention), the causes of their affliction cannot be fully explored until we have more fully documented their behavior and attitudes toward women.

A great deal more basic research is called for if we are to gain a clear picture of the origins and ramifications of sexism and racism. But our perception suggests that little advance in our understanding will be made by concentrating on describing particular cases of discrimination or exploitation. Rather, what is called for are studies which link situations of discrimination to their broader institutional and ideological context. As we noted above, it simply makes no sense to discuss the plight of low-level health workers outside of the dynamics and traditions of the American labor market and class system. Linking cases of discrimination to their historical and institutional foundations will generate insights that are useful to both academicians and social reformers.

The literature which we have summarized is useful and has been an important contribution to this goal. Nevertheless, it helps to foster and sustain the notion that the exploitation and inequality suffered by nurses or blacks or the elderly, regardless of sex or race, call for special and separate action. An example of this kind of particularism is provided by Cleland (93): "Sex discrimination is very different from race discrimination in that, with the former, the 'enemies' have so much day to day contact." In the first place, men are not "enemies." This kind of simple-minded thinking reflects the same inability to distinguish opponents from the unenlightened which led some orthodox Marxists to warn Mao that he could never build a base of support among the Chinese peasants because they were reactionary class enemies. The Chinese experience demonstrates the fallacy of Cleland's type of generalization.

The more significant issue is the assertion that the condition of women and minorities is basically different. Such thinking engenders particularism and competition ("We are worse off than you are, so subordinate your interests and demands to ours!") which lead to endless disputes. Such partisanship takes attention away from the broad issues of strategy and the relative powerlessness of individual efforts. As we saw above, the operations of the secondary labor market exploit individuals caught in it whether they are women or men, Anglo or minority. The fact that minorities are more cruelly exploited should not blind reformers to the fact that power or lack of it is based on the number of one's resources, not the severity of one's situation. It is both historically unenlightened and politically bankrupt to charge that feminism is a threat to minority advancement because women want jobs which are just opening up to minority men; and it is equally shortsighted to fail to be sensitive to the needs and aspirations of minority women. Who but the prevailing power elite benefits from such particularisms? Yet this is precisely the consequence of emphasizing the superficial and insignificant differences between the plight of women and minorities at the hands of the health industry.

REFERENCES

1. Suter, E., and Miller, P. Income differences between men and career women. *American Journal of Sociology* 78: 962-974, 1973.
2. Blaxall, M., and Regan, B. B., editors. Women and the workplace: The implications of occupational segregation. *Signs* 1(3, part 2): topical issue, 1976.
3. Marshall, R. The economics of racial discrimination: A survey. *Journal of Economic Literature* 12(3): 849-871, 1974.
4. Knowles, L. L., and Prewitt, K. *Institutional Racism.* Prentice-Hall, Englewood Cliffs, N.J., 1969.
5. U.S. Bureau of the Census. *The Social and Economic Status of the Black Population in the United States, 1974.* Series P-23, No. 54. Government Printing Office, Washington, D.C., 1975.
6. Stern, R. S., Walter, G. R., and Galle, O. R. Equality for blacks and women: An essay on relative progress. *Social Science Quarterly* 56(4): 664-672, 1976.
7. Almquist, E. M. Untangling the effects of race and sex: The disadvantaged status of black women. *Social Science Quarterly* 56(1): 129-142, 1975.
8. Women M.D.'s—What we have here (maybe) is a revolution. *Am. Med. News* 15: 11-13, 1974.
9. Medical education. *JAMA* 236 (26): topical issue, 1976.
10. Thompson, T. Curbing the black physician manpower short. *J. Med. Educ.* 49(10): 944-950, 1974.
11. Wilensky, H. Women's work: Economic growth, ideology. *Journal of Industrial Relations* 7: 265-288, 1968.
12. Krauss, W. R. Political implications of gender role: A review of the literature. *Am. Pol. Sci. R.* 58(4): 1708-1711, 1974.
13. Counseling coeds on their role in medicine (students). *Medical World News* 15: 91-92, 1974.
14. Roberts, P., and Plunkett, R. A. Selected keys to the door to minority student participation in health careers. *Journal of Allied Health* 40-49, 1974.
15. Roessler, R., Collins, F., and Mefferd, R. B., Jr. Sex similarities in successful medical school applicants. *American Medical Women's Association Journal* 30(6): 254-265, 1975.
16. Fruen, M. A., Rothman, A. I., and Steiner, J. W. Comparison of characteristics of male and female medical school applicants. *J. Med. Educ.* 49(2): 137-145, 1974.
17. Rothman, A. I., et al. An empirical definition of a medical school's admissions procedure. *J. Med. Educ.* 49(1): 71-73, 1974.
18. Ortiz, F. I. Women in medicine: The progress of professional incorporation. *American Medical Women's Association Journal* 30(6): 18-30, 1975.
19. Benedek, E. P. Training the woman resident to be a psychiatrist. *Am. J. Psychiatry* 130(10): 1132, 1973.
20. Campbell, M. A. *"Why Would a Girl Go into Medicine?" Medical Education in the United States: A Guide for Women.* The Feminist Press, Old Westbury, N.Y., 1973.
21. Kaplan, H. Women physicians: The more effective recruitment and utilization of their talents and the resistance to it—The final conclusions of a seven year study. *Women Physician (American Medical Women's Association Journal)* 25(9): 561-570, 1970.
22. Haynes, M. A. Problems facing the Negro in medicine today. *JAMA* 209: 1068, 1969.
23. Notman, M. T., and Nadelson, C. Medicine: A career conflict for women. *Am. J. Psychiatry* 130(10): 1123-1126, 1973.
24. Medical education: Those sexist putdowns may be illegal. *Science* 186: 450, 1974.
25. Roeske, N. A. Women in psychiatry: Past and present areas of concern. *Am. J. Psychiatry* 130(10): 1127-1131, 1973.

26. Medical education. *JAMA* 234(13): 1351, 1975.
27. Johnson, D., and Smith, V. Recruitment and progress of minority medical school entrants 1970-1972. *J. Med. Educ.* 50: 711-755, 1975.
28. Have women advanced in medicine? *Med. World News* 65-66, 1975.
29. Pool, J. G., and Bunkee, J. P. Women in medicine. *Hospital Practice* 7:109-116, 1972.
30. Navarro, V. Women in health care. *N. Engl. J. Med.* 292(8): 400, 1975.
31. Seham, M. *Blacks and American Medical Care*, p. 69. University of Minnesota Press, Minneapolis, Minn., 1973.
32. Curtis, J. L. *Blacks, Medical Schools and Society,* pp. 21-25. University of Michigan Press, Ann Arbor, Mich., 1971.
33. Ehrenreich, B., and English, D. *Witches, Midwives, and Nurses: A History of Women Healers.* The Feminist Press, Old Westbury, N.Y., 1972.
34. Walsh, M. R. Doctors wanted: No women need apply. In *Sexual Barriers in the Medical Profession, 1835-1975.* Yale University Press, New Haven, Conn., 1977.
35. Dube, W. F. Women students in U.S. medical schools: Past and present trends. *J. Med. Educ.* 48(2): 186-189, 1973.
36. Carpenter, E. S., and Walker, S. Women in Male-Dominated Health Professions. Paper presented at the 1974 Annual Meeting of the American Public Health Association.
37. Pennel, M. Y., and Renshaw, J. E. Distribution of women physicians, 1970. *American Medical Women's Association Journal* 27: 197-200, 1972.
38. Lopate, C. *Women in Medicine,* pp. 127-128. Johns Hopkins University Press, Baltimore, 1968.
39. Hendrickson, R. M. Women physicians: Where they rank on the money tree. *Prism* 20-21, 1975.
40. Jacobson, B., and Jacobson, W. Only eight percent: A look at women in medicine. *Civil Rights Digest* 7(4): 20-28, 1976.
41. Dolson, M. Where women stand in administration. *Modern Hospital* 108: 100-105, 1967.
42. Womanpower in hospital administration. *FAH Review* 5: topical issue, 1972.
43. Pecarchik, R., and Mather, W. G. Lack of business skills threatens women administrators. *Modern Nursing Home* 24(5): 58, 1970.
44. Weaver, J. L. *Conflict and Control in Health Care Administration.* Sage Publications, Beverly Hills, 1975.
45. Elling, R. H., and Shepard, W. P. A study of public health careers: Hospital administrators in public health. *Am. J. Public Health* 58(5): 915-929, 1968.
46. D'Antonio, W. V., and Samora, J. Occupational stratifications in four southwestern communities: A study of ethnic differential employment in hospitals. *Social Forces* 41: 18-24, 1962.
47. Applewhite, H. L. Blacks in public health. *J. Natl. Med. Assoc.* 66: 505-510, 1974.
48. Rice, H. To cure racism. *Hospitals* 47(9): 54-56, 1973.
49. Jonas, S. Health, health care and racism. *Hospitals* 48(4): 72-75, 1974.
50. Alarming lack of black administrators confirmed. *Modern Nursing Home* 25: 37, 1970.
51. Bullough, B. New militancy in nursing: Collective bargaining activities by nurses in perspective. *Nurs. Forum* 10(3): 273-288, 1971.
52. Grand, N. K. Nursing ideologies and collective bargaining. *Journal of Nursing Administration* 3(2): 29-32, 1973.
53. Erickson, E. H. Collective bargaining: An inappropriate technique for professionals. *Nurs. Forum* 10(3): 300-311, 1971.
54. Health Policy Advisory Center. *Health Workers.* Health/PAC, New York. (A packet of Health/PAC *Bulletin* March 1970, July-August 1970, April 1972.)
55. Ehrenreich, J., and Ehrenreich, B. Hospital workers: A case study in the "new working class." *Monthly Review* 24(8): 12-27, 1973.
56. Langer, E. Inside the hospital workers: The best contract anywhere. *N. Y. Review of Books* 16(9): 25-33, 30-37, 1971.
57. Cleland, V. Sex discrimination: Nursing's most pervasive problem. *Am. J. Nurs.* 71: 1542-1543, 1971.
58. Bullough, B., and Bullough, V. Sex discrimination in health care. *Nurs. Outlook* 23: 40-45, 1975.
59. Roberts, J. I., and Group, T. M. The women's movement and nursing. *Nurs. Forum* 12(3): 303-322, 1973.
60. Winder, A. E. Why young black women don't enter nursing. *Nurs. Forum* 10(1): 56-63, 1971.
61. Miller, M. On blacks entering nursing. *Nurs. Forum* 11(3): 248-263, 1972.
62. Levinson, R. Sexism in medicine. *Am. J. Nurs.* 76(3): 431, 1976.

63. Piore, M. J. *Notes for a Theory of Labor Market Stratification*, p. 2. Working Paper No. 95. Massachusetts Institute of Technology, Cambridge, Mass., 1972.
64. Weaver, J. L. *National Health Policy and the Underserved: Ethnic Minorities, Women, and the Elderly.* C. V. Mosby, St. Louis, Mo., 1976.
65. Ehrenreich, B., and English, D. *Complaints and Disorders: The Sexual Politics of Sickness*, pp. 34-36. The Feminist Press, Old Westbury, N.Y., 1973.
66. Seidenberg, R. Drug advertising and perceptions of mental illness. *Mental Hygiene* 55: 21-31, 1971.
67. Linn, L. S., and Davis, M. S. The use of psychotherapeutic drugs by middle-aged women. *J. Health Soc. Behav.* 12(4): 331-340, 1971.
68. Bunker, J. P. Surgical manpower: A comparison of operations and surgeons in the United States and in England and Wales. *N. Engl. J. Med.* 282(3): 135-144, 1970.
69. Mudd, J. W., and Heiss, J. L. Physical examinations of hospitalized adults. *J. Med. Educ.* 48(12): 1140-1147, 1973.
70. Howell, M. C. What medical schools teach about women. *N. Engl. J. Med.* 291(13): 304-307, 1974.
71. McDonald, M. Sex discrimination—Subtle and pervasive. *Psychiatric News* 26-27, 1975.
72. Jean, K., and Lennane, R. J. Alleged psychogenic disorders in women—A possible manifestation of sexual prejudice. *N. Engl. J. Med.* 288(6): 288-292, 1973.
73. Broverman, I. K., et al. Sex-role stereotypes and clinical judgments of mental health. *J. Consult. Clin. Psychol.* 34: 1-7, 1970.
74. Chester, P. *Women and Madness.* Avon, New York, 1972.
75. Scully, D., and Bart, P. A. A funny thing happened on the way to the orifice: Women in gynecology textbooks. *Am. J. Sociol.* 78: 1045-1050, 1973.
76. Cornely, P. B. Segregation and discrimination in medical care in the United States. *Am. J. Public Health* 46(9): 1074-1081, 1956.
77. Snyder, J. D. Race bias in hospitals: What the civil rights commission found. *Hospital Management* 96(5): 52-53, 1963.
78. Seham, M. Discrimination against Negroes in hospitals. *N. Engl. J. Med.* 271(18): 940-943, 1964.
79. Jackson, O. J. Medicine in the black community. *California Medicine* 113(4): 57-61, 1970.
80. Hines, R. H. The health status of black Americans: Changing perspective, p. 43. In *Patients, Physicians, and Illness*, Ed. 2, edited by E. G. Jaco, Free Press, New York, 1973.
81. Robertson, L. S., et al. Race, status, and medical care. *Phylon* 28(4): 353-360, 1967.
82. Roth, J. A. The treatment of the sick, p. 218. In *Poverty and Health: A Sociological Analysis*, edited by J. Kosa, A. Antonovsky, and I. K. Zola. Harvard Universtiy Press, Cambridge, Mass., 1968.
83. Powell, L. *Studies in the Use of Health Services by Families on Welfare.* PS-190 391. National Technical Information Service, Springfield, Va., 1970.
84. La Farge, J. P. Role of prejudice in rejection of health care. *Nurs. Res.* 21(1): 53-58, 1972.
85. Shaw, C. T. A detailed examination of treatment procedures of whites and blacks in hospitals. *Soc. Science Med.* 5: 251-256, 1971.
86. Yamamoto, J., Dixon, F., and Bloombaum, M. White therapists and Negro patients. *National Medical Association Journal* 64(4): 312-316, 1972.
87. Madsen, W. *Mexican-Americans of South Texas*, p. 92. Holt, Rinehart, and Winston, New York, 1964.
88. Jones, B. E., et al. Problems of black psychiatric residents in white training programs. *Am. J. Psychiatry* 127(6): 798-803, 1970.
89. Sabsin, M., et al. Dimensions of institutional racism in psychiatry. *Am. J. Psychiatry* 127(6): 787-793, 1970.
90. Gordon, D. M., editor. *Problems in Political Economy: An Urban Perspective*, p. 328. D. C. Heath, Lexington, Mass., 1971.
91. Bullough, B., and Bullough, V. *Poverty, Ethnic Identity, and Health Care*, pp. 160-161. Appleton-Century-Croft, New York, 1972.
92. Davis, K. *National Health Insurance: Benefits, Costs, and Consequences*, The Brookings Institution, Washington, D.C., 1975.
93. Cleland, V. S. To end sex discrimination. *Nursing Clin. North Am.* 563-571, 1974.

CHAPTER 5

Women Workers in
The Health Service Industry

Carol A. Brown

Health work is women's work. Over 85 per cent of all health service and hospital workers are women. The largest occupation in health work—nursing—is almost entirely female.

The increase in health employment over the past decades has been primarily an increase in women employees. Weiss(1) showed that the occupations that were predominantly female were expanding fastest, and that most occupations were becoming increasingly female. He showed the reason to be that the greatest increase has been at the lower ends of the ladder, where there are more women. Between 1960 and 1970 the number of physicians in practice increased by only 25 per cent, registered nurses by 39 per cent, and practical nurses by 80 per cent (2).

The health service industry is run by a small minority. It is run primarily by physicians, who have traditionally held the power, but also by the increasingly powerful hospital administrators, insurance company directors, government regulators, medical school educators, and corporation managers. Most of these people are men (3).

Aside from this top level in which industrial power is concentrated, men are found largely at the bottom—as kitchen helpers, janitors, and porters—and in a few technical fields such as laboratory and x-ray. Men at the bottom experience the same lack of power as their female coworkers, and, like the women, the further down the professional ladder they are the more likely they are to be non-white.

Health service is women's work, but not women's power. It is not unusual to find industrial power concentrated at the top echelon of an industry, nor to find the policy or practice of "men only" at the top echelon. It *is* unusual to find an industry requiring a complex mix of highly technical skills in which most of the skilled as well as the unskilled workers are women. In health service the conflict between "management" and "workers" is a conflict mainly between men and women.

Three main areas are dealt with in this paper. First, why are health workers women? Second, how is the overlap of sexual and occupational status upheld, and with what effects on the field? Third, what struggles take place that may lead to change in the future?

THE EMPLOYMENT OF WOMEN

Many apparent advantages to physicians and other elites in the health industry accrue to the hiring of women. First, women are an inexpensive source of labor. Health care is a costly but essential commodity, with labor constituting the biggest expense. Health service only became big business with the rise of hospitals. Hospital services are expensive and the biggest expense is labor. If costs are beyond the reach of consumers, the industry suffers, and with it the incomes of physicians and service organizations. Public financing has been put forth as one solution to high health costs; keeping labor costs low is another. A labor force composed mostly of women can be hired more cheaply than one composed mostly of men. Women can be paid less than men would be paid for the same work. In addition, women are believed to be dedicated to service and not self-interest (4), and are expected to drop out of the labor force to raise families—thus obviating the need for promotions or increased pay for seniority (5).

Second, women are available. Rapid expansion of labor requires an easily available labor force to draw on, and women are the last major reservoir of unemployment (6).

Third, women are safe. They pose no threat to physicians who, in order to expand their own services and therefore their incomes, must be assured of subordinates who will stay subordinate. Women do not have the social power—that is, access to capital, access to specialized education, freedom from family responsibilities, and respect of political leaders—to become organized competition to physicians in the medical marketplace, whereas other men and other male-dominated professions such as optometry or osteopathy do provide competition to physicians (7). Women's efforts to open medical schools to more women students have had limited success for the same reasons. At an interpersonal level, physicians are (or hope to be) assured of respect and willing service in members of subordinate occupations in part because they are men and the others are women.

Why do women accept the low pay and interpersonal subordination of the health service industry? If asked, many would say they went into health service to help people, to care for the sick, rather than to earn a high salary or to enjoy prestige. Caring for others is seen as women's work by society at large, and is seen by many women as their vocation. But physicians and surgeons also help the sick. The answer to women's acceptance of poorly paid subordinate occupations lies outside the health service industry in the economic opportunities available to women elsewhere. Women are "willing" to accept subordinate conditions of work because they have little choice in the matter.

Few occupations are open to women, whereas many are open to men. Out of 80 major occupational categories listed in the 1970 United States Census, seven occupations contain 43 per cent of all women workers. One of these occupations is nursing (8). Non-white women are concentrated in service and labor occupations. Discrimination is endemic, and few can afford to spend years pressing anti-discrimination suits at every barrier. When people need jobs they have to take what is open to them. When they need skill training, they learn what skills are offered. In addition, most women work because they need the money. The majority of women workers are single, are sole supports of households, or have husbands with incomes below $4000 a year (9).

The low pay for high skills found in health service is only low compared to white *men's* opportunities elsewhere. From the point of view of women, the pay is relatively good. Pay rates are low in all occupations in all industries for women. Median full-time earnings in hospital employment are *above* the median for workers in all industries for the categories of white women, black men, and black women. Median earnings in hospital employment are well below the median only for white men (10). One black woman from the South described to this author her entry into health service as a nurses' aide as an "incredible opportunity," because it was steady work and good wages. In getting further education, the average woman does not have a choice between nursing school and medical school, but between nursing school and, for example, computer programming school.

The lack of promotion opportunities in health careers over a lifetime does not compare unfavorably to the lack of promotion opportunities everywhere else for women. Of all the managers and non-farm administrators at all levels in the economy, only 16 per cent are women and 1 per cent non-white women (11).

Women's low wages compared to men's make a wife-mother necessarily dependent on her husband for her livelihood and that of her children (12). Her husband has the economic power to insist that she give up any other job. Thus, because of her tenuous position, long-term upward mobility opportunities within one organization, as much as she might want them, become unavailable to her. More relevant are good starting pay and certified skills for jobs that she can leave, reenter, and move to a new location. In many health occupations, one-half of entrants have left after five years; those who remain often change jobs for marginally higher pay, better working conditions, or family responsibilities, rather than for nonexistent promotion opportunities (13, 14).

Women accept the interpersonal subordination assigned to them in health service for the same reasons they accept low pay: there is a lack of alternatives. Few women are in decision-making positions in the polity or the economy, making women dependent on men's decisions. A woman cannot afford to demand her rights or to walk off the job if she is treated like an inferior. She will be treated like an inferior everywhere else, and like an unemployed inferior to boot.

Thus the limitations on women's opportunities everywhere else make it possible for the health service industry to offer low wages for high skills and to keep women down. The outside limitations lead women to accept subordination within health service. Health service, at least, is an area in which they can get skills, get jobs, and have the self-respect of making an important contribution to society.

MAINTAINING THE SYSTEM

Health service, then, has a sex hierarchy as well as an occupational hierarchy. The decision makers are almost entirely males and the workers are largely female. It is generally assumed that women as workers are satisfied with their positions in both hierarchies within the industry, that women workers will not fight for their economic welfare as men would, and that as women they accept the leadership of the male sex. The assumption is false.

The labor force pattern of women is now changing. More women are able to continue working despite childbearing, or to drop out for shorter periods of time. More women have a long career ahead of them, and they are increasingly in a position to demand the opening of high-level positions to them (5). Women now fight for position when they can. The modern health service industry has been permeated with internal economic conflict since it began, and the conflicts have grown as the industry has expanded.

To understand the peculiar nature of some of the conflicts in health service, we should examine the way the system is maintained. Health service is somewhat like the construction industry in having separate specialized crafts, with work performed on a custom basis in a large number of small work units (15, 16). Each health occupation above the unskilled level has a separate training program and special entry procedures, often culminating in registration or licensing procedures. Each occupation has a national professional society which tries to function like a craft union.

Unlike the construction industry, however, many highly skilled health occupations are relatively low paying and dead-end. In addition, the "crafts" are not independent of each other; they are hierarchically organized with rigid barriers between levels. The top male occupation—physician—controls the female occupations, not only on the job but in the educational programs. The American Medical Association and its affiliate medical societies have the right to set the curriculum, direct the training programs, control professional certification, and sit on the state licensing boards of (at last count) 16 other occupations. Through the Joint Commission for Accreditation of Hospitals, the American Association of Medical Colleges, the American Hospital Association, American Medical Association (AMA), and the Commission on Medical Education, for example, physicians can decide to create new occupations and control the division of labor. In the dental area the American Dental Association controls dental hygienists, assistants, and technicians. Bullough (17) has shown that historically the development of medicine as an elite profession depended on the patronage of socially powerful institutions external to health service, such as universities. This continues to be true. State legislatures, federal funders, government regulators, college and university administrators, and others support the power of physicians to control other occupations through, for example, hospital staffing regulations, Medicare funding regulations, rights of accreditation, and licensing laws (18).

The nursing profession has escaped total medical control only by its self-conscious determination to be an independent profession, yet organized nursing has far less power in the health service industry than one would expect of an occupation of so many workers and so key to the industry. The American Nursing Association (ANA) and the National League for Nursing (NLN) are generally ignored by the health service industry elite and its outside supporters on questions of public policy with respect to health care. The ANA and the NLN have no voice on the Joint Commission for Accreditation of Hospitals in regulating occupations and hospitals. On the job, nurses are very much subordinate to doctors. Although some of the middle-ranking occupations assert some controls over lower-ranking occupations following the physicians' model, they cannot assert power because they have little or none to assert (see below).

The formal controls on occupations are reinforced by the personal relations between employers and employees, superiors and subordinates at the work site. Who is allowed to work and who is allowed to make decisions are controlled by the same interlocking mechanisms explained above.

Both the ranking system and the ranks of each individual are as obvious in hospitals as in the armed forces. The individual's position is identified by distinctive uniforms and name tags which list occupation and department. As in the armed forces, a superior rank carries weight across departments—a physician on one medical service can often endanger the job of a technician or assistant on another service. Since jobs are insecure, everyone knows not to cross a superior, even though many acts of arrogance or unfairness in superiors can be traced to sexism or racism rather than to mere bureaucratic superiority. Those who complain fear being charged with insubordination, bad work attitudes, or disrespect to the superior.

In case individuals might begin with bad attitudes, training programs for the subordinate occupations include "professional ethics," in which they are taught primarily how to respect the physician and be loyal members of "the team." One chief radiologic technologist at a training hospital complained to this author that the radiologic technologists allow themselves to be pushed around by the doctors, but then he said ruefully, "But I suppose it is our own fault—that's what we teach them to do in the ethics courses."

To a certain extent teaching such "ethics" is unnecessary. Individual placements in the occupational hierarchy reflect the placements in the social hierarchy—men over women, whites over non-whites—and each has spent a lifetime learning how to act toward the other. When an intern is coached on how to handle nurses to get what he wants (19) he is simply relearning at a higher level his teenage lessons on how to handle girls.

The overlap between occupational and sexual status is so great it is sometimes hard to tell which is which. If a male physiologist ignores a female physical therapist's suggestion, is this because the physical therapist knows less, or because women don't know anything worth listening to? When she does not make the suggestion in the first place, has she learned her ethics as a physical therapist or has she learned her place as a woman? When a black nurses' aide talks back to a white nurse, is she being an uppity nurses' aide or is she being an uppity black?

Lest we think that the bureaucratic hierarchy is the primary reason for the superior-subordinate interaction, let us consider what happens when the two hierarchies do not overlap.

Nurses know how to respond to doctors because women know how to respond to men. But what if the doctor is a woman or the nurse a man? Suppose in our previous example the physiologist were a woman and the physical therapist a man? Suddenly the standardized behaviors that were presumed to flow from occupational hierarchies are thrown into turmoil. Much of the "natural" behaviors between occupations turn out to be based on the sex of the incumbent rather than the status of the occupation. Male doctors do not treat male subordinates the same way they treat female subordinates (20). Studies of female doctors show that they often try to identify with their occupational superiority and are perceived as "arrogant" in trying to get the same assistance from nurses and other women subordinates that the men get automatically (21, 22). Similar problems arise when a women chief technician runs a partly male department, or a black therapist supervises white therapy aides. Male orderlies often resent orders given by female nurses. The behavior patterns seen in hospitals between women and men of different occupations are very much sex-status patterns, just as the interpersonal relations between blacks and whites of different occupations are racial relations.

CONFLICTS

While it would appear that male physicians and hospital administrators have the upper hand through their ability to control other occupations, their ability to go outside the system for support, and the deference imposed on subordinates, the apparently iron-clad control system does not necessarily work. Women do fight for opportunities, and have most commonly followed the physicians' model of a professional society fighting for the status of its members.

Because occupational and sexual segregation overlap, conflict often revolves around the shape and structure of the occupations and can best be characterized as maneuvering for "turf" - for control of occupational territory.

Historically, physicians fought hard to suppress midwifery, and by World War Two finally won for physicians the right to deliver babies (23). Now general practitioners are being prevented from assisting at hospital deliveries by obstetricians. Both general practitioners and obstetricians have fought against public health nurses and nurse-midwives giving service in rural areas and urban slums, but this fight presents a dilemma for physicians. Maternity, like most medical specialties, is on a fee-for-service basis. Obstetricians may want to assure that they alone have the right to the fee for this service, but few want the reciprocal obligation of giving the service where there is no fee to be gained. As a result, there is an appallingly high maternal death rate from lack of medical care. Nurse-midwives, after years of struggle, have gained "permission," we might say, to become the inexpensive substitute for the expensive private practitioners, but only in the rural and urban areas that obstetricians do not want (24). Organized medicine keeps a careful watch to see that nurse-midwifery does not expand into serving the more affluent population. Nurse-midwifery services are as yet a controlled threat to a lucrative medical specialty (25). Similarly, nurse-anesthetists are a real threat to anesthesiologists, who have attempted without success to abolish the occupation (26).

The nursing profession has developed other clinical specialists whose skills and training with that specialty are greater than the average physician's, and who can undercut the physician-specialists' high wage rates. Physicians on their part attempt to undercut the threat of nurse specialists by creating lower-skilled substitutes such as obstetrical technicians and operating room assistants who are under AMA control and physicians' authority.

The occupation of licensed practical nurse (LPN) or licensed vocational nurse was consciously created over the objections of the nursing profession by physicians in medical schools and university-affiliated hospitals, who sought a less-trained, lower-paid, and more controllable alternative to the registered nurse, and the LPN was quickly accepted by hospitals and state licensing boards for the same reasons (3). The nursing profession was not able to prevent the development of the LPN, but was able to incorporate LPNs into the National League for Nursing structure and to obtain some control over licensing. Simultaneously with the LPN movement the three-year registered nurse programs were terminated in hospitals and two-year community college programs were created, although the nursing profession favored and has developed four-year B.S. training for nurses (27, 28).

With the shortage of physicians and the high cost of care by physicians, nurses began to develop nurse-practitioners, thus moving into the physicians' territory of diagnosing and curing. Physicians countered with the physician assistant, an occupation completely controlled by physicians, as nurses are not. The occupation was first advertised as a means by which physicians in private practice could increase their patient load and boost their incomes by letting someone else do the work. In this it was similar to the development by dentists of the dental assistant and dental hygienist occupations. The physician assistants were intended to be on a higher level than mere nurses—better paid and possessing medical skills and some decision-making power, but functioning only under the control and direction of physicians (29). They were also intended to be men, especially Vietnam-veteran medics. However, men are expensive and not automatically respectful of the physician's male status, and men can get better-paying, more responsible jobs elsewhere. The physician assistant programs are now primarily training women, taking the same amount of time as nurses' training, and currently at issue is whether physician assistants, standing *in loco medicus*, can give orders to nurses or whether nurses, as independent professionals, can give orders to physician assistants (30).

The sex identification of the occupations is an important component in many of the struggles. Physicians attempt to stamp out lower-level male professions such as podiatrist and optometrist, and attempt to develop women's occupations that can be controlled. Since women have little social power, men are assured of their own primacy. In any other industry a professional society or union which represents half the workers would not be as blithely ignored as is the ANA. Governments and educators simply do not pay attention to mere women. Although 40 per cent of medical technologists are men, the American Society of Medical Technologists (ASMT) is collectively referred to by the clinical pathologist leadership as "the girls." The organization is treated as men treat women—as not very serious and not needing to be taken into account when decisions are made that affect them. When the ASMT elected its first male president, one prominent woman technologist wondered if the ASMT would now be called "the girls and boys."

The pathologists' belief in women's collective subordination has backfired, as did belief in the collective subordination of nurses. The men might not wish to take the women seriously, but the women find their situation to be no laughing matter. Conflict in laboratory technology is rampant (31).

Although medical technologists, with college graduation and a year of clinical training behind them, are the official subordinate profession in pathology laboratories, pathologists have hired lower-paid technicians, usually with a year or two of college and no formal training. To protect themselves, the medical technologists attempted to create an occupation subordinate to themselves in the laboratory assistant, a high school graduate with one year of training who was intended to squeeze out technicians. The pathologists, however, refused to sponsor that level. Desiring a less troublesome but still skilled assistant occupation, the pathologists began to develop an official technician program, requiring two years of college and one year of training, which the technologists refused to sponsor. Pathologists subsequently sought tighter control over technologists' schools and registration. Technologists then sued the pathologists as a combination in restraint of trade. The best efforts of the AMA and out-of-court mediators have not brought a satisfactory solution. The ASMT has begun developing master's degrees in laboratory management, an area the pathologists consider to be their exclusive prerogative, and the American Society of Clinical Pathologists has withdrawn some financial support from ASMT and its related organizations.

INDUSTRIALISM

The change to hospitals and clinics as the first line of medical defense has weakened the independent power of physicians, who no longer control the market. The AMA's lessened influence on national medical policy is indicative of this. Increasing financial involvement of government, insurance companies, and other corporations has inevitably brought increased power to those institutions at the expense of hospital administrators as well as physicians (32). These third parties, as they are known in the trade, are not as interested in supporting the status quo as in providing inexpensive, efficient, and often profitable health service.

This increasing industrialization will clearly restructure the health occupational system, although if it follows current trends the structuring will be downward. Lesser-skilled and lesser-paid subordinates will replace the higher-skilled, higher-paid subordinates, just as the semi-skilled factory workers have replaced craftsmen in other industries. The current rigid occupational structure does enable women to retain some exclusive occupational territory and to attempt to move up by group mobility into the higher slots. However, the rigid segregation produced the high-skilled, low-paid, dead-end nature of health work in the first place. The likelihood of success through this strategy is questionable.

Other changes may be more productive of upward mobility. Clinics, hospitals, and Health Maintenance Organizations are now increasingly replacing the private physician even in formerly lucrative areas, and physicians more and more are adopting the role of backup personnel and paid staff rather than that of controllers of medical care. The administrative side of medicine then becomes more important, and produces a different potential for the lower occupations.

For one thing, the physician loses the personal incentive to keep down the training and wages of subordinates as he had in private practice. Since the wages are being paid by hospitals rather than by the physician, the physician wants the best assistants money can buy. Hospital-based physicians sometimes side with the upwardly mobile women's occupations against the hospital administrators and private practitioners (33).

In addition, most physicians have not perceived administration as a career ladder to success or as a major means to industrial power.[1] Members of subordinate occupations are developing hierarchies within their occupations and are moving upward there and in the administrative hierarchy. This permits them a certain amount of occupational self-control and even some bureaucratic control over the practice of physicians. The subordinate occupations are taking steps to enhance mobility by writing administrative positions into their own staffing guides, adding management courses to their training programs, and adding articles about administration to their professional society journals.

However, these new bureaucratic opportunities tend to benefit the men and the whites within the lower occupations more than they benefit the women and blacks.

---

[1] A past governor of the American College of Surgeons perceives the development as follows: "Nurses originated as helpers for doctors but over the years they have assumed more and more administrative functions until they occupy a position midway between administrative and professional staff. Many doctors regret this development but it has come about because of the laissez-faire attitude of doctors so that they have no real basis for complaint. As long as nurses realize and remember their primary mission of assisting the doctor in the care of his patients, no real harm results" (34).

Lower-level administrators are appointed from above and the top tends to choose its own kind. For example, chief radiologic technologists, who are promoted by administration, are twice as likely to be men as are radiologic technologists as a whole. The form of the stratification may change, but the membership composition by race and sex at each level may remain the same. As long as control flows from the top down, and the top is a small minority of white males in a system that fosters racism and sexism, the relative positions of white men, non-white men, white women, and non-white women will (or may) remain the same.

UNIONISM

As the private office and small hospital are replaced by the large hospital and clinic, there is not only an increasing number of occupations, but also an increased number of workers within each occupation, in national communication with each other. Health service has become a major form of employment. These are the ideal conditions for unionization. Both craft unionism, in which workers are organized by occupation, and industrial unionism, where workers are organized by employing unit, have increased (35).

Nurses' strikes are an example of what craft unionism can accomplish (36, 37). This kind of militance is only possible when there are enough members of an occupation in positions that can bring the hospitals to a halt. Hospital technicians on both the east and west coasts, mostly male, have attempted similar unionism and have largely failed, because their numbers are too small and the skills can be bought elsewhere. Nurses' strikes are aided not only by sufficient strength and number but also by the militance that the subordinate position of women can create. Having no future to lose, they can risk a strike, and they are brought together by their mutual identity as women as well as nurses. In addition, nurses who have carefully developed the identity of nursing as a profession giving service to patients are outraged by their treatment as assembly-line workers giving skilled labor to employers.

Industrial unionism is typified by hospital strikes, in which all the employees of one hospital or one city's hospitals are organized as a unit. Such organizing is aided by the development of large medical centers employing hundreds and even thousands of low-paid workers (38).

There is tremendous hostility to strikes in the health sector, in part because strikes interfere with treatment but in part because of the sex and often race of the striking workers. The enormous hostility to the hospital workers' strike in New York City in the early 1960s resulted in large part from the fact that the strikers were mostly non-whites and women and identified themselves with the civil rights struggle. "How dare they?" would best characterize the response of hospital administrators and the informed public. Similar upper-level sentiment against the San Francisco nurses' strikes was outrage that women would do such things. The California Nurses Association sees its struggle as a woman's struggle. In many cases, hospital strikers realize that their problems within the work setting are based partly on their sex and race status in the community (39).

Although people can unite around their sexual and racial oppression, these factors can also hold back organization, as can the segregation of occupations (40). Workers often feel more solidarity with their occupational colleagues in other hospitals than they do with their fellow workers in their own hospital, some of whom are in competing occupations and some of whom are of occupations, races, or sex perceived as inferior.

Strikes have failed because white strikers ignored black workers and black strikers ignored white workers, or because of male-female hostility. All these differences are exploited by the upper level. One major hospital union was not able to organize the nurses, technicians, and therapists into an industrial union until they developed a separate professional guild for these higher-level workers. In one hospital I studied which was undergoing a unionism drive, a technician explained her opposition to the union with, "Why should I have to go on strike because a porter throws a broom against a wall?" This same argument was given me by the laboratory administrator as a reason "his girls" should not join the union, leaving me with a strong impression about where the argument originated. The objection to the porter was not merely occupational. All of the porters who might have thrown their brooms against the wall were black men; all the technicians were white women. Thus race, sex, and professionalism combined against the union.

Professionalism is often seen as the antithesis of unionism and is used in this way. Said the chairman of the radiologists' Committee on Technician Affairs (41):

> Better trained and better paid technologists have a more professional attitude and are less likely to seek unionization and licensing as solutions for their problems. They also more properly appreciate their role in medicine and their relationship to their radiologists.

Nevertheless, in the attempt to push away unions, the professional societies are themselves having to respond to the rising demands of their members, and have taken actions resembling those of unions, partially in fear that their members will desert them in favor of unions. The radiologic technologists instituted a salary study "to meet head-on the encroachment of unionization. . . ."(42). The resulting salary proposals were so far above prevailing wage rates as to resemble nothing so much as the bargaining demands of a union.

Unionism seems promising, and hospital unions have been successful in raising the wages and bargaining position of hospital workers across occupational, race, and sex lines, and many have been making efforts to open mobility channels for low-level workers. However, unionism as a whole in this country has been both racist and sexist and has tended to become subordinate to management. If unions are to solve the problems, women must have power within them (43). The unions must remain aware of the need for equality for women and non-whites, and aware of the need to challenge management's right to rule.

CONCLUSION

A successful struggle against sexism in health service, as against racism, requires the unification of women and non-whites at all occupational levels in a common struggle not only against particular hospitals or occupations but against the entire structure of the health service industry that sustains low wages for the majority of workers and poor quality of care for the general population.

REFERENCES

1. Weiss, J. The Changing Job Structure of Health Manpower. Unpublished dissertation, Harvard University, Cambridge, 1966.
2. National Center for Health Statistics. *Health Resources Statistics: Health Manpower and Health Facilities 1971.* U.S. Department of Health, Education, and Welfare, 1972.
3. Reverby, S. Health: Women's work. *Health-PAC Bulletin* 40: 1-3, April 1972.
4. Rosenberg, M. *Occupations and Values.* Free Press, Glencoe, Ill., 1957.
5. Kreps, J. *Sex in the Marketplace.* Johns Hopkins Press, Baltimore, 1971.
6. Oppenheimer, V. K. *The Female Labor Force in the United States.* Population Monograph Series No. 5, University of California, Berkeley, 1970.
7. Greenfield, H. I., with Brown, C. A. *Allied Health Manpower: Trends and Prospects.* Columbia University Press, New York, 1969.
8. Women's Bureau. *Handbook on Women Workers.* U.S. Department of Labor, 1969.
9. Women's Bureau. *Facts about Women Workers.* U.S. Department of Labor, 1974.
10. Flaim, P. O., and Peters, N. I. Usual weekly earnings of American workers. *Monthly Labor Review* 95(3): 28-38, 1972.
11. Bureau of the Census. *General Social and Economic Characteristics, United States Summary, 1970.* U.S. Department of Commerce, 1972.
12. Mitchell, J. *Woman's Estate.* Pantheon, New York, 1972.
13. Ladinsky, J. Occupational determinants of geographic mobility among professional workers. *Amer. Sociol. Rev.* 32: 253-264, April 1967.
14. Smith, P. D. *Influence of Wage Rates on Nurse Mobility.* Graduate Program in Hospital Administration, University of Chicago, Chicago, 1962.
15. Kissick, W. *Health Manpower in Transition.* U.S. Public Health Service, 1966.
16. Coggeshall, L. T. *Planning for Medical Progress through Education.* Association of American Medical Colleges, Evanston, Ill., April 1965.
17. Bullough, V. L. *The Development of Medicine as a Profession.* S. Karger, Basel and New York, 1966.
18. Spieler, E. Division of laborers. *Health-PAC Bulletin* 46: 1-2, 4, November 1972.
19. Nolen, W. A. *The Making of a Surgeon.* Simon and Schuster, New York, 1972.
20. Cooper, V. The lady's not for burning. *Health-PAC Bulletin* pp. 2-3, March 1970.
21. Lopate, C. *Women in Medicine.* Johns Hopkins Press, Baltimore, 1968.
22. Kosa, J., and Cocker, R. E., Jr. The female physician in public health: Conflict and reconciliation of the sex and professional roles. *Sociology and Social Research* 49(3): 294-305, 1965.
23. Ehrenreich, B., and English, D., editors. *Witches, Midwives, and Nurses: A History of Women Healers.* Feminist Press, Old Westbury, New York, 1973.
24. *The Training and Responsibilities of the Midwife.* The Josiah Macy Jr. Foundation, New York, 1967.
25. *The Midwife in the United States,* Josiah Macy Jr. Foundation, New York, 1968.
26. Stevens, R. *American Medicine and the Public Interest.* Yale University Press, New Haven, 1971.
27. Levine, E. Some answers to the nurse shortage. *Nursing Outlook* 12(3): 30-34, 1964.
28. Levine, E., Siegel, S., and De La Prente, J. Diversity of nurse staffing among general hospitals. *Hospitals* 35(9): 42-48, 1961.
29. Lippard, V., and Purcell, E., editors. *Intermediate-Level Health Practitioners.* Josiah Macy Jr. Foundation, New York, 1973.
30. Reverby, S. Sorcerer's apprentice. *Health-PAC Bulletin* 46: 1-2, November 1972.
31. Brown, C. A. The division of laborers: Allied health professions. *Int. J. Health Serv.* 3(3): 435-444, 1973.
32. Ehrenreich, B., and Ehrenreich, J. *The American Health Empire: Power, Profits and Politics.* Random House, New York, 1970.
33. Brown, C. A. The Development of Occupations in Health Technology. Unpublished dissertation, Columbia University, New York, 1971.
34. Bowers, W. F. *Interpersonal Relationships in the Hospital.* Charles C Thomas, Springfield, Ill., 1960.
35. Gershenfeld, W. J. Labor Relations in Hospitals. Paper presented at Emerging Sectors of Collective Bargaining Seminar No. 4, Temple University, Philadelphia, March 28, 1968.
36. The male-feasance of health. *Health-PAC Bulletin,* March 1970.

37. Gaynor, D., Blake, E., Bodenheimer, T., and Mermey, C. RN strike: Between the lines. *Health-PAC Bulletin* 60: 1-2. 5, September-October 1974.
38. Davis, L. State of the Union. *1199 Drug and Hospital News,* pp. 20-23, March 1969.
39. Institutional organizing. *Health-PAC Bulletin* No. 37, January 1972.
40. Fragmentation of workers: An anti-personnel weapon. *Health-PAC Bulletin* No. 46, November 1972.
41. Soule, A. B. Trends in training programs in radiologic techology. *Radiol. Technol.* 38: 70-73, 1966.
42. Proceedings of the thirty-ninth annual convention. *Radiol. Technol.* 39: 98, September 1967.
43. Bergquist, V. A. Women's participation in labor unions. *Monthly Labor Review* 97(10): 3-9, 1974.

PART 4

Women's Work, Women's Health

CHAPTER 6

Employment and Women's Health: An Analysis of Causal Relationships

Ingrid Waldron

Interest in the effects of employment on women's health has been stimulated by the substantial increase in the employment of women in the United States (1) and by evidence suggesting that the male role as bread-winner may contribute to men's higher mortality (2). An analysis of the evidence concerning possible causal links between employment and health in women is presented in this paper.

There are three basic types of causal links which could affect the relationship between employment and health. These are effects of employment on health, effects of health on employment, and effects of a common factor (such as education) on both health and employment. Evidence concerning each type of causal link will be presented in the subsequent sections of this paper. This introductory section will briefly summarize evidence concerning differences in morbidity between employed women and housewives. The data presented in this section are morbidity data for national samples in the United States in the last two decades.

Housewives are more likely than employed women to report having a chronic condition, such as asthma, allergies, or heart disease (Table 1), or activity limitation due to chronic conditions (Table 2). This difference has been observed in national

An earlier version of this paper was presented at the Annual Meeting of the American Psychological Association held in Toronto, Canada, in 1978.

Table 1

Relationship between employment status and prevalence of self-reported chronic conditions, United States, 1965-1966[a]

Employment Status (by sex)	Percent with Any Chronic Condition[b]		
	Actual	Expected, Based on Age Distribution	Difference (Actual minus Expected)
Women			
Currently employed	59.5	62.7	-3.2
Unemployed (looking for a job)	59.2	59.5	-0.3
Housewives and other women not in the labor force	69.4	67.1	+2.3
Men			
Currently employed	59.0	59.6	-0.6
Unemployed (looking for a job)	57.2	58.0	-0.8
Not in the labor force	75.6	71.2	+4.4

[a] Source, calculated from data in references 3 and 4.
[b] Chronic conditions include specified conditions such as allergies, arthritis, cancer, diabetes, heart trouble, high blood pressure, or ulcers, in addition to any condition which has persisted for more than three months. Data are for women or men 17 years of age and over. Rates for currently employed women, for housewives, and for men not in the labor force are significantly different from expected ($p < 0.01$).

Table 2

Relationship between employment status and prevalence of self-reported activity-limiting chronic conditions, by age, United States, 1974[a]

	Percent with Chronic Condition Which Limits Activity[b]	
	Age 17-44	Age 45-64
All women	8.0	21.3
Housewives	10.4	28.7

[a] Source, calculated from data in reference 5.
[b] The percentages given exclude about 1 percent of women who were unable to carry on a major activity, most of whom were neither keeping house nor employed. Rates for housewives are significantly different from rates for other women ($p < 0.01$).

surveys dating from the early 1960s to the mid-1970s (3, 5-7). Since these findings are based on self-report data, they could reflect differences between employed women and housewives in a tendency to report illness, rather than differences in actual physical morbidity. However, data from physicians' examinations also suggest that employed women have fewer chronic conditions than housewives. The prevalence of diagnosed rheumatoid arthritis among employed women was only three-quarters of the expected prevalence for women with their age distribution (8), and the prevalence of definite coronary heart disease among employed women was less than two-thirds of the expected prevalence (9). (Due to small numbers, the difference for arthritis was not statistically significant, and the difference for coronary heart disease was only marginally significant.) Hypertension also appears to be somewhat less prevalent among employed women than among housewives (10, 11).

When employed women and housewives are asked to rate their health, a higher proportion of the employed women rate it as excellent or good (12), or as better than the health of other women their age (13). A follow-up study of one sample of middle-aged women found evidence of a correlation between changes in self-rated health and changes in employment status (14). Women who reported an improvement in health were more likely to have entered the labor force, while women who reported a deterioration in health were more likely to have left the labor force. Among whites, employed women also report fewer symptoms than housewives (15, 16). These differences in symptom reporting and subjective health status must be interpreted with caution, since both measures may reflect factors such as psychological distress, in addition to physical illness.

Employed women report fewer days of restricted activity or bed rest due to illness than housewives (17-19). This difference has been observed in national surveys throughout the period from 1960 to 1975. The reported differences are probably not due solely to differences in health, since it is probably easier for a housewife to reduce activity or to take a day of bed rest when she is ill. The differences between employed women and housewives increase with age, with housewives reporting 20 percent more days of restricted activity or bed rest at ages 17-44 and 80-90 percent more at ages 45-64 (17).

Differences in the rates of acute conditions reported by employed women and housewives have been variable, depending on the year and the age group (20-22). For acute conditions which resulted in medical attention or restricted activity, employed women have reported slightly higher rates than other women in each year since 1968 (20, 21). In conclusion, in recent national surveys employed women have reported slightly more acute conditions but fewer chronic conditions, fewer symptoms, better general health, and fewer days of bed rest or restricted activity than housewives.

EFFECTS OF HEALTH ON EMPLOYMENT

Data from national surveys indicate that health has a significant impact on women's decisions to seek a job or to leave a job. About 6 percent of women who are not in the labor force give ill health or disability as their reason for not seeking a job (1).

For women who have left the labor force within the previous year or two, about 10 percent give ill health as their reason for having left their last job (23-25). In both types of survey, the proportion of women who give ill health as their reason for not being employed rises steeply with age (23-25). Women who have permanently retired from the labor force frequently give poor health as their reason for retirement (5, 13, 26).

The results from these surveys may overestimate the importance of the effects of health on women's employment. Poor health may be given as the reason for not being employed by some women for whom other, less socially acceptable reasons may actually be more important (27). A more satisfactory estimate of the effects of health on employment could be derived from longitudinal studies which analyze the relationship between health and subsequent changes in employment status. For example, a study of this type for men has shown that, among older men, those who reported health problems were substantially more likely to retire within the next few years (28). Men who are not in the labor force report more chronic illness (Table 1) and have higher mortality (29) than employed men, and indirect epidemiological evidence indicates that the primary reason why employed men are healthier is that healthier men are more likely to seek and to keep a job (29). This effect of health on employment is frequently called the "healthy worker effect." Although very little evidence of this type is available for women, studies of disability suggest that poor health is probably as strong a deterrent to employment for women as it is for men (30, 31).

The effects of health on employment may be a major determinant of the reported health differences between employed women and housewives. This hypothesis is supported by the finding that several major features of the reported morbidity differences between employed women and housewives can be accounted for by the expected effects of health on women's employment. First, the proportion of housewives who give poor health as their reason for not being employed (1, 23-25) is about the right magnitude to account for the reported excess in prevalence of chronic conditions among housewives (Tables 1 and 2). In addition, the differences between housewives and employed women in rates of reported chronic conditions and disability days increase with age (Table 2) (17), and this age gradient would be expected, since older women more often give illness as their reason for not being employed (23-25). The differences between housewives and employed women in the prevalence of reported health problems are generally larger for black women than for white women (10, 12, 14, 32). This racial difference would be expected, since black women more frequently give ill health as their reason for leaving their last job or for not seeking a new job (24, 25). This may reflect greater difficulty in finding a job which is compatible with poor health, because job options may be limited by discrimination and poor education.

Another finding which can be accounted for by the expected effects of health on employment is the observation that, although differentials in self-reported chronic conditions consistently show higher rates for housewives (3, 5-7), differentials for acute conditions have been more variable and in recent years have indicated slightly higher rates for employed women (20, 21). Since acute conditions are by definition of short duration and exclude incidents due to potentially chronic conditions such as asthma (20), it seems reasonable to expect that these acute conditions would, in general, have little effect on women's decisions to join or to leave the labor force, and thus the healthy worker effect would not be expected to produce substantial or consistent differentials in rates of acute conditions.

These observations suggest that the effects of health on women's employment may be a major determinant of the reported health differences between employed women and housewives.

EFFECTS OF EMPLOYMENT ON HEALTH

It is not possible at present to assess the overall effects of employment on the health of women in the contemporary United States. Much of the available evidence is derived from cross-sectional studies which compared self-reported health of employed women and housewives, and these data do not provide an adequate basis for estimating the effects of employment on women's health. One major problem is that health differences between housewives and employed women are influenced not only by the effects of employment on health, but also by the effects of health on employment, and it will require longitudinal rather than cross-sectional data to distinguish these effects and to estimate their magnitudes. Also, it is not known to what extent the self-reported health data may be influenced by differences between employed women and housewives in the propensity to report health problems. In this section, attention is turned to a review of evidence concerning several specific types of effects which employment may have on women's health.

Physical, Chemical, and Biological Occupational Hazards

As can be seen from Figure 1, a large proportion of employed women work in occupations which appear not to entail serious physical, chemical, or biological hazards. Over one-third of women employed in the United States work in clerical occupations, and an additional 14 percent work as saleswomen or teachers (33). Even these apparently safe occupations may be associated with significant hazards (34, 35). For example, clerical workers may be exposed to hazardous levels of ozone, methanol, or other chemicals from copying and duplicating machines (35, 36). Sales workers appear to have an increased risk of leukemia (37), possibly due to increased exposure to infectious agents (38).

Approximately two million women, or about 7 percent of employed women in the United States, work as health care workers (33). Occupational hazards for such workers include increased risk of infections such as viral hepatitis (39), back strain and injuries from lifting patients (40), and, for operating room personnel, increased risk of cancer and spontaneous abortion due to exposure to anesthetic gases (41).

A substantial number of employed women are exposed to occupational carcinogens. Currently available data do not permit any precise estimate of the extent of risk, but Table 3 shows the number of women employed in six manufacturing industries in which workers have a relatively high risk of exposure to carcinogens. The risk of exposure is greatest for blue-collar workers; about half a million women are blue-collar workers in these industries. Substantial numbers of women in other occupations,

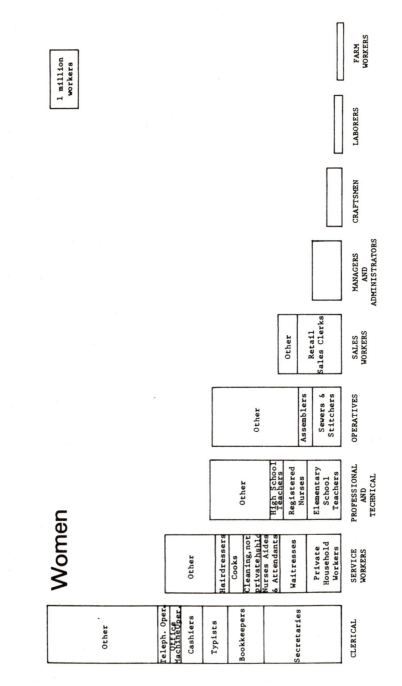

Women

1 million workers

CLERICAL
Other
Teleph. Oper.
Office Machine Oper.
Cashiers
Typists
Bookkeepers
Secretaries

SERVICE WORKERS
Other
Hairdressers
Cooks
Cleaning, not private hshld
Nurses Aides & Attendants
Waitresses
Private Household Workers

PROFESSIONAL AND TECHNICAL
Other
High School Teachers
Registered Nurses
Elementary School Teachers

OPERATIVES
Other
Assemblers
Sewers & Stitchers

SALES WORKERS
Other
Retail Sales Clerks

MANAGERS AND ADMINISTRATORS

CRAFTSMEN

LABORERS

FARM WORKERS

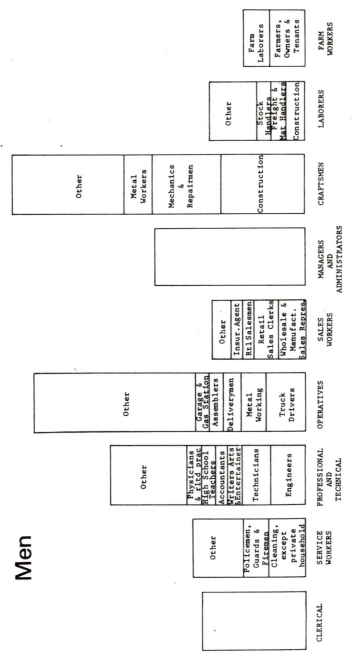

Figure 1. Occupations of employed women and men in the United States, 1970. This figure shows the number of women and men employed in nine broad occupational categories and in specific categories in which more than 400,000 women or men were employed. Source, data from reference 33.

Table 3

Employment in manufacturing industries with relatively high exposure to
known or suspected carcinogens, United States, 1972[a]

Industry	Examples of Carcinogens Used	Number Employed (Thousands)	
		Women	Men
Instruments and related products	Asbestos, thallium oxide	179	-293
Petroleum and petroleum products	Benzene, polycyclic aromatics	17	172
Leather and leather products	Chrome salts, benzene	180	123
Ordnance and accessories	Asbestos, benzene	42	156
Transportation equipment	Vinyl chloride, benzene	194	1624
Fabricated metal products	Chromates, lube and cutting oil mists	261	1151
		873	3519

[a] Source, data from references 37, 42-44.

not related to manufacturing, are also exposed to occupational carcinogens. For example, 100,000 women work in dry-cleaning and laundry establishments, and excess cancer mortality has been reported for women in these occupations, probably due primarily to exposure to tetrachloroethylene (45).

Approximately 300,000 women work with cotton fibers and thus are exposed to cotton dust and the risk of developing brown lung or byssinosis (35). Early symptoms of byssinosis include chest tightness and shortness of breath, which in some workers progresses to severely disabling and even fatal deterioration of pulmonary function (46). The prevalence of byssinosis in cotton mill workers is generally in the range of 5-10 percent, with prevalence rates of 20 percent common for workers in the dustiest areas (46, 47). It is estimated that roughly 20,000 women in the United States have byssinosis as a consequence of current or former occupational exposure to cotton dust.

Hairdressers and beauticians have been found to have an increased risk of respiratory disease, probably due to exposure to hairsprays (48). Exposure to chemicals which can cause skin or eye irritation, as well as a variety of more serious conditions, is common in a number of industries, including the textile, apparel, and electronics industries, which together employ nearly two million women (35).

Two hundred thousand women in the United States are disabled to some extent as a result of injuries received in accidents on the job (49). However, women have substantially more accidents at home than on the job (49, 50), and the risk of accidents may be as high for housewives as for employed women (20).

This account indicates some of the more serious known or probable occupational hazards which are present in the work environments of substantial numbers of employed women. Many other physical, chemical, and biological hazards are known or suspected (34, 35). Due to limited data, it is not possible to make an accurate estimate of the overall effect of occupational hazards on the health of women workers. On the basis of current data, it appears that many women are employed in relatively safe occupations with relatively minor health risks due to physical, chemical, and biological hazards, but a substantial fraction of employed women are exposed to serious occupational hazards.

Social Support

Psychological aspects of employment may also affect physical health. On the positive side, there is the possibility that increased social contact and social support may improve the health of employed women. Many women value social contact on the job as an important benefit of employment (51, 52). In a study of older factory workers, 40 percent of the women reported that their workmates were their closest friends (52). In another study of married women, employed women were only half as likely as housewives to report that they often felt lonely (53). A number of studies have shown that social support is associated with a reduced risk of illness or death (54-56). Social contact on the job may be of greater importance for unmarried women than for married women, and this would lead to the prediction that employment would be associated with a greater health advantage for unmarried women than for married women. This predicted pattern has been observed in the one study which reports relevant data (57).

Stress

Although it is difficult to define stress or to measure it satisfactorily, there is much evidence that a situation which is perceived as a threat to the well-being of an individual can elicit substantial physiological changes (58, 59), and repeated or prolonged stress can lead to increased susceptibility to illness (59, 60).

Many employed women experience stress due to the heavy time pressures and role conflicts associated with combined responsibility for job and the care of family and home (61-63). On the other hand, many housewives experience stress because they find housework monotonous and unrewarding and because of the social isolation and low status commonly associated with the housewife role (51, 64). These findings indicate that employed women and housewives may experience different types of stress, but it is not clear if either group experiences more stress than the other. The next few paragraphs summarize evidence from studies which compare the psychological health of employed women and housewives. This evidence must be interpreted with caution, because the observed differences in psychological health may reflect not only differences in the stress experienced by housewives and employed women, but also possibly differences in susceptibility to psychological problems in response to stress (65), differences in the propensity to report psychological symptoms, and a tendency for women in poor psychological health not to seek employment.

For a number of psychological measures, differences between housewives and employed women are favorable to employed women for samples of higher socioeconomic status, but not for samples of lower socioeconomic status. For example, for samples which were predominantly college educated, employed women reported more general satisfaction or happiness than housewives (26, 66, 67). In contrast, in all but one study (51) of less-educated women, housewives reported as much (16, 26, 67, 68) or more (26, 67) satisfaction or happiness than employed women. Similarly, marital satisfaction was slightly higher for employed women in a sample of college graduates (26), but slightly higher for housewives in samples of lower-class women (66). Psychosomatic symptoms such as insomnia, perspiring hands, or inertia were reported less frequently by employed white women than by white housewives, but this difference was not observed for blacks (15).

Although the psychological advantage associated with employment has generally been found to be greater for women of higher socioeconomic status, there are exceptions to this pattern. Housewives appear to be slightly more likely than employed women to be users of minor tranquilizers, of sedatives, of sleeping pills, or of antidepressants (69-71), and it appears that the excess of regular use of minor tranquilizers and sedatives may be greatest for housewives of low socioeconomic status (70). Suicide rates appear to be higher for housewives than for employed women in general (72), but elevated suicide rates have been found for women physicians (73) and psychologists (74). This suggests that women employed in these demanding and male-dominated professions may have experienced increased stress and social isolation, at least during the period of the 1960s. The number of women in these professions is too small to have a significant influence on the findings for general samples of college-educated women discussed in the previous paragraph.

Most studies (53, 65, 75, 76), although not all (77), have found that employed women report fewer symptoms of psychiatric impairment than housewives do. Interestingly, no significant differences between employed women and housewives have been reported for employed women who began employment during the previous year (75), or for mothers of preschool children (53, 75). The latter finding suggests that the combination of employment with heavy family responsibilities may result in relatively greater stress. Further suggestive evidence for this hypothesis is the finding that women who had three or more children and had been employed more than half their adult years had a significantly higher incidence of coronary heart disease than either childless women with similar employment experience or housewives with three or more children (78). It is possible that there is an interaction between family responsibilities and type of job, since the incidence of coronary heart disease was highest for women who had children and worked in clerical and sales occupations.[1]

Women who are employed part-time may have the best overall psychological health (51, 62, 66, 67, 75), although some evidence (26, 68) does not support this suggestion.

---

[1]The incidence of new cases of coronary heart disease appears to be higher for certain groups of employed women than for housewives (78), but, in contrast, its prevalence appears to be lower among employed women (9, 79). This contrast suggests that employed women who develop coronary heart disease are more likely to leave the labor force. These observations provide additional, suggestive evidence for the importance of the effects of health on employment.

(Limited data have not revealed differences in physical health between part-time and full-time workers [75, 80, 81].)

Based on the data currently available, it is not clear whether there are significant differences in the average stress experienced by employed women and housewives. However, the data do suggest that part-time employment may be associated with relatively less stress, while the combination of employment with heavy responsibilities for care of children may be associated with relatively more stress. An additional hypothesis is that the jobs held by less-educated women may be more stressful on the average than the jobs held by more-educated women. This hypothesis is compatible with findings from studies of men which have shown that workers in unskilled, highly repetitive jobs with a rapid, externally controlled pace of work have higher levels of adrenalin and noradrenalin secretion (82), more feelings of exhaustion and depression, more sleep problems, more dissatisfaction (83), and poorer mental health (84).

Health-related Behavior.

It could be argued that employed women have less time available to visit doctors or to take a day of rest when ill, and that consequently employed women may not be able to care for their health as well as housewives do. Employed women do take fewer rest days than housewives (17-19), and this probably reflects the time constraints imposed by employment as well as lower illness rates for employed women. Lack of rest may be related to future health problems. One study has shown that adults who did not take any days of rest due to illness during a one-year period had higher mortality during the subsequent five years than adults who took one to three days of rest (85).

Studies of differences in the rate of doctor visits between employed women and housewives have yielded somewhat variable results. In a national survey in the early 1960s, a higher proportion of housewives reported having visited a physician within the past year, but differences between housewives and employed women were very small except at ages 17-24 and 65-74 (86). Another study in the United States (Rivkin, cited in reference 87) and one in England and Wales (81) have both reported that, contrary to expectation, employed women who have children appear to make greater use of medical services than comparable housewives. Doctor visits may be to some extent a substitute for rest days, which were less frequent for employed women. Two-thirds of the excess of doctor visits by employed women were due to visits for the common cold or flu (81). For many of the more serious types of illness, employed women had fewer doctor visits. Another reason why employed women with children may visit doctors more often than comparable housewives may be that employed mothers feel a more urgent need to maintain their health in order to meet their multiple role responsibilities (87).

The Type A or Coronary-prone Behavior Pattern is a hard-driving, time-pressured style of life which is associated with approximately a two-fold elevation in the risk of coronary heart disease (88, 89). Employed women are more Type A than housewives on the average (11, 89). Pressures to perform on the job and time pressures due to combined responsibilities for job, housework, and child care may increase Type A behavior (11, 90) and consequently may increase the risk of coronary heart disease among employed women. In addition, a woman who has the hard-driving Type A behavior pattern appears to be more likely to seek a job or to keep a job even when she feels overburdened by the combined demands of job and home responsibilities (11). Thus, Type A behavior may play a role in a causal relationship of the type considered in the next section, as a characteristic which influences both employment and health.

Cigarette smoking substantially increases the risk of many chronic diseases (91). However, it is unclear whether employment has any significant effect on women's smoking behavior. Women who are in the labor force are somewhat more likely to be cigarette smokers, particularly at the oldest ages (Table 4). At young ages, women in the labor force are somewhat less likely to be heavy smokers (Table 4). Thus, employment is associated with higher rates of cigarette smoking primarily among women over 65. In the period when these older women entered the labor force and when they began smoking, both employment and smoking were somewhat deviant behaviors, and both may have been more common in somewhat rebellious or independent-minded women (1, 2, 93). The prevalence of cigarette smoking by occupation varies from over 40 percent for waitresses or hairdressers to less than 20 percent for elementary school teachers (92). These differences may reflect differential effects of these occupations on cigarette smoking and/or selection of certain types of women into certain occupations.

Table 4

Relationship between employment status and smoking habits of women, United States[a,b]

Age	Percent Who Are Current Smokers		Percent of Smokers Who Smoke More Than a Pack a Day	
	Women in Labor Force	Women Not in Labor Force	Women in Labor Force	Women Not in Labor Force
17-24	32.1	30.3	53	66
25-34	40.8	37.0		
35-44	39.8	38.8	NA[c]	NA
45-54	36.3	36.7	NA	NA
55-64	29.6	28.2	NA	NA
65 and over	17.6	10.4	NA	NA
Total	34.9	28.2	51.2	52.6

[a] Source, calculated from data in references 4, 92, and 93.
[b] Data are for 1970, except for heavy smoking among young women, which are for 1975.
[c] NA indicates data were not available.

SOCIOECONOMIC CHARACTERISTICS WHICH INFLUENCE
BOTH HEALTH AND EMPLOYMENT

Several socioeconomic characteristics influence both the health and employment of women, and thus could influence the relationship between health and employment. More educated women have better health and are also more likely to be employed (1, 5, 66, 94), so this would tend to result in better health for employed women. On the other hand, women who are white or married in general report better health but are less likely to be employed (1, 5, 17, 66, 95, 96), and this would tend to result in better health for housewives.

A preliminary estimate of the possible importance of these relationships has been calculated, based on data from national surveys of self-reported chronic illness. To estimate the expected effects of educational differences on the health differences between housewives and employed women, I calculated the expected difference in the prevalence of activity-limiting chronic conditions between populations of women which were identical except that one had the distribution of educational levels observed for housewives and the other had the distribution of educational levels observed for employed women. Similar calculations were made for marital status and race (1, 5, 66, 94-96). These calculations indicate that the expected effects of race are very small. The expected effects of marital status and education are about equal: approximately a 1 percent difference in the prevalence of activity-limiting chronic conditions at younger ages and approximately a 2 percent difference in prevalence at older ages. Since the marital status effect predicts better health for housewives and the educational effect predicts better health for employed women, the net effect appears to be very small.

These results suggest that differences in the socioeconomic characteristics of employed women and housewives may make only a minor contribution to the differences between employed women and housewives in self-reported chronic morbidity. This conclusion is supported by the finding that, in national samples, rates of self-reported morbidity are significantly higher for housewives than for employed women, even after controlling for education, marital status, and race (16), or education, marital status, and family size (97), or marital status and race (13, 14). However, it should be noted that studies of more local samples have not always found significant differences in morbidity between housewives and employed women after controlling for socioeconomic characteristics (74).

DISCUSSION

Figure 2 presents a preliminary model which summarizes some of the more important causal relationships which may link employment and health in women. This model was developed on the basis of the morbidity data summarized in the preceding sections of this paper. The model can also account for the major findings from studies of mortality in employed women (Table 5). Factors which are important in the interpretation of these mortality data include the effects of exposure to

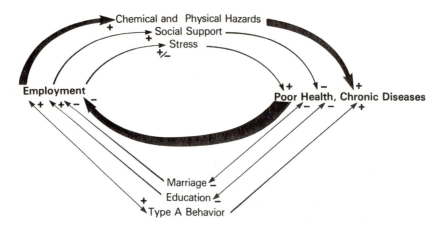

Figure 2. A preliminary model of the causal relationships which may link employment and morbidity in women. This model must be considered preliminary, primarily because the available data do not provide an adequate basis for estimating the actual quantitative importance of the suggested causal links or of other possible causal links which may prove to be equally important. Although different types of morbidity are not distinguished in this model, there are differences in the causal relationships for different types of morbidity, as discussed in the text. For example, Type A behavior is associated specifically with an increased risk of coronary heart disease, and apparently not with a general increase in morbidity.

chemical and physical hazards and the healthy worker effect, that is, the effect of poor health in deterring women from being employed.

The evidence reviewed in this paper indicates that the effects of employment on women's health vary, depending on the type of job and probably also on the family situation of the woman. Adverse effects seem most likely for women in time-pressured, highly repetitive jobs which involve exposure to occupational hazards. Positive effects seem most likely for women without heavy family responsibilities who have jobs which provide social contact and social support with no exposure to occupational hazards.

Thus, this review has found evidence for both positive and negative effects of employment on women's health and no clear evidence of a substantial overall effect of employment on women's health on the average. In contrast, analyses of sex differences in mortality have presented evidence that men's role as breadwinner is an important cause of men's higher mortality in the United States (2, 105). It appears that employment may have a more adverse effect on the health of men than on the health of women for several reasons. Because of the types of jobs typically held by men and women, men are more likely to be exposed to serious physical and chemical hazards. For example, substantially more men than women are employed in manufacturing industries with relatively high exposure to occupational carcinogens (44) (Table 3). Many more men than women are employed as operatives, craftsmen, laborers, and farm workers (Figure 1), and, as would be expected, men have much higher rates of job accidents resulting in disabling injuries (49, 106). In addition, a

Table 5

Mortality of employed women

Employed Group	Standardized Mortality Ratio[a]	Comments
Asbestos workers[b]	151	Substantial exposure to major hazard
Rubber plant production workers[c]	103	Exposure to chemical hazards
Professors and other career women at colleges[d]	103	Study design tends to minimize healthy worker effect; more likely to have been single than comparison group (wives of professors)
Railroad employees[e]	94	Comparison group: wives of railroad employees
Physicians[f]	84	Employed women had higher socioeconomic status than comparison group
Rubber plant salaried and production workers[g]	78	Exposure to chemical hazards, but some underreporting of deaths for employed women
White women having Social Security earnings in 1965[h]	60-83	Study design results in large healthy worker effect; some underreporting of deaths for employed women

[a]The Standardized Mortality Ratio is the ratio of mortality for the employed women to the age-standardized mortality of a comparison group, multiplied by 100. The comparison groups were women in the general population, with two exceptions which are noted in the comments.
[b]British sample, 1936-1968 (98).
[c]U.S. sample, 1964-1973 (99).
[d]U.S. national sample, 1965-1970 (100).
[e]U.S. national sample, 1968-1970 (101).
[f]U.S. national sample, 1969-1973 (102).
[g]U.S. national sample, 1940-1974 (103).
[h]U.S. national sample, 1965-1972 (104).

major effect of employment on men's health may be indirect—the effect that expectations of the male role have on the socialization of boys. For example, boys may be encouraged more than girls to develop Type A behavior, since hard-driving, competitive behavior appears to contribute to vocational success, but not to success in traditional female roles (11, 90, 107). Increasing employment of women may lead to changes in the socialization of girls, but these changes will develop slowly and would be expected to affect women's mortality only after a lag of decades. These arguments suggest that the immediate effects of women's employment on women's health do not necessarily provide an accurate basis for predicting the long-term health consequences of contemporary trends in women's employment.

Acknowledgments—I would like to thank Dr. Michelle Forman, Dr. Suzanne Haynes, and Dr. Nancy Woods for helpful criticisms of earlier drafts of the paper.

REFERENCES

1. U.S. Department of Labor. *1975 Handbook on Women Workers.* Women's Bureau Bulletin 297. U.S. Government Printing Office, Washington, D.C., 1975.
2. Waldron, I. Why do women live longer than men? *Soc. Sci. Med.* 10: 349-362, 1976.
3. U.S. Department of Health, Education, and Welfare, National Center for Health Statistics. Limitation of activity and mobility due to chronic conditions, U.S., 1965-1966. *Vital and Health Statistics,* Series 10, No. 45, 1968.
4. U.S. Department of Labor. *Handbook of Labor Statistics.* U.S. Government Printing Office, Washington, D.C., 1969 and 1977.
5. U.S. Department of Health, Education, and Welfare, National Center for Health Statistics. Limitation of activity due to chronic conditions, U.S., 1974. *Vital and Health Statistics,* Series 10, No. 111, 1977.
6. U.S. Department of Health, Education, and Welfare, National Center for Health Statistics. Chronic conditions and activity limitation, U.S., 1961-1963. *Vital and Health Statistics,* Series 10, No. 17, 1965.
7. U.S. Department of Health, Education, and Welfare, National Center for Health Statistics. Limitation of activity due to chronic conditions, U.S., 1969 and 1970. *Vital and Health Statistics,* Series 10, No. 80, 1973.
8. U.S. Department of Health, Education, and Welfare, National Center for Health Statistics. Rheumatoid arthritis in adults, U.S., 1960-1962. *Vital and Health Statistics,* Series 11, No. 17, 1966.
9. U.S. Department of Health, Education, and Welfare, National Center for Health Statistics. Coronary heart disease in adults, U.S., 1960-1962. *Vital and Health Statistics,* Series 11, No. 10, 1965.
10. Franti, C. E., Blaszkowski, T. P., Brandon, B., et al. Trends in High Blood Pressure Control Related to Employment Status. Paper presented at Annual Meeting of the Society for Epidemiological Research, Iowa City, 1978.
11. Waldron, I. The coronary-prone behavior pattern, blood pressure, employment and socio-economic status in women. *J. Psychosom. Res.* 22: 79-87, 1978.
12. Shea, J. R., Spitz, R. S., Zeller, F. A., et al. *Dual Careers: A Longitudinal Study of Labor Market Experience of Women,* Vol. 1. Center for Human Resources Research, Ohio State University, Columbus, Ohio, 1970.
13. Sherman, S. R. Labor-force status of nonmarried women on the threshold of retirement. *Soc. Sec. Bull.* 37(9): 3-15, 1974.
14. Kim, S., Roderick, R., and Shea, J. R. Dual Careers, Vol. 2. *Manpower Research Monograph,* No. 21. U.S. Government Printing Office, Washington, D.C., 1973.
15. U.S. Department of Health, Education, and Welfare, National Center for Health Statistics. Selected symptoms of psychological distress. *Vital and Health Statistics,* Series 11, No. 37, 1970.
16. Feld, S. Feelings of adjustment. In *The Employed Mother in America,* edited by F. I. Nye and L. W. Hoffman, pp. 331-352. Rand McNally, Chicago, 1963.
17. U.S. Department of Health, Education, and Welfare, National Center for Health Statistics. Disability days, U.S., 1975. *Vital and Health Statistics,* Series 10, No. 118, 1978.
18. U.S. Department of Health, Education, and Welfare, National Center for Health Statistics. Disability days, U.S., 1961-1962, 1963-1964, 1968, and 1971. *Vital and Health Statistics,* Series 10, Nos. 4, 24, 67, and 90, 1963-1974.
19. U.S. Department of Health, Education, and Welfare, Disability days, U.S., 1959-1960. *Health Statistics,* Series B, No. 29, 1961.

20. U.S. Department of Health, Education, and Welfare. National Center for Health Statistics, Acute conditions: Incidence and associated disability, U.S., 1976-1977. *Vital and Health Statistics,* Series 10, No. 125, 1978.
21. U.S. Department of Health, Education, and Welfare, National Center for Health Statistics. Acute conditions: Incidence and associated disability, U.S., 1961-1978. *Vital and Health Statistics,* Series 10, Nos. 1, 10, 15, 26, 38, 44, 54, 69, 77, 82, 88, 98, 102, 114, 120 and 132, 1963-1979.
22. Nathanson, C. A. Sex roles, employment status and patterns of disease. Paper presented at Annual Meeting of the American Psychological Association, Toronto, 1978.
23. Rosenfeld, C., and Perrella, V. C. Why women start and stop working: A study in mobility. *Monthly Labor Review* 88(9): 1077-1082, 1965.
24. Flaim, P. O. Persons not in the labor force: Who they are and why they don't work. *Monthly Labor Review* 92(7): 3-14, 1969.
25. U.S. Department of Labor, Bureau of Labor Statistics. Employment and unemployment in 1976. *Labor Force Report* 199, 1977.
26. Campbell, A., Converse, P. E., and Rodgers, W. L. *The Quality of American Life.* Russell Sage Foundation, New York, 1976.
27. Cole, S., and Lejeune, R. Illness and the legitimation of failure. *Am. Sociol. Rev.* 37: 347-356, 1972.
28. Parnes, H. S., et al. The pre-retirement years, Vol. 4, A longitudinal study of the labor market experience of men. U.S. Department of Labor, *Manpower Research and Development Monograph* No. 15. U.S. Government Printing Office, Washington, D.C., 1975.
29. McMichael, A. J. Standardized mortality ratios and the "healthy worker effect." *J. Occup. Med.* 18: 165-168, 1976.
30. Makarushka, J. L. Workers' compensation: The long-term consequences of work-related injury for women. In *Proceedings of Conference on Women and the Workplace,* edited by E. Bingham, pp. 292-301. Society for Occupational and Environmental Health, Washington, D.C., 1977.
31. Schechter, E. S. Employment and work adjustments of the disabled: 1972 survey of disabled and nondisabled adults. *Soc. Sec. Bull.* 40(7): 3-15, 1977.
32. Parnes, H. S., et al. Years for Decision: A Longitudinal Study of the Educational and Labor Market Experience of Young Women, Vol. 2. *Manpower Research Monograph* 24. U.S. Government Printing Office, Washington, D.C., 1970.
33. U.S. Bureau of the Census. *Census of the Population: 1970, Subject Reports, Final Report PC(2)-7A, Occupational Characteristics.* U.S. Government Printing Office, Washington, D.C., 1973.
34. Stellman, J. M. *Women's Work, Women's Health.* Pantheon Books, New York, 1977.
35. Hricko, A., with Brunt, M. *Working for Your Life: A Woman's Guide to Job Health Hazards.* Labor Occupational Health Program, Berkeley, 1976.
36. Allen, R. J., Wadden, R. A., and Ross, E. D. Characterization of potential indoor sources of ozone. *Am. Ind. Hyg. Assoc. J.* 39: 466-471, 1978.
37. Williams, R. R., Stegens, N. L., and Goldsmith, J. R. Associations of cancer site and type with occupation and industry from the Third National Cancer Survey Interview. *J. Natl. Cancer Inst.* 59: 1147-1185, 1977.
38. Neth, R., Gallo, R. C., Mannweiler, K., et al. *Modern Trends in Human Leukemia II.* J. F. Lehmanns Verlag, Munich, 1976.
39. Pattison, C. P., Maynard, J. E., Berquist, K. R., et al. Epidemiology of hepatitis B in hospital personnel. *Am. J. Epidemiol.* 101: 59-64, 1975.
40. Magora, A. Investigation of the relation between low back pain and occupation. *Indust. Med.* 39: 465-471 and 504-510, 1970.
41. Ad Hoc Committee on the Effect of Trace Anesthetics on the Health of Operating Room Personnel, American Society of Anesthesiologists. Occupational disease among operating room personnel. *Anesthesiology* 41: 321-340, 1974.
42. Hickey, J. L. S., and Kearney, J. J. Engineering Control Research and Development Plan for Carcinogenic Materials. U.S. Department of Health, Education, and Welfare, National Institute for Occupational Safety and Health, Division of Physical Sciences and Engineering, Cincinnati, 1977.
43. U.S. Department of Labor. *Employment and Earnings* 19(8), 1973.
44. Bridbord, K., Decoufle, P., Fraumeni, J., et al. Estimates of the Fraction of Cancer in the United States Related to Occupational Factors. National Cancer Institute, National Institute

for Occupational Safety and Health, National Institute of Environmental Health Sciences, Research Triangle Park, North Carolina, 1978.

45. Blair, A., Decoufle, P., and Grauman, D. Mortality among laundry and dry cleaning workers. *Am. J. Epidemiol.* 108: 238, 1978.

46. Harris, T. R., Merchant, J. A., Kilburn, K. H., et al. Byssinosis and respiratory disease of cotton mill workers. *J. Occup. Med.* 14: 199-206, 1972.

47. Merchant, J. A., Lumsden, J. C., Kilburn, K. H., et al. Dose response studies in cotton textile workers. *J. Occup. Med.* 15: 222-230, 1973.

48. Palmer, A. Respiratory disease prevalence in beauticians and its relationship to aerosol sprays. In *Women and the Workplace,* edited by E. Bingham, pp. 184-188. Society for Occupational and Environmental Health, Washington, D.C., 1977.

49. Krute, A., and Burdette, M. E. 1972 survey of disabled and nondisabled adults: Chronic disease, injury and work disability. *Soc. Sec. Bulletin* (April): 3-16, 1978.

50. U.S. Department of Health, Education, and Welfare, National Center for Health Statistics. Persons injured and disability days by detailed type and class of accidents. *Vital and Health Statistics,* Series 10, No. 105, 1976.

51. Ferree, M. M. Working-class jobs: Housework and paid work as sources of satisfaction. *Social Problems* 23: 431-441, 1976.

52. Jacobson, D. Rejection of the retiree role: A study of female industrial workers in their 50's. *Human Relations* 27: 477-492, 1974.

53. Gove, W. R., and Geerken, M. R. The effect of children and employment on the mental health of married men and women. *Social Forces* 56: 66-76, 1977.

54. Cobb, S. Social support as a moderator of life stress. *Psychosom. Med.* 38: 300-314, 1976.

55. Berkman, L. F., and Syme, L. Social networks, host resistance, and mortality: A nine-year follow-up study of Alameda County residents. *Am. J. Epidemiol.* 109: 186-204, 1979.

56. Gore, S. The effect of social support in moderating the health consequences of unemployment. *J. Health Soc. Behav.* 19: 157-165, 1978.

57. Hochstim, J. R. Health and ways of living. In *The Community as an Epidemiological Laboratory,* edited by I. J. Kessler and M. L. Levine, pp. 149-176. Johns Hopkins University Press, Baltimore, 1970.

58. Mason, J. W. Clinical psychophysiology—Psychoendocrine mechanisms. In *American Handbook of Psychiatry,* Vol. 4, Part 2, *Psychosomatic Medicine,* edited by M. F. Reiser, pp. 553-582. Basic Books, New York, 1975.

59. Selye, H. *Stress in Health and Disease.* Butterworth, Boston, 1976.

60. Cassel, J. The contribution of the social environment to host resistance. *Am. J. Epidemiol.* 104: 107-123, 1976.

61. Johnson, C. L., and Johnson, F. A. Attitudes toward parenting in dual-career families. *Am. J. Psychiatry* 134: 391-395, 1977.

62. Rapoport, R. N., and Rapoport, R. Dual-career families: Progress and prospects. *Marriage and Family Review* 1: 1-12, 1978.

63. Lein, L., Durham, M., Pratt, M., et al. *Work and Family Life.* Final Report to the National Institute of Education, Center for the Study of Public Policy, Cambridge, Mass., 1975.

64. Oakley, A. *The Sociology of Housework.* Random House, New York, 1974.

65. Brown, G. W., Bhrolchain, M. N., and Harris, T. Social class and psychiatric disturbance among women in an urban population. *Sociology* 9: 225-254, 1975.

66. Hoffman, L. W., Nye, F. I., et al. *Working Mothers.* Jossey-Bass, San Francisco, 1974.

67. Nye, F. I., and Hoffman, L. W. *The Employed Mother in America.* Rand McNally, Chicago, 1963.

68. Bradburn, N. M., and Caplovitz, D. *Reports on Happiness.* Aldine, Chicago, 1965.

69. Chambers, C. D. An assessment of drug use in the general population. In *Drug Use and Social Policy,* edited by J. Susman, pp. 50-123. AMS Press, New York, 1972.

70. Parry, H. J., Balter, M. B., Mellinger, G. D., et al. National patterns of psychotherapeutic drug use. *Arch. Gen. Psychiatry* 28: 769-783, 1973.

71. U.S. Department of Health, Education, and Welfare, National Center for Health Statistics. Use habits among adults of cigarettes, coffee, aspirin, and sleeping pills. *Vital and Health Statistics,* Series 10, No. 131, 1979.

72. Cumming, E., Lazer, C., and Chisholm, L. Suicide as an index of role strain among employed and not employed married women in British Columbia. *Canadian Rev. Sociology Anthrop.* 12: 462-470, 1975.

73. Steppacher, R. C., and Mausner, J. S. Suicide in male and female physicians. *J.A.M.A.* 228: 323-328, 1974.

74. Mausner, J. S., and Steppacher, R. C. Suicide in professionals: A study of male and female psychologists. *Am. J. Epidemiol.* 98: 436-445, 1973.
75. Welch, S., and Booth, A. Employment and health among married women with children. *Sex Roles* 3: 385-397, 1977.
76. Lowenthal, M. F., Berkman, P. L., et al. *Aging and Mental Disorder in San Francisco.* Jossey-Bass, San Francisco, 1967.
77. Radloff, L. Sex differences in depression—The effects of occupation and marital status. *Sex Roles* 1: 249-265, 1975.
78. Haynes, S. G., and Feinleib, M. Women, work and coronary heart disease: Prospective findings from the Framingham Heart Study. *Am. J. Public Health* 70: 133-141, 1980.
79. Bengtsson, C., Hallstrom, T., and Tibblin, G. Social factors, stress experience and personality traits in women with ischaemic heart disease, compared to a population sample of women. *Acta Med. Scand.,* Suppl. 549: 82-92, 1973.
80. Hauenstein, L. S., Kasl, S. V., and Harburg, E. Work status, work satisfaction and blood pressure among married Black and White women. *Psychology of Women Quarterly* 1: 334-349, 1977.
81. Logan, W. P. *Morbidity Statistics from General Practice.* Vol. 2. Occupation Studies on Medical and Population Subjects No. 14. General Register Office, London, 1960.
82. Johannson, G., Aronsson, G., and Lindstrom, B. O. Social psychological and neuroendocrine stress reactions in highly mechanised work. *Ergonomics* 21: 583-599, 1978.
83. Karasek, R. A. Job demands, job decision latitude and mental strain: Implications for job redesign. *Admin. Sci. Quart.* 24: 285-308, 1979.
84. Kasl, S. V. Epidemiological contributions to the study of work stress. In *Stress at Work,* edited by G. L. Cooper and R. Payne, pp. 3-48. John Wiley and Sons, Chichester, Great Britain, 1978.
85. Berkman, P. L. Survival and a modicum of indulgence in the sick role. *Med. Care* 13: 85-94, 1975.
86. U.S. Department of Health, Education, and Welfare, National Center for Health Statistics. Physician visits, interval of visits and children's routine checkup, U.S., 1963-64. *Vital and Health Statistics,* Series 10, No. 19, 1965.
87. Nathanson, C. A. Illness and the feminine role: A theoretical review. *Soc. Sci. Med.* 9: 57-62, 1975.
88. Haynes, S. G., Feinleib, M., and Kannel, W. B. Prospective study of psychosocial factors and coronary heart disease in Framingham. *Am. J. Epidemiol.* 108: 229, 1978.
89. Haynes, S. G., Feinleib, M., Levine, S., et al. The relationship of psychosocial factors to coronary heart disease in the Framingham Study—II. Prevalence of coronary heart disease. *Am. J. Epidemiol.* 107: 384-402, 1978.
90. Waldron, I., Hickey, A., McPherson, C., et al. Type A Behavior Pattern—Relationships to variation in blood pressure, parental characteristics, and academic and social activities of students. *J. Human Stress* 6(1): 16-27, 1980.
91. U.S. Department of Health, Education, and Welfare. *Smoking and Health—A Report of the Surgeon General.* DHEW Publication No. (PHS) 79-50066. U.S. Government Printing Office, Washington, D.C., 1979.
92. Sterling, T. D., and Weinkam, J. J. Smoking characteristics by type of employment. *J. Occup. Med.* 18: 743-754, 1976.
93. National Cancer Institute. *Cigarette Smoking Among Teen-agers and Young Women.* DHEW Publication No. (NIH) 77-1203. U.S. Government Printing Office, Washington, D.C., 1977.
94. U.S. Department of Labor. *Handbook on Women Workers.* Women's Bureau Bulletin 294, U.S. Government Printing Office, Washington, D.C., 1969.
95. U.S. Department of Health, Education, and Welfare, National Center for Health Statistics. Differentials in health characteristics by marital status. *Vital and Health Statistics,* Series 10, No. 104, 1976.
96. U.S. Department of Commerce. *Social Indicators 1976.* U.S. Government Printing Office, Washington, D.C., 1977.
97. Ross, E. Differences in illness between employed married women and full-time housewives. Paper presented at the Annual Meeting of the Eastern Sociological Association, 1978.
98. Newhouse, M. L., Berry, G., Wagner, J. C., et al. A study of the mortality of female asbestos workers. *Br. J. Ind. Med.* 29: 134-141, 1972.
99. Andjelkovich, D., Taulbee, and Blum, S. Mortality of female workers in a rubber manufacturing plant. *J. Occup. Med.* 20: 409-413, 1978.

100. Duncan, R. M. Untitled mimeo from Teachers Insurance and Annuity Association, New York, 1972.
101. Railroad Retirement Board. Life expectancy of railroad retirement beneficiaries. *R. R. B. Quart. Rev.* (Jan.-Mar.): 4-7, 1973.
102. Goodman, L. J. The longevity and mortality of American physicians, 1969-1973. *Milbank Mem. Fund. Q.* 53: 353-375, 1975.
103. Monson, R. R., and Nakano, K. Mortality among rubber workers–II. Other employees. *Am. J. Epidemiol.* 103: 297-303, 1976.
104. Decoufle, P. Statistically speaking. *J. Occup. Med.* 19: 582-584, 1977.
105. Waldron, I. Sex differences in longevity. In *Proceedings of Second Conference on Epidemiology of Aging,* edited by S. G. Haynes and M. Feinleib, National Institute of Aging. DHEW Publication No. (NIH) 79-969. U. S. Government Printing Office, Washington, D.C., 1979.
106. Akman, A., Brooks, M., and Gordon, J. Use of work injury rate tables in estimating disabling work injuries. *Am. J. Public Health* 62: 917-923, 1972.
107. Waldron, I. Sex differences in the Coronary-prone Behavior Pattern. In *Coronary-prone Behavior,* edited by T. M. Dembroski, S. M. Weiss, J. L. Shields, et al., pp. 199-205. Springer-Verlag, New York, 1978.

CHAPTER 7

Do Men and Women Have Different Jobs Because of Their Biological Differences?

Karen Messing

Working women in North America are usually found in "employment ghettos," that is, areas in which women workers represent a large majority. In Quebec, women constitute 36 percent of the "active" population (those who are working or looking for work), but these women are distributed unequally across the job market. In the primary and secondary sectors (agriculture, forestry, fisheries, manufacturing) a quarter of the workers are women, while in the tertiary (services) sector 43 percent of the work force is female. Moreover, the sex distribution is uneven within these sectors. For example, within the services sector, only 18 percent of workers in transport and communications are female, but women constitute 57 percent of those employed in finance and 56 percent of those in personal services (1).

As we look more closely at where women work, the workplace reveals itself as a checkerboard of employment ghettos, some male and some female. In her analysis of positions in the Quebec Ministry of Social Affairs, Dominique Gaucher (2) found, first, that the ministry itself is a female employment ghetto (73 percent). This is explainable by the fact that the ministry employs most of the health care and social workers in the province. But within the ministry, the job category "stores" (care of hospital pharmacies and chemical supplies in laboratories) is a male ghetto (85 percent). And within this male mini-ghetto, there are micro-ghettos: 80 percent of store clerks (light work) are women but 86 percent of storekeepers are men.

A preliminary version of this article was published in French in the Montreal-based journal *Cahiers du Socialisme* (No. 7, 1981). Part of the research was supported by the Institutional Research Fund of the University of Quebec at Montreal.

Many other examples of this kind of segregation can be found in Gaucher's study, and in our daily lives. We can see that women are secretaries, telephone operators, laundresses and sewing machine operators, while men are mechanics, truck drivers, welders, and miners. There seems to be a social consensus about what is a man's job and what is a woman's job. And there is a vague impression that these definitions come from our biology, from the different "nature" of men and women.

In fact, the prevailing ideology gives us a sort of syllogism:

1. Women and men are biologically different. Each sex has its strengths and weaknesses.
2. We can not assign the same tasks to women as to men; women can not do men's jobs, and vice versa.
3. We must protect women by giving them tasks which are adapted to their physical capacities and by excluding them from jobs which endanger their health.
4. The process of adapting job assignments to physical capacity, related as it is to biology, gives rise naturally to concentrations of women employees in those jobs which pose the least risk to their health.

Let's examine this familiar logic. As a biologist, I would like to ask the question, what are the biological differences between men and women, and do they in fact justify the existence of employment ghettos?

According to a modern textbook of occupational medicine (3, p. 932):

> In general, women's size and weight are less than men's; the hand is smaller, finer and suppler, with greater dexterity. Physical force is less developed, although it must be said that women can furnish an intense effort during a brief period of time, so that [the doctor] must not take into account any short-time measurements. The difference consists mainly in prolonged efforts for which women are more easily tired. From a genital point of view [*sic, d'un point de vue génital*] the [menstrual] periods cause physical and nervous fragility. Pregnancy and lactation get in the way of the accomplishment of industrial tasks. Women seem to be more sensitive than men to toxins. In any case their sensitivity increases when pregnant. Also, certain toxins cross the placental barrier; we must take into account the risk to the foetus. . . .
> Altogether, except for dexterity, women are physiologically disadvantaged compared to men.

Unfortunately, the textbook fails to furnish scientific findings to back up these conclusions. What are the relevant data concerning the assertions made above?

STRENGTH—THE "WEAKER SEX" MYTH

The first and most widespread argument used to justify the allocation of women to different tasks and jobs is that, since women are weaker, they must be given the jobs which are physically the least exacting.

What do biologists know about the respective strengths of men and women? First, they know that "strength" is not a simple concept. Strength, defined as "bodily or muscular power" (4), is a characteristic of a muscle or group of muscles. Women's muscles work the same way as men's; in both cases, the strength of a muscle is proportional to its cross-section (5). Muscles are groups of fibers which can contract, and their strength depends on the number of fibers and the energy used to contract them. Different muscles are used when lifting, lowering, pushing, or pulling an object.

The ergonomists (specialists in the use of energy) Snook and Ciriello (6) examined the physical force used in industrial tasks and found that six components are involved: raising, lowering, pushing, pulling, carrying, and walking. Each action consists of two or more of these components. They then tested men and women by asking them to perform these tasks while varying load weights, distance transported, and speed. They recorded the largest weight each individual would accept to manipulate. For the great majority of tasks, the scales of weights men and women would accept overlapped. The average man accepted 1.5 times the weight accepted by the average woman. For pushing and pulling, the figure was 1.2 times as high; for walking, the sexes accepted equal weights. The longer the effort was sustained, and the faster the speed, the more the two sexes resembled each other.

A few points should be noted here. Even where the differences were most pronounced—in lifting—the weight acceptable to 50 percent of women was too heavy for 20 percent of men. In other words, it is incorrect to say that "women" can lift less weight than "men." Also, the dimensions of the weights were the same for the two sexes. This is the norm in industrial tasks; that is, tasks are not adapted to make them manageable by smaller people, but they could be if the will were there. Finally, data on *average* differences should not be used to justify allocating women to job ghettos. It would be just as logical to exclude all men from jobs requiring heavy lifting on the grounds that they are statistically more likely to have heart attacks.

Strength is not just a matter of a momentary effort. We should also consider the question of endurance, which is a function of the capacity of muscles to contract repeatedly before tiring. Since muscles get their food energy and oxygen from the blood, endurance is directly related to the efficiency of the respiratory and cardiovascular systems. On the average, men have 5 percent more red blood cells than women, and a lung capacity 30 percent greater (5). However, these biological differences are not necessarily either innate or unchangeable. As weight-trainers have found, people can increase the cross-sectional area of their muscles and thereby their strength. Joggers know that it is possible to improve cardiovascular and respiratory capacities. We also know that the critical period in which the number of red cells and lung capacity are determined is between 8 and 11 years of age (5), a time when girls are not encouraged to participate in sports, and when public facilities for their activities are lacking. Thus, it is possible that with changes in attitudes toward female performance, the difference between average male and female capacities will diminish.

In fact, if we consider Olympic performances by males and females, we observe that women are improving more rapidly than men in many sports. For example, in 1924, when women were first allowed to compete in the 400 meter swim, the best man's time was 58 seconds faster than the best woman's; in 1972, women's time had come to equal that of men in 1956 and was only 19 seconds slower than that of men in the 1972 competition. Similarly, in the 100 meter run, men improved by 0.66 seconds between 1928 and 1972, while women improved by 1.13 seconds (7). There is no way of knowing whether these tendencies will eventually result in men and women competing on an equal basis. The physical differences which now exist between men and women may result from nature more than environment, or vice versa.

Contrary to the myth that women's lesser strength requires that they be given less strenuous jobs, a close look at some of these jobs shows that they have not been designed to be particularly easy physically. Exertion of effort is not in itself damaging to the organism. But to furnish a sustained effort during which the muscles have no time to relax, is a stress which first tires the body and in the long term wears it out. The sewing machine operator, cramped in a fixed position, holding her fabric in one hand while she manipulates the machine with the other, contracts her shoulder muscles all day. The assembly line worker in a slaughterhouse, who spends her whole day cutting up chickens at the rate of 60 *per minute*, forced to stand without moving her legs, is not protected against backache and sore legs any more than is the stevedore (8).

Moreover, many "feminine" occupations require women to lift very heavy weights. For example, nurses' aides in homes for the aged or handicapped frequently lift their patients, some of whom weigh over 250 pounds. "On force comme des chevaux!" ("We strain like horses"), I was told by a group of these workers (9).

We must not forget the biology of the male worker in this discussion. Women are not alone in risking their health by lifting weights too heavy for them. Seventy percent of adults, males as well as females, suffer from backache (10). Because of a mythology that says that a "real" man can do anything, men are encouraged to lift weights which are dangerously heavy. In a Quebec firm which distributes merchandise to retailers, the young truck loaders lift 75-pound boxes at the rate of 22 tons per day. Few men can do a job like this without developing back problems.

The owner of a South Shore (Montreal) steel pylon company recently explained to me, "I could never hire a woman to work in the shop. The work is too hard. All the *men* who work here have back problems. You couldn't ask me to send a woman in there!" It seems that this employer's remarks are an excellent argument for changing the nature of the jobs in his factory, rather than a justification for employment ghettos.

DEXTERITY—THE "FAIRY FINGERS" MYTH

The average woman's hand is smaller than that of the average man—9 percent shorter, 12 percent narrower, and 16 percent thinner, to be exact (11). This difference in size is supposed to confer a greater dexterity which, in turn, is used to justify the fact that assembly of tiny electronics components and typewriting are traditionally female jobs. Women's supposed greater manual dexterity does not explain why surgery, mechanics, and the great symphony orchestras are male employment ghettos, however.

Again, jobs calling for a woman's "fine touch" are by and large not good for her health. "Carpal tunnel syndrome" is a work-related ailment characterized by wrist pain and loss of manual sensitivity. Often it ends in loss of manual capacity. These symptoms are caused by rapid manipulation of precision tools (12). According to scientific studies (e.g. 13), the syndrome is 2 to 10 times more frequent in women than in men.

In addition, tasks which demand great dexterity often have a large visual component. Referring to electronics industry workers, an ophthalmologist notes (14), "It is true that in a significant number of cases an intense and prolonged visually demanding task results in visual fatigue, shown by conjunctival hyperemia [reddened eyes], tearing, a feeling of burning or pain in the eyes." Ninety percent of telephone operators who get their information from reading microfiche suffer from headaches; 55 percent experience pain in their eyes and 20 percent have visual hallucinations which persist after work (15). In this context, the fact that women are 20 percent more likely than men to wear corrective lenses is possibly significant (16).

Thus, we can not say that certain tasks are reserved for women because of their great dexterity. It is more accurate to say that the jobs "reserved" for women are those in which the fine manipulations are repetitive, boring, and extremely demanding visually as well as manually. In fact, these may be jobs for which male workers would not apply.

THE MENSTRUAL CYCLE—THE "RAGING HORMONES" MYTH

Dr. Edgar Berman, former surgeon advisor to the U.S. State Department, said publicly what many people think, that women cannot be trusted to hold high office since their "raging hormonal imbalances" make them unstable. As this stereotype is widespread, many studies have been done attempting to relate productivity to the stage of the menstrual cycle.

In one well-known experiment, male and female chimpanzees vied with each other for a banana. According to the researcher, R. M. Yerkes (quoted in 17, p. 8):

> When the female is not sexually receptive, the naturally more dominant member of the pair almost regularly obtains the food; whereas during the female's phase of maximal genital swelling, when she is sexually receptive, she claims or may claim the food and take it regularly even though she be the naturally subordinate member of the pair.

Ruth Herschberger found that the scientific analysis of the results of this experiment left something to be desired. She speculates on how the female chimpanzee regarded Yerkes' analysis of her behavior (17):

> Those words [naturally subordinate member] look like somebody decided I was subordinate way in advance. The referees are practically saying any gains I make while I'm "sexually receptive" can't be registered because the phase of maximal genital swelling is out of bounds! . . . *Why don't they ask what the score was?* . . . I was top man at the food chute for fourteen days out of the thirty-two. Jack was top man for eighteen. This means I won 44% of the time, and Jack won 56%. He's champion, I'll grant you that, but still it's almost fifty-fifty. If Jack hadn't been dragged in as the *biggest* male in the whole colony. . . .

This is a good example of how scientists allow their conception of male and female roles to influence their interpretation of data relating hormonal status to behavior. In fact, many studies of human motor function show no variation in performance with stage of the menstrual cycle (e.g. 18). One study did show that women who were wrongly led to believe they were at a "premenstrual" stage of their cycle performed and perceived themselves in the same way as women who were really premenstrual and knew they were (19). The relationship between hormones and human behavior can be safely characterized as complex, and the stereotypes as so far unsupported by evidence.

As far as women's jobs are concerned, data do not confirm the hypothesis that women are given tasks requiring little sustained energy or physical and emotional stability. The *Dictionary of Occupational Titles* of the U.S. Department of Labor gives the following description of the job of housewife ("foster mother"): "Rears children in own home as members of family. Oversees activities, regulating diet, recreation, rest periods, and sleeping time. Instructs children in good personal and health habits. Bathes, dresses and undresses young children. Washes and irons clothing. Accompanies children on outings and walks. Takes disciplinary action when children misbehave. . . ." And this, all day long. It would be hard to imagine a profession which gives less respite when a woman is feeling under par—whether sick, menstruating, depressed, or otherwise—especially when there are young children. Yet the position of housewife, a 59-hour-a-week job (20), is a female ghetto (97 percent), as are all jobs which involve care of small children. We could also cite the positions of teacher, nurse, receptionist, or telephone operator [where women must respond cordially to over 200 calls per hour (15)] as examples of so-called female jobs which demand stability and emotional endurance of a high order.

It must be added that women are not alone in having biological cycles. The study of biological clocks is an active research area: an increasing number of biological parameters have been shown to vary in both sexes with time of day and over weeks or months. Women and men have cyclical patterns of sleep, temperature, urine production, cardiac rhythm, and production of sex and other hormones (21-23). In Japan, administrators in the public transport service were able to lower accident rates by changing the work schedules of their male drivers to conform with their energy peaks (24).

In general, the organization of most jobs respects neither male nor female cycles. Night shifts (nurses, bookkeepers in banks, telephone operators, night cleaners, mothers of infants) gravely affect the basic biological cycles such as the sleep-wake cycle, temperature variations, digestive system cycles and eating schedules (25). A cleaning woman at the CBC radio service told us how, as a result of 10 years on the night shift, she has lost her appetite, suffers from chronic constipation, and has to take sleeping pills to get to sleep in the morning and drink lots of coffee to stay awake at night.

And as far as the menstrual cycle is concerned, a study of poultry slaughterhouse workers has shown that 75.7% of the women employees suffer from menstrual cramps, and that this is statistically correlated with, among other things, high speed of assembly line and very cold temperatures inside the building, two factors which impede blood circulation (8, p. 93).

REPRODUCTION—"PROTECTING" PREGNANT WORKERS

There is one certain biological difference between males and females which cannot be explained away as a difference between statistical means or as a stereotype—only women get pregnant. This fact has two consequences for the pregnant woman: (a) the woman changes physically during her pregnancy and (b) the unborn child is brought into the workplace and is exposed to chemicals, radiation, and germs.

First, how does pregnancy change women's bodies? During pregnancy, blood volume increases to feed the fetus, the heart has to work harder to pump the increased amount of blood, the excretory and digestive systems must work harder to clean the blood and process the extra food, and the respiratory system must supply the fetus with oxygen (26).

Does this mean that pregnant women can not work? No one has ever proposed that pregnant women with small children take nine months off from their housework and child-care duties, so we must conclude that our society is not convinced that effort is dangerous for pregnant women. During the early months of pregnancy, women remain physically fit. In fact, 10 of the 26 Soviet women gold medalists in the 1964 Olympics were pregnant (27). Nevertheless, during the last months of pregnancy, women have more difficulty moving around, and jobs which force women into confining positions or to make abnormally intense sustained efforts can cause problems, reflected, for example, in the greater rates of premature births among mothers whose jobs were physically exacting (28). A paid pregnancy leave is obviously a biological necessity for these workers, as is a paid leave for the final weeks of pregnancy for all women. However, employers do not yet feel sufficiently protective toward women workers as to grant such leaves.

As far as chemical contamination is concerned, pregnant women are at a definite disadvantage in polluted workplaces. Their respiratory, digestive, and excretory systems cooperate to rid the body of toxins; the nasal hairs and the lungs filter the air; the liver and kidneys clean the blood. In an unhealthy work environment, these organs are overworked and suffer, just as an alcoholic's liver, unable to rid the body of all the accumulated alcohol, is poisoned by it, resulting in cirrhosis. The bodily systems which are overworked in a polluted work environment are the same ones which are asked to work harder to take care of the fetus.

Lead, mercury, and cadmium are a few of the many substances which are dangerous for the pregnant woman (10). These substances are also dangerous for the fetus. Contrary to what scientists used to believe, most toxic substances can cross the placental barrier and affect the fetus of an exposed mother. A good number of the substances which we call teratogenic (giving rise to malformations in a fetus) are used in various workplaces which employ women: lead by workers on automobile batteries, mercury by dental technicians, anesthetic gases by anesthesiology technicians, ionizing radiations by radiotherapists, 2,5 diaminotoluene by hairdressers using tints, carbon tetrachloride by laundresses, etc. (29). Many of these substances find their way into the milk of nursing mothers as well.

Given that many women's jobs are not suitable for pregnant women, the traditional "solution" has been to protect them by sending them home without pay for the duration of pregnancy and lactation. But this policy has been "modernized." The period of greatest danger for the fetus has now been identified as extending between 21 and 45 days of pregnancy, a time when few women even know they are pregnant (10). This discovery has been used to justify the exclusion of all fertile women from certain factories (30).

But this is not a very efficient way to protect the children of exposed workers. The women are replaced by male workers who may someday be fathers. And sperm (as well as eggs) can undergo mutations which threaten the life and health of the child. In most cases, substances which are teratogenic for the fetus are mutagenic for the eggs and sperm before conception. Groups of male workers who have been identified as having undergone damage to their sperm include anesthesiologists (31), radiologists (32), pesticide workers (33), and workers exposed to vinyl chloride (34). It must be added that most of the agents named in the preceding paragraphs have also been shown to cause cancer among male and female workers, since the mechanisms of cancer production, mutation, and teratogenesis are very similar.

We can safely say that it is not out of a yearning to protect workers and their children that certain companies have excluded fertile women; if that were the case, they would also have to exclude potential fathers. Besides, women are not excluded from *all* unhealthy workplaces. If there is one problem which has been well studied in regard to the possibility of damage to fetuses, it is the effects of radiation on pregnant women. Yet the profession of radiology technician (radiodiagnostics) is a female ghetto (83 percent), as are radiotherapy (97 percent) and nuclear medicine (76 percent) (2). In fact, several other female employment ghettos involve recognized dangers for unborn and future children: laboratory technician, packager of contraceptive pills, printshop worker. But employers do not attempt to exclude fertile women from these jobs, since there are no men who would replace them.

The following examples show something about the bases on which these decisions are made. In Quebec, all radiology technicians are employed by the government (since medicine is socialized) and their working conditions are regulated by collective agreement. In 1979, women government workers were able to win a contract clause saying that a pregnant woman exposed to a risk for herself or her fetus has the right to a transfer, or if this is not possible, to be sent home at full pay. Among the first workers to take advantage of this clause was a radiology technician who had had two children with congenital malformations since she had started work. The employer contested her request on the grounds that there was no danger to the fetus in working as a radiology technician. The case is presently under arbitration (35). It is interesting that, in the United States (where there is no cost to the *employer* who sends a pregnant worker home, but where the *fetus* could potentially sue for damages if harmed), it was the employer who insisted in a recent case that a pregnant radiology technician be sent home without pay for the duration of her pregnancy on the grounds that her job was dangerous for her fetus. (This case was heard by the Equal Employment Opportunities Commission (36), which ruled that the employer had to transfer the technician to less-dangerous work.)

Could it be that the desire to protect women and children in the workplace is less related to altruism than to who foots the bill? We must also wonder whether the recent policy of excluding fertile women from certain factories has more to do with affirmative action programs and with the unemployment rate among men than with an intention to protect unborn children. A policy genuinely concerned with protecting workers and their children would provide full, paid maternity leave and clean up all dangerous workplaces.

CONCLUSIONS

The prevailing ideology attempts to justify employment ghettos by invoking a necessity to protect the health of women by respecting their biological specificity.

But we can now reject the syllogism this ideology presents us and substitute one based on research evidence:

1. It is impossible to prove that all women are biologically weaker, less stable, or have more manual dexterity than all men.
2. It is moreover impossible to prove that the differences in mean performances of men and women are the result of biology rather than education and training.
3. Women's jobs are not particularly healthful; on the contrary, many conditions to which working women are exposed are dangerous for their health.
4. Working conditions which are used to justify the exclusion of women (exposure to pollutants, lifting of heavy weights) are also dangerous for male workers.

If the prevailing ideology hasn't deduced its myths from a knowledge of biology, they must come from another source. We can perhaps find their origin in the effect which the ideology has on the behavior of women and men workers. For example, salaries in female employment ghettos are notoriously low; on the average, full-time women workers receive less than 60 percent of the average man's salary (37). Yet women are told that they should not try for the jobs which are more interesting and pay more, since these are not suitable for them; a "real" woman doesn't compete with men.

At the same time, men work in conditions of deafening noise, smothered with dust, exposed to the danger of fatal accidents. They are told that they are big and strong and able to "take" it; a "real" man doesn't cry.

In this way, by keeping men and women in their respective ghettos, the employers can legitimize the exploitation of both women and men in interdependent ways.

Acknowledgments—I would like to acknowledge the importance of conversations I have had with Donna Mergler, Monique Simard, Dominique LeBorgne, and Luc Desnoyers, and the assistance of Raymonde Pelletier.

REFERENCES

1. Martin, C. Unpublished study drawn from data in *Statistics Canada* (Census of Canada, Ottawa, 1971).
2. Gaucher, D. L'égalité des femmes: une lutte à finir. Master's thesis, Department of Sociology of Health, University of Montreal, 1979.
3. Desoille, H., Sherrer, J., and Truhaut, R. *Précis de médecine du travail.* Masson, Paris, 1978.
4. Barnhart, C. L., ed. *The American College Dictionary.* Random House, New York, 1961.
5. Wyrick, W. Biophysical perspectives. In *The American Woman in Sport,* edited by E. W. Gerber et al. Addison-Wesley, Reading, Mass., 1974.
6. Snook, S. M., and Ciriello, V. M. Maximum weights and work loads acceptable to female workers. *J. Occup. Med.* 16: 527-534, 1974.
7. Chester, D. *The Olympic Games Handbook.* Scribner, New York, 1975.
8. Mergler, D., Vézina, N., Beauvais, A., and Everell, J. Etude des effets des conditions de travail dans les abattoirs sur la santé des travailleurs et travailleuses. Confederation of National Trade Unions, Canada, 1980.
9. Statement given at the Annual Meeting of the Central Council of Haut-Rive of the Confederation of National Trade Unions, Baie-Comeau, Canada, October 18, 1980.
10. Hunt, V. *The Health of Women at Work.* CRC Press, Boca Raton, Fla., 1978.
11. Garret, J. *Anthropometry of the Air Force Female Hand.* Aerospace Medical Research Laboratory, Aerospace Medical Division, Air Force Systems Command, Wright-Patterson Air Force Base, Ohio, 1970.

12. Tichauer, E. R. Some aspects of stress on forearm and hand in industry. *J. Occup. Med.* 8: 63-71, 1966.
13. Armstrong, T. J., and Chaffin, D. B. Carpal tunnel syndrome and selected personal attributes. *J. Occup. Med.* 21: 481-486, 1979.
14. Imbert, J. P. Les aides optiques dan l'industrie électronique. In *International Colloquium on Vision and Work,* edited by G. E. Lambert. Rodez-Toulouse, 1978.
15. Teiger, C., Laville, A., Desors, D., and Gadbois, C. Renseignements téléphoniques avec lecture de microfiches sous contrainte temporelle. Report No. 54, Laboratoire de Physiologie de Travail et Ergonomie, Paris, 1977.
16. Department of Health, Education and Welfare. *Characteristics of Persons with Corrective Lens.* DHEW Publ. No. (HRA) 75-1520, Rockville, Md., 1974.
17. Herschberger, R. *Adam's Rib.* Harper and Row, New York, 1948.
18. Gamberale, R., Strindberg, L., and Wahlberg, I. Female work capacity during the menstrual cycle. *Scand. J. Work Envir. Health* 1: 120-127, 1975.
19. Ruble, D. N. Premenstrual symptoms: A reinterpretation. *Science* 197: 291-292, 1977.
20. Vanek, J. Time spent in housework. *Sci. Amer.* 231(5): 116-120, 1974.
21. Beauvais, A. Les rythmes biologiques et le travail de nuit. Unpublished, 1975.
22. Brown, F. A. *Biological Clocks.* Academic Press, New York, 1970.
23. Briscoe, A. M. Hormones and gender. In *Genes and Gender:* I, edited by E. Tobach, and B. Rosoff. Gordian Press, New York, 1978.
24. Ramey, E. Men do have monthly cycles. *Ms. Magazine,* Spring 1972, pp. 8-14.
25. Bernier, C. *Le travail par équipes.* Bulletin No. 15, Institut de Recherche Appliquée sur le Travail, 1979.
26. Al-Aidroos, K. and Mergler, D. La femme et la santé au travail. *Cahiers de la femme* 1: 86-87, 1979.
27. Scott, A. C. Closing the muscle gap. *Ms. Magazine,* October 1979, p. 55.
28. Mamelle, N., Munoz, F., Collin, D., Charvet, F., and Lazar, P. *Fatigue professionnelle et prématurité. Unité de recherches épidémiologiques et statistiques sur l'environnement et la santé.* U-110, INSERM, Villeurbanne, France, 1981.
29. Shepard, T. H. *Catalog of Teratogenic Agents,* 3rd edition. Johns Hopkins University Press, Baltimore, 1980.
30. Rawls, R. L. Reproductive hazards in the work place. *Chemical and Engineering News,* February 18, 1980, pp. 35-37.
31. Knill-Jones, R. P. et al. Anesthetic practice and pregnancy. *Lancet,* October 25, 1975, pp. 807-809.
32. Macht, S. H., and Lawrence, P. S. Congenital malformations from exposure to roentgen radiation. *Am. J. Roentgen.* 73: 442-446, 1955.
33. Kapp, R. et al. Y-Chromosomal non-disjunction in dibromochloropropane-exposed workmen. *Mut. Res.* 64: 47-51, 1979.
34. Infante, P. F. et al. Genetic risks of vinyl chloride. *Lancet,* April 3, 1976, pp. 734-739.
35. Arbitration Hearing on the Case of Mme. Adrienne Robichaud, Before Judge Jean-Jacques Turcotte, Québec, 1980-1981.
36. Equal Employment Opportunity Commission. Decision 6443.
37. Conseil du Statut de la Femme du Québec. *Pour les Québécoises, Egalité et Indépendance.* Gouvernement du Québec, 1979.

PART 5

The Professional Control
Of Social Conflict

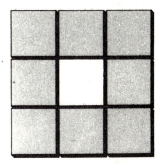

CHAPTER 8

The Politics of Birth Control, 1920-1940: The Impact of Professionals

Linda Gordon

Birth control can have three major social purposes: to increase the individual freedom of women; to control overall population trends; and to improve and protect health. When the modern birth control movement began in the early 20th century, the first was its dominant motive. Organizations demanding the legalization of birth control were formed by feminists and other radical political activists concerned with women's rights. The medical and population control motivations for supporting birth control came primarily from other sources which entered the birth control movement later but ended by dominating it.

Beginning in the 1920s birth control as a cause was taken over by male professionals, many of them physicians, in a "planned parenthood" campaign that made women's equality and autonomy a secondary issue. In the 1970s a revived feminist movement reentered the birth control cause, mainly through campaigns for legal abortion. The existence once more of an approach to birth control primarily concerned with individual human rights has created an historical context in which it is appropriate to reexamine the historical legacies behind birth control.

In this article I argue that the influx of professionals into the cause changed the goals of the birth control movement, from a campaign to increase the area of self-determination for women and all working-class people to a campaign infused with elitist values and operated in an elitist manner. These professionals were mainly of two groups: doctors and eugenists. The latter group was not, of course, a professional occupation in itself, but was mainly composed of university professors and researchers. However, professional eugenics organizations brought them together and gave them a collective consciousness as strong as that among doctors. Despite important differences, the two groups had an ultimately similar influence on birth control.

The need to identify and analyze the influence of doctors and eugenists is not merely a question of setting the historical record straight. Their impact on birth control has left serious problems today for anyone concerned with that issue. The identification of the birth control movement with the demographic theories of the population controllers and the small-family ideal of white, prosperous Americans has created antagonism to birth control among many poor people, and especially the non-white poor, in the U.S. and abroad. They often perceive population control programs as coercive, imposing alien cultural values. That antagonism to birth control is sometimes associated with an antagonism to feminism, especially since feminism until recently has been primarily a movement of educated and prosperous women. I would argue, on the contrary, that birth control has failed to cross class lines because it has not been feminist enough. A feminist birth control movement would struggle to expand women's options, to extend their right to choose, not to impose a certain economic or political theory upon them. For example, in the first agitation for birth control, feminists argued for the legitimacy of having children, in or out of marriage, and for mothers' and children's rights to a decent standard of living, as well as for women's rights not to have children.

After a brief survey of the state of the birth control movement in the early 20th century, I will discuss first the general meaning of professionalization and then the roles of doctors and eugenists separately. There will not be space here for an evaluation of the new birth control movement that those groups created, mainly associated with Planned Parenthood, but I will offer some tentative conclusions.

THE BIRTH CONTROL MOVEMENT IN THE EARLY 20TH CENTURY

In 1915 the issue of birth control came out into public rather suddenly, as radicals like Emma Goldman and Margaret Sanger deliberately defied obscenity laws by distributing information on contraception. By late 1916 there was a nationwide campaign of agitation and direct action for birth control. By 1917 there were national and local organizations, run almost entirely by women, devoted to the legalization of contraception. Most of these groups considered themselves within the feminist tradition, concerned with women's right to reproductive self-determination. In many instances these organizations were connected to the Socialist Party or to local socialist and anarchist groups.

Nineteenth-century feminists had argued that involuntary child-bearing and child-rearing was an important cause of women's subjection. Their agitation for "voluntary motherhood" (1), beginning in the 1870s, was limited by the prudish sexual fears and moralities that pervaded capitalist society at that time.[1] In the first decades of the 20th century a loosening in acceptable standards of sexual conduct, particularly in the cities, made public advocacy of mechanical contraceptive devices politically possible.

Still, birth control did not immediately become respectable. Not only was it illegal, but its militant advocates were occasionally arrested on obscenity charges, though none were heavily sentenced. By the outbreak of the First World War Margaret Sanger had become the chief spokesperson for the cause. In her regular column in the *New York Call*, a Socialist Party paper, she began in 1911 to write about birth control, venereal disease,

[1]This does not mean that contraception was not practiced in the 19th century. In fact, there was widespread use of douches, male withdrawal, abortion, and vaginal pessaries to prevent or interrupt pregnancy.

and other previously unmentionable topics. In 1914 she published seven issues of a revolutionary feminist paper, *The Woman Rebel,* which advocated birth control, printed the views of Emma Goldman, and attacked the suffrage movement for its irrelevance to working-class women. Sanger wrote that she saw birth control primarily as a means to alleviate the suffering of working-class and poor women from unwanted pregnancies, and in the long run she identified the demand for birth control as an important weapon in the class struggle.

Rejecting the path of lobbying and winning over influential people, Sanger chose direct action. In October 1916 she, her sister, and a few other women opened a birth control clinic in Brownsville, Brooklyn. She and her sister were arrested, and the publicity around their trial and imprisonment gave them a public platform from which to present their ideas. Largely through their influence, direct action became a part of the tactics of the large network of local birth control organizations that existed by 1917.

World War I, however, brought with it a sharp and effective attack on the American Left. One of the fatalities of the rightward political swing of this period was the feminist movement. Although the woman suffrage organizations went on to victory after the war, they lost their Left wing—those whose analysis of women's oppression led them to demand social change more fundamental than extension of the franchise. In 1916 the birth control activists had been politically connected to the Left wing of the feminists and to pro-feminist groups of socialists and anarchists. When these political groupings were broken up, the birth control advocates—mostly educated women and some even upper-class—floundered politically. Losing confidence in the legitimacy of the rebellion of women of their own class, they fell back into an orientation as social workers, in the tradition of the settlement houses. Their own class position often led them to isolate the birth control issue from other social and economic pressures working-class people faced; this separation made their appeals unconvincing to the working-class women they hoped to win over. The continued existence of organized feminism might have reinforced their inclination to fight for *themselves* (as the abortion movement of the 1960s and 1970s has been powerful because it has been essentially a movement of women fighting in their own interests). Without it, the birth controllers remained social workers, with the tendency to think that they knew best what was good for their "clients." Given this orientation, it was not unnatural that the birth controllers, despite their feminism, welcomed the aid of professional experts and, in many cases, sought them out.

Of those among the original birth controllers who resisted the rightward swing of the War and postwar era, many deserted the birth control movement. For most socialists, the War itself, and then the Russian Revolution and the defense of the American Left against repression, seemed the most pressing issues after 1918. They were able to change causes because most of them had seen birth control as a reform issue rather than a revolutionary demand, something requiring less than fundamental change in the society. The tendency to distinguish between fundamental and superficial change, between revolution and reform, was characteristic of those influenced by a Marxist analysis of society. Historical and material determinism argued that certain aspects of social reality determined others, and the traditional Marxist interpretation had placed matters of sexual and reproductive relations in the "superstructure," among other cultural phenomena determined ultimately by the "substructure" which was economic relations. Liberal reformers, however, did not share this view, and several groups of professionals perceived birth control as especially fundamental. Doctors saw it as a health measure, and increasingly a preventive health measure; and naturally doctors viewed human health as a fundamental, not a superficial, condition of social progress. Eugenists saw it as a race health measure; their hereditarian views led them to consider reproduction the fundamental condition of social progress. Both groups considered reproduction fundamental, and once converted, could devote themselves to the birth control cause with passion and perseverance.

PROFESSIONALISM

Professionals entering the birth control movement brought with them a unique self-image and consciousness that made their reform work an integral part of their careers. They believed, by and large, that they worked not only to earn a living but simultaneously to help humanity, to improve society. Since they saw the content of their work as important, not merely its function in earning wages, they saw unity between their paid work and their volunteer activities. Clearly, this view is produced by the opportunity professionals have to do creative, self-directed work. There is no mystery about the relative absence of this consciousness among working-class people or businessmen. The professional attitude toward work is largely dependent on not being paid by the hour and, for higher professionals, the opportunity to determine their own work schedules. Furthermore, many of the professionals active in birth control, particularly doctors, were not wage workers at all, but self-employed. For both kinds of professionals—employed and self-employed—participation in reform activities if respectable enough could add to their prestige in their vocation and among their colleagues.

The desire to make a contribution to civilization led many professionals to go beyond their places of employment to seek wider social influence. For many professionals, seeking political influence seemed a contribution, not an indulgence, because they believed society needed them. Especially in the early 20th century, many professionals believed that their superior intelligence and education entitled them to a larger share of political leadership than their numbers in the population would automatically create in a true democracy. Their view of democracy was meritocratic. Edward L. Thorndike, a eugenist educator, wrote in 1920: "The argument for democracy is not that it gives power to men without distinction, but that it gives greater freedom for ability and character to attain power!" (2, p. 122). Henry Goddard, who introduced the intelligence test in the United States, thought that democracy was "a method for arriving at a truly benevolent aristocracy" (3).

Behind these politics was, first of all, the assumption that superior intelligence and education were coincident with superior political virtue. Hereditarian analyses of the causes of crime supported this view, from the theory that feeble-mindedness was a major cause of crime to the more general attitude that if crime flowed from poverty, poverty in turn was caused by lesser ability and/or laziness. Professional psychologists in the 1920s were engaged in developing intelligence tests, and the bias of these tests was consistently hereditarian and meritocratic: they measured ability to solve the kinds of problems urban professionals met with the kinds of solutions urban professionals would approve. Indeed, the Stanford-Binet test, for years the standard, classified intelligence in terms of what was "required" for five occupational groupings, the professions considered the highest. (The remaining were semiprofessional work, skilled labor, semiskilled labor, and unskilled labor, in descending order (2, p. 121).)

Professionals did not assume that their intellectual superiority came entirely from innate ability. On the contrary, they perceived that rigorous training in intellectual discipline, general knowledge, and tested methodologies had given them skills unavailable to the masses. They did not see their monopolization of this expertise and knowledge as special privilege because they were committed to equal opportunity. They did not usually perceive the effective social and economic barriers that kept most people from these opportunities. But they never doubted that their expertise and knowledge were useful guides for social policy. They did not hesitate to build professional organizations, institutions, and programs of self-licensing which excluded others from their privileges and influence because they had confidence in the universality, objectivity, and social value of the expertise they possessed. Conscious, many of them, of having rejected aristocratic and plutocratic values, they did not think that their meritocratic values were antisocial or unjust. Their basic assumption was that greater intellectual ability, learned and innate, should be rewarded and entrusted with public power.

In the birth control movement, professionals behaved much as they did throughout the society. They sought to solve what had previously been ethical and political questions by objective study. In order to lend their support or even their names to the cause, they needed to be satisfied that it was honest, its strategies careful, and its tactics appropriate to their dignity. Even inside of voluntary associations, therefore, they distrusted leaders who did not share their own values, skills, and social status. Inevitably, their influence transformed birth control leagues from participatory, membership associations into staff organizations.

Had the professionals merely changed the structure and methods of the birth control movement, their influence could not have worked. Structure and methods in social movements cannot be separated from goals. Despite their posture as reformers who sought changes for the benefit of the whole society, or for the less fortunate in it, in fact professional men brought to the birth control movement their own political beliefs and social needs. Molded by professional training and practice but also by class origin and individual experiences, these beliefs were by no means identical among professionals and even within one profession. But leading professionals shared a common set of values, with meritocracy at its root. The professionals of the 1920s believed that some individuals were more valuable to society than others. Whether environmentalists or hereditarians or both, they doubted that superior individuals were equally distributed within all classes and ethnic groups, and believed that scientific study could determine where talent was most likely to be born. Birth control appealed to them as a means of lowering birth rates *selectively* among those groups less likely to produce babies of great merit.

Professionals also perceived themselves as social benefactors, eager not just to legalize birth control for themselves and their wives, but anxious also to install it as social policy. Their commitment to individual liberty was tempered by their recognition that some people were wiser than others, and that good social policy would not necessarily result from allowing each individual to make private decisions about such matters as birth control. Furthermore, many professionals were placed by their jobs in positions of influencing people—doctors, social workers, educators, and psychologists, for example. Accepting meritocratic political views, they naturally taught them to others. They not only disapproved of but feared a democracy that meant that all individuals, despite their educational or intellectual qualifications, would have equal power in the society; they genuinely feared the unfortunate political decisions that might result. Goddard wrote in 1920: "The disturbing fear is that the masses—the seventy or even eighty-six million—will take matters into their own hands." Rather, he argues, they should be directed by the four million of superior intelligence (2, p. 122). This self-conscious elitism reflected not only fear but also an effort to reassure themselves of their differences from the "masses."

DOCTORS

Most physicians remained opposed to contraception in the early 1920s. The predominant position among prestigious doctors was not merely disapproval, but revulsion so hysterical that it prevented them from accepting facts. As late as 1925 Morris Fishbein, editor of the *Journal of the American Medical Association,* asserted that there were no safe and effective birth control methods (4).

In 1926 Frederick McCann (5) wrote that birth control had an insidious influence on the female, causing many ailments previously regarded as obscure in their origins; and that while "biology teaches" that the primary purpose of the sexual act is to reproduce, the seminal fluid also has a necessary and healthful local and general effect on the female. Many doctors believed that they had a social and moral responsibility to fight the social degeneration that birth control represented. George Kosmak, a prominent gynecologist, asked rhetorically: "Is this movement to be ascribed to an honest intent to better the world, is it another expression of the spread of feministic doctrines . . . or is it merely another instance of one of those hysterical waves with which our civilization is so frequently assailed?" (6). The social values underlying Kosmak's opposition were extremely conservative:

> . . . fear of conception has been an important factor in the virtue of many unmarried girls, and . . . many boys are likewise kept straight by this means . . . the freedom with which this matter is now discussed . . . must have an unfortunate effect on the morals of our young people. It is particularly important . . . to keep such knowledge from our girls and boys, whose minds and bodies are not in a receptive frame for such information.

Running throughout Kosmak's attack was an expression of strong elitism:

> . . . those classes of our social system who are placed in a certain position by wealth or mental attainments, require for their upkeep and regeneration the influx of individuals from the strata which are ordinarily regarded as of a lower plane . . . it is necessary for the general welfare and the maintenance of an economic balance that we have a class of the population that shall be characterized by "quantity" rather than by "quality." In other words, we need the "hewers of wood and the drawers of water" and I can only repeat the question that I have already proposed to our good friends who believe in small families, that if the "quantity" factor in our population were diminished as the result of their efforts, would they be willing to perform certain laborious tasks themselves which they now relegate to their supposed inferiors? Might I ask whether the estimable lady who considered it an honor to be arrested as a martyr to the principles advocated by Mrs. Sanger, would be willing to dispose of her own garbage at the river front rather than have one of the "quantity" delegated to this task for her?

Kosmak's concern to guard accustomed privilege also applied to the particular prerogatives of his profession, and reflected the professional ideology that expertise should decide social values (6):

> . . . the pamphlets which have received the stamp of authority by this self-constituted band of reformers . . . are a mixture of arrant nonsense, misinformation, false reports, and in addition, in some cases, seditious libels on the medical profession. These publications are not scientific and in most instances have been compiled by non-scientific persons. . . . Efforts to impress the public with their scientific character need

hardly be dignified by further professional comment, and yet they are a source of such potential danger that as physicians we must lend our assistance in doing away with what is essentially indecent and obscene. . . . Shall we permit the prescribing of contraceptive measures and drugs, many of which are potentially dangerous, by non-medical persons, when we have so jealously guarded our legal rights as physicians against Christian Scientists, osteopaths, chiropractors, naturopaths and others who have attempted to invade the field of medical practice by a short cut without sufficient preliminary training such as is considered essential for the equipment of every medical man? Will we not by mere acquiescence favor the establishment of another school of practice, the "contraceptionists," . . . if as physicians we do not raise our voices against the propaganda which is spreading like a slimy monster into our homes, our firesides, and among our young people?

In protecting his profession Kosmak was very like a craft unionist. But in his sense of responsibility for morality, his point of view was uniquely professional. The sexual values that the anti-birth-control doctors cherished were not so different from 19th-century conservative values: that the major function of women and sexual intercourse both was reproduction of the species; that the male sex drive is naturally greater than the female, an imbalance unfortunately but probably inevitably absorbed by prostitution; that female chastity is necessary to protect the family and its descent; and that female chastity must be enforced with severe social and legal sanctions, among which fear of pregnancy functioned effectively and naturally.

Toward Medical Birth Control

A significant minority of physicians, however, did not share these conservative values. Arguments for a higher valuation of human sexuality as an activity in itself, separate from reproduction, were expressed not only by radicals such as Dr. William Josephus Robinson but by liberal physicians as well in the early 1920s. A leading spokesman of this point of view among prestigious physicians was gynecologist Robert Latou Dickinson. He had applied his medical expertise to social problems for several decades already. He believed that mutual sexual satisfaction was essential to happy marriage. He shared the view of Kosmak and the anti-birth-controllers that doctors ought to assert moral leadership, but chose a more flexible approach. Dickinson encouraged his Ob-Gyn colleagues to take greater initiatives as marriage and sex counsellors. In his 1920 address as President of the American Gynecological Society he recommended that the group take an interest in sociological problems. He too disliked the radical and unscientific associations of the birth control movement. But unlike Kosmak he preferred to respond not by ignoring the movement but by taking it over, and he urged his colleagues to that strategy as early as 1916 (7, p. 179).

Sensitive to the difficulties of pulling his recalcitrant colleagues into a more liberal view of contraception, Dickinson began his campaign with a typical professional gambit. In 1923 he organized a medical group to *study* contraception, with the aim of producing the first scientific and objective evaluation of its effectiveness and safety. He consciously used anti-radicalism to win support for the plan. "May I ask you . . . whether you will lend a hand toward removing the Birth Control Clinic from the propaganda influence of the American Birth Control League . . .," he wrote to a potential supporter in 1925 (8). So firm was Dickinson's insistence that the group would merely study, without preformed opinion, that he was able to get Kosmak himself to serve on the committee. He got financial support from wealthy Gertrude Minturn Pinchot and a qualified endorsement from the New York Obstetrical Society.

Dickinson did not merely *use* anti-radicalism; it was in part his genuine purpose. His

Committee on Maternal Health (CMH), as his "study" project was called, was a reaction to Margaret Sanger's efforts to open and maintain a birth control clinic (8). Continuing her search for medical acceptance, when she planned a second clinic beginning in 1921 she projected it primarily as a center for the medical study of contraception; the women who would receive contraception would be its research subjects. When it opened in January 1923, she called it the Clinical Research Bureau. It had a physician as its supervisor, but she was a woman, not a gynecologist but formerly employed as a public health officer by the State of Georgia—in other words, she did not have professionally impressive credentials. Furthermore, Sanger had insisted on considering social and economic problems as sufficient indications for prescribing contraception. Thus because of Sanger's alternative, many doctors, while remaining suspicious of birth control, supported Dickinson's endeavor as a lesser evil.

At first Dickinson's group was hostile to the Sanger clinic. They tried to get Sanger and Dr. Bocker, head of the Clinical Research Bureau, to accept the supervision of a panel of medical men, but failed. In 1925 Dickinson wrote a report scathingly critical of the value of Bocker's scientific work (7, p. 191). But several factors intervened to lessen this hostility and even bridge the gap between Sanger and the Committee on Maternal Health. One was the fact that the CMH clinic found it difficult to get enough patients with medical indications for contraception. The CMH insistence on avoiding publicity and open endorsement of birth control made women reluctant to try the clinic, anticipating rejection and/or moralistic condemnation of their desire for birth control. Furthermore, it was still extremely difficult to obtain diaphragms, which had to be smuggled into the country. By 1926, three years of work had produced only 124 incomplete case histories. Meanwhile, Sanger's clinic saw 1655 patients in 1925 alone, with an average of three visits each (7, p. 190; 9; 10).

Another factor leading toward unity between the two clinics was Sanger's conciliatory, even humble, attitude toward Dickinson and other influential doctors. The American Birth Control League (ABCL), which united some of the local birth control leagues into a national propaganda and lobbying staff organization, primarily under Sanger's control throughout the 1920s, had been courting medical endorsement since its establishment in 1921. The League accumulated massive medical mailing lists, for example, and sent out reprints of pro-birth-control articles from medical journals (11, p. 280). Sanger got her millionaire husband to pay a $10,000 yearly salary to a doctor, James F. Cooper, to tour the country speaking to medical groups for the ABCL (12). Although even he was not immune from attacks as a quack (13), he commanded the attention of male physicians as no woman agitator could ever have done. And Cooper's prestige was enhanced by sharing the speakers' platform with prestigious European physicians at the International Birth Control Conference held in New York in 1925 under ABCL auspices. Indeed, the prestige of the Europeans—whose medical establishment was far more enlightened on the birth control question than was the American—was sufficient to entice the President of the American Medical Association, William A. Pusey, to offer a lukewarm endorsement of birth control at that conference (14). The ABCL kept exhaustive files, not only of letters but also from their clipping service, on every physician who appeared even mildly favorable to birth control. By 1927 they had 5484 names (11, p. 280). Sanger's standard procedure in response to letters asking for information on contraceptives was to send the writer the names of nearby sympathetic doctors. In response to criticism of her clinic from the Dickinson group in 1925 Sanger, avoiding any defensive reaction, asked the Committee on Maternal Health to take over and run the clinic, hoping in return to be able to get licensing from the New York State Board of Charities. Dickinson demanded in return the removal of all propagandistic literature and posters, to which Sanger agreed. The scheme failed anyway, because Sanger's radical reputation and opposition from the Catholic Church led the State Board to refuse a license (7, pp. 193–196). Dickinson, on the other hand, made his professional influence clear and useful to Sanger by procuring for her a $10,000 grant from the Rockefeller-backed Bureau of Social Hygiene.

Undoubtedly the largest single factor drawing doctors into the birth control movement, however, was Sanger's support for a "doctors only" type of birth control legislation, legislation that would simply strike out all restrictions on doctors' rights to prescribe contraception, giving them unlimited discretion. A corollary to Sanger's support for federal and state "doctors only" bills was her work on birth control conferences at which nonmedical personnel were excluded from the sessions which discussed the technique of contraception. At birth control conferences in 1921 and 1925 organized by the ABCL, sessions on contraception were for physicians only and by invitation only.

Meanwhile, other birth control groups, such as the Voluntary Parenthood League, continued to campaign for open bills, exempting discussion of contraception from all restrictions for anyone. These groups had substantial objections to the "doctors only" bill. In a letter to members of the Voluntary Parenthood League, President Myra Gallert wrote (15):

> Yes, of course we believe in medical advice for the individual, but again how about the large mass of women who cannot reach even a clinic? . . . Mrs. Sanger's own pamphlet on methods finds its way through the American mails . . . *and it is not a physician's compilation.* . . . Mrs. Sanger herself testified "that the Clinical Research Department of the American Birth Control League teaches methods so simple that once learned, any mother who is intelligent enough to keep a nursing bottle clean, can use them."

Furthermore, the "doctors only" bills left "the whole subject . . . still in the category of crime and indecency" (16). Not only did they accept the definition of sexuality without reproduction as obscene, but they also removed the technique of birth control from a woman's own control. If women could not have direct access to birth control information, they would have to get their information from doctors accompanied by censorship at worst and moral guidance at best.

Tactically, the "doctors only" bill also had serious repercussions. As Dr. Antoinette Konikow (17) wrote, the very advantage that its supporters liked—that it would make birth control seem safely controlled—was its worst feature "because it emasculates enthusiasm. To the uninformed the exemption seems hardly worth fighting for. . . ." The very substance of the politics doctors brought to the birth control movement tended to squash widespread participation in the movement.

Many doctors, of course, believed that they had weighty reasons to oppose an "open bill." Sharing the views expressed by Kosmak in 1917, their sense of professional responsibility and importance led them to anticipate all sorts of moral and physiologic disasters should contraceptive information and devices be generally available.

A Local Birth Control League: The Massachusetts Case

The effect of concentration on a "doctors only" bill can be seen by examining the work of a local birth control league. While there were of course many differences in the histories of the local leagues, we are emphasizing here certain developments that were common to most of them while illustrating them with specifics from the Massachusetts case. A birth control group had emerged in Boston in 1916 with the arrest of a young male agitator, a Fabian socialist, for giving a police agent a pamphlet entitled "Why and How the Poor Should Not Have Many Children." Supporters of the accused, Van Kleeck Allison, organized a defense committee which later became the Birth Control League of Massachusetts (BCLM). The League members were from the beginning a coalition of radicals (Allison's fellow Fabians and members of local Socialist Party groups) and liberals (social workers and eugenics reformers in particular). As elsewhere, no doctors—with the exception of the revolutionary socialist Dr. Antoinette Konikow—were conspicuous in the movement in its first years (18).

The BCLM members agreed in 1916 and 1917 on tactics designed to make birth control a public issue and a popular cause. They tried and often succeeded in getting publicity in the popular press, they held mass meetings and public debates, and they contacted 900 women's clubs around the state in efforts to recruit supporters. They accepted support from all quarters, and featured speakers identified as radicals. From the beginning, however, some of the socialists in the BCLM encountered a tension between offering a genuinely radical social alternative and using the support of conservative but powerful people to win immediate gains. Cerise Carman Jack, a Harvard faculty wife of radical leanings, expressed her conflicts about the tension between her radical ideas and her desire to win (19):

> It is the same old and fundamental question that everyone who has any independence of mind encounters as soon as he tries to support a really radical movement by the contributions of the conservative. . . . The Settlements have . . . found it out and have become . . . crystallized around activities of a noncreative sort; the politician has found it out and is for the most part content to lose his soul in the game. . . . [But] half-baked radicals . . . [tend to] have nothing to do with any movement that savors of popularity and . . . think that all reforms must be approached by the narrow path of martyrdom.

Cerise Jack was typical of many women of similar views when she decided in 1918 that the most important and strategic direction for her political efforts should be defense work against political repression. Birth control could wait; it would come anyway after the revolution, would "come so spontaneously wherever the radicals get control of the government, just as the war has brought suffrage . . . now is the time to work for the fundamentals and not for reform measures" (20).

In Massachusetts, as in many places, the immediate effect of the defection of radicals and the entrance of professionals into the birth control league was a period of inactivity. In 1918, birth control supporters among high professionals were still the minority. Most doctors, lawyers, ministers, and professors found birth control too radical and improper a subject for public discussion. Besides, they feared "race suicide" among their own class. But throughout the 1920s quiet but steady concentration on a "doctors only" bill by remaining birth control activists transformed medical opinion. Despite Massachusetts' special problem of strong Catholic pressure against birth control, the League got 1200 doctors to endorse its bill (21). The principle of doctors' rights even led the by now exclusively liberal and conservative Massachusetts Birth Control League to defend radical Dr. Antoinette Konikow. She regularly lectured on sex hygiene to women, demonstrating contraceptives as she discussed birth control, and was arrested for this on February 9, 1928. She appealed to the now defunct League and her defense in fact rehabilitated the League under its old President, Blanche Ames Ames. Konikow was a difficult test case for the League to accept: a Bolshevik, and a regular contributor to revolutionary socialist periodicals, she lacked a refined personal style and was rumored to be an abortionist. Nevertheless, the principle at stake was too important for the doctors to ignore: the prosecution of any physician under the obscenity statutes would have set a dangerous precedent for all physicians. The Emergency Defense Committee formed for Konikow worked out an extremely narrow line of defense: that she was not exhibiting contraceptive devices within the meaning of the law but was using them to illustrate a scientific lecture and warn against possible injuries to health (21). This line worked and Konikow was acquitted.

The verdict stimulated renewed birth control activity and a new BCLM nucleus drew together with the goal of persuading doctors to support birth control and passing a "doctors only" bill in Massachusetts. A new board for the BCLM was chosen, and 10 of the 16 new members were physicians. The lobbying activities took all the League's time, and there was virtually no public visibility in this period. Konikow herself was extremely critical of this policy. She saw that commitment to it required maintaining a low profile and specifically meant giving up the project of a clinic. She argued, in fact, that opening a clinic would in the long run do more to bring the medical profession around than a long, slow legislative lobbying campaign (17). Konikow's criticisms angered the League people. Possibly in retaliation, they refused to lend her the League mailing list of 1500 names to publicize her new book, *The Physicians' Manual of Birth Control*. Konikow's angry protests condemned what she saw as a new kind of organization quite different from that of the original local birth control leagues (21): "the relations between the Executive Board and the membership are so distant that the members do not know what the official policy of the organization is . . . ."

As Konikow had predicted, one of the consequences of this new kind of organization was failure. While the BCLM had become narrow and elitist, the opposition from the Catholic Church was based on mass support. The Birth Control League, meanwhile, had become less an organization than a professionals' lobbying group. Furthermore, no matter how decorous and conservative the League's arguments for birth control, they could not escape red-baiting and other forms of scurrilous attack. Cardinal O'Connell said that the bill was a "direct threat . . . towards increasing impurity and unchastity not only in our married life but . . . among our unmarried people . . . ." The chief of obstetrics at a Catholic hospital said that the bill was "the essence and odor that comes from that putrid and diseased river that has its headquarters in Russia." Another opponent made the direct charge that this was a campaign supported by Moscow gold (22). A broad opposition defeated the doctors' bill. Even non-Catholic attackers recognized the radical potential of birth control: separation of sex from reproduction, and removal of one of the main sanctions for marital chastity—involuntary pregnancy. Even had birth control never had its reputation "damaged" by association with socialists, anarchists, and Free Lovers, its content could not be disguised. This was the weak point in the conservative strategy of the BCLM, even measured against its own goals. If birth control was inherently radical, subversive of conventional morality in its *substance*, no form of persuasion could bring around those who needed and benefited from the conventional morality. The meaning of birth control could not be disguised by coating it as a medical tool.

While the Catholic Church played a particularly large role in Massachusetts, "doctors only" bills were defeated in every state in which they were proposed, even in states without large Catholic populations (16, pp. 72-93). Indeed, the whole pattern of development of the BCLM was echoed in many local birth control leagues. After the radical originators of the movements left because of the War and other causes that seemed to them more pressing (or in a few instances, were pushed out by professionals and conservatives), the birth control leagues fell into much lower levels of activity and energy. The impact of professionals—particularly doctors—on birth control as a social movement was to depress it, to take it out of the mass consciousness as a social issue, even as information on contraceptives continued to be disseminated. Furthermore, the doctors did not prove successful in the 1920s even in winning the legislative and legal gains they had defined as their goals. While some birth control organizers, such as Cerise Jack of the BCLM, felt that they were torn between radical demands and effectiveness, in fact there is reason to question whether the surrender of radical demands produced any greater effectiveness at all.

The Problem of Clinics

The Massachusetts example, while typical of the national struggle for legislation legalizing birth control, was not representative of the development of birth control clinics. By 1930 there were 55 clinics in 23 cities in 12 states. In Chicago in 1923 a birth control clinic was denied a license by the City Health Commissioner, but the League secured a court order overruling him and granting a license. Judge Fisher's decision in this case marked out important legal precedents. His opinion held that the project was a clinic under the meaning of the law; that there existed contraceptive methods not injurious to health; that the actions of the Health Commissioner (who had cited biblical passages in his letter of refusal to license!) amounted to enforcing religious doctrines, an illegal use of power; that the obscenity statutes only sought to repress "promiscuous" distribution of contraceptive information; and that "where reasonable minds differ courts should hesitate to condemn" (23).

As the clinic movement mushroomed around the country, however, conflict raged about how and by whom the clinics should be controlled. Margaret Sanger still resisted relinquishing personal control of her New York clinic to the medical profession. No doubt part of her resistance came from a desire to control things herself, especially since she had lost control of the American Birth Control League and its publication the *Birth Control Review* by 1929. (Sanger was undoubtedly a difficult person who did not thrive on cooperative work. Her personal struggles within the birth control movement are well described in Kennedy (7).) But part of her resistance, too, came from disagreement with the doctors' insistence on requiring medical indications for the prescription of contraceptive devices. Her Clinical Research Bureau had consistently stretched the definition of appropriate indications; and if an appropriate medical problem that justified contraception could not be found, a patient was often referred to private doctors whose prescriptions would be less dangerous (7, p. 197). Sanger was willing to avoid an open challenge to the law on the question of indications, but she was not willing to allow close medical supervision to deprive physically healthy women of access to contraception.

She still wanted a license to guarantee the safety and stability of her clinic. When she withdrew the clinic from the auspices of the ABCL in 1928, Sanger once again approached Dickinson, requesting that he find her a medical director whose prestige might help obtain a license. Dickinson in reply demanded that the clinic be entirely turned over to a medical authority, suggesting New York Hospital. Sanger was convinced that such an affiliation would hamstring her work and refused it. Then, in April 1929, the clinic was raided by the police. A plainclothes policewoman asked for and was supplied with a contraceptive device. She even came for her second checkup to make sure her diaphragm was fitting her well, and then returned five days later with a detachment of police who arrested three nurses and two physicians, and confiscated the medical records. The last action was a mistake on the part of the police, for it could not help but unite the medical profession behind Sanger, in defense of confidential medical records. Furthermore, the policewoman had been a poor choice because the clinic doctors had indeed found pelvic abnormalities that provided a proper medical indication for giving her a diaphragm. The case was thrown out of court. (Some time later the policewoman returned to the clinic, off duty, to seek treatment for her pelvic disorders! (24, pp. 402–408).)

This episode produced good feelings between Sanger and the doctors who supported her, and Dickinson followed it up with a last attempt to persuade her to give up the clinic—this time into the hands of the New York Academy of Medicine rather than a hospital. Sanger was probably closer to acceding now than she had ever been and might have done so had it not been for countervailing pressure she was getting from another group of professionals—the eugenists. Though easily as conservative as the doctors in terms of the feminist or sexual freedom implications of birth control, they were solidly in Sanger's camp on the issue of indications. They could not be content with a medical interpretation of contraception, i.e. that its function was to prevent pathologies in mothers. The eugenists sought the kind of impact birth control might have when disseminated on a mass basis; they wanted to improve the quality of the whole population, not just protect the health of women. They also felt a certain amount of professional rivalry with the physicians. Eugenists had been among the earliest of the nonradicals to support birth control, and some of them had spoken out for it publicly even before the War. They perceived the doctors as joining the cause after it was safe, and trying to take it over from its originators (25). Though politically conservative, their intensity of commitment to their reform panacea—selective breeding—allowed them to accept Sanger's militant rhetoric and her willingness to challenge and stretch the law. At the same time the eugenists had a great influence not only on Sanger but on the whole birth control movement.

EUGENISTS

Eugenics attitudes had attracted reformers of all varieties for nearly a century. Lacking a correct genetics, 19th-century eugenics was largely utopian speculations based on the assumption that acquired characteristics could be inherited. This assumption meant that there was no necessary opposition between environmentalism and heredity. The scientific discrediting of the theory of the inheritance of acquired characteristics changed the political implications of eugenics, and more narrow applications of it became dominant. Margaret Sanger described the development of eugenics succinctly: "Eugenics, which had started long before my time, had once been defined as including free love and prevention of conception .... Recently it had cropped up again in the form of selective breeding" (24, p. 374). The new eugenics, "selective breeding," was rigidly elitist, intended to reproduce the entire American population in the image of those who dominated it politically and economically. The "new" eugenics was not a reform program but a justification for the status quo. Its essential argument—that the "unfit," the criminal, and the pauper were the products of congenital formations—suited the desire of its upper-class supporters to justify their own monopoly on power, privilege, and wealth.

Eugenics Ideology

New genetic theories provided reliable methods of prediction, and therefore control, of the transmittal of some identifiable physical traits, and they stimulated a great deal of scientific research into human genetics. The first eugenics organizations were research centers, such as the Eugenics Record Office and the Station for Experimental Evolution. As eugenics enthusiasts developed specific political and social proposals for action, they established organizations to spread the gospel generally and do legislative lobbying specifically. The first of these was the Eugenics Section of the American Breeders Association, set up in 1910; in 1913 human breeding became the main focus of the Association which changed its name to the American Genetic Association. Several other organizations were established in the next decade.

In no academic field was the coalition between corporate capital and scholars developed more fully than in eugenics. By the 1920s eugenics was a required course in many American universities. The development of eugenics as a scholarly field represented the capitulation of university scholars to a fad, allowing their skills to become a commodity for sale to a high bidder. The backers of eugenics research and writing included the wealthiest families of the country. The Eugenics Record Office was established by Mrs. E. H. Harriman (26). The Station for Experimental Evolution was funded by Andrew Carnegie (26). Henry Fairfield Osborn, a gentleman scholar and founder of the New York Museum of Natural History, was a main financial backer of the eugenics societies; in the late 1920s Frederick Osborn, nephew of Henry Fairfield, assumed leadership in the cause and financed a research program for the Eugenics Research Association (27).

Despite the direct influence of big business on eugenics, the cause carried with it some of its historic aura of radicalism for many years, an aura which sometimes disguised its fundamentally conservative content. For example, eugenists identified themselves as crusaders for reform, and argued their case with apocalyptic warnings (e.g. "race suicide," "menace to civilization") and utopian promises ("a world of supermen"). They advocated techniques, such as sterilization and marriage licensing, which were often repulsive to traditional and religious people. Equally important, many radicals remained interested in eugenics programs. Socialists, feminists, and sex-radicals continued to use eugenics ideas. Mainly outside academic and scientific circles, these followers of a traditional "popular eugenics" continued to offer analyses and proposals that assumed the inheritance of acquired characteristics well into the 1920s. They endorsed programs to lessen suffering through the prevention of birth defects; they included demands for prenatal medical care for women under the aegis of eugenics.

After the First World War, however, academic eugenists consistently avoided all except strictly hereditarian interpretations of eugenics. In clinging to their hereditarian assumptions,[2] they stood in opposition to the tradition of social reform in America. Eugenists justified social and economic inequalities as biological; their journals featured articles about "aristogenic" families, as if the existence of several noted gentlemen in the same family proved the superiority of their genes. Their definitions of what was

---

[2] I call these assumptions because nothing in the genetic theory they relied upon, even as it progressed to Mendel's mathematically sophisticated and predictive models, provided any basis for judgment about the relative impact of heredity and environment in producing characteristics such as feeble-mindedness, insanity, laziness, and other common eugenic bugaboos.

socially worthy naturally used their own professional and upper-class standards of success. The professional bias can be seen particularly clearly in their emphasis on intelligence. Standard eugenics concepts of inferiority, such as "degeneracy," consistently equated lack of intelligence with viciousness and intelligence with goodness (2, pp. 115-116). "Among the 1000 leading American men of science," eugenist Paul Popenoe (28) wrote, "there is not one son of a day laborer. It takes 48,000 unskilled laborers to produce one man distinguished enough to get in *Who's Who,* while the same number of Congregational ministers produces 6000 persons eminent enough to be included...."

Aristogenic stock was missing not only from the working class as a whole, but also from non-Yankees in particular. Here is a typical explanation of the problem from a standard eugenics textbook first published in 1916 (29):

> From the rate at which immigrants are increasing it is obvious that our very life-blood is at stake. For our own protection we must face the question of what types or races should be ruled out ... many students of heredity feel that there is great hazard in the mongrelizing of distinctly unrelated races.... However, it is certain that under existing social conditions in our own country only the most worthless and vicious of the white race will tend in any considerable numbers to mate with the negro and the result cannot but mean deterioration on the whole for either race....

Consider the following—typical—passage from *Revolt Against Civilization: The Menace of the Under Man* by Lothrop Stoddard (30), one of the most widely respected eugenists:

> But what about the inferior? Hitherto we have not analyzed their attitude. We have seen that they are incapable of either creating or furthering civilization, and are thus a negative hindrance to progress. But the inferiors are not mere negative factors in civilized life; they are also positive—in an inverse destructive sense. The inferior elements are, instinctively or consciously, the enemies of civilization. And they are its enemies, not by chance but because they are more or less uncivilizable.

The eugenics movement strongly supported immigration restriction (27, p. 55) and contributed to the development of racist fears and hatreds among many Americans. In 1928, the Committee on Selective Immigration of the American Eugenics Society recommended that future immigration be restricted to white people (31). The movement also supported the enactment of antimiscegenation laws throughout the South (32), and Southern racists used the respectability of eugenics to further the development of segregation. For example, the Virginia State Board of Health distributed a pamphlet among schoolchildren entitled "Eugenics in Relation to the New Family and the Law on Racial Integrity," published in 1924. It explained in eugenic terms the valiant and lonely effort of Virginia to preserve the race from the subversion fostered by the 19 states plus the District of Columbia which permitted miscegenation. It concluded, "Let us turn a deaf ear to those who would interpret Christian brotherhood to mean racial equality."

Toward Eugenical Birth Control

When they turned their attention to "positive eugenics," most eugenists were antagonistic toward birth control. To appreciate this conflict fully, one must remember that the eugenists were concerned not only with the inadequate reproduction of the "superior," but also with a declining birth rate in general. As late as 1940, demographers worried that the net reproduction rate of the U.S. was below the replacement level (33). Many eugenists clung to mercantilist notion that a healthy economy should have a steadily growing population. In addition, they adopted the "race suicide" analyses that birth control was being practiced in a particularly dysgenic way, the best "stock" producing the fewest children. In the area of "negative" eugenics, they approved of birth limitation, of course, but preferred to see it enforced more permanently—through sterilization and the prohibition of dysgenic marriages.

The feminist content of birth control practice and propaganda was especially obnoxious to the eugenists. They feared the growing "independence" of women. Eugenists were frequently involved in propaganda for the protection of the family, and in anti-divorce campaigning. The most common eugenics position was virulently antifeminist, viewing women primarily as breeders. One typical eugenist wrote in 1917: ". . . in my view, women exist primarily for racial ends. The tendency to exempt the more refined of them from the pains and anxieties of child bearing and motherhood, although arising out of a very attractive feeling of consideration for the weaker individuals of the race, is not, admirable as it seems, in essence a moral one" (34).

While most eugenists were opposed to birth control, some were not, and all saw that they had certain common interests with the birth controllers. Some believed that while sterilization would be necessary in extreme cases, birth control could be taught to and practiced by the masses. Especially the younger eugenists and the demographer-sociologists (demography was not at this time a distinct discipline) were convinced that the trend toward smaller families was irrevocable, and the only thing to do to counteract its dysgenic tendency was to make it universal. Finally, they shared with birth controllers an interest in sex education and freedom of speech on sexual issues.

If these factors contributed to close the gap between eugenists and birth controllers, the attitudes of the birth controllers contributed even more. While eugenists by and large opposed birth control, birth controllers did not make the reverse judgment. On the contrary, almost all birth control supporters, both leaders and followers, agreed with eugenics goals and felt that they could gain from the popularity of eugenics.

Identification with eugenics goals was, for many birth controllers, based on familiarity with the 19th-century radical eugenics tradition. Most of them did not immediately apprehend the transformation of eugenics by the adoption of exclusively hereditarian assumptions. Some radicals were critical of the class basis of eugenics programs, as was socialist Henry Bergen (35) in 1920:

> Unfortunately eugenists are impelled by their education and their associations and by the unconscious but not less potent influences of the material and social interests of their class to look upon our present environment . . . as a constant factor, which not only cannot be changed but ought not to be changed.

But most socialists accepted the fundamental eugenics belief in the importance of congenital characteristics. Thus British birth controller and socialist Eden Paul (36) wrote in 1917 that the "socialist tendency is to overrate the importance of environment, great as this undoubtedly is. . . ." Furthermore, on issues of race or ethnic differences the Left shared with the Right deep prejudices. In the same article in which Bergen identified the class function of eugenics, he endorsed the goal of using eugenics programs to improve the white race (35). In a socialist collection of essays on birth control published in 1917 (37) we find passages like this:

Taking the coloured population in 1910 as ten millions; it would in 1930 be twenty millions; in 1950, forty millions; in 1970, eighty millions; and 1990, one hundred and sixty millions. A general prohibition of white immigration would thus, within the space of about eighty years, suffice to transform the Union into a negro realm. Now, although individual members of the Afro-American race have been able, when educated by whites, to attain the highest levels of European civilisation, negroes as a whole have not hitherto proved competent to maintain a lofty civilisation. The condition of affairs in the black republic of Haiti gives some justification for the fear that negro dominance would be disastrous.

Like the rest of the Left, the feminist birth controllers tended to accept racist and ethnocentric attitudes. As did most middle-class reformers, the feminists also had a reservoir of anti-working-class attitudes. The American feminist movement had its own traditions of elitism, in the style of Elizabeth Cady Stanton's proposal (38) for suffrage for the educated. Many feminists had been active in the temperance movement, and saw immigrants and working-class men as drunken undesirables. Anti-Catholicism particularly had been an undercurrent in the women's rights movement for decades, stimulated by Catholic opposition to prohibition and women's rights. Southern feminists used the fear of the black vote as an argument for suffrage, and were supported by the national woman suffrage organizations in doing so (39). Birth control reformers were not attracted to eugenics *because* they were racists; rather, they had interests in common with eugenists and had no strong tradition of anti-racism on which to base a critique of eugenics.

Sanger, too, had always argued the "racial" values of birth control, but as time progressed she gave less attention to feminist arguments and more to eugenical ones. "More children from the fit, less from the unfit—that is the chief issue of birth control," she wrote in 1919 (40). In *Woman and the New Race* (41), published in 1920, she put together statistics about immigrants, their high birth rates, and low literacy rates in a manner certain to stimulate racist fears. In *The Pivot of Civilization* (42), published in 1922, she urged applying stockbreeding techniques to society in order to avoid giving aid to "good-for-nothings" at the expense of the "good." She warned that the masses of the illiterate and "degenerate" might well destroy "our way of life." She developed favorite eugenical subthemes as well, such as the cost to the society of supporting the "unfit" in public institutions, and the waste of funds on charities that merely put band-aids on sores rather than curing diseases. Society is divided into three demographic groups, she argued: the wealthy who already practiced birth control; the intelligent and responsible who wanted birth control; and the reckless and irresponsible, including "the pauper element dependent entirely upon the normal and fit members of society" (43). She shifted her imagery about such social divisions, for later in the 1920s she cited a "Princeton University authority" who had classified the U.S. population as 20 million intellectual, 25 million mediocre, 45 million subnormal, and 15 million feeble-minded (44). The racism and virulence of her eugenical rhetoric grew most extreme in the early 1930s. In 1932 she recommended the sterilization or segregation by sex of "the whole dysgenic population" (45). She complained that the government, which was so correctly concerned with the quality of immigrants, lacked concern for the quality of its native-born (44).

Eugenics soon became a constant, even a dominant, theme at birth control conferences. In 1921 at the organizational conference of the American Birth Control League there were many eugenics speakers and exhibits of charts showing the dysgenic heritage of the infamous Jukes and Kallikak families. In 1922 Sanger went to London for the Fifth International Neo-Malthusian and Birth Control Conference as its only female honored guest. Yet not a single panel was devoted to birth control as a woman's right nor did Sanger raise this point of view (46). In 1925 Sanger brought the Sixth International Conference to New York under the sponsorship of the ABCL. The impact of ABCL control was to make the emphasis more eugenical and less neo-Malthusian, but there was no increase in concern with women's rights. Not a single session was chaired by a woman; about one out of ten speakers was a woman. Four of the total of eleven sessions focused specifically on eugenics, none on women's problems (14).

Meanwhile the propaganda of the ABCL was becoming more focused on eugenics at the expense of women's rights. The introductory brochure used during the 1920s lists the first point of "What This Organization Does To Inform the Public" as publishing and distributing literature and conducting lectures "on the disgenic [sic] effects of careless breeding." The program of the ABCL included a sterilization demand and called for "racial progress."

The *Birth Control Review*, the ABCL publication, reflected eugenics influence from its inception in 1917. While eugenists of the older, radical tradition dominated in its first years, it also printed without editorial comment a eugenical anti-birth-control argument, virtually a "race suicide" argument, in its very first volume (47). By 1920 the *Review* published openly racist articles (48). In 1923 the *Review* editorialized in favor of immigration restriction on a racial basis (49). In the same year the *Review* published a study on "The Cost to the State of the Socially Unfit" (50). In 1920 Havelock Ellis favorably reviewed Lothrop Stoddard's *The Rising Tide of Color Against White World-Supremacy* (51). Stoddard was at this time on the Board of Directors of the American Birth Control League. So was C. C. Little, another openly racist eugenist. President of the Third Race Betterment Conference, he justified birth control as an antidote to the "melting pot," a means of preserving the purity of "Yankee stock" (52). Also closely involved with the ABCL and writing regularly for *Review* was Guy Irving Burch, a director of the American Eugenics Society and leader in the American Coalition of Patriotic Societies. He supported birth control, he wrote, because he had long worked to "prevent the American people from being replaced by alien or Negro stock, whether it be by immigration or by overly high birth rates among others in this country" (7, p. 119). A content analysis of the *Review* showed that by the late 1920s only 4.9 per cent of all its articles for a decade had had any concern with women's self-determination (11, p. 232).

The Decline of a People's Birth Control Movement

It is important to understand correctly the birth controllers' conversion to eugenics and their desertion of feminism. They did not disavow their earlier feminism so much as find it not useful because of the more general change in the country's political climate. Had they had deeper feminist or anti-racist convictions, they might have found eugenics ideas more uncomfortable. But feeling no discomfort, they found eugenics ideas useful. They could get from the eugenists a support that they never got from the Left. The men who dominated the socialist movement did not perceive birth control as fundamental to their own interests, and their theory categorized it as a reform peripheral to the struggle of the working class. Eugenists, on the other hand, once they caught on to the idea of urging birth control upon the poor rather than condemning it among the rich, were prepared to offer active and powerful support.

Nevertheless, the professionalization of the birth control movement was identical with its takeover by men. Although women remained the majority of the membership of the large birth control organizations, the officers and the clinic directors more and more frequently became men. By 1940 Margaret Sanger had been kicked upstairs to being "honorary chairman." Men came to occupy the positions of President, General Director, and all the five Vice-Presidents. Two of them were noted eugenists and authors of explicitly racist tracts—anti-immigrant and anti-black.[3] The only remaining woman on the board was Mrs. Mary Woodard Reinhardt, Secretary.

The men, however, did not all agree. While doctors and eugenists could mesh their concerns for individual and racial health in propaganda, they did not see eye to eye on the practice of the clinics. Particularly as regards indications, as we have seen, the doctors wanted to preserve narrow medical justifications for prescribing contraceptives, while eugenists and many lay birth controllers wanted to use contraception to ameliorate social, psychologic, and economic problems as well. Beyond this, eugenists were eager to use birth control clinics to collect data on family patterns, birth control use, changing attitudes, sexual behavior, and genetic history (7, p. 200). The eugenists were there in the forefront of the social sciences. Many eugenists (e.g. Lewis Terman and Edward Thorndike) were leaders in the development of improved quantitative and statistical techniques in the social sciences. The foundations generously funded such statistical studies (53-55). Eugenists feared and opposed medical supervision of clinics because it threatened to interfere with their data collection (7, p. 202).

Most birth control clinics appreciated the eugenists' support for disseminating contraceptives in the absence of pathologic indications. The clinics also acceded to eugenists' research interests. Many clinics conducted inquiries into the hereditary histories of their patients, and presumably advised the women as to the desirability of having children (53, p. 44). In 1925, responding to suggestions from her eugenist supporters, Sanger reformed her clinical records to show the nationality, heredity, religion, occupation, and even trade union affiliation of patients (7, p. 200). A review of the work of 70 birth control clinics in Britain and the U.S., published in 1930, proudly demonstrated that they reached a disproportionately large number of working-class women, and claimed a eugenic effect from doing so (56, Ch. IV).

The birth controllers also influenced the eugenists, of course. As Sanger described the relationships (24, pp. 374-375):

> ... eugenics without birth control seemed to me a house built upon sands. It could not stand against the furious winds of economic pressure which had buffeted into partial or total helplessness a tremendous proportion of the human race. The eugenists wanted to shift the birth control emphasis from less children for the poor to more children for the rich. We went back of that and sought first to stop the multiplication of the unfit.

---

[3] Dr. Richard N. Pierson, President; Dr. Woodbridge E. Morris, General Director; Vice-Presidents were Dr. Robert Latou Dickinson, Henry Pratt Fairchild, Frederick C. Holden, Clarence C. Little, and Charles-Edward Amory Winslow. Little and Fairchild were eugenists. Winslow was closely associated with Rockefeller family enterprises.

Thus in one paragraph is condensed the transformation of birth control politics: the poor, "buffeted into partial or total helplessness" by economic pressure, are rechristened the unfit.

With such an attitude toward the poor, it is not surprising that the clinics encountered difficulties in teaching working-class women to use birth control properly. Some such women were unteachable, Sanger and several other birth control leaders agreed. They particularly had trouble with "the affectionate, unreflecting type known to housing experts, who, though living in one room with several children, will keep a St. Bernard dog." For these women, sterilization was recommended (56, pp. 50-52). Another area in which the snobbery of the birth control workers was manifest was in their attitude toward working-class men. They projected an image of these husbands as uncontrolled, uncontrollable, sex-hungry, violent sexual aggressors, with no regard or respect for their wives, who would never agree to contraception. Certainly the reasons such men might have for hostility to birth control clinics were not taken seriously.

But medical supervision of the clinics had created similar problems in reaching the poor with birth control, and Sanger and other clinic partisans ultimately saw more usefulness in the propaganda of eugenics than in the more reserved, "soft sell" style of doctors. Furthermore, the eugenists could not exercise the kind of direct control over clinics that the doctors could, lacking the institutions such as hospitals or medical academies, and were thus willing to share control with birth controllers like Sanger. If Sanger and her colleagues ultimately chose to work with the eugenists, it was because it seemed to them the only realistic option. They would greatly have preferred cooperative working relationships with both groups; and perhaps, had this been possible, they might have retained more direct power in their own hands by playing off the two groups of professionals against each other. As it was, the ideological disagreements, and, even more, the jurisdictional rivalry of the two professions prevented this.

Ultimately, the rivalry held back the clinic movement. Although contraception became widespread in the 1930s, most middle-class people continued to get their help from private doctors. Working-class people, on the other hand, often did not get it at all. Many studies have shown that poor people have more excess fertility—in terms of their *own* preferences—than more prosperous people (57). It is equally clear that poor people have little access to birth control services. This last is, of course, part of the general inadequacy and unequal distribution of medical care in the United States. Poverty generally tends to limit the use of medical facilities to the treatment of emergencies and acute or painful conditions, and minimizes access to preventive health services. While the right to birth control is not a medical issue, the actual delivery of most contraceptives must be done in medical situations. The movement for birth control clinics was thus in itself a break with the private capitalist medical system in the U.S., and its failure was a part of a general failure of American medicine.

Physicians' attitudes toward the birth control movement—their demand for exclusive control and restrictive distribution—represented a microcosm of the general attitude taken by the medical profession. The attitude of many doctors toward their private patients continued, well into the mid-20th century, to parallel that of many elite 19th-century doctors: while they opposed the "promiscuous," "indiscriminate" dissemination of contraception, they did not question their own discrimination and even thought it important that private doctors should be able to make exceptions to the policies they supported as general rules. Well-to-do women were able to secure diaphragms without medical indications from doctors who may themselves have opposed making it possible for clinics to use the same principles. The discretionary right of the individual doctor was a privilege as cherished by the profession as that of privacy—and the latter, of course, protected the former.

In the 1930s eugenics went into eclipse as a mass cause. Nazi eugenic policies tarnished the image of the movement, and scientific criticisms of Galtonian genetics stripped away much of the academic respectability that had clothed eugenical racism. On the other hand, the success of birth control also contributed to the decline of eugenics.

Birth control had become a movement that could do much of the eugenists' work for them. Henry Pratt Fairchild, former President of the American Eugenics Society, told the annual meeting of the Birth Control Federation (successor to the ABCL) in 1940 (58):

> One of the outstanding features of the present conference is the practically universal acceptance of the fact that these two great movements [eugenics and birth control] have now come to such a thorough understanding and have drawn so close together as to be almost indistinguishable.

CONCLUSION

Birth control emerged as a movement in the 1910s among radicals, especially feminists, who sought basic social change in sexual and class relations. By the end of the 1930s birth control was no longer a popular movement but had become a staff organization of experts lobbying for reforms in behalf of a larger constituency. I have argued that this transformation was accomplished by the large-scale entrance of professionals into the birth control cause; in this article I have singled out doctors and academic eugenists, but in the book-in-progress from which this is an excerpt[4] I have also discussed the important role of social workers.

The organization that today dominates birth control in the U.S., the Planned Parenthood Federation, originated in 1942 out of a merger of birth control groups, and is beyond the scope of this article. Nevertheless, it represents the culmination of the tendencies which the professionals introduced in the 1920s and 1930s: removing the focus of birth control education from women's rights to family stability, social unity, and population control. For example, Planned Parenthood continued the efforts of the original birth controllers in promoting sex education, but its content was subtly changed. Planned Parenthood spokespeople avoided the connotation that women might wish to remain childless, affirming motherhood as the main source of women's fulfillment, and arguing merely for the economic and health benefits of small families. They offered a male-centered sex education which perpetuated many existing myths about female sexuality, such as the vaginal orgasm and dangers of promiscuity. Planned Parenthood long clung to a policy of offering birth control services only to married women. That policy in practice supported the prevailing ethic that sex belonged only with marriage; it also supported in effect the double standard, the view that unmarried women who "went all the way" had to "take their chances." Choosing not to challenge conventional norms about women's roles in society—full-time wifehood and

---

[4]The book, tentatively entitled Sexuality, Feminism and Birth Control, will be published by Grossman/Viking in 1976.

motherhood as primary—Planned Parenthood therefore had to argue for birth control in terms of health and population control primarily. And these two themes, as we have seen, were interpreted to the public under the influence of doctors and eugenists. The experts defined good social policy for the public. They held up small families as a model for all people, regardless of other economic and psychologic needs, and without relating family size to the overall quality of life. The planned parenthood-population control merger of the 1950s reflected the experts' sense of their responsibility for offering the small family as a solution for poverty all over the world, with increasing insensitivity to the personal and cultural preferences of other people.

None of these criticisms should obscure the fact that the availability of efficient birth control provided the basis for a radical change in women's possibilities. Lack of control over pregnancy (except through avoiding marriage, which was not an economic or social possibility for most women) and the great burdens of child-raising had represented the single most important factor in women's inequality, probably from the beginning of the species. Placing reproduction under individual control has the potential of making any opportunity available to men open to women also. But the vast majority of women never won these advantages. It is precisely because the liberating potential of birth control for women was so great that the failure of the birth control movement thus far to reach its potential seems regrettable, and is worth analyzing.

Part of the problem lies in the inadequate quantity of birth control services available. But many women do not take advantage of birth control techniques available to them: their problem is social and economic, not merely technologic. For women to desire limiting their pregnancies and to be able to take the responsibility for contraception, they must have a new way of looking at what women should be, a new image of femininity and a new set of actual possibilities that do not require sexual passivity, maternalness, domesticity, self-sacrifice, and the absence of ambition. It was this new sense of womanhood that the birth controllers of the early 20th century were after. Margaret Sanger believed in 1916 that birth control was revolutionary because it could provide the technologic basis for women to control not only their pregnancies, but their destinies.

Historically, the technology of birth control did not lead, but followed, the social demand for it. Today too women have tended to use contraception to the extent that they have other activities that they find preferable to child-raising. The birth control movement was once part of an overall feminist movement, struggling for more opportunities for women in many areas simultaneously, for a total self-determination for women. Lacking that overall movement, birth control has become a part of the technologic revolution, attempting to create social reform through a single invention, and without the process of liberation that is entailed in a movement of people struggling for their own interests.

Because birth control became removed from a larger social movement, it lost the political content that identified it with the struggle for human liberation. Indeed, one of the problems birth control advocates face today is that many associate birth control with the opposite of liberation—with elitist and racist policies leading even to genocide. There is truth in that belief. Population controllers have used coercion and trickery to impose birth control, often in the form of permanent sterilization, upon Third World peoples such as Puerto Ricans and Indians. Many poor people associate birth control with feminism and disapprove of both. They have experienced feminism as the struggle of privileged women for equality with the men of their privileged classes. It is true that the feminist movement primarily reflected the needs of privileged women in the past; it is also true that the discrimination such women faced, within the birth control movement, for example, paralleled that directed against working-class people. The birth control professionals felt confident that they knew how to arrange the social advancement of less privileged groups, and offered contraception as a panacea. In fact for women and all poor people birth control represents a major step forward only when it is combined with campaigns for equality on many fronts.

The struggle for birth control today offers opportunities for those concerned with the welfare of women and of the poor—for those concerned with social equality in general—to change its previously elitist direction. The history of the birth control movement suggests that it is possible to make of it a popular cause that reaches people of all classes if its basic principle is self-determination through increasing the real choices that people have. Legalized abortion that remains out of the price range of most women does not, for example, represent real self-determination. Offering women contraceptives without thorough, female-centered sex education does not represent self-determination. Offering women inadequately tested pills, and testing those pills on poor and non-white women as has been the custom of the drug companies, does not represent self-determination nor is it likely to make poor people favorably inclined toward birth control as a reform. Similarly, it makes no sense to offer advice or contraceptives without adequate general medical care, or to offer it through disrespectful and condescending doctors. Self-determination must mean a birth control program that is part of an overall program of good medical care, education, respect, and equal opportunity for all women.

REFERENCES

1. Gordon, L. Voluntary motherhood. *Feminist Studies* I(3-4): 5-22, 1972-1973.
2. Karier, C. J. Testing for order and control. In *Roots of Crisis: American Education in the Twentieth Century*, edited by C. J. Karier, P. Violas, and J. Spring. Rand-McNally, Chicago, 1973.
3. Goddard, H. *Psychology of the Normal and Subnormal*, p. 234. Dodd, Mead, New York, 1919.
4. Fishbein, M. *Medical Follies*, p. 142. Boni & Liveright, New York, 1925.
5. McCann, F. Presidential address to League of National Life. *Medical Press and Circular*, p. 359, November 3, 1926.
6. Kosmak, G. In *Bulletin, Lying-In Hospital of the City of New York*, pp. 181-192, August 1917.
7. Kennedy, D. *Birth Control in America: The Career of Margaret Sanger*. Yale University Press, New Haven, 1970.
8. Dickinson, R. L. Letter to J. Bentley Squier, November 10, 1925. Dickinson Manuscripts, Countway Library, Harvard University Medical School, Boston.
9. Reed, J. Birth Control and the Americans: 1830-1970, Part III: Robert L. Dickinson and the Committee on Maternal Health, pp. 77-82. Ph.D. dissertation, Harvard University, unpublished, 1974.
10. Lader, L. *The Margaret Sanger Story*, p. 216. Doubleday, Garden City, N.Y., 1955.
11. Vreeland, F. M. American Birth Control League files. In The Process of Reform with Especial Reference to Reform Groups in the Field of Population. Ph.D. dissertation, University of Michigan, unpublished, 1929.
12. Sanger, M. Letter to J. Noah Slee, February 22, 1925. Sanger Manuscripts, Library of Congress, Washington, D. C.
13. Wishard, W. N., Sr. Contraception: Are our county societies being used for the American Birth Control League propaganda? *J. Indiana State Med. Assoc.*, pp. 187-189, May 1929.
14. *Proceedings, Sixth International Birth Control Conference*, Vol. III, pp. 19-30, 49-60. American Birth Control League, New York, 1925.
15. Mimeographed letter to Voluntary Parenthood League members from President Myra P. Gallert, December 2, 1925. Alice Park Manuscripts, Stanford University Library, Stanford, California.

16. Dennett, M. W. *Birth Control Laws*, pp. 72-93. Frederick H. Hitchcock, New York, 1926.
17. Konikow, A. F. The doctor's dilemma in Massachusetts. *Birth Control Review* XV(1): 21-22, 1931.
18. Jack, C. C. In *Birth Control Review* II(3): 7-8, 1918.
19. Jack, C. C. Letter to Charles Birtwell, June 17, 1917. Ames Manuscripts, Sophia Smith Collection, Smith College Library, Northampton, Massachusetts.
20. Jack, C. C. Letter to Blanche Ames Ames, January 7, 1918. Ames Manuscripts, Sophia Smith Collection, Smith College Library, Northampton, Massachusetts.
21. Birth Control League of Massachusetts Records, Schlesinger Library, Radcliffe College, Cambridge, Massachusetts.
22. *Boston Post*, July 25, 1916. Quoted in The Birth Control League of Massachusetts, p. 21, by D. McCarrick Geig. Unpublished B.A. Thesis, Simmons College, 1973.
23. Birth Control and Public Policy, Decision of Judge Harry M. Fisher of the Circuit Court of Cook County, November 23, 1923. Illinois Birth Control League, 1924 (pamphlet).
24. Sanger, M. *Autobiography*, pp. 374, 402-408. W. W. Norton, New York, 1938.
25. Little, C. C. Letter to Robert L. Dickinson, October 28, 1925. Sanger Manuscripts, Library of Congress, Washington, D.C.
26. Pickens, D. K. *Eugenics and the Progressives*, p. 51. Vanderbilt University Press, Nashville, 1968.
27. Haller, M. *Eugenics: Hereditarian Attitudes in American Thought*, p. 174. Rutgers University, New Brunswick, N.J., 1963.
28. Popenoe, P. *The Conservation of the Family*, pp. 129-130. Williams and Wilkins, Baltimore, 1926.
29. Guyer, M. F. *Being Well-Born. An Introduction to Eugenics*, pp. 296-298. Bobbs-Merrill, Indianapolis, 1916.
30. Stoddard, L. *Revolt Against Civilization: The Menace of the Under Man*, p. 21. Scribners, New York, 1922.
31. Fourth Report, Committee on Selective Immigration, American Eugenics Society, June 30, 1928, p. 16. In Anita Newcomb McGee Manuscripts, Library of Congress, Washington, D.C.
32. Popenoe, P., and Johnson, R. H. *Applied Eugenics*, pp. 294-297. Macmillan, New York, 1918.
33. Lorimer, F., Winston, E., and Kiser, L. K. *Foundations of American Population Policy*, pp. 12-15. Harper and Brothers, New York, 1940.
34. Halford, S. H. Dysgenic tendencies of birth-control and of the feminist movement. In *Population and Birth Control*, p. 238, edited by Eden and Cedar Paul. Critic and Guide, New York, 1917.
35. Bergen, H. Eugenics and the social problem. *Birth Control Review* IV(4): 5-6, 15-17, 1920.
36. Paul, E. Eugenics and birth-control. In *Population and Birth Control*, p. 134, edited by Eden and Cedar Paul. Critic and Guide, New York, 1917.
37. Quessel, L. Race suicide in the United States. In *Population and Birth Control*, edited by Eden and Cedar Paul. Critic and Guide, New York, 1917.
38. Letter of December 20, 1865, from Elizabeth Stanton to Martha Wright. In *Elizabeth Cady Stanton as Revealed in Her Letters, Diary and Reminiscences*, edited by T. Stanton and H. Stanton Blatch. Harper and Brothers, New York, 1922.
39. Kraditor, A. *Ideas of the Woman Suffrage Movement 1890-1920*, Ch. 7. Columbia University Press, New York, 1965.
40. Sanger, M. Why not birth control clinics in America? *Birth Control Review* III(5): 10-11, 1919.
41. Sanger, M. *Woman and the New Race*, p. 34. Brentano's, New York, 1920.
42. Sanger, M. *The Pivot of Civilization*, pp. 177-178. Brentano's, New York, 1922.
43. Stenographic Record of the Proceedings of the First American Birth Control Conference, 1921, p. 24. American Birth Control League, New York, 1921.
44. The Necessity for Birth Control. Speech by Margaret Sanger in Oakland, California, December 19, 1928. Stenographic Record in Sanger Manuscripts, Library of Congress, Washington, D.C.
45. My Way to Peace. Speech by Margaret Sanger to New History Society, January 17, 1932. In Margaret Sanger Manuscripts, Smith College Library, Northampton, Massachusetts.
46. *Report, Fifth International Neo-Malthusian and Birth Control Conference*, edited by R. Pierpont. Heinemann, London, 1922.
47. Popenoe, P. In *Birth Control Review* I(3): 6, 1917.
48. Thompson, W. Race suicide in the United States. *Birth Control Review* IV(8): 9-10, IV(9): 9-10, IV(10): 10-11, IV(11): 14, 1920; V(1): 16, V(2): 9-12, V(3): 11-13, 1921.
49. Immigration and birth control (editorial). *Birth Control Review* VII(9): 219-220, 1923.
50. Winsor, M. The cost to the state of the socially unfit. *Birth Control Review* VII(9): 222-224, 1923.

51. Ellis, H. Review of Lothrop Stoddard's *The Rising Tide of Color Against White World Supremacy. Birth Control Review* IV(10): 14-16, 1920.
52. Little, C. C. Unnatural selection and its resulting obligations. *Birth Control Review* X(8): 243-244, 257, 1926.
53. Davis, K. B. *Factors in the Sex Life of Twenty-Two Hundred Women.* Harper and Brothers, New York, 1929.
54. Terman, L. *Psychological Factors in Marital Happiness.* McGraw-Hill, New York, 1938.
55. Hamilton, G. V. T. *A Research in Marriage.* A & C Boni, New York, 1929.
56. Robinson, C. H. *Seventy Birth Control Clinics.* Williams and Wilkins, Baltimore, 1930.
57. Jaffe, F.S., and Polgar, S. Family planning and public policy: Is the "Culture of Poverty" the new cop-out? In *Readings in Family Planning,* p. 169, edited by Donald V. McCalister, Victor Thiessen, and Margaret McDermott. C. V. Mosby, St. Louis, 1973.
58. Fairchild, H. P. Speech in Planned Parenthood Federation of America Manuscripts, p. 169. Sophia Smith Collection, Smith College Library, Northampton, Massachusetts.

CHAPTER 9

Medicine and Patriarchal Violence: The Social Construction of a "Private" Event

Evan Stark, Anne Flitcraft, and William Frazier

INTRODUCTION

By conservative estimate, between 3 and 4 million women are brutally beaten each year in the United States.[1] Some of these beatings are administered by strangers, occur in public, or remain unrecorded. And for probably fewer than 10 percent of

---

[1] Straus (1) estimates that 1.8 million women living in couples are beaten in the U.S. each year. But we found that almost half of the battered women in the emergency service sample were divorced or separated and this figure was confirmed in a community-based sample by Flynn (2). We can guess, therefore, that as many as 2 of the 6 million women in the U.S. who are separated or divorced, or who are married but whose spouses are absent, are at risk for battering. A similar figure can be derived from studies that show one-third to a half of all divorces may involve violence (3, 4), and that for a woman, once married, the risk of being battered falls only with widowhood (5).

these women, the beating is an isolated event speedily followed by either effective intervention or permanent estrangement from the aggressor. But women receive the vast majority of these beatings in their homes as part of an identifiable pattern of systematic and escalating abuse that often extends over their lifetime (6-17).

The fact that "wife-beating" is so frequently reported in the United States and England and yet remains widespread, systematic, and long-term, marks it as social and deliberate. Despite this, social service workers, researchers, victims, and even their attackers portray battering as a "private" event determined in the arena of family life either by such individual peculiarities as alcoholism, psychopathology, and "learned helplessness," or by the tensions inherent in family interaction (18-37). Of course, a complex of personal or interpersonal problems may characterize any given abusive incident. But the immediate problems and motives from which identical patterns of brutal subjugation arise are too varied to suggest an adequate explanation or solution to battering on any but the social realm (38-39).

Our primary objective in this paper is to illustrate the extent to which battering is broadly social in its construction, its dynamic, and its consequences, and to which, further, the picture of abuse as "private" or "peculiar" supports this social construction. By "social construction" we mean that the key determinants of battering—from its prevalence in a given population to the point in the life-cycle when it intensifies—are conceived largely outside the medical system, the family, and private life, amidst class and sexual struggles for the most fundamental resources in the society. Of course, as these struggles become embedded in the structures of the family and the medical system, they are shaped to meet the immediate needs of these institutions. On a more important level, however, they respond to increasing tensions between the needs of an expanding capitalist economy and the often contradictory pressures to sustain traditional patriarchal privileges. The thrust of our argument is that a strategy that neglects the social determinants of abuse can neither reduce nor prevent battering.

Three problems have guided our inquiry. First, how are individual instances of physical abuse shaped into the phenomenon we recognize as battering? Second, how is medicine (and, by extension, the other "helping" services) implicated in this process? And, finally, if medicine and other services help sustain violent families, what can this teach us about the overall constitution of patriarchy in this society?

In the first part of this article, we use visits to the emergency service and the medical histories of battered women to show that battering typically includes, in addition to multiple physical injuries, a pattern of self-abuse and of associated problems which emerge only after the first recorded instances of abuse. These problems appear to be the consequence of battering and can hardly be considered its cause. The sequence that leads from physical abuse through self-abuse to an escalation of physical abuse reflects the diminishing realm of options available to women as their abuse turns into battering. Indicative of this is the fact that in one study of domestic homicide, 80 percent of the cases had been preceded by 1 or more complaints of assault to the police and 50 percent by 5 calls or more (cited in 29).

An "index of suspicion" is used in the first section to contrast the actual prevalence of abuse in the emergency population with the cases physicians positively identify. But the index tells us little about what motivates physician bias or how medicine's collective response to abuse contributes to the emergence of what we call "a battering syndrome." As Cicourel argues persuasively, to properly read data we must gauge its meaning to its recorders and in the system that generates it (40). Thus, in the second section, we treat the medical record less as a scientific report of female brutalization than as a social product which can be examined archeologically to learn about its "producers" and the stages involved in its construction. This examination suggests that the emerging pattern of abuse derives as much from the individualistic bias of the medical paradigm and the structural constraints imposed on the physician's response to abuse by the medical system's need to control a persistent patient population as it does from the tragic encounter between a male aggressor and a female victim.

Cicourel's work, however valuable, is limited by his primary focus on the situational context. He misses the extent to which the recorder's behavior and the social system where he works are comprehensible—as specifically social behaviors—only in relation to larger class and sexual dynamics which constrain the medical system in its entirety. The ultimate meaning of the process by which a pathological syndrome is created in the guise of "treatment" lies in the reproduction of broadly enforced social divisions. Regardless of the personal reasons that lead physicians to abandon scientific logic as they approach health problems that defy classification within their individualist, pathophysiological model, the process of labelling directly contributes to the exploitation and oppression of patients elsewhere because of their race, sex, age, or class (32, 33, 41-43). Others have severely criticized the medical system for commodifying health delivery in response to pressure from a multi-million-dollar health industry and for enforcing "the patient role" as a dependent status that serves to support subservient relations more generally (44-50). But our focus is on how medicine *as* medicine, as a process of presumably scientific diagnosis, referral, and treatment, codetermines traditional sex and class hierarchies and contributes, despite contrary intentions among health providers, to the suppression of struggles to overcome these hierarchies.

In the third section, the limitations of current theoretical perspectives on battering are discussed and an alternative conceptualization is proposed. Both Straus' findings about the frequency with which women assault men and evidence that women widely report their abuse expose as fraudulent the stereotype of battered women as either "helpless," masochistic, or otherwise "sick" (1, 2, 16, 18, 20-26). Although some psychiatric researchers continue to justify a pharmaceutical approach to battering because, not surprisingly, the majority of victims are "depressed," most researchers adopt a cultural approach and trace women's tolerance of repeated abuse to norms establishing female dependence, passivity, and weakness (1, 3, 5, 6, 10, 20, 32-37). "Sexism" appears in the cultural approach though, not as a materially based consequence of ongoing struggle, but as a static dimension of a socialization process which trains and permits men to be aggressive and women to act as "objects." While allegedly shifting the emphasis from "the victim" to "the male-dominated system," like the psychological approach, the cultural view also accepts the premise that women's failure to act on their own behalf leads to battering. Here we take the opposite tack, arguing that it is the contradictory nature of women's status and their struggles to overcome these contradictions and resist their status that makes battering intelligible.

In the concluding sections, we suggest that medicine's contribution to battering is merely one instance of the general determination of male domination in the home from "outside." From the bourgeois standpoint, the current "crisis in the family" results either from its penetration by the market (with a consequent increase in narcissistic impersonality) or from the costly assumption of its traditional economic tasks (e.g. education and health care) by social services. But official attempts to at least maintain the shell of family life are predictable from the contradictory interests in female subordination expressed by business and government. For alongside "workfare" and "pro se divorce," policies designed to set aside the obstacles posed to efficient market behavior by traditional family commitments and pull women out of their traditional roles into low-wage services and marginal industry, other policies, e.g. the refusal to federally fund day care or abortion, appear to reaffirm women's traditional family role and maintain their dependence as reserve labor. When we add the declining empirical importance of the father-husband—last year, no adult male was present in the majority of low-income households in the U.S.—to the disappearance of family property as a material basis for patriarchal power in the home, it becomes obvious that outside intervention is needed to sustain female subordination in the household, even when violence is employed (51).

But if the family has always played an important economic role, its major work, the early socialization of children and the formation of personality, is "a labor of love" and never reducible to purely economic principles (52). Nor is the importance of this work diminished by its exclusive assignment to women. Indeed, several historians have argued that this distortion of roles stimulated an autonomous "women's sphere," an extended community of intimates in marked contrast to the emerging capitalist world where social connectedness among men appeared mainly in fetishistic forms (53-56). The demands made by this community tore the veil from the domestic imagery that linked women's biological and cultural identities and made it possible to reconceptualize the family as part of an extended community of love between equal subjects. It is in response to this unfolding possibility that traditional patriarchal relations are now imposed through means which turn the family into a veritable battlefield and provide the contemporary context within which battering (as well as rape, child abuse, and other forms of "family pathology") must be understood.

The disappearance of the family's traditional economic and social roles, the "decline of the patriarchy" as a specific familial form, contrasts markedly with the subjective and objective extension of male domination throughout every aspect of life in the U.S. We conclude by arguing that this seeming paradox is reconciled when we appreciate the extent to which the social services, broadly construed to include education, religion, and recreation as well as medicine, law, police, and welfare, function today as a reconstituted or extended patriarchy, defending the family form "by any means necessary," including violence, against both its internal contradictions and women's struggles.

Neither privacy, nor personal life, nor social connectedness remains in the millions of homes where women are systematically beaten. For this reason, "the violent family" provides us with a point of departure, what might be termed a boundary case, to see how the family is reproduced in the final instance, when one adult member tries to escape.

THE PILOT STUDY: ABUSE IN A MEDICAL SETTING

Emergency services in the United States are increasingly organized for high-technology interventions in extreme trauma and illness. To the poor, minorities, and large segments of the white working class, however, they remain the only available primary care facilities (57). This discrepancy is part of a broad power struggle over how scarce health resources should be used, a struggle that is further reflected in the tendency for emergency physicians to view minor, chronic, or social ills as "inappropriate" and to diagnostically fragment complex social ailments into a myriad of visible, apparently isolated, and relatively treatable symptoms. The pattern was apparent in Kempe's initial work on child abuse (58). Not only did physicians in the early 1960s fail to recognize familial assault as the etiology of children's medical problems but, on the contrary, they often turned to extensive medical workups in an attempt to discover blood and metabolic disorders which could explain an accumulating history of multiple bruises and fractures.

Although abused women who may hesitate to call on police or social workers for help will, nonetheless, use emergency services when they are seriously injured, they consistently report that physicians refuse to accept their claims of brutalization. For this reason, and because of Cicourel's argument about methods, accurate retrospective case identification depends upon reviewing recorded trauma incidents with a critical eye, considering not only recognized instances of domestic abuse but also other instances of assault and incidents where the recorded etiology cannot adequately explain the injury pattern (e.g. bilateral facial contusions from "walking into a door"). When the research began, little data were available to indicate to what extent battering was an ongoing process. Still, the legitimacy of including estimates of prevalence of women who were not identified on medical records as battered depended upon finding not only that many suspicious incidents appeared in the records of women who were injured by their husbands but also that these records would be substantially the same as those of women "assaulted, punched, or kicked" and those who allegedly "walked into doors."

Although this initial study was primarily designed to measure the extent of abuse in the emergency population, it became gradually clear that physician behavior played an important part in actually bringing the observed pattern of violence into existence.

Methods

Our goals were to measure the prevalence of abuse, to develop a sociomedical profile of its victims, and to evaluate medicine's response to 520 women who sought aid for injuries at a major urban emergency room during 1 month. Medical records were analyzed for 481 of these women (92.5 percent). These records included previous emergency visits, hospitalizations, clinic records, and social and psychiatric service notes. Each episode of injury was examined, some 1419 trauma events ranging in frequency from 1 to more than 20 per patient, and the women were subsequently classified according to the following criteria:

- *positives*: at least one injury was recorded as inflicted by a husband, boyfriend, or other male intimate;
- *probable*: at least one injury resulted from a "punch," "hit," "kick," "shot," or similar and deliberate assault by another person, but the relationship of assailant to victim was not recorded;
- *suggestive*: at least one injury was inadequately explained by the recorded medical history;
- *reasonable negative*: each injury in the medical record was adequately explained by the recorded etiology, including those recorded as sustained in "muggings" or "anonymous assaults."

Summary of Findings

Prevalence and Frequency. During the sample month, physicians identified 14 battered women (2.8 percent), although an additional 72 women (16 percent) had injuries we considered "probable" or "suggestive." However, from the full medical histories, almost 10 percent of the 481 women could be positively identified as battered at least once and an additional 15 percent had trauma histories pointing toward abuse (Table 1, Columns I and II).

It is difficult to make accurate statements concerning the relationship between racial and economic variables and battering from this emergency room sample, in large part because the geographical location of the emergency room in the midst of a poor and minority community ensures that most outpatient service utilization rates will be skewed (59). However, white and minority women and welfare and medically insured women are all significantly represented in the battered subset of this sample.

Of the more than 1400 injuries these women had ever brought to this hospital, physicians had identified 75 abusive incidents, although an additional 340 or 24 percent fell into the "probable" or "suggestive" categories of this methodology. But, since almost half of the "probable" and a quarter of the "suggestive" incidents appeared in the histories of women identified elsewhere as abused, it was clear that only the tendency to disaggregate social ailments prevented the emergence of battering as an ongoing process of repeated brutalization. Indeed, once an "index of suspicion"

Table 1

Description of battering risk groups (BRG)

BRG	I % of Women by Sample Visit N = 481	II % of Women by Trauma History N = 481	III % of Injuries N = 1419	IV Injuries per Woman	V Injuries per Year
Positive	2.8	9.6	22.5	6.35	.973
Probable	5.2	4.8	10.7	6.26	1.127
Suggestive	9.8	10.6	13.6	3.08	.822
Negative	82.2	75.0	53.2	1.83	.346

was applied to overcome physician blindness, almost half (46.8 percent) of all injuries ever brought to this hospital by these 481 women appeared to have been brought by battered women (Table 1, Column III).

The hypothesis that battering is ongoing is supported by the finding that "positives" were injured three times as frequently as nonbattered women (6.35 injuries/1.83 injuries). Note that while "probables" and "positives" have almost identical trauma histories, "suggestives" have similar rates of injury (.82 compared to 1.127 and .97 incidents per year) but only half as many injury episodes (Table 1, Columns IV and V). This may indicate that the "suggestive" category includes many women whose abusive relationships are just beginning.

In sum, where physicians saw 1 out of 35 of their patients as battered, a more accurate approximation is 1 in 4; where they acknowledged that 1 injury out of 20 resulted from domestic abuse, the actual figure approached 1 in 4. What they described as a rare occurrence was in reality an event of epidemic proportions.

Duration. Once it is shown that battering is widespread—approximately 10 times more frequent than physicians acknowledge—and that its victims have numerous injuries, we confront the popular impression that it results from an extended lover's quarrel, but that it is speedily resolved. If this were true, the number of sample women who are still being abused would be significantly lower than the number who had ever been beaten. But when we compare the women who had ever been abused (25 percent of the sample) to the number whose injuries during the sample month still suggested abuse (18 percent), we see that, at a maximum, no more than 28 percent of the cases have been resolved. Unfortunately, the more realistic estimate is far lower. For if we compare the overall prevalence (25 percent) with the incidence of violence suggestive of abuse during the last 5 years (23 percent) we can see a resolution rate of just 8 percent. Or, conversely, in all likelihood 92 percent of the women who have ever been in an abusive relationship are still subjected to violence.

Sex-specific Character of Abuse. The deliberate, sexual, and familial dimensions of abuse are reflected in the predominance of injuries to the face, chest, breast, and abdomen and by the high rate of violence during pregnancy. While we can assume that a pregnant woman is generally more likely to view any injury as an "emergency," battered women were 3 times more likely than nonbattered women to be pregnant when injured. Consequently, these women evidenced a significantly greater number of miscarriages. And, once the child was born, they were 10 times more likely than nonbattered women to report child abuse or to fear it. Perhaps the most surprising finding was that 50 percent of all rapes reported within the medical history of the sample population occurred to women at risk for battering. And in a follow-up study to determine the frequency of rape within an ongoing "intimate" relationship, Roper and Frazier (60) found that of the 174 rape victims who came to the emergency room during the previous 2 years, almost a third had documented histories of battering. In fact, of the rape victims over 30, 58 percent were battered women.

Self-abuse and Associated Problems. In addition to the serious physical injuries associated with battering, researchers have pointed to other psychosocial problems evidenced by victims of abuse (14). The question remains: Does battering primarily arise among women who suffer significant psychiatric disorders or, to the contrary, do these disorders evolve during the course of an abusive relationship and, indirectly, as a consequence of inadequate service intervention? Prior to the onset of abuse, with the single exception of alcoholism, there are no statistically significant differences between battered and nonbattered women in their rates of psychiatric disorders, mental health service utilization, or in the appearance of psychosocial "labels" in their medical records (Table 2).

However, there is no question from our findings that physical abuse is quickly followed by psychiatric disorders, self-abuse, and personal stress. As Table 3 indicates, 1 of every 4 battered women attempted suicide at least once; 1 in 7 abused alcohol; 1 in 10 abused drugs; and more than 1 in 3 were referred to emergency psychiatric services and the community mental health center, while 1 in 7 was eventually institutionalized at the state mental hospital. Again, in the vast majority of cases such problems emerge only *after* the first incident suggestive of abuse.

Table 2

Problem incidence and referrals of nonbattered women and of battered women prior to first recorded assault (per 100 women)

Problem/Referral	Nonbattered Women	Battered Women Before Assault
Suicide attempt	3	6
Drug abuse	1	2
Alcohol abuse	1	7*
Psychiatric emergency service	7	9
Community mental health center	3.6	4
State mental hospital	1	2
Psychosocial labels	2	4

*x^2 significant at < .001.

Table 3

Overall problem incidence and referrals of nonbattered and battered women (per 100 women)

Problem/Referral	Nonbattered Women	Battered Women
Suicide attempt	3	26*
Drug abuse	1	7*
Alcohol abuse	1	16*
Psychiatric emergency service	7	37*
Community mental health center	3.6	26*
State mental hospital	1	15*
Psychosocial labels	2	22*

*x^2 significant at < .001.

Patterns of Medical Response. The medical response to battering takes two forms in the emergency room. On the one hand, nearly 1 in 4 (24 percent) battered women receive minor tranquilizers or pain medications, while fewer than 1 in 10 (9 percent) non-battered women receive these prescriptions. This response is not simply a poor therapeutic choice given the previously presented evidence of the ongoing nature of domestic violence but a dangerous one as well, given the record of attempted suicides by victims of battering. On the other hand, medicine disposes of battering by characterizing it as a psychiatric problem for the victim. Psychiatric referrals follow nonbattering injuries only 4 percent of the time, while the largely unidentified victims of battering were referred 15 percent of the time to emergency psychiatric facilities, clinics, local community mental health centers, or the state mental hospital.

Beyond this, pseudopsychiatric labels in the medical record such as "patient with multiple vague medical complaints" or "multiple symptomatology with psychosomatic overlay" suggest the already noted tension between patient demand for help and medicine's frustration in the absence of overt physiological disorder. Of course, once such phrases are used to characterize a patient, it becomes even more difficult for her to get sympathetic, quality treatment.

From the standpoint of the emergency service, therefore, battering appears as a widespread and ongoing problem that includes a host of derivative psychosocial problems as well as repeated acts of physical injury and self-abuse. Since the pattern is invisible to medicine and emerges primarily only after the first apparent incident of abuse, and since repeated medical interventions are ineffective at best and at worst may contribute to the victim's diminishing options, the medical encounter must be carefully considered in an analysis of the evolving pattern of abuse.

MEDICINE CONSTRUCTS THE BATTERING SYNDROME

Jacoby (61) has argued that the search for a working model of "cure" to guide psychoanalytic practice in the post-World War I United States led the neo-Freudians to deliberately "forget" the radical insights of their master, particularly his uncompromising notions of sexuality. In medicine too, a kind of "social amnesia" has accompanied the combination of an individually oriented, physiology based therapeutics with the image of the healthy body as an efficient machine performing its assigned tasks in functional isolation from a determinant social universe (50, 62). In fact, Koch's proof of the germ theory upon which Flexnerian medicine is based gained popularity in 19th-century scientific circles only as part of the broader conservative reply to the political theories of illness-causation developed by Virchow and other radical epidemiologists (44, 63, 64). And the categories of post-Flexnerian medicine are neither less political nor more adequate today, when, with every alternative approach to sickness reduced to quackery, they are accepted unreflectively.

The aim of medical diagnosis is to aggregate immediate symptoms with the history of the symptoms and relevant physiological data (lab tests, x-rays, and physical findings) into preexisting "scientific" disease categories. These, in turn, suggest a particular therapeutic response in accord with recognized precepts of medical practice. The response typically completes a single process, particularly in the emergency service where any follow-up care is rare, and legitimates "the symptom" as the appropriate object and "the individual" as the appropriate limit of "the medical gaze" (62). On a broad historical plane, as has been shown elsewhere (64-67), medicine's "conquest of disease" depended on the prior control of the major infections by improvements in the diet and other living conditions. In the immediate treatment context, meanwhile, medicine's apparent "success," particularly against health problems with no clearly identifiable natural cause, rests on a general acceptance of its categorical assumptions about the basis of disease and the limits of intervention (50). Conversely, the suppression of alternative definitions of health and illness legitimates the assumption that medicine is the only appropriate intervention even where, as with most cancers, it fails to stem the course of a disease (67), or proves, as with "mental illness," no more effective than placebos or no intervention at all.

When medicine is faulted, it is for its technical limitations (68) and rarely because its limited appropriation of symptomatic variables excludes the social causes of ailments, hence any approach based on primary prevention. And, when billions are invested so medicine can upgrade the technical means it uses to control particular symptoms, its ideological focus on the anatomical individual is reproduced on an ever-wider scale.

The aggregation of symptoms at any given "presentation" constitutes "a medical event" and the aggregation of isolated events makes up "the medical history." In this framework, the symptoms are not read to illuminate a person's history, but the reverse. The social dimensions of the patient's experience, her history as she has lived it in the presence of the medical system, disappear behind a developing catalogue of prior symptoms and medical events which are continually reorganized in the doctor's mind, ostensibly to illuminate a discrete pathophysiological moment. The fact that the physician-patient contact is fraught with political meaning is reflected in the ideological content of seemingly objective conclusions and referrals.

The movement of the medical diagnosis from a focus on specific symptoms toward its outer boundary, the focus on "the individual," occurs only if the normal processes break down. The persistence of particular patients, the failure of well-tested therapies to control a given set of symptoms, the epidemic prevalence of particular symptoms in a given population, or the incongruity of symptoms and available physiological explanations, all create a "crisis of the cure" and force medicine to the limits of its perception. But even here the medical object is conceived not as a socially mediated being but as the fictional persona of 19th-century liberal propaganda, as the individual wholly in control of her situation, hence completely responsible for it (50, 69). Disease continues to be viewed as a natural process but one for which the patient is held accountable and for which she may even be punished with what consequences we will see momentarily.

Battered women pose enormous problems to medicine, not only because they are persistent and appear in such large numbers at the emergency service, but also because no apparent physiological event links one injury to another, or one presentation to the next. At first, their wounds are treated as legitimate medical problems. But as it becomes clear that neither the women, nor their injuries, on an aggregate, will respond to treatment, their problems are reaggregated as symptoms of particular social or psychopathologies, alcoholism or depression, for example. At this point the woman herself, rather than her assailant, appears as a legitimate object of medical control.

These diagnoses are a response to the problems the abused woman poses to the medical system and paradigm, not primarily to her physical complaints. The most common diagnoses, e.g. "alcoholic," "drug-abuser," "hysteric," "hypochondriac," "depressive," function as "labels" because they are often applied with no therapeutic intent and used widely to suppress the "inappropriate" demands for help of those victimized elsewhere (41).

The "label" explains the failure of the medical paradigm and the continued suffering of the abused woman in a way that is intelligible, even acceptable, to the physician. Meanwhile, in the process of salving the wounds of the medical system, strong, health-seeking women are transformed into apparently helpless objects available for brutalization by particular men, and, beyond this, for subordination under prevailing class and sexual divisions. The convergence of medical care and forms of suffering such as battering has little to do with individual physician behavior, however, even when it is clearly motivated by sexism. For in order to reaffirm its own peculiar brand of mystification, medicine as a whole must align its structure, procedures, and ideology with the overall structure of domination in bourgeois society.

In the final analysis, it is this alignment process, what might be termed "the socialization of medical perception," that marks the medical construction of battering as social and which we can observe, at various stages, in the medical histories of battered women. While the following discussion of stages is intended primarily to illustrate the objective character of medical intervention in battering, it also highlights actual moments in the evolving experience of abused women.

Stage I – The "Injury" Appears

When the battered woman first comes to the emergency service, her discrete individual injury is defined as the only appropriate object for medical care. The fact that the injury was caused by a "punch" is no more significant than that it resulted from a "fall" and, if the cause is recorded, there is no comment. The woman's history may be considered, but only if it can help resolve an apparent diagnostic dilemma. For instance, if the physician is confused by the coexistence of abdominal pain and a broken arm, he may ask, "Did he also hit you in the abdomen?" But if no incongruity arises from the physical evidence, there will be no question. This helps explain why only 1 of every 10 battered women who come to the emergency service is officially "recognized" (5). This statistic is an artifact and reflects neither the unwillingness of women to admit their abuse nor any mere underestimate of its actual incidence. Rather, it is constructed to reflect the number of pragmatic problems battering has posed to physicans constrained to analyze discrete, individual symptoms.

The limited repertoire of interventions at the physician's disposal bounds his perception of what is wrong with the woman. On the one hand, these strategic limits are imposed through the medical definition of the situation to displace any alternative interpretation of their situation women often bring with them to the emergency service. On the other hand, lacking a coherent physiological explanation and prevented by a host of factors from accepting the patient's explanation, particularly when it points to social factors such as unemployment as the cause, the physician records the early consequences of abuse as another "accident." Thus, from the first encounter with the patient, under seemingly "normal" conditions, the reconstruction of her situation begins.

Even *within* the individualized diagnosis, it is possible to discover the sexual origins of physical abuse and its link to women's status. These "accident" victims are more likely to have facial injuries and 13 times more likely than other victims of accidents who came to the emergency service to have been injured in the breast, chest, or abdomen (5). But the sex-familial specificity of battering is perhaps best revealed by the shocking frequency with which abuse is administered to women during pregnancy. Eleven of the 44 "violent families" Gelles studied (70) reported beatings during pregnancy. In another small sample, half the victims of abuse indicated they had been assaulted while pregnant (26). And Flitcraft (5) found that battered women were 3 times as likely as controls to have been pregnant when injured.

Then, too, medicine should be able to aggregate the perpetrators of injuries in the same way epidemiological methods are used to track down the chemical origins of a cancer or the carrier of typhus. Of the women whose battering is recorded, notes also reveal that 54 percent are beaten by their husbands, 34 percent by boyfriends, and the remainder by sons or relatives. Nor does the family lose its clinical significance as the source of injury simply because it has been legally dissolved. Indeed, divorced or separated women risk battering as much as married women and, once married, the risk of abuse falls significantly only for the widowed (2, 5). In an independent sample of battered women in the same emergency population studied by Flitcraft, two-thirds of the victims were divorced or separated (26).

Five cases of leukemia in a single high school make national headlines. A single recorded death from "swine flu" stimulates a campaign costing hundreds of millions to identify and control the virus. The typhus victim and carrier *are* identified. But the battered woman and her attacker are not, although battering accounts for up to half the serious injuries women bring to the emergency service, and although the procedures used to get this reading of the medical record are elementary, even with the prevailing ahistoric, individualized, and symptomatic orientation.

Just when battering might emerge from the multiplying and discrete "accidents" women "present" before medicine's eyes, "something else" comes to mind instead.

Stage II – From Injury to "Self-Abuse"

We have argued that the psychosocial problems that appear in association with physical abuse follow the initial assault and its presentation. Here, what concerns us is not the actual sequence of these problems but the sequence in which they appear to medicine, that is, their existence as stages in the organization of medical perception. Insofar as the medical definition of her situation impacts on the abused woman's self-perception, and, more importantly, on her access to resources she might otherwise use to get out of danger, it determines the overall organization of her "disease" as well.

Of course, the symptomatic treatment offered to victims of domestic assault does nothing to prevent subsequent injury. Intervention may have been more effective in the past. From 1900 through the 1920s, for example, major cities employed women police officers with social work training to help find emergency housing for battered women (71). And in the emergency service we are studying, before the widespread use of antidepressants in the 1950s, social work referrals may have significantly curtailed the course of abuse. Today, however, the battered woman returns again and again to the emergency service. At first, her visits are recognized simply by recording her repeated trauma. Gradually, however, the accumulation of injuries is supplemented by physician notes about "vague medical complaints." And, finally, a complex of problems is recognized, including "trouble with neighbors," alcoholism, drug abuse, attempted suicide, depression, "fear of child abuse," and a variety of alleged mental illnesses.

By recording the woman's secondary problems, medicine in effect acknowledges what the patient has recognized from the start, namely that therapy designed only to provide symptomatic relief to emergency complaints is wholly ineffective against her "condition." Until now, the woman has suffered the burden of symptomatic treatment in isolation. Her persistence, however, reflected on the medical record by the aggregation of incongruous injuries presented to the emergency service, forces the medical system to assume "the failure of the cure" and to recognize that the collection of trauma has been borne by a particular woman.

To the individual physician, patient persistence presents a problem in "cooperation," not simply in diagnosis and response. To the medical system persistence guarantees steady income but it also poses problems in controlling "demand." Physician and hospital interests now converge: from the relative standpoints of the medical paradigm and the hospital's flow-charts, the solution to the problems the patient *has* suddenly appears to lie in the problem the patient *is*. The secondary problems the abused woman has developed in the course of her "treatment" provide medicine with labels they can use to "organize" a history of otherwise unrelated "accidents." She is, after all, a drug abuser, or an alcoholic, or she is suffering from one of a myriad of such "female disorders" as depression, hysteria, hypochondrias, etc. And this explains not only why she has had so many injuries but also why she occasionally appears to have had "fights" or why she has such a poor self-image. In other words, she is hurt because this is what hapens when persons abuse drugs or alcohol, or are emotionally unstable. The key to understanding the attractiveness of the label to medicine is that, by subjecting the patient to hospital control within the classic categorical limits of the medical paradigm, it solves two problems at once. Even if the actual source of the patient's repeated injuries becomes unavoidable, her "battering" is only acknowledged as a tragic but inevitable consequence of her "more basic" problem with drugs or emotional control. Before assessing the full impact this process has on the abused woman, it must be described in more detail.

Ironically, even as the medical system recognizes that the woman is a unique person, it turns her volitional capacity into an instrument used to control, not cure her. To paraphrase Esterson and Laing (72, 73), the process by which she was injured is described within a field over which she is presumed to have decision-making responsibility, as if it resulted from her deliberate *praxis*. But, in the same breath, her praxis is defined as pathological, as a "weakness" that must be treated, suppressed, or otherwise removed. In all likelihood this definition of her praxis is shared by her brutal husband or boyfriend as well. Her persistence leads to her recognition as a person, not simply as a complex of incongruous symptoms; but her personhood is acknowledged as itself symptomatic of a more profound disorder.

It is impossible, in our opinion, to separate the "natural" etiology of physical abuse in personal or family pathology from etiological factors created as the result of institutional neglect and intervention. It is sufficient to recognize that soon after her initial report of abuse, the patient develops other "symptoms" associated with her battering but separable from it, from the standpoint of the medical system at least, in both time and space. These symptoms may actually result from prior medical attempts to control the woman's complaints with classic psychiatric methods (e.g. she may "abuse" her antidepressants); they may involve headaches or other suffering directly attendant upon repeated beatings, or they may reflect the isolation that leads victims of institutional and family abuse to turn anger inwards that might otherwise be directed at assailants and "helpers." Whatever the source or actual time sequence, the appearance of "self-destructive" behavior alongside the emotional and physical effects of abuse permits the physician to integrate the woman's demand to be seen as a whole person and his own desire to reestablish clinical control within his individ- ualistic bias. Whereas for the woman, the symptom of sociopathology signals entrap- ment within a predictable syndrome associated with "battering," for the physician, it offers a "solution," a cognitive and therapeutic strategy for encompassing otherwise unintelligible experience.

Medicine's contribution to these secondary disorders cannot be lightly dismissed. Although physicians rarely record "battering" as the source of a woman's injuries, nevertheless, they do respond differently to the victims of physical abuse than to other "accident" victims. For instance, victims of abuse are more likely to leave the emergency service with a prescription for pain medication and/or minor tranquilizers *in spite* of the fact that such medication may be contraindicated by the head and abdominal injuries prevalent among these patients. Only 1 in 10 of the nonbattered accident victims receives these prescriptions, but 1 in 4 of the women we found to be battered did. In a British sample of 100 battered women, 71 had received antidepres- sant medication (14). And another study recommends such medication for 80 percent of abused women (26). In addition, despite the central injuries battered women suffered, physicians were less likely to follow them clinically. In short, even where battering was not officially recognized, physicians made a collective (if inexplicit) diagnosis which not only selected abused women from the general patient population but treated them in ways which differ from the standard pattern of good medical practice.

The ideological tendency toward control inherent in the shift of the diagnostic focus from "the symptom" to the individual's sociopathology is actualized through patterns of labeling and psychiatric referral. As the depth of the family crisis generates "accidents" at rates which overwhelm the piecemeal therapeutic response, physicians draw from their arsenal of cultural labels those which permit them to treat the victim of abuse as a stereotypic female. At the time of injury, abused women are referred to psychiatric staff 5 times more frequently than victims of "accidental" trauma. These women, who present with frequent headaches, bowel disorders, painful inter- course, and muscle pains, but whose x-rays and lab tests are normal, are labelled "neurotic," "hysteric," "hypochondriac" or "a well-known patient with multiple vague complaints." One nonbattered woman in 50 leaves with one of these labels; 1 battered woman in 4 does, and is given tranquilizers, sleeping medication, or further psychiatric care (5). The epidemiological reflection of these labels is the appearance of "characteristic urban female disorders," the "obvious" prevalence of which helps justify expanded funding for the medical system that does the labeling.

Stage III — From Self-Abuse to Battering

Whatever physicians intend these therapies to accomplish, their general consequence is to cool the abused woman out, to reduce her capacity to understand, adequately respond to, or to resolve her crisis by leaving the violent home or by struggling through to autonomy against the hurt inflicted by a malevolent other. If the woman's repeated efforts to get help or, failing that, to "escape" from the most painful aspects of her situation through self-abuse, are defined as her primary problem, the "cure" typically involves the reimposition of traditional female role behavior and, more often than not, within the same male-supremacist context in which she is being beaten.

Among the primarily female patients with whom she is now categorized, the woman's price of cure is a prior admission of total dependence. Even as the medication helps the woman "forget" her abuse as a political-ethical issue, it reminds her daily that she cannot survive "on her own." Legally, too, being labelled mentally ill or alcoholic ensures that she must depend on the good will of the "helper" in such future attempts at independence as working outside the home or gaining custody of her children. The woman's isolation in the treatment context aggravates the isolation that may have driven her to self-abuse in the first place and generates the very symptoms alleged by her label. The abused woman continues to talk to herself. Only now, she believes that what she is saying is foolish.

Our research is not sufficiently advanced to describe the exact interaction between medical labelling and the high incidence of drug abuse, suicide, rape, child abuse, or actual mental breakdown among abused women. What is clear, however, is that applying the label and its associated therapy both gives the woman an added incentive to escape from her situation (including now her relation to the medical system) and reduces her capacity to do so realistically. The abused woman is often labelled at the height of her vulnerability, during a particularly severe crisis, for instance, when the signs of her outward collapse readily suggest the inner illogic or pathological determinancy implied by the label. Because of this, the label is far more than a simple misrepresentation of her existential condition and may easily be read as an alternative interpretation of her entire experience as a woman. Now, she as well as the physician may perceive her life with an abusive male as another symptom of her dependency and helplessness. Under the sway of this interpretation, whatever courage she has mustered to survive her beatings, whatever integrity she hoped to salvage by "making a bad relationship work" or even by helping someone she once loved solve *his* problem, is lost and she is urged to accept the idea that it is she who is "sick," perhaps even requiring *his* help. In this light, the suicide attempts of nearly 1 battered woman in 3, often with the antidepressants they have been given to "help them cope," can be read as acts of autonomy, as expressions of what Marcuse calls "the Great Refusal" to choose between equally pathological alternatives, objectification at the hands of a violent other, or self-alienation within an allegedly benign medical definition. The final irony is that what is often a last desperate act of existential responsibility, a refusal to live sanely in an intolerable milieu, is recorded by medicine to confirm its diagnosis of pathology and to justify subjecting the woman to even further degradation (5, 74, 75).

In addition to clinically replicating the means and determinants of isolation and self-abuse, medicine now recognizes battering as part of a "syndrome" to which it gives a distinct materialist content and social form. If medical ideology helps create an actual set of sociopathic symptoms, medicine's response to these symptoms, its "cure," is to reimpose "women's work" and to reconstitute the family as the setting within which the abused woman must be treated.

Battered women are typically referred to "de-tox" programs, drug dependence units, mental health clinics or mental hospitals, and to a variety of counselling agencies, all of which typically presume their clients have been led to "deviance" by an inability (or "refusal") to accept and perform the work normally associated with their sex-role assignments. In one sense, this analysis is accurate since, as the Dobashes (76) and others suggest, domestic violence occurs most frequently in arguments about child care, sex, housework, and money. At the state mental hospital to which 1 battered woman in 8 is eventually committed, female stereotypes are enforced with a vengeance. Here release is often conditional upon a willingness to perform efficient housework routinely ("won't dearie clean her room today?") and to "look pretty" (77). In addition to reaffirming the idea that doing housework for men without wages is "normal" and should not create conflicts, even when the housework is added to marginal labor in factories, the negative experience of institutionalization permanently hangs in the memory as the alternative to "making things work" (78).

The repressive aspects of referral to a case worker or to agency counseling are less dramatic but may be no less damaging. Abuse is rarely selected as the focus of intervention (16), even when batterers seek help along with their victims. Instead, physical abuse appears amidst a myriad of problems which are not only as damaging as physical violence, but far easier to treat with traditional therapeutic means. Before long, from the morass of personal and interpersonal disorders described by "the client," the case worker sees what she has been taught to expect from the beginning, the "multi-problem family." Not only are women beaten because they drink. More broadly, both alcoholism and violence are defined as inextricable parts of a peculiar family constellation characteristic of many low-income milieus (25, 27, 79). The family is not the battered woman's problem. To the contrary, she is a problem for it to handle.

The maintenance of the multi-problem family is viewed, almost universally, as the appropriate goal of social work intervention. Although social reformers have identified family reconciliation as an economical alternative to making women and children wards of the state since at least the 1890s (80, 81), in fact, of course, by reinforcing families within which there is ongoing abuse, the permanent dependence of women and children on agency support is guaranteed. Now, a vicious cycle is complete. Every new and serious incident of violence leads the "helper" to an unresolved secondary problem; each new label calls for a reinvigorated effort to stabilize families which would otherwise be torn apart by internal contradictions; and, the new combination, family/agency, accepts the woman's abuse as an unfortunate, but necessary aspect of "working" together. All family members, including the victims of abuse, may define violence as a natural part of their collective identity. The woman, locked irretrievably into "the violent family," is no longer abused only occasionally. She now is regularly and systematically battered.

If the general form of "treatment" is family maintenance, the substance of therapy revolves around submissiveness as an essential aspect of female health. Mounting evidence suggests that, throughout the 19th century, batterers were periodically singled out by vigilante groups, including the Klan, as particularly noxious "scoundrels." Even the law, however, readily distinguished "the gentle, fragile, and submissive" woman whose abuse earned her a divorce, for example, from "the amazon," the woman who acted "disobediently," who "countered violence with violence" or who, in the words of one judge, "chooses to unsex herself and forget she is a female" (82). For such women, there was no protection. Criteria for appropriate female behavior have changed since the 19th century, but the basic principles of patriarchal dominance are still reflected in therapeutic models. Thus, although batterers are far more frequently unfaithful to their wives than the reverse (22), a recent article on battering in the *British Journal of Psychiatry* concluded, "most abused wives were unfaithful and deserved to be beaten" (83). Others cite the growth of the woman's movement as a prime cause of battering and frankly suggest the reestablishment of a patriarchal status quo to eliminate abuse (22). In another study, a group of women who chose to fight their husbands physically and neither to leave them nor to call for agency help were labelled "immature" and "impulsive" (84). The classic justification for female role maintenance in the context of family therapy has been offered by Parsons, for whom "the sick role" is readily intelligible only as an escape from social or family "responsibilities." Says Parsons,

> It is easy to see . . . how the wife-mother, for example, might choose the sick role as an institutionalized way out of her heavy "human relations management" responsibilities in the family; or how she might seize upon illness as a *compulsively feministic* way of reacting to her exclusion from the life open to a man (quoted in 85, p. 17) [italics in original].

What is being posited by Parsons is nothing more than what medicine has been saying to the abused woman all along—namely, that resistance to subordination is "sick," not subordination itself.

TOWARD A THEORY OF SOCIAL CAUSATION

Current Theoretical Approaches

Rarely do physicians record that patients injured during "a fall" are any different than patients whose trauma resulted from physical abuse. And yet, in each encounter, over a lifetime, and on an aggregate basis, abused women *are* treated differently. To respond to the clinical dilemmas abuse poses to medicine, individual physicians draw on diagnostic, referral, and treatment strategies which extend a woman's suffering and mystify its cause. However, the fact that this process meets medicine's need to reaffirm control over persistent patients and otherwise incomprehensible injuries does not adequately explain either the substance of the medical response, the use of labels to reinforce female stereotypes, or its consequence, the constitution of a "battering syndrome."

By referring to a "syndrome," we only mean that from the vantage of medicine battering appears as a unitary phenomenon whose individual components are interdependent and wherein the logic of interdependence can be specified (86). This does not imply, of course, that immanent biological, or even psychosocial, principles account for battering, although they may explain isolated incidents of abuse. To the contrary, behind the construction of the violent family as a relatively stable historical formation we have discovered a social logic which now illuminates medicine's otherwise illogical case-by-case response to physical abuse. If the abused woman's problem is actually heightened by the clinical response so that her dependence on "helpers" becomes inevitable, the specific substance of this intervention, the reconstitution of her family, reproduces and extends an untenable clinical situation which is resolved only by the gradual substitution of patriarchal for medical logic. And, although the structural alignment of medicine and the patriarchy is only actualized over time, in the unfolding interaction between particular women and particular helpers, the patriarchal spectre is present in the very first encounter.

But if patriarchal logic overdetermines the medical response to abuse, neither medicine nor the family alone or even in combination control the resources required to organize so widely destructive an event as battering. Attempts by "exchange theory" and "victimology" to paint a unified picture of battering by aggregating familial and personality characteristics into portraits of "typical" victim-participants have been largely unrewarding (19, 25, 26, 84, 87). The actual variety of abused women is simply too great to fit the profile that emerges from personality research of the victim as helpless, ineffectual, and masochistic (20, 24, 35-37, 84). Meanwhile, the "typical" batterer seems to be an inarticulate, frustrated man, unhappy with his work, economically insecure, and easily angered, who resents his children, abuses alcohol, and was severely disciplined as a child. In short, he is a parody of the American male, that peculiar combination of depersonalized artifact and pathetic, if deeply felt, reality whose overwhelming needfulness and frustration are reproduced at work and on the market (8, 14, 21-23, 25, 84, 88).

Aside from the methodological problems that make attempts to generalize from discrete data suspect, the incredibly high statistical incidence in the general population of problems associated with abuse, such as divorce, alcoholism, drug addiction, depression, child abuse, and so forth, suggests that what researchers are calling "the violent family" is really the American family as such, not an aberrant subtype. Or, put more critically, although researchers often claim they will reach a general explanation by aggregating individual cases and proximate causes of abuse, the ideological thrust of their work is often to disaggregate normative experiences in ways that make them even less susceptible to explanation, management, or change. Worse, as the emerging stereotypes of abused women as powerless victims and of batterers as multi-problem deviants are incorporated into the logic of kitsch melodrama on the mass media, a pervasive sense of estrangement results. Victim and batterer see themselves in the projected imagery, but as isolates and grotesques, not as persons for whom recognition is a step toward a collective solution.

Recent evidence (1, 30, 31) indicates that, although women are the prime targets of domestic beatings, women also attack and kill men almost as frequently as they are attacked and killed. So, for example, in the only national survey of family violence to date, Straus (1) reports that the overall incidence rate of domestic violence by women is 11.6 percent, within a percentage point of the overall male incidence rate of 12.1 percent, and the median frequency with which "violent women" annually attack men at home (3.0 percent) is higher than the frequency with which abusive men assault their wives or girlfriends (2.5 percent). And yet, "battered men" rarely show up in police or medical records. In a survey of all police cases reported in Edinburgh in 1974 involving domestic violence, the Dobashes (6) found that a mere 3.6 percent of cases concerned women who attacked men while 94 percent (841 of 873 cases) involved "wife-beaters."

While the discrepancy between Straus' record of abused men and their invisibility on social agency reports may result from the stigma attached to male "weakness" or from inadequate identification techniques, we suspect that it reflects two quite different experiences: the private nature of family fights (in which women may clearly be as aggressive as men), and the social character of battering created when male aggression in the home is given implicit or explicit support from "outside." The broad enforcement of female subjugation distinguishes battering from fighting, causes women to show up at helping sites far more frequently than men, and generates the almost paralyzing terror and overvaluation of male power typical of many female victims (6, 17, 38). And whereas fighting may occur frequently without destroying the extended relations of family, community, or cultural life, "battering" appears only when persons have been forcibly isolated from potentially supportive kin and peer relations and virtually locked into family situations where their objectification and continued punishment are inevitable. Isolated instances of physical abuse are transformed into the escalating pattern we recognize in battering because the abused woman cannot escape even if she wants to and she cannot because her situation—unlike the man's—is mediated by the enforcement of a dependent status that is reproduced throughout the social totality. It is the reimposition of this status after women are hit, or hit back, and often in the context of repeated "helping" encounters that seems to determine that women, not the men with whom they are fighting, will be "battered" (39).

More fruitful than the attempts to reduce battering to personality or family dynamics has been the identification of broad social factors to which abuse is tied. Since domestic abuse accounts for a consistently high percentage of all serious assaults (29, 31, 89, 90), the criminal assault rate can serve as a proxy variable for battering. When this is done, battering can be linked to the business cycle (29, 91), to class and occupational situations (79, 92-99), to cultural or national differences (34, 97, 100-102), to race (5, 101, 103), and to stages in the life-cycle (29, 88). But even here, conclusions are often contradictory.

Brenner and others (8, 104) think the frustration unemployed and underemployed men experience in the job market explains high assault and homicide rates. Using much the same data, however, Eyer (91) and Henry and Short (103) identify violence against others with the peak in the business cycle and attribute this correlation to the relative stress in a highly competitive, expansive labor market. Studies linking battering to class show that there is a higher incidence of violence among working-class than among middle-class individuals and families (105); that class (income and occupation) is a more important predictor of violence than race (93); and that the "occupational environment," not wage levels alone, contributes to probable abuse (94). But other studies show that as much abuse is reported in wealthy as in poor communities (5, 106); that middle-class and professional men are frequent batterers

(20, 107, 108), and that there is little difference in the use of force among working-
and middle class-parents (109). Nor is it easy to weigh these results since methodological bias in class analyses works in both directions. So, while Straus rationalizes his
failure to discover a violent pattern among the working-class parents he studies by
arguing that, since they have children in college, their socialization "anticipated"
upward mobility (109), anecdotal material in the popular media shows "it can happen
to anyone," like romance or success (35, 99, 110). In an attempt to pinpoint the
rationality of physical force, Goode (111) argues that battering results when men
convert the superior economic resources they command outside the home into the
privilege of beating their wives to resolve domestic disputes. And Lachman (29)
argues that domestic violence peaks at the point in the life-cycle when economic
pressure and family pressures coincide, for example after the birth of a second child.
But when the market model is applied to family affairs, important questions are left
unanswered. For instance, why is sex, rather than ability, a key to economic power
in liberal societies? And exactly what do men "win" when they beat their wives?
In fact, it is the existence of the family as a sphere "outside" the purely economic
world of work and consumption that partially explains the persistence of patriarchal
privilege in the home. Finally, the appearance of battering as a public problem at the
present, when female economic power relative to male power seems to be increasing,
suggests that at best "the resource theory" is static.

Adding a cultural dimension to these economic explanations fails to account for
contradictory evidence, but it does point toward the importance of subjective as well
as objective factors in any adequate analysis. Though women's work is certainly as
degrading as men's, violence may be peculiar to the felt ineffectualness men suffer
in this society as they vainly try to fulfil male roles on or off the job (8, 95). By pro-
jecting images of manhood that are always beyond reach, the mass media encourage
the internalization of role models that lead men to work harder and, simultaneously,
to blame their inevitable failure on "others," including women, who appear in the
background of ads as part of the general world of objects. Indeed, the "morbid
jealousy" that may lead men to beat their wives often seems to contain a fetishistic
dimension. On numerous medical records the victim appears to have been kicked
repeatedly like a broken TV, a commodity in which a large emotional investment has
been made but which now symbolizes the world of "false promises" (112). When
men blame women for not being their perfect things ("*my* woman") and for failing
to return to them through love or sex their own alienated subjectivity (e.g. the self-
esteem appropriated at work), battering can be traced to yet another dimension of
the mysterious process Marx called "the fetishism of commodities" (113).

Violence among the poor has been tied to cultural values which lead low-income
persons, in pursuit of immediate gratification, to strike out impulsively even against
kin (114, 115). And others argue that for poor and working Americans "a marriage
license is a hitting license" and battering simply a normative means of settling disputes
(33). In the pilot study, however, Flitcraft (5) found that the poorest women in the
emergency service sample exhibited patterns of deviance and self-abuse generally
identified with the "culture of poverty" only after the first recorded incident of
battering, possibly as a result of their isolation from cultural supports, including
potentially supportive peer and kin networks. Conversely, battering appeared amidst

an already established pattern of social problems mainly among the more affluent patients. Then, too, as Fanon (101) has argued, many so-called "deviant" behaviors can best be understood as ways of resisting poverty, not as its result.

The most common cultural explanation of battering, that "violence is as American as apple pie," is no explanation at all. Not only does the argument miss the key fact about violence in modern societies, namely that it is punished under some conditions and positively sanctioned, even organized, under others, but it conceals both the varied political substance of violence, e.g. the sex-specific dynamic of battering, and the different uses to which it is put in different periods. Moreover, even in the case of battering, what medicine encourages is not violence as such but obedience to hierarchical relations. To be sure, these relations take their meaning from given material circumstances. Thus, the realization of male power depends on the actual and direct appropriation of women's labor, i.e. housework, sexuality, child care, etc. But violence is necessary only when this appropriation is threatened in particular families or on a broad social plane.

Social science first recognized battering in the 1960s, after a growing feminist movement called attention to misogyny embodied in the ritual abuse of women (84, 100-116). The feminists typically focused on "sexism" as the cultural attribute which unified women's experience of oppression and otherwise scattered assessments of male domination in the family, economy, and service sector. According to this view, the sexual divisions of labor and opportunity, like women's subordination at home, were mere objectifications and rationalizations of a male chauvinism that appeared sometimes learned, sometimes almost innate. Physically more powerful than women, men are trained to solve their problems forcibly, while women passively accept their status as male property. To this extent battering is the domestic counterpart to rape, a reminder of the privileges seemingly given to men by Nature, the political imperative behind the "normal" inequality (8, 35, 99, 108, 117, 118).

The acceptance of wife-beating in biblical and medieval times and in 19th-century Europe highlights the continuity of female oppression and the inadequacy of approaches to abuse which neglect its persistence or downplay struggles about domesticity. Still, though force may always have been used to guarantee female dependence, to avoid what Juliett Mitchell calls "simplistic materialism" (quoted in 119), this truth must be specified historically in ways that permit us to chart its changing meaning under different conditions and the appropriateness of different strategies of resistance. Contrasts like the one drawn by 19th-century feminist Frances Power Cobbe between "the kicking districts" of working-class Liverpool and the relatively "mild" beatings administered to London women suggests that complex social factors may determine whether and in what combination physical, ideological, political, or economic force will be used to control women and to what particular end (9). Because the forcefulness of the sexist critique derives from reducing the range of variation within and between societies in order to universalize gender identity, it obscures this complex determination, including the determinants of sexism itself. The consequence is that sexism seems as immutable a part of the social fabric as "poverty," for instance, too deeply embedded in character to respond to more than personal or temporary remedies. Beyond this, because feminists often equate society-as-a-whole with "patriarchy," they miss what we think are often decisive tensions between specific patriarchal forms and the political economy in which they are embedded. Conversely, by using familial power relations to analyze overall patterns of domination, the argument can mistake as progressive shifts in family roles such as women's "freedom" to do wage work outside the household, which may prove as detrimental to women as male chauvinism.

These criticisms of a certain feminist position are particularly important for an understanding of battering. Preliminary research indicates that abuse occurs most often when women refuse their work at home—cleaning, cooking, or child care, refuse sex, or demand money, not when they are passive (39, 76). In addition, battering escalates as a function of increased tension between the economic demands made on women and their family roles (29, 88). In each of three modern periods when battering has been widely noted and juridically controlled—during the 1830s and 40s, in the late 19th century, and in the 1960s and 70s—we find an expansion of business dependent, in part, upon large numbers of new female workers, effecting a major shift in family power. And, concurrently, we find important political expressions of women's awakening consciousness (54-56, 120-122). Within families during these periods, men use violence primarily to defend traditional prerogatives since subordination no longer appears "natural" to women earning an independent wage. Complaints about the changes wrought by factory work among previously domesticated Lowell mill girls are frequent in antebellum reform literature. And even Engels, sounding like a bourgeois moralist, reports among Manchester operatives, an "incapacity as housekeepers, neglect of home and children, indifference, actual dislike of family life, and demoralization" (quoted in 123).

Legal control of abuse may reflect business interest in protecting a new source of profits as well as the power of working women to influence legislation. Although individual men can still employ violence successfully to isolate women from popular social currents and to actually intensify housework alongside wage work, in modern societies the tendency to treat women as "private property" is always contested by women themselves as well as by the economic interest in women as laborers "free" to sell their labor power to the highest bidder. In the contemporary U.S., finally, the impact of economic change on family violence is reflected in the increase of rape and assault by younger males (124), the frequency of abuse where women have higher occupational status than their mates (10), and the importance of money to distinguish women who escape abuse from women who do not (7, 20).

Patriarchy versus Capitalism

In part, the contradictory conclusions about abuse reflect the methodological problems confronting researchers with little conception of how personality and family are socially formed. But the persistence of ambiguity even when battering is studied in a cultural or economic milieu suggests the findings may reveal an important truth about the reality itself, namely, that at the level of personality structure, family interaction, or attitude formation, battering is a multidimensional phenomenon that can be traced to diverse, perhaps even contradictory influences. Battering takes on a unitary appearance only insofar as the various layers at which it is constructed are themselves organized around a common interest. And the task of organization is typically assumed by the helping services.

Thus far, in our attempt to understand why medicine responds to abuse in the ways that it does, two layers of social construction have been roughly identified, the patriarchal or familial, and the economic. The immanent determination of violence in the family may derive from perceived threats posed to the exercise of male privilege or, put into materialist terms, from threats to the continued appropriation by particular males of women's work at home. These threats may originate from sources as various as male jealousy or women's refusal to make love or do housework during pregnancy. But when the economy in which the family is embedded simultaneously undermines the economic basis of family autonomy (e.g. household production) and requires and preferentially rewards female labor outside the home, the threat to male power in the home is constituted on a broad social plane. And it is precisely this tendency that both characterizes the expansive phase of capitalist development and defines its "revolutionary" impact on women and the family in contrast to all previous modes (85, 119, 123, 125, 126). In this context, whatever its roots in individual pathology or family dynamics, on a social plane, domestic violence now assumes an apparently contradictory character which reflects the opposing social purposes to which it is put. By sustaining female subordination and forcing women to continue their domestic duties despite their new independence on the labor market, abuse keeps otherwise obsolete "private" relations from being reduced to pure economic exchange. At the same time, however, abuse reflects the family's penetration by the market and the resulting competitive antagonism between persons whose creative powers, including their power to love, have meaning primarily as commodities put up for sale. Thus, the same man who at one moment may jealously covet his wife as if she were unique and irreplaceable, may beat her in the next instant as if she were a mere commodity, i.e. no different than any other woman and entirely disposable.

Of course, if domestic violence could contain the disruptions occasioned in the family by economic change associated with capitalist growth, medicine's role or the role of the social services in battering would be unintelligible. In fact, the assistance social services give the patriarchal family is required by its eroding autonomy and the corresponding political organization of women, developments whose importance can only be noted here.

Since the dawn of industrial capitalism, despite major ideological efforts in the opposite direction, both the father's power to command and the family's power of social constitution have been repeatedly compromised by at least these simultaneous processes: the dissolution of household production (the material basis for patriarchal command and family autonomy); the assumption of socialization by the state (hence the disappearance of the family's key "private" function); and the reconstitution of the family's internal life as a function of the marketing and reproductive needs of business (127-129). Alongside such oft-noted consequences of these factors as rising divorce and desertion rates (85, 130), declines in the birth rate and in family size (131, 132), and a shift from "work" for a "master" to nurturance and consumption as a "social" obligation (129), several feminist historians suggest that we add the emergence of "a woman's sphere" (53-56). Formed in and strengthened by the major transitions in capitalist development, the homosocial networks of friendship and affiliation women forged included the home to which they were typically confined but went beyond it to generate a collective politics that made domesticity and the patriarchal family increasingly untenable (54). As a consequence, feelings of inferiority among women gradually were displaced by an analysis of subjugation, an analysis, coincidentally, which business periodically encouraged to win female loyalty away from traditional values and relations to new products, ideas, and responsibilities (128).

Although the case is far from proved, it may be useful to view the social services, including medicine, as both an embodiment and an attempt to contain the increasingly political demands posed by working-class women primarily, i.e. as an "extended patriarchy" which functions, given the problems created for the family by capitalist growth, to reconstitute the diminishing sphere of private life and patriarchal privilege and to supplement the market's uneven regulation of female labor. To be sure, the principles of the social services, their specific substance (health, education, and welfare), and their predominantly female labor force, reflect the socialization of nurturance and extend the ideals and practices of the traditional family without reducing them to a "wage" for which specific quantities of labor power must be regularly exchanged. At the same time, however, the social services also inherit the generalized authoritarian character of the patriarchal family and so undermine in practice the very ideals they are theoretically established to socialize. As medicine's role in battering suggests, the private sphere is reproduced by the services not as a space where self-hood can be apprehended and developed but where it can be denounced, managed, and even eliminated. To this extent, far from extending the family's ideals into a liberating public space, the services achieve the opposite, the social construction of privacy as a living hell.

The Reconstitution of Patriarchy

One anthropological conception of patriarchy emphasizes its exclusive applicability to preindustrial societies where male power is either synonymous with fatherhood (133) or where the political and economic status of women is defined primarily by their dependent relation to husbands, fathers, and brothers (49, 134). While patriarchy may appear to be the sole determinant of social life only when it is embedded in a system of household production, even under preindustrial conditions the relative power of women in the sphere of production may significantly alter the constitution of the patriarchy (135-136). Nor is the critical force of the term lost where male power in the home is merely "relatively autonomous" and survives only by aligning with more advanced forms of production and reproduction located outside the family. Perhaps as many as half of the American women battered each year have no blood or legal ties to the men who assault them (2, 5, 26). Yet, they are clearly oppressed as a group, not simply as single victims. And the logic medicine adopts to support violent households is nonetheless patriarchal because the bonds that link physicians to batterers are not personal or subject to the control of men whose power lies in the household. Thus, medicine's response to abuse becomes a necessary constituent of male power in the home precisely to the extent that blood ties and the household have lost their centrality in the productive and reproductive process. If we disentangle the patriarchy from kin-production surrounding the home, we find that the present combination of medicine and the violent family resembles the traditional patriarchy in its source of power (male-bonded networks); its ideology (sexism); its means (the sexual division and subordination of female laborers and their primary assignment to household and reproductive tasks); its goal (the appropriation of female labor as the exclusive prerogative of specific men); and its consequence (the subordination and degradation of women). But although there is a certain formal continuity in the construction of the patriarchy, capitalism completely transforms its substantive meaning, its mode of determination, and its ultimate viability.

As has been suggested already, organized male domination in the household, community, and workplace often persists in present day institutions in forms apparently opposed to the immediate goals of business. As Hartmann puts it:

> The emergence of capitalism in the fifteenth to eighteenth centuries threatened patriarchal control based on institutional authority as it destroyed many old institutions and created new ones, such as a "free" market in labor. It threatened to bring all women and children into the labor force and hence to destroy the family and the basis of the power of men over women (i.e., the control over their labor power in the family) (123, p. 139).

At the same time, economic discrimination against women in capitalist societies—job segregation by sex, marginal employment, and lower wages—drives women to marry, apply their undervalued labor time to household drudgery, and to remain dependent on men generally, if not on a specific husband, boyfriend, or father (50, 123, 137). As important, while individual industrialists may treat the family as an obstacle to profit making, *social* capital (capital-as-a-whole) understood as a circuit of value realization which includes, in addition to production, the sale of goods, and the reproduction of laborers, benefits from a host of biosocial, psychosocial and sociopolitical functions the family performs (122-123, 128, 138). The services gain their widespread legitimacy from their juridical appearance as part of a "public sector," a world apart from the spheres of commodity circulation and profit making, organized to serve and protect the "private" spheres of family and property (139). But, as important, they are supported by business in order to manage the crises that arise from the inherent antagonisms between the development of private life and the growth of private property. The services effect this management in part, by ideologically and politically displacing crises from the social to the interpersonal or individual spheres. So, although the incidence of coronary disease is a function of the "stress" between work and emotional life, it is disaggregated at a host of medical sites into a myriad of personal problems allegedly brought on by "bad habits" (66, 69). And battering appears not as a normative response to the conflict between economy and patriarchy, but as a paradoxical consequence of too much love, i.e. men who are pathologically jealous and women who love too much to leave home.

Constructed according to such traditional criteria as skill or gender, the services are nonetheless permeated by the strictest economic criteria (140). Although female subordination in the public sector reflects a normative system, namely sexism, whose logic can be abstracted from the rationality of pure profit taking, the private appropriation of social wealth ultimately determines the meaning of public experience in capitalist societies, the form and substance of the work done in families, and the limits to which the expression of any traditional principle can go—including the professional autonomy of physicians and male dominance at home—before it must align its logic with the more fundamental logic of accumulation.

If the patriarchy's survival into the present as a governing principle of the private and public sphere was facilitated by the need for "a world apart," the specific circumstances which produced modern medicine and the other services in America insured their sexist content (49, 140, 141). Once we recognize the material basis of patriarchy as a system of social reproduction based on the appropriation of women's labor through male-dominated networks, we can follow "the male principle" in its historical flight from the home and into the public sphere where, by embedding itself in the services and professions, it functioned to overcome growing female resistance and to compensate for the declining power of the patriarchal family in turn-of-the-century America (49, 140, 142). Even as 19th-century business undermined domesticity and the patriarchal family, it required their reconstitution in order to sustain the highly profitable sex-segregated division of labor, regulate female labor in and out of the home, reproduce male and female labor power, pacify tendencies toward antisocial behavior by youngsters and male workers, organize individual consumption, and compensate for disintegrating kin and peer networks (122, 123, 126-129). Equally important, as women exploited the deterioration of patriarchal authority and extended their resistance to wageless "private" subordination into opposition to economic exploitation as well, the social services were used increasingly to reconstruct the private sphere, disregarding the resulting brutality when necessary, in order to unify previously opposed patriarchal and economic interests (143).

CONCLUSION

At the dawn of capitalism, the personal power of men was typically invested with the added authority given the father because of his role as head of the economic unit. So long as household production prevailed, the formation of male-bonded political institutions appeared to be a natural extension of family relations whose patriarchal character could be concealed by ideologically identifying social well-being and family stability. Within the family, the treatment of women and children was constrained only by the rituals of interpersonal obligation and by the rough limits suggested by the greater importance of women in certain forms of household production than in others (133-136). In any event, the priority placed on protecting the autonomy of the patriarchal family permitted wife-beating to arise in one family for reasons which might have little to do with its emergence in another, according to the peculiarities of interpersonal life. Society took no interest unless resistance posed a collective obstacle to male/private power (e.g. in a "revolt of witches").

By contrast, the very survival of a capitalist social order requires the universal emancipation of laborers from the traditional bonds of personal life to sell their labor power on the market. Though capital may continue to mediate its power through such male-bonded networks as "the army" or "the professions," it must, at the same time, continually "revolutionize" the social relations within these networks as well as relations within families. The disappearance of household production and the rise of industrial production controlled by a small class of entrepreneurs divests the patriarchal role of its economic authority and, simultaneously, subordinates the family's interpersonal needs to capital's general interests in pacification, lowering the costs of socialization, and facilitating consumption.

But the family's redefinition cannot bestow a new stability. Instead, the contradictions that govern capitalist development as a whole thoroughly destabilize everyday life as well. The universalization of the wage and its movement through "boom" and "bust" cycles periodically disaggregates and reconstitutes the family unit as a function of the changing shares of income household members command in the market. More important, in addition to suppressing basic needs for nurturance, the tendency to reduce family life to an economic calculus contradicts an opposing tendency inherent in but undeveloped by capitalist expansion, namely, the potential to expand the realm of personal relations and reduce the effort expended to produce life's necessities (139). Meanwhile, stripped of its economic legitimacy within the family, the patriarchal role must either yield to the prevailing pressure to equalize oppression (women into factories and offices, men into nurseries and kitchens) or be reconstituted through the investment of outside resources in opposition to dominant tendencies. Violence may emerge in response to any of these contradictions, but it is primarily in this last instance, when the patriarchy is systematically reconstructed with outside aid, that "battering" appears.

Bourgeois ideology continues to portray the family as a "haven" from an anarchic market and a dehumanizing workplace (85, 128). But the illusion that "family" and "factory" are opposite poles dissolves, particularly for working-class women, before an elaborate network of power that combines the diminishing realm of personal life and the expanding economy into an "antagonistic unity." The precariousness of this unity is revealed in the interface between medicine and the victims of domestic abuse and when we aggregate the outcome of women's encounters with the services into a picture of "the violent family," a world apart which must continue to assume the costs of progressive irrationality as its private burden. By socializing heretofore private functions of health, protection, and welfare, the services ostensibly fulfil traditional feminist demands and technology's age-old promise that labor will be employed for its own social well-being, i.e. "unproductively." But this benign face proves merely to have been a mask behind which the services assume the traditional patriarchal task of imposing female labor in the family. Viewing only the mask, it is easy to conclude that increased investment in the services will save the family from its erratic tendencies toward violence and abuse. We mourn progress because the continuation of wife-beating reveals that for women, at least, the old maxim is true: "everything changes so that things can remain the same." But when the mask is removed, we find merely the spectre of the self-confident patriarch of precapitalist days, given the appearance of strength only by his dependence on the "helping" services.

Thus, battering arises today as the services attempt to reprivatize "women's work" in a context of patriarchal domination against counter-tendencies to socialize the labor of love. From this standpoint, the women's movement must be considered not simply a means to an end, but as part of a process which already embodies much of the reality that must eventually be universalized, the abolition of patriarchy, the reconstitution of the "family" with an extended network of loving equals, and the cooperative organization of child care and women's other traditional household chores.

The possibility to extend this process derives, in part, from the urban-based networks of female resistance that persist among blacks, Puerto Ricans, ethnics, Chicanos, and working-class whites (97, 102, 143-146). In addition to providing the base for explicitly political demands for housing, welfare rights, educational reform, health and child care, these networks challenge the ideological hegemony of the social services and the mass media. By offering women a strategic repertoire based on inherited principles of female prowess, they help them to understand their relations to men and children, to respond to crises in everyday life, including domestic violence, and to sustain their physical and mental health against capital, the patriarchy, and the "helping" services. The most tragic consequence of battering is that it effectively isolates women from these networks, cutting them off from any chance for collective subjectivity. It is this isolation primarily that makes the abused woman seem like a "helpless victim."

By contrast with a strategy that focuses on resolving domestic violence by strengthening these indigenous networks of resistance, an appeal to social services to be "more sensitive" to women is completely hollow. And, of course, such an approach misses the main conclusion of this research, namely, that since the services themselves are socially constructed for, among other purposes, the reimposition of patriarchal domination in the private sphere, their reform, and the alteration of their logic, requires the most fundamental social revolution. But a strategy which relies primarily on providing battered women with "shelter" must also be carefully weighed. To be sure, the shelter movement emerged from the attempt by women to institutionally solidify networks of resistance against the fracturing and isolation imposed by domestic violence and the social services. At the same time, the image of the shelter as a concealed refuge from the horrors of male-dominated family life, its treatment of women in crisis as "victims," and its simulation of "community" to raise consciousness in lieu of direct political intervention to change the realities of the working-class communities that already exist, replicate the popular conception of the "good" family. As the shelter becomes an "alternative" service, it also apes other treatment programs for the "disadvantaged": a few "successful" women get jobs and may even join the staff, but the vast majority find their lives unchanged, still lacking the political skills and contacts to extend the momentary solidarity experienced in the shelter into the neighborhoods where their daily struggles are waged (147).

We make no claim that it is easy to balance the organization of indigenous networks of resistance with the provision of individually based emergency service to women in crisis. One step in this direction involves thinking of "shelter" less as a single facility than as a political space opened up for women-in-crisis within their own neighborhoods or communities, a "liberated" church basement or hotel, for instance, or a protective ring, provided perhaps by the abused woman's kin or friendship network, within which she appears less like a helpless object than as a courageous subject vulnerable only so long as she is isolated from her peers. Of course, many battered women will eventually return to their homes, often naively expecting that things will be different. In these instances, our task is not to denigrate the romantic ideal which so many battered women hold close, even in the face of physical crises unimaginable to persons who live more safely. Our task rather is to extend this ideal politically to help forge a world which can sustain it.

Acknowledgments—Support for this research was provided by a grant from the National Institute of Mental Health, "Medical Contexts and Sequelae of Domestic Violence" (MH 30868-01A1), as well as the Trauma Program of the Department of

Surgery, Yale University School of Medicine, and the Institution for Social and Policy Studies of Yale University. For critical and technical help we would like to thank particularly Karen Baar, Anne Grey, Heidi Hartmann, Kim Hopper, Judy Robison, Martha Roper, and members of the East Coast Health Discussion Group.

REFERENCES

1. Straus, M. A. Wife beating: How common and why? *Victimology: An International Journal* 2(3-4): 443-458, 1977-1978.
2. Flynn, J. P. Recent findings related to wife abuse. *Social Casework* 13-20, January 1977.
3. Levinger, G. Sources of marital dissatisfaction among applicants for divorce. *Am. J. Orthopsychiatry* 883-897, October 1966.
4. O'Brien, J. E. Violence in divorce prone families. *Journal of Marriage and the Family* 692-698, November 1971.
5. Flitcraft, A. Battered Women: An Emergency Room Epidemiology with Description of a Clinical Syndrome and Critique of Present Therapeutics. Doctoral thesis, Yale University School of Medicine, 1977, Sterling Medical Library, Yale University, New Haven, Conn.
6. Dobash, R., and Dobash, R. E. Wives: The appropriate victims of marital violence. *Victimology: An International Journal* 2(3-4): 426-442, 1977-1978.
7. *Battered Women: Issues of Public Policy.* U.S. Commission on Civil Rights, Washington, D.C., 1978.
8. Martin, D. *Battered Wives.* Pocket Books, New York, 1977.
9. Davidson, T. *Conjugal Crime.* Hawthorn Books, New York, 1978.
10. Gelles, R. J. *The Violent Home: A Study of Physical Aggression Between Husbands and Wives.* Sage Publications, Beverly Hills, Cal., 1974.
11. Gelles, R. J. Abused Wives: Why do they stay? *Journal of Marriage and the Family* 38, November 1976.
12. Warrior, B. Battered wives. *Houseworker's Handbook.* Women's Center, Cambridge, Mass., 1976.
13. Pizzy, E. *Scream Quietly or the Neighbors Will Hear.* Penguin Books, London, 1974.
14. Gayford, J. J. Wife battering: A preliminary survey of 100 cases. *Br. Med. J.* XXV: 194-197, January 1975.
15. Petro, J., Quann, P. L., and Graham, W. P. Wife abuse: The diagnosis and its implications. *JAMA* 240(3): 240-241, 1978.
16. Nichols, N. The abused wife problem. *Social Casework* 27-32, January 1976.
17. Hilberman, E., and Munson, K. Sixty battered women: A preliminary survey. *Victimology: An International Journal* 2(3-4), 1977-1978.
18. Rounseville, B. J. Battered Wives: Very Common but Difficult to Reach. Unpublished paper, Connecticut Mental Health Center, New Haven, Conn., 1977.
19. Snell, J. E., Rosenwald, R. J., and Roby, A. The wifebeater's wife: A study of family interaction. *Arch. Gen. Psychiatry* 107-113, August 1964.
20. Walker, L. *The Battered Woman.* Harper & Row, New York, 1979.
21. Whitehurst, R. Violence potential in extramarital sexual responses. *Journal of Marriage and the Family* 683-691, November 1971.
22. Whitehurst, R. Violently jealous husbands. *Sexual Behavior* I(4): 32-41, 1971.
23. Renvoize, J. *Web of Violence.* Routledge & Kegan Paul, London, 1978.
24. Reich, A. A contribution to the psychoanalysis of extreme submissiveness in women (1940). *Psychoanalytic Contributions.* Int. University Press, New York, 1973.
25. Hanks, S. E., and Rosenbaum, P. Battered women: A study of women who live with violent alcohol-abusing men. *Am. J. Orthopsychiatry* 47(2): 291-306, 1977.
26. Rounseville, B., and Weissman, M. M. Battered women: A medical problem requiring detection. *International Journal of Psychiatry in Medicine* 8(2): 191-202, 1977-1978.
27. Chalfant, P. The alcoholic in magazines for women. *Sociological Focus* 19-26, Fall 1974.
28. Wiseman, J. An alternative role for the wife of an alcoholic in Finland. *Journal of Marriage and the Family* 37: 172-179, February 1975.
29. Lachman, J. A. A theory of interpersonal conflict with application to industrial disputes. Discussion paper. Institution of Public Policy Studies, Ann Arbor, Mich., January 1978.
30. Lundsgaarde, H. P. *Murder in Space City: A Cultural Analysis of Houston Homicide Patterns.* Oxford University Press, New York, 1977.

206 / Stark, Flitcraft, and Frazier

31. Wolfgang, M. E. Husband and wife homicides. *Corrective Psychiatry and Journal of Social Therapy* 263-271, 1956.
32. Firestone, S. *The Dialectic of Sex.* William Morrow & Company, New York, 1970.
33. Steinmetz, S., and Straus, M. The family as a cradle of violence. In *Violence in the Family,* edited by S. Steinmetz and M. Straus. Harper & Row, New York, 1975.
34. Straus, M. Cultural and social organizational influences in violence between family members. In *Configurations: Biological and Cultural Factors in Sexuality of Family Life,* edited by Prince and Barrier. Lexington Books, Lexington, Mass., 1974.
35. Gingold, J. One of these days—Pow! Right in the kisser: The truth about battered wives. *Ms.* V(2): 51, August 1976.
36. Abrams, S. The battered husband bandwagon. *Seven Days* II(14), September 29, 1978.
37. Steinmetz, S. The battered husband syndrome. *Victimology: An International Journal* 2(3-4): 499-509, 1977-1978.
38. Stark, E. Which sex is batter. *Seven Days* 11(16): 3, October 27, 1978.
39. Schecter, S. Psychic Battering: The Institutional Response to Battered Women. Paper presented at Midwest Conference on Abuse of Women, St. Louis, 1978.
40. Cicourel, A. *Method and Measurement in Sociology.* Free Press of Glencoe, New York, 1964.
41. Mollica, R., and Redlich, F. Equity and Changing Patient Characteristics in South Central Connecticut, 1950-1975. Unpublished paper, Yale University, New Haven, Conn., 1978.
42. Kelman, S. The social nature of the definition problem in health. *Int. J. Health Serv.* 5(4): 625-642, 1975.
43. Blum, J. D. On changes in psychiatric diagnosis over time. *American Psychologist* 33(11): 1017-1031, November 1978.
44. Berliner, H. S. A larger perspective on the Flexner Report. *Int. J. Health Serv.* 5(4): 573-592, 1975.
45. Health Policy Advisory Center. *The American Health Empire.* Random House, New York, 1970.
46. Krause, E. A. *Power and Illness: The Political Sociology of Health and Medical Care.* Elkevier, Amsterdam, 1977.
47. Waitzkin, H. B., and Waterman, B. *The Exploitation of Illness in Capitalist Society.* Bobbs-Merrill Studies in Sociology, Bobbs-Merrill, New York, 1974.
48. Cleaver, H. Malaria, the politics of public health and the international crisis. *Review of Radical Political Economics* 9(1): 81-103, 1977.
49. Ehrenreich, B., and English, D. *For Her Own Good.* Anchor Doubleday, New York, 1978.
50. Turshen, M. The political ecology of disease. *Review of Radical Political Economics* 9(1): 45-60, 1977.
51. Sawhill, I. Discrimination and poverty among women who head families. *Signs* 1(3, part 2): 201-212, Spring 1976.
52. Levine, D., and Levine, L. Personality Structure and the Family: Historical and Theoretical Studies, in progress.
53. Smith-Rosenberg, C. The female world of love and ritual: Relations between women in 19th century America. *Signs* 1: 1-31, Autumn 1975.
54. Cott, N. F. *The Bonds of Womanhood, "Women's Sphere" in New England, 1780-1835.* Yale University Press, New Haven, Conn., 1977.
55. Farrager, J., and Stansell, C. C. Women and their families on the overland trail, 1842-1867. *Feminist Studies* 2, November 1975.
56. Sklar, K. K. *Catherine Beecher, A Study in American Domesticity.* W. W. Norton, New York, 1976.
57. Skinner, E., and German, P. S. Use of ambulatory health services by the near poor. *Am. J. Public Health* 68(12): 1195-1202, December 1978.
58. Kempe, G. H. The battered-child syndrome. *JAMA* 181(1): 17-112, 1962.
59. Zonana, H., Henisz, J., and Levine, M. Psychiatry emergency services a decade later. *Psychiatry Med.* 4(3): 273-290, 1973.
60. Roper, M., and Frazier, W. The Interrelation of Rape and Battering. Unpublished report, Yale Trauma Program, New Haven, Conn., 1977.
61. Jacoby, R. *Social Amnesia.* Beacon Press, Boston, 1976.
62. Foucault, M. *The Birth of the Clinic: An Archeology of Medical Perception.* Pantheon Books, New York, 1973.
63. Ackerknecht, E. H. *Rudolf Virchow.* University of Wisconsin Press, Madison, 1953.
64. Berliner, H., and Salmon, J. Toward an understanding of holistic medicine. *HMO Packet #4: Ideology and Medicine* 71-99. Health-PAC, New York, 1978.

65. McKeown, T. *The Modern Rise in Population.* Academic Press, New York, 1977.
66. Stark, E. The epidemic as a social event. *Int. J. Health Serv.* 7(4): 681-705, 1977.
67. Powles, J. The Effects of Health Services on Adult Male Mortality in Relation to Effects of Social and Economic Factors. Paper delivered to the International Conference on Priorities for the Use of Resources in Medicine. Fogarty International Center, Bethesda, Md., 1976.
68. Fuchs, V. *Who Shall Survive?* Basic Books, New York, 1974.
69. Crawford, R. You are dangerous to your health: The ideology and politics of victim blaming. *Int. J. Health Serv.* 7(4): 663-680, 1977.
70. Gelles, R. J. Violence and pregnancy: A note on the extent of the problem and needed services. *The Family Coordinator* 81-86, January 1975.
71. Roberts, A. R. Police social workers: A history. *Social Work* 294-299, July 1976.
72. Esterson, A. *The Leaves of Spring: Schizophrenia, Family and Sacrifice.* Penguin Books, Middlesex, England, 1970.
73. Esterson, A., and Laing, R. D. *Sanity, Madness and the Family.* Penguin Books, Middlesex, England, 1970.
74. Marcuse, H. *Eros and Civilization.* Vintage Books, New York, 1958.
75. Guttmacher, S., and Hopper, K. Suicide in the social etiology of disease. *HMO Packet #2.* Health-PAC, New York, 1977.
76. Dobash, R., and Dobash, R. E. Violence between Men and Women within the Family Setting. Paper presented at the VIIth World Congress of Sociology, Toronto, Canada, 1974.
77. Chessler, P. Women as psychiatric and psychotherapeutic patients. *Journal of Marriage and the Family* 746-759, November 1971.
78. Radical Therapist Collective. *The Radical Therapist.* Ballentine Books, New York, 1971.
79. Wolfgang, M., and Ferracuti, F. *The Subculture of Violence.* Tavistock Publications, London, 1967.
80. Davis, A. F. *Spearheads for Reform: The Social Settlement and the Progressive Movement, 1890-1914.* Oxford University Press, New York, 1967.
81. Platt, T. *The Childsavers: The Invention of Delinquency.* University of Chicago Press, Chicago, 1969.
82. Pleck, E. Wife-Beating in 19th Century America, Unpublished paper, University of Michigan, May 1977.
83. Alani, A. The battered husband. *Br. J. Psychiatry* 129: 96, 1976.
84. Pfouts, J. H. Violent families: Coping responses of abused wives. *Child Welfare* VLVII(2): 101-111, 1978.
85. Lasch, C. *Haven in a Heartless World.* Basic Books, New York, 1977.
86. Selye, H. *The Stress of Life.* McGraw-Hill Book Company, New York, 1956.
87. Hendriz, M. H., LaGodna, G., and Bohen, C. A. The battered wife. *Am. J. Nurs.* 650-653, April 1978.
88. Gove, W., and Grimm, H. W. The family life cycle: Internal dynamics and social consequences. *Sociology and Social Research* 57: 182-195, January 1973.
89. Richardson, L. F. *Statistics of Deadly Quarrels.* Boxwood Press, Chicago, 1960.
90. Voss, H. L., and Hepburn, J. R. Patterns in criminal homicide in Chicago. *Journal of Criminal Law, Criminology and Police Science* LIX: 499-508, 1968.
91. Eyer, J. Prosperity as a cause of death. *Int. J. Health Serv.* 7(1): 125-150, 1977.
92. Stark, R., and McEvoy, J. Middle-class violence. *Psychology Today* 30-31, November 1970.
93. Lystad, M. Violence at home. *Am. J. Orthopsychiatry* XLV(3): 328-345, 1975.
94. Steinmetz, S. Occupational environment in relation to physical punishment and dogmatism. In *Violence in the Family,* edited by S. Steinmetz and M. Straus, pp. 116-172. Harper & Row, New York, 1974.
95. Sennett, R., and Cobb, J. *Hidden Injuries of Class.* Vintage Books, New York, 1973.
96. Rubin, L. *Worlds of Pain: Life in the Working Class Family.* Basic Books, New York, 1976.
97. Miller, W. B. Lower class culture as a generating milieu of gang delinquence. *Journal of Social Issues* XIV: 5-19, 1958.
98. Fannin, L. F., and Clinnard, M. B. Differences in the conception of self as male among lower and middle-class delinquents. *Social Problems* XII: 205-214, 1965.
99. Moran, R. Criminal homicide: External restraint and subculture of violence. *Criminology* IV: 357-374, 1971.
100. Safilios-Rothschild, C. The study of family power structure: A review 1960-69. *Journal of Marriage and the Family* 539-552, November 1969.
101. Fanon, F. *The Wretched of the Earth.* Grove Press, New York, 1971.
102. Caulfield, M. D. Imperialism, the family and cultures of resistance. *Socialist Revolution* 20, October 1974.

103. Henry, A. F., and Short, J. F., Jr. *Suicide and Homicide.* Free Press, Chicago, 1964.
104. Brenner, M. H. Health costs and benefits of economic policy. *Int. J. Health Serv.* 7(4): 581-624, 1977.
105. Chester, R., and Streather, J. Cruelty in English divorce: Some empirical findings. *Journal of Marriage and the Family* 706-711, November 1972.
106. Bard, M. The study and modification of intrafamilial violence. In *The Control of Aggression and Violence: Cognitive and Psychological.* Academic Press, New York, 1971.
107. Household Violence Study. Connecticut Task Force on Abused Women, Hartford, 1977.
108. Marsden, D. Sociological perspectives on family violence. In *Violence and the Family,* edited by J. M. Martin, pp. 103-135. John Wiley & Sons, New York, 1978.
109. Straus, M. Some social antecedents of physical punishment: A linkage theory interpretation. *Journal of Marriage and the Family* 658-663, November 1971.
110. Britain: Battered Wives. *Newsweek* 39, July 9, 1973.
111. Goode, W. J. Force and violence in the family. *Journal of Marriage and the Family* 683-691, November 1971.
112. Aronowitz, S. *False Promises.* McGraw-Hill Book Company, New York, 1973.
113. Marx, K. *Capital: A Critical Analysis of Capitalist Production,* Vol. I, edited by F. Engels. International Publishers, New York, 1967.
114. Lewis, O. *La Vida.* Vintage Books, New York, 1965.
115. Levy, C. *Spoils of War.* Houghton-Mifflin, Boston, 1974.
116. Hicks, M. W., and Platt, M. Marital happiness and stability: A review of the research in the sixties. *Journal of Marriage and the Family* 553-574, November 1970.
117. Brownmiller, S. *Against Our Will.* Simon and Schuster, New York, 1975.
118. Straus, M. Sexual inequality, cultural norms, and wife beating. *Victimology: An International Journal* VI(1): 54-70, Spring 1976.
119. Zaretsky, E. *Capitalism, the Family and Personal Life.* Harper & Row, New York, 1976.
120. Gilman, C. P. *The Living of Charlotte Perkins Gilman, An Autobiography.* D. Appleton-Century Company, New York, 1935.
121. Sochen, J. *The New Woman in Greenwich Village, 1910-1920.* Quadrangle Books, New York, 1972.
122. Hartmann, H. *Capitalism and Women's Work in the Home: 1900-1930.* Temple University Press, forthcoming.
123. Hartmann, H. Capitalism, patriarchy and job segregation by sex. *Signs* 1(3, part 2): 137-169, Spring 1976.
124. Silberman, C. *Criminal Violence, Criminal Justice.* Random House, New York, 1978.
125. Mead, M. Social change and cultural surrogates. In *Personality in Nature, Society and Culture,* edited by C. Kluckhohn and H. Murray. Alfred Knopf, New York, 1953.
126. Benjamin, J. Authority and the family revisited: Or, a world without fathers? *New German Critique* 13: 35-59, Winter 1978.
127. Marcuse, H. The obsolescence of the Freudian concept of man. In *Five Lectures,* pp. 44-61. Beacon Press, Boston, 1970.
128. Ewen, S. *Captains of Consciousness.* Vintage Press, New York, 1977.
129. Horkheimer, M. *Authority and the Family in Critical Theory,* translated by M. J. O'Connell. Herder & Herder, New York, 1972.
130. Krishnan, P. and Kavani, A. Estimates of age specific divorce rates for females in the U.S. 1960-1969. *Journal of Marriage and the Family* 36: 72-76, February 1974.
131. Sweet, J. A. Differentials in the rate of fertility decline: 1960-1970. *Family Planning Perspectives* 6: 103-107, Spring 1974.
132. Glick, P. Some recent changes in American families. *Current Population Reports,* Series P-23, No. 52. U.S. Bureau of the Census, Washington, D.C., 1975.
133. Rubin, G. The traffic in women. In *Toward an Anthropology of Women,* edited by R. Reiter. Monthly Review Press, New York, 1975.
134. Muller, V. The formation of the state and the oppression of women. *Review of Radical Political Economics* 9(3): 7-22, 1977.
135. Stack, C. B., Caulfield, M., and Estes, V. et al. Review essay on anthropology. *Signs* 1(1): 147-159, 1975.
136. O'Laughlin, B. Mediation of contradiction. In *Women, Culture and Society,* edited by M. Rosalda and L. Lampere. Stanford University Press, Stanford, 1974.
137. Safilios-Rothchild, C. Dual linkages between the occupational and family systems: A macrosociologial analysis. *Signs* 1(3, part 2): 51-61, 1976.
138. Marx, K. *Capital: A Critical Analysis of Capitalist Production,* Vol. II, edited by F. Engels. International Publishers, New York, 1967.

139. Knödler-Bunte, E. The proletarian public sphere and political organization: An analysis of Oskar Neat and Alexander Kluge's *The Public Sphere and Experience. New German Critique* 4: 51-75, 1975.
140. O'Connor, J. Fiscal crisis of the state. *Socialist Revolution* 1(1) and 1(2), 1970.
141. Barker-Benfield, G. J. *The Horrors of the Half-Known Life.* Harper Brothers, New York, 1976.
142. Haller, J. S., and Haller, R. *The Physician and Sexuality in Victorian America.* University of Illinois Press, Urbana, 1974.
143. Della Costa, M., and James, S. *The Power of Women and the Subversion of the Community.* Falling Wall Press, London, 1972.
144. Stack, C. *All Our Kin: Strategies for Survival in a Black Community.* Harper & Row, New York, 1975.
145. Williams, M. Strategies of Migrant Farmworkers. Ph.D. dissertation, University of Illinois, Urbana, 1975.
146. Lewin, H., Kobak, S., and Johnson, L. Family, religion and colonialism in central Appalachia. In *Growing Up Country,* edited by J. Axelrod, Calintwood, Va., 1973.
147. Flitcraft, A. Shelters: Short-term needs. In *Battered Women: Issues of Public Policy,* pp. 113-115. U.S. Commission on Civil Rights, Washington, D.C. 1978.

PART 6

Biology, Nature, And The Construction Of Knowledge

Chlorosis and Chronic Disease in 19th-Century Britain: The Social Constitution of Somatic Illness in a Capitalist Society

Karl Figlio

"A civilization . . . ultimately has only the diseases it agrees to sustain."

Dagognet, *Le catalogue de la vie,* p. 9

The ambiguity in the phrase "the social constitution of illness" is intentional. It is intended to convey that the disease as a clinical object structures a cluster of social relations, and that at the same time it is itself socially constructed. There are two aspects of this socioclinical phenomenon: the social relations of disease and the embodiment of social relations in the concepts of disease. They may be isolated for analysis, but they must be reunited to understand the disease in the concrete historical case. This is another way of saying that medicine mediates social relations, and is itself constructed in the process. Thus, to explain the social relations of medicine, we must look not to the behavior of individual practitioners, but to their social position as a class, and to their systems of concepts and practice as reflections of that position.

This article is a revised form of one which has appeared in *Social History* 3(2): 167-197, 1978.

Medical sociologists and historians have already touched on relevant aspects of this thesis. The sociologists have delineated social "roles" which characterize the public features of illness, and professional roles which define the socially sanctioned behavior of physicians (1). Similarly, historians of medicine have moved toward a social history by studying topics such as professionalization, the social impact of disease, and the politics of public health (2). Both sociologists and historians of medicine, however, hold to a distinction between behavior and the ideas of nature which justify that behavior. For them, the "sick role" refers, not to the social construction of disease, but to illness behavior; and professionalization is formulated, not as an integral aspect of scientific medicine, but only of occupational behavior. They see no necessary homologies between the structure of social relations and the structure of conceptual systems. So, while I doubt that there is much disagreement about the importance of the "social" for our understanding of medicine—either in its historical or its contemporary context—I suspect that the social rootedness of medical ideas can always be affirmed with just enough generality to empty it of meaning. A point is always reached in the argument at which a line is drawn between the social realm of practice, behavior, influence, etc., and an *autonomous* natural world of scientific/medical concepts/facts.

The boundary drawn around the ideas has put a limit on the extent to which medicine can be historicized. Because the essentially scientific/medical is withdrawn from the historical arena, only the application or misapplication of theory remains to be contextualized. On scholarly grounds alone, this separation of the natural from the social cannot be sustained. Whatever the issue, the historian's interest remains fastened on human activity. To work historically demands that we extend our analysis without prior constraint and without regard for areas called natural. Indeed, the distinction between natural and human should itself be treated as an historically rooted phenomenon, made by people in the service of interests.

But there are more pressing reasons for insisting that we socialize the putatively natural realm of medical ideas. Theoretical systems reproduce and transmit the forms of domination in social relations, such as hierarchical class stratification. By retaining in our analyses an autonomous natural part of medicine, we perpetuate that domination by concealing an important channel through which it is sustained. If our scholarship is to be humanistic, it must criticize the symbolic, as well as the overt, forms of repression.

History is potentially a powerful critical method. We can look at the emergence of concepts and practices at the times when their social meanings were most clear, from a vantage-point which makes the present appear strange rather than self-evident, and at a time when we can see the science/medicine in the making. In this way, history encourages us to see the ideas as the products of human activity.

To historicize everything raises complicated and contentious issues, and we must proceed judiciously with both theoretical refinements and empirical studies. But although we must be cautious, we must also refuse to be drawn repeatedly into sterile philosophical disputes over the existence of value-free facts or neutral observations. Interesting as those questions may be, they can also be an intellectual distraction.

I am not suggesting that there is nothing outside human control—no "nature" in our common usage—but I am taking as the basis of my analysis the Marxian view that there is no raw nature for us. Everything we take to be nature is, one way or the other, appropriated by us, and the form of this appropriation is historically contingent. At one level, this position is well known. Philosophers and sociologists of science have attacked the positivistic assumption of natural objects which can be observed and theoretically treated with increasing precision (3-6). It is a commonplace among them to dispute the existence of neutral observations and facts which are not theory-laden. The binding of particular presuppositions about nature to concrete historical circumstances, however, remains to be done. With the path opened by their epistemological analyses, we need not continually justify the attempt to discover the social, and the significance of the forms it took, in what people assumed to be objective nature. In Robert Young's words, "Our world view includes conceptions both of nature and of society, with 'society' as a category which is more fundamental than, and more basic to, that of 'nature' (Lukács). It must follow that our science, however unobtrusively, is an expression of our social relations" (7, p. 71).

Marxist historians of science have begun to explore the relationships between the mode and social relations of production on the one hand, and the terms in which nature was conceived on the other. For Sohn-Rethel (8), even the apparently timeless logical framework underlying fundamental physical laws is a representation of the pure abstraction embodied in commodity exchange, and that exchange characterizes capitalist society. Just as the laws of the market appear to be autonomous from social relations, so do medical/scientific facts/theories. As a result, we tend to believe that things are related *immediately* to other things in nature, rather than *mediately* through human relations. For Marx, the objective quality of the commodity concealed its essence as production and the relations enforced between people for that production. In the commodity, the variety of human differences was abstracted into the market-determined "exchange value," and with that process was also lost the sense of human control over an increasing domain of "reified" phenomena which appeared to people as natural rather than human. We can extend his argument (Marx himself hinted at it (9, p. 162)) to the thinginess of facts and theories by seeing them as concealing social relations as well—by seeing them as "frozen" social relations (7, pp. 70-79).

This does not mean that all statements about nature only reveal something about the particular social order, but it does mean that all statements about nature do express aspects of the social order. It would be a crude idealism or fetishism to imagine either nature subsumed wholly under social relations, or social relations subsumed wholly under an unappropriated, raw nature (10).

We are now able to formulate an approach to historicizing medicine in such a way as to include all of it, not just the social behavior of its practitioners. The social history of medicine has looked at social relations between people—or people as class representatives—such as those between doctor and patient. One way to go beyond that approach would be to discover the symbolic representation of the social relations, and then to extend that analysis to include those forms of symbolic representation taken to be scientific/medical knowledge. The very facticity of knowledge of nature, with the correlative objective neutrality of the practitioner, powerfully reinforces the social relations symbolized by them. They, too, become natural (necessary) and the practitioners are at the same time put beyond criticism by that neutral stance—unless, of course, they misuse the knowledge. Seen in this way, medical knowledge carries ideology within it, whether or not it is "misused." Indeed, it is ideologically more powerful if it is *not* misused.

In answer to the question, "How do we historicize medicine?", my answer is that we treat its concepts as symbolic systems whose political function is to reinforce social relations necessary to the capitalist mode of production. The symbolic systems will make those relations appear natural, and this naturalness will both reinforce those relations and render the symbolic system apparently autonomous from its social roots. Finally, they will conceal the origins of social relations in the mode of production, and thus hide the roots of structural domination and hierarchy in society. In Pierre Bourdieu's (11) formulation, the dominant culture produces a specific ideology which:

> ... contributes to the real integration of the dominant classes ... to the fictitious integration of society as a whole, and hence to the demobilization ... of the dominated classes; and to the legitimation of the established order by the establishment of distinctions (hierarchies) and the legitimation of these distinctions.

If society is organized by production, and if class ownership of the means of production entails domination, then medical knowledge as ideology will hide that domination, make a hierarchical stratification appear natural, and conceal its own social roots.

This sort of analysis may lead us to an expectation of how things work, but it cannot be argued on theoretical grounds alone. I would like to make my analysis more concrete. After reviewing the literature on the history of women's illness, I shall use for my material a feminine disease of adolescence common in the 19th century (chlorosis), along with chronic ill health and the theoretically central notion of "constitution," to treat 19th-century medical thought as "frozen" social relations.

HISTORICAL WRITING ON WOMEN'S ILLNESS

The analysis of the social roles of medical ideas has been pursued most actively by feminist scholars, whose work stands out as an example both of the attempt to contextualize medical concepts and of committed history (12-15). Many of these writers emphasize the common 19th-century view that women were frail and prone to disorder. Their frailty, it was argued, was mainly a function of their weak nervous systems, which rendered them unsuited to intellectual or competitive work. Their tendency to go wrong could be demonstrated easily in the large number of menstrual diseases they suffered—indeed, in menstruation itself. Thus, they were fragile beings, subject to periodic waves of even greater susceptibility. And their nervous systems were not only too weak for masculine activity, but also more primitive—more suited to sentiment, emotion, and sympathy than to reason. Women were bound to their special, delicately balanced physiology from "puberty to menopause" (16).

Women were to stay at home for their own health. This was a general theme of medical ideology, but it was also one located in specific historical conditions. Feminist historians have associated the use of medical ideas about the nature of women with conservative middle-class reactions to specific demands for an equal place for women in a man's world. Traditional bourgeois roles were threatened by the increasingly strident call for women's suffrage, by the number of women in men's jobs as a result of the American Civil War, and by their demand for secondary and university education. The perceived explosion of female diseases during the 19th century measured the strain on bourgeois values more than it reflected an increase of clear, physical pathology (17-19).

The literature I have précised tends to associate a particular historical event (for example, educational reform) with a specific and explicit use of medically legitimated social control (for example, that the menstrual cycle revealed a biological instability which masculine work might overbalance). Paradoxically, this concrete linking of the conceptual mythologizing with the conditions it sought to legitimate can undermine itself. Although it was (and is) used for social control, to analyze such biomedical mythologizing this way invites criticism of a conventional sort. Medical theories have sources internal to medical thought and practice, the argument would run, and these sources both antedated and survived the events to which they were applied. If medical myths were so obviously oppressive, that was because the medicine was practiced badly, not because the medicine itself was oppressive. Thus, the behavior, but not the medicine, was socially rooted.

Sometimes, even feminist historians of medicine are led implicitly to accept the reactionary position that individual doctors could mistreat women because the undeveloped state of reproductive physiology enabled them to propagate mythologies (20). But in trying to understand the tools of oppression, male aggressiveness or anxiety in the presence of women is misleading. Ultimately, the relationship of medical ideas to their social roots must be interpreted in terms of mediations whose presence and mode of working will not be apparent. These mediations bring social control to bear upon people in ways which are powerful because they seem right, and they seem right precisely because they seem also to lie outside immediate social relevance; they appear not to be social, but to be "natural." This apparent relationship of social to natural is also an inversion, one which brings the expertise of medicine to bear irresistibly upon people and one which is also a *source* of medical concepts which are themselves oppressive. It is the re-inversion of this process—making the "natural" reappear as "social"—that I am advocating.

Hysteria is a good example. Looking at the compatibility between disease and the social position of women, Smith-Rosenberg (21) related the prevalence of hysteria in 19th-century America to role conflict, that of a "child-woman" in an egalitarian society, born of the coincidental ideals of freedom and dependency. From a psychoanalytic perspective, hysteria was the psychosomatically plausible reaction to an intolerable social position. In acting out their situation according to apparently autonomous laws, women hid its conventional nature behind an illness—they "naturalized" their social condition.

With the psychoanalytic interpretation of hysteria we have also an example of the reinversion of the social/natural relationship. First the disease, and the 19th-century interpretation of it, hide the relationships between people by appearing natural, not social. Then psychoanalysis reverses the priority. The "natural" disease process is actually the expression of the "social" environment of women in a man's world. Used historically, psychoanalysis reinterprets the "real" explosion of hysteria in the 19th century as a crisis in the relationships between men and women.

In contemporary theory, hysteria, though expressed physically, is psychological. A person unconsciously converts the stress of irreconcilable pressures into overt behavior meant both to conceal and to reveal the conflicts within. It is literally a construction of illness. But because we have no equivalent to hysterical conversion to make transparent the social relations which may underlie the morbid phenomena we classify as physical disease, there are not many cases where such a model could be applied easily. Nonetheless, I think we should take seriously Smith-Rosenberg's approach. The division and abstraction of living phenomena into two types, the psychological and the physical, is itself a product of our bourgeois age, and it would be a fetishism to accept such a dualism as ahistorical (8, pp. 50-55; 10, pp. 107-123). Thus, the historicizing of disease and medicine remains in spite of the fact that medicine, reflecting its bourgeois basis, has not developed sociopsychosomatic foundations. What matters is not the medical legitimation of our procedure, but the intention of seeing how an unqualified nature—inchoate symptoms, mannerisms, appearances—was appropriated in specific social settings, and formed into a specific nature—diseases—which obscured those very conventional origins.

CHLOROSIS: A PHYSICAL ILLNESS

I would like to turn to a disease which was taken to be physical, so that the separation between behavior and hard facts of medicine, the one social, the other scientific, cannot be sustained. Chlorosis (22) (the green sickness) was tersely and technically defined in 1925 (23):

> A primary anaemia [having no known cause] commencing at puberty, especially in girls, and characterized by pallor, symptoms of secondary anaemia, absence of wasting, and rapid improvement on treatment with iron. Now rare.

In addition to elaborate clinical details, a battery of physicochemical criteria identified chlorosis with increasing specificity during the 19th century. By 1832, chemical analysis of chlorotic blood had shown a decreased hemoglobin content. Protein and serum level determinations, red cell counts, sedimentation rates, and urinalysis were also applied. Even the pathological anatomy of chlorosis was described (24, 25, 26, pp. 52-54). But clinical acumen still came first (25, pp. 519-523):

> ... extreme anaemia of the skin and visible membranes, without impairment of the previous state of nutrition (sometimes with an actual increase in the amount of subcutaneous fat); dropsical symptoms comparatively rare, and when present always inconsiderable; power of continued muscular exertion very limited; fatigue speedily experienced; great tendency to dyspnoea and palpitation whenever any considerable exertions are made.... The pulse is usually small and compressible.... [There are often] loud systolic murmers.... She is liable to ... perverted cravings (picae) for such things as coffee beans, highly-spiced dishes, salads, and sour articles of food; sometimes for all sorts of indigestible things, such as slate-pencils, lead-pencils, eggshells, cotton-wool.... The patient may suffer from obstinate constipation.... The urine ... is pale, of low specific gravity, and contains but little urea or uric acid.... The state of the menstrual function requires especial notice because ... the invasion of the malady often coincides with the first appearance of the catamenia and the approach of the female organism to sexual maturity.... Nervous disorders are commonly, nay, very constantly associated with the chlorotic state.

Many clinicians also differentiated chlorosis from anemia, a discrimination which shows their clear perception of a discrete entity (27). The Parisian clinician, Trousseau

(28, p. 100) considered blowing sounds in the neck, detectable with the stethoscope, pathognomic:

> ... it appears to me that there are two classes of blowing sounds in the neck; viz. the simple sounds, purely arterial, and double-current sounds. ... The first belong to anaemia, whatever may be the cause of the anaemia: the others are peculiar to chlorosis.

Although chlorosis was, and is, described as an anemia, that can be misleading. Anemia is a symptom of many diseases, including chlorosis. Reduced red-cell size and hemoglobin levels are common in anemia, but to call chlorosis just an iron-deficiency anemia would be an oversimplification. Indeed, there is little correlation between the iron content of hemoglobin and nervous symptoms in iron-deficiency anemia (29). Physicians (30, 31) knew that the normal diet contained adequate iron, so that the efficacy of large doses of iron in treating chlorosis depended upon factors other than simply supplementing an iron-poor diet. Chlorosis was a "constitutional" disease which meant that it affected certain types of people—both physiological and psychological. Iron was more a tonic for constitutional torpor than a specific replacement therapy (32-34).

I mention the discrimination between chlorosis and anemia, partly to emphasize the precision of clinical analysis which reinforced belief in its objective reality, but also to cut short any suggestion that chlorosis is a disease still seen today, obscured only by a change in label. Chlorosis seems to have arisen and declined at definite times. Although the Hippocratic corpus refers to symptoms which were later interpreted as chlorotic, and the occasional modern author has used the word, chlorosis emerged in the 16th century; it was first described clearly in the early 18th century and became common in the 19th century; it peaked around mid-century and was rare by the 1920s. Explanations of its disappearance vary, but authors did reject the possibility that chlorosis vanished simply because it had received another name (35-41). According to the *British Encyclopaedia of Medical Practice* in 1936 (42):

> Chlorosis was a very common hypochromic anaemia occurring usually in young women, but during the last thirty years it has almost entirely disappeared, for which there is no explanation. ... Although the treatment and the response obtained are identical with those described under idiopathic hypochromic anaemia, the two diseases are not identical. ...

To go into these reasons in detail would get us into the risky business of retrospective diagnosis. But more important even than the explanations proposed to interpret its decline is the fact that the need met by attaching a medical label, with all the consequences that followed, was now either met in some other way, or no longer existed. We are led to accept the probable existence of a disease limited to a definite life-span, and the consequent suggestion that its presence depended upon factors which had their clearest expression in that period.

DISEASE AND SOCIAL CLASS: CHLOROSIS AS AN ILLNESS OF BEING "BETTER-OFF"

In 1928, the Marxist historian of medicine, Henry Sigerist (43, p. 63), suggested that:

> The symptom complex of chlorosis appears to be bound up with a definite type of young girl, as it is most clearly recognizable roughly in the *Biedermeier* period. With the disappearance of this type, the disease also disappeared. The history of chlorosis is the history of young girls in society.

Sigerist directs us not just to the period from the 1820s to the 1850s, but to a feature of German society. *Biedermeier* (44, 45) was a satirical term used to depict a narrow-minded, self-satisfied, conservative, law-abiding domestic class and mentality. Perhaps "petit bourgeoisie" would be an apt term—a group on the margin of the middle class whose very marginality engendered an exaggerated aping of "respectable" behavior.

Social class, such as petit bourgeoisie (used interchangeably with the "middle strata" and "lower middle class"), is really a dynamic concept—a frozen moment of social relations (46). By taking that relational characteristic into account, we can refine Sigerist's insight into the class associations of chlorosis. Medical conceptualization should be seen as the product of two analytically distinct features of class relations: the physician in his class, and the patient in hers.

The physician was a marginal member of the middle class, in that his social position derived from service to his patron-patients[1] (47-49). In terms of his economic relation to capital and his source of status, his professional position was structurally similar to the middle strata; both lived on service to better-off employers. The important issue was not occupation, but marginality in the bourgeoisie. While this marginality derived from being neither capitalist nor worker, it could be shifted in accordance with property, family connections, and clientele (50, pp. 134-136).

Marginality in both income and the sharpened quest for respectability can be seen in the hostility of physicians to female midwives. Midwifery provided both an entree for building up a family practice and an income supplement, so that general practitioners feared their competition. But because midwifery was a manual skill dealing with a normal feminine function, medical men—at least the elites—also thought it beneath the dignity of an educated gentleman. As a compromise, Sir Anthony Carlisle, council member and president of the College of Surgeons, recommended that the physicians' female relations take up midwifery. Thomas Wakely, editor of the *Lancet* and champion of general practitioners' interests, ridiculed the proposal because the employment of their relatives would have both excluded them from respectable society and been disreputable for the physicians (51).

The leading aspiration—most evident in the middle strata—was for upward social mobility. Since social class is both imprecise and relational, we might expect a continuum of aspiration throughout the middle class, exaggerated at points of marginality.

Turning to the patient (analytically distinct), I shall emphasize class dynamics in a similar way. "Bourgeois" meant nonworking women, trained to their station during the prolonged in-between period of adolescence. As a feature of aspiration rather than of financially determined reality, this feminine stereotype was an important part of lower-middle-class, and even of upper-working-class, consciousness (52, p. 83; 53).

Medicine recast social norms into the form of health. The physician's marginality supported an exaggerated normativeness of middle-class values, now medically

---

[1] Professor J. Peterson has carried out a detailed investigation of the social status of the medical profession, especially the London medical elites, in the 19th century. Her book is being published by the University of California Press, and should be available in 1978.

reformulated. Stereotyped class characteristics, such as uncontrolled, improvident, immoral working class; provident, hard-working, self-reliant middle class; idle, self-indulgent, luxurious upper class, could be construed as normal versus pathological. Pathology then became the naturalized measure of deviation from either side of the middle-class norm.

I shall take up the better-off deviation first. Cominos (54) has argued that upward social mobility in the middle class—especially at the lower end—demanded a self-denying, ascetic working life, and that these values found expression in a life of "sexual respectability." Sexual respectability meant late marriage and sexual restraint, the saving of sperm as well as money. Although Cominos does not say so, it seems as if sexual respectability helped to define "middle class," especially among the marginally middle class, by characterizing this distinctive, self-denying sexual ideal as "not working class." Delayed marriage and premarital restraint, the argument goes, were prerequisites for successful middle-class status. The working class showed little concern for either one. Thus, the distinction seems to have been more a definition than a description of middle-class behavior. Such a view is compatible with the interest in the age of puberty in girls seen in the writings of John Roberton (55). Since cross-cultural studies revealed that the age of puberty did not depend on the physical environment, he argued, the different ages of marriage in different cultures reflected social, not biological, factors. The late marriages in the West, therefore, signified advanced civilization, with its respect for women and the responsibility of motherhood.

Concrete historical changes lay beneath the idealization of sexual asceticism in the 19th century. Laslett (56) has shown that the age of puberty declined during the century, and has suggested that earlier sexual maturity upset authority in the family. The age at marriage of members of the working class also declined with industrialization, and stereotyped sex roles were eroded (57-59, 60, Ch. 9). Girls were physically and economically more likely to act autonomously and to set up independent households. Such promiscuous behavior in the working- and lower-middle classes must have threatened the stability of the middle-class ideal and have engendered an exaggerated reinforcement of its boundaries. It is likely that the focus of attention would have been on the sexuality of young adults, and especially on the purity of the better-off youth. The medical attention to sexually based pathology then became part of the overall discrimination between social classes.

Chlorosis was one form of sexually based pathology—in this case it was marked by asexuality (25, p. 563; 28, pp. 112-113). Associated not just with adolescence, but with being unmarried (31, p. 34), it had even been called the "virgin's disease" (61). It was also associated not just with disappointed vanity, but with disappointed sexual feelings (62, p. 69). The regimen for its treatment—early hours, regularity, open air, exercise, controlled diet and emotional life—was wholesomely childlike. A rejection of affectation comes out in discussions of chlorosis among the better-off. Late 18th- and 19th-century writers scorned the luxurious habits of well-to-do town ladies, who led idle, ornamental lives (62, p. 68). William Buchan, author of the popular *Domestic Medicine*, spoke of the dangers to them at puberty (63, pp. 526-527):

> A lazy indolent disposition proves likewise very hurtful to girls at this period. One seldom meets with complaints from obstructions among the more active and industrious part of the sex; whereas the indolent and lazy are seldom free from

them. These are, in a manner, eat up by the chlorosis, or green sickness, and other diseases of this nature.

Thomas Laycock, a prominent writer on nervous system physiology and pathology, blamed forced mental training, sedentary employments without enough outdoor exercise, music, dancing, vivid colors and odors, and "the excitement and competition of social life, excited love, ungratified desire, disappointed vanity as well as affecting late hours, long and late indulgence in sleep, and the excessive use of stimulants . . ." (64). These authors paint with a broad brush a picture of young women living artificially and without anything worthwhile to fill their time. Girls fallen into frivolous idleness weakened their delicate constitutions. Indeed, Buchan feared a future with women incapable of bearing healthy children or of caring for them (63, pp. 25-31).

Chlorosis emerged as a disease of refinement at a time when physicians would have seen mainly a well-to-do clientele. It seems also to have delineated a discrete stage in the life cycle, in that the occurrence of symptoms around the time of puberty became pathognomic for the new disease. Age, along with symptoms which might have been found in a wide variety of people, indicated chlorosis almost by definition (25, pp. 504-506, 545-546, 554-557; 36; 37). Chlorosis and unfinished puberty went together. In a girl apparently developed physically, but not yet menstruating, "a struggle is evidently taking place to bring about the sexual functions" (62, p. 68). If they are not treated, the early symptoms lead to chlorosis. Thus, chlorosis marked a new social group, the fashionable female adolescent, by physical illness. The worry over the disease was an appreciation of the vulnerability of the adolescent. But knowing and controlling go together (65). Constructing an illness which then needed attention and treatment was one aspect of discovering adolescence which needed to be watched and controlled.

Chlorosis belongs with the 19th-century literature of innocence, which praised the unspoilt virtues of youth. Adolescence took its place in this literature as a natural stage between childhood and adulthood (66, 67). If we see them as part of the bourgeois ideal of delayed marriage, the connection between chlorosis and adolescence becomes clearer. Adolescence was inserted between sexual maturity and delayed marriage; chlorosis described and attended to the delicacy of this state by throwing its features into sharp relief.

Physicians condemned the refinement and luxury which led to disease. That was partly a class condemnation directed at the idle aristocrats. Since class is relational, we have to look at the importance of class in the medical perception of chlorosis. By rebuking aristocratic behavior through the naturalized mode of disease, the middle-class physician threw into relief the normativity of his own position. It was not so much the negative reaction to the better-off as the positive reinforcement of bourgeois identity. As at once a servant and an equal to his better-off patron-patients, the physician lived concretely the ambivalent position of an upwardly mobile bourgeoisie. Its medicalized condemnation of luxurious habits expressed a class hostility—one which concealed aspiration to the same style.

In *Middlemarch* George Eliot vividly portrays the class ambivalence of the doctor in the character of Lydgate, who indulges, indeed needs, the ornamental triviality of his wife, Rosamund. Rosamund comes from the Vincy family, which was a good

English equivalent of the *Biedermeier* type. Lydgate does not like what he sees, as Rosamund expresses her frustration in increasingly child-like behavior and material demands, but he cannot allow anything else either. Refinement became a hallmark of mobility, a defining characteristic in the aping behavior of a still unstable group.

We can see the same pattern in the anger of physicians over dress. In addition to scorning luxurious habits and refined taste, doctors admonished chlorotic girls for wearing constricting clothing (19, pp. 79-80; 36, pp. 183-184; 39, p. 34; 68). This case is curious, however, in that the styles of the well-to-do became increasingly plain and free during the century. Although tight-lacing and fashionable, constricting dress has been associated with Victorian sexual repressiveness and respectability (a view shared by contemporary physicians), it was really a lower-middle-class practice. It was an act of defiance which, far from being sexually repressive as the restriction of movement would suggest, was considered sexually titillating and a little vulgar. Corsetting for the Victorians was "part of the sociosexual initiation of puberty." The corsetted waistline was a sign of an insecure, not a stable leisured, class (69).

In this example of dress styles, we see another characterization of the pathology of puberty and adolescence. Although physicians attributed the pathology to the better-off by equating these styles with fashion and therefore with luxury, tight lacing actually referred to the lower-middle class. The physicians and the lower-middle-class girls shared the aping of respectability which derived from their marginal positions. But in their mimicry of respectability, the dress styles flaunted the sexuality which respectability was meant to conceal. The better-off in the middle class saw it as vulgar; the doctors, who were part of the scientific edge of this class, saw it as pathological. The medical judgment was simply the naturalized reformulation of the same reaction to the distorted co-option of its norms. The outrage expressed the instability of the upwardly mobile middle class which, we might reasonably argue, saw the lower-middle-class styles as a covert mockery of its own pretensions; saw chlorosis as a mockery of its aspiration to refinement; and saw hysteria as a mockery of its idealized modesty (70, p. 10).

This edginess about lower-class behavior was, therefore, a feature of the marginality of physicians and the aspirations to refinement of the bourgeoisie. Their very negativeness about aspiration and refinement shows their emphasis on bourgeois values as normative—the zero point or standard—in the face of their own mobility. While lower-middle-class aping might have invited their scorn by exposing their own aspiration, working-class aspiration, symbolized by activities such as eating meat (46, p. 349), needed their guidance and control. Doctors were concerned about the health of the working class, whose inclination to eat above its station could only do harm (71).

In this section, I have given the impression that the middle class enforced control of both the upper and lower classes through medical knowledge. That puts it all negatively, in the form of social control. It might be put positively in terms of reinforcing class identity. I would like to suggest an even stronger formulation. Since that identity was formed in relation to other classes, it included not only the perceived or defined distinctions which cement and structure it, but also factors close to concrete conditions dependent on the mode of production. After all, there was a material basis for these class distinctions. Concepts like social control are useful, but applicable generally to all societies. The particular society we are looking at was one which was perfecting the means of extracting surplus value from workers, so that the organization of that process and the associated class relationships (on which class identity depends) are especially important. I would, therefore, now like to develop that aspect more fully.

THE OTHER SIDE: CHLOROSIS AND THE WORKING CLASS

So far I have stressed one side of the picture, disease and refinement. This aspect is bound up with the position of the physician as a marginal man with aristocratic aspirations and patrons. The "naturalized," reified expression of the social relations involved here emerged in the medical literature in the form of theorizing about etiology. But refined adolescence was clearly only half the story. It seems a strange emphasis in describing the youth of the mid-19th century, when chlorosis exploded into visibility. During this period, physicians increasingly came into contact with working people in hospitals, dispensaries, and the Poor Law infirmaries. These institutions must have changed the perception of morbidity and mortality drastically by uncovering a vast field never seen in aggregate before (72-74).

Even the briefest look at hospital statistics shows that physicians regularly diagnosed chlorosis among the working-class people who came to them. To find chlorosis entered as a separate category in the disease classifications of even large general hospitals reinforces my argument that it was seen to be a discrete clinical entity. Since chlorosis was a nonfatal and usually minor illness, its appearance in the inpatient records of large British general hospitals suggests that the levels in the population were substantial. A good example of the two sides of chlorosis shows through the analysis of data from a study of idiopathic anemia among patients at the Victoria Park Hospital in London (30). During 1884, roughly 8 percent of 2087 were diagnosed anemic; of these 159 patients, 140 were idiopathic, of which 114 were female. No males were definitely idiopathic. More than half were 15-20 years old; less than a third 20-30; only 10 were 30-40. "Thus most of the cases would come under the head of what is called chlorosis," according to the reporting physician, Vincent Harris, who went on to say (30, p. 87):

> A very notable fact about this was the great number . . . who had no occupation, that is to say, who lived at home. The patients at the hospital are, as a rule, of rather a better class than those at ordinary general hospitals, and of the whole number observed, very few could have their condition traced to their occupation. This will certainly accord with the experience of most, that chlorosis is a condition observed among the well-to-do classes. . . .

But his table of occupations does not convincingly support his conclusion. In many cases, only a small proportion of the patients had no occupation;[2] instead, they were servants, dressmakers, boot sewers, machinists, etc. Although he takes his hospital experience to confirm the common view that chlorosis was a disease of well-to-do adolescent girls, his own data show that it was found among the working class as well (30, p. 88).

The source of the contradiction between the data and the interpretation may lie in a socially structured perception of illness which excluded occupation as an exciting

---

[2] It was common to underestimate the extent of female working, so that "no occupation" is misleading (75, pp. 63-66).

cause. Hackney was a new district in 19th-century London. It was an upwardly mobile lower-middle-class area with a high proportion of service to other female occupations (leaving out wealthy areas). Areas like Hackney were major immigration points for country girls coming into domestic service in the city (52, p. 139). Servants were prized because they released the family women from domestic work, and thereby signified respectability (53). Given the aping, exaggerated respectability characteristic of middle-strata values, we would expect Harris' sample to be archetypal in terms of marginality. We would therefore expect to find the contradictory presence of both strong, normative standards of behavior reinforced by the pathology of deviation, and aspiration toward those same deviant, luxurious styles. Thinking of the field of disease and the corresponding social background of the people which the doctor would have seen, we might guess that there were many working girls whose chlorosis did not appear to be work-related because the image of the area was "respectable."

It may be significant, therefore, that the majority of the working women in Harris' study were domestic servants. If we add to them the other trades, such as needlework, which, like service, were done in households, the numbers would be even greater. The physician then would have seen chlorosis as a disease of young women of respectable households; his perception would have been of the group, rather than of individual cases associated with concrete working and nonworking conditions. The physician may even have seen the family girls in his private practice and the working girls at the hospital to which the family subscribed. If a household was the social unit which produced chlorosis from the physician's point of view, it is also possible that chlorosis was a shared self-perception among the women themselves. Symptoms reinforced by such a common self-image could have combined with the medical perception based on the household unit to form the stereotype of an illness of nonworking young women. (Remember that Harris seemed to equate nonworking with staying at home.) With girls in households making up a large proportion of chlorotic girls, the stereotype could have spread easily.[3]

Such an analysis applies most readily to the household case. Indeed, one can find references to chlorosis as a disease of domestic servants (31, p. 34; 34, p. 378), the majority of whom in London were between 15 and 25 years old, the typical chlorotic age (75, p. 98). But writers also referred explicitly to its prevalence among the manufacturing working class (34, p. 378):

> In some manufacturing districts, chlorosis and some affections strictly allied to it, may, from the habits of the people, be justly said to be endemic.

But even so, the possible recognition of illness related primarily to occupation was often deflected onto an account of urban versus rural conditions, or onto the personal habits of the people. Stating that chlorosis was the most common menstrual disorder, Thomas Ashwell, obstetrician at Guy's Hospital, added (76, p. 534):

> The registrars of hospital and of private practice will fully confirm this statement; more especially, if we include the female youth of the higher ranks, where delicacy and disease are so prevalent, and the young females inhabiting large cities and towns,

---

[3] My comments are derived from suggestions offered by Professor M. Jefferys in response to the version of this paper which I presented to the Society for the Social History of Medicine, Summer Conference, July 9-11, 1977, University of Cambridge.

> in many of which, unhealthy employments, crowded and densely-peopled streets and houses, together with bad air, irregular diet and excess, inevitably produce an enfeebled and diseased offspring.

Although he did mention working-class conditions, Ashwell put a particular slant on his interpretation (76, p. 551):

> Chlorosis is a rare affection in rural districts; where female youth are much in the open air, where is it not unfashionable to walk and run, and where it is not considered a gross violation of good breeding to sport and play with activity and vigour.

In spite of explicitly referring to the working class, he emphasized urban versus rural conditions and personal behavior associated with respectability.

What is striking about the etiological discussions of chlorosis in the 19th century is the persistence of the image of the idle, well-to-do girl. The tenacity of this perception of the socioclinical entity, the chlorotic young woman, in the face of the discovery of a similar entity in the working class, needs some explanation. One interpretation follows the lines I have developed in discussing marginality, aspiration, and upward mobility. Along with marginality went strongly normative values of self-reliance, character, and respectability which distinguished the middle strata from the working class. This separation was reinforced by sexually based diseases which stressed both the innocence of the better-off girl and the pathology of aspiration (as in the case of working-class eating habits). The aspiration of the middle class, exaggerated at points of marginality, led to a contradiction, in that those who rejected it in principle were living it in fact. Medicine, reformulating this contradiction in theories of disease, concealed this aspiration by condemning both aspiration and luxurious habits in the language of diseases of refinement.

The household case was an example of marginality in a concrete situation. There the aspiration of the family and the exploitation of the worker were not only economically related, they were actually located in the same place. In the general case where the economic relationship between leisured respectability and exploitative work held, but where there was no equivalent to a household unit to structure both behavior and medical perception, this example might not provide a mechanism adequate to explain chlorosis as a socioclinical entity. But the perception was still the same. The illness of working-class girls was interpreted in terms inappropriate to their working conditions. Moreover, the etiological emphasis on refinement made illness into a personal failing. Idleness was voluntary; diseases of refinement were also voluntary—ultimately. The effect of this etiological inappropriateness was to conceal the relations between illness and work by defining them out of existence. That was also its ideological function. The marginality argument located the place in society where delineation from the working class was sharpest and middle-class values were most clearly expressed, and showed how it contributed to chlorosis. But I want to make a general point about the ideological work of medicine—that it privatized illness and thereby concealed the social relations and social consequences (illness) of work.

Chlorosis was only one example of this ideological power. One can also see it in the discussions of the increasing burden of chronic illness which differentiated the new urban industrial areas from the country. There were no clear causes and, curiously, that very absence of an etiology made these illnesses potentially potent as social criticism. There was no way to treat them as accidents of an otherwise healthy system. Reporting on dressmakers and milliners in London for the Privy Council, William Ord found symptoms of brain distress, dyspepsia, phthisis, chlorosis, hysteria, and affections of vision. Although these symptoms appeared to condemn the conditions of work, they were not associated with any clear pathology, not even of occupational disease (77, pp. 370-371):

> Of diseases therefore specially dependent upon the nature of their occupation we find few among the dressmakers and milliners; we find nothing like the jaw disease of the match-makers, or the mercurial tremors of the looking-glass makers, or the lung disease of the stone grinders. . . .

What was becoming evident was a state of ill-health, rather than disease. Even the traditionally recognized relations between disease and the particular condition of work faced by miners or the workers referred to above were less apparent in the new industrial setting. Health/ill-health was a different axis from health/disease (77, p. 371):

> . . . but we find, in place of such well defined instances of cause and effect, the terrible fact that thousands of women in London are pursuing their occupations under conditions which constantly undermine their vital and physical powers, and contract, with fatal certainty and by large per-centage, their measure of years.

Acute disease was not the problem. Chronic illness was becoming endemic, and its potential for exposing the sick-making conditions inseparable from the labor process itself was high. Acute disease fired controversy over specific causes, such as the nature of contagion; chronic illness, expressing a depletion of vitality, implicated the working conditions.

In 1863 there was the sensational newspaper story of the death of Mary Anne Walkely, who worked in a respectable dressmaking establishment. The attending physician reported to the coroner's jury that she "had died from long hours of work in an over-crowded work-room, and a too small and badly-ventilated bedroom." But the jury refused to accept his opinion, and instead ruled that she had died of apoplexy accelerated by these conditions (78, 79, p. 475). This case is extreme, but its lesson holds for the more routine examples—responsibility was deflected away from working conditions.

In his report on the diseases of printers, Edward Smith (80) noted the picture of chronic illness: exhaustion due to defective alimentation and assimilation, or defective appetite and digestion, lassitude, weakness, feeble heart action, lessened respiration, headache, bilious derangements, swelling feet, and piles. He went on to say (80, p. 410):

> The diseases of printers are commonly ascribed more to their unsteady habits than to the conditions of their occupation; but whilst it may readily be admitted that excess will predispose the system to the attacks of disease, the nature of the diseases, as above mentioned, show that they are less due to the habits of the operatives than to the conditions of their labour.

Like Ord, Smith noted that there was little specific disease, but insisted that there was nonetheless major ill-health which could not be measured by the printers themselves. Smith and Ord were warding off the manipulative neglect of the conditions producing ill-health as opposed to disease, and Smith was clearly aware of how the responsibility for their state could be put onto the workers themselves.

Benjamin Richardson, senior physician to the Royal Infirmary for Diseases of the Chest and prolific writer on health, wrote a series of articles on overwork (81). One can see in this enlightened writer the way medical writers "liberalized" the understanding of disease, i.e. they cautiously introduced all the relevant factors in such a way as to make a consistent criticism impossible. It was a setting of the terms of discussion so as to eliminate the extension of a "purified" medical account into the social dimension. Richardson's articles by and large neglected the overwork of anyone but middle-class people, except for an article on physical overwork, "the work that kills" (81, pp. 193-202). Conceding here that "people die *at* their calling," he was careful to distinguish that from dying *from* it (81, p. 193, Richardson's italics). People had a definite reserve of vital energy, which could be exhausted quickly or slowly. He condemned the organization of work which, in the interest of greed, extracted that energy rapidly from workers. He had in mind the baker, compositor, needleworker, "and the representative indeed of every trade, or art, or profession, from which some product has to be furnished within a given period of time, and where indifferent remuneration for work done, or greed on the part of an employer, prevents due distribution and division of toil. . . ." Even strikes he saw as a "solemn protest against the violation of natural laws."

But Richardson also mixed the professions into his account. He saw in the protest mentioned above a lesson for those who *voluntarily* overstrained themselves. Similarly, while his accounts of overwork included the exploited workers, they tended to emphasize cases like that of the athlete (e.g. the Oxford and Cambridge boat race led to premature death). His very generousness in pointing out causes of ill-health smothered the detailing not only of the impact of exploitation, but also of the conditions of unhealthy work which were irradicable. The fragmentation of work as labor power from concrete work in a concrete structure and the mixing together of the problems of the boatman with the industrial worker both separated off an apparently legitimate domain of medical concern and deflected the terms of discussion from the specific to the abstractions of the quantitative depletion of an inborn supply of vitality.

The background for these examples was an apparent decline in acute disease and the increase in chronic illness in urban areas, which was interpreted in terms of town versus country environment. Indeed, town versus country was an explicit redirection away from industrial versus nonindustrial work (82). Even the apologist for the industrial system, Andrew Ure, acknowledged the changing pattern, or at least part of it. Noting the decline in acute diseases among the town population, but not mentioning the increase in chronic illness, he proclaimed the advantages of industrial life for the workers (83, 84). Ure's pronouncement tells us about medicine as well. As a bearer of bourgeois ideology, medicine was reinforcing the legitimacy of Ure's statement, not by guaranteeing better health, but by redefining the health problems in terms unconnected with the labor process.

MEDICAL THEORY AND PERSONAL
RESPONSIBILITY FOR ILLNESS

I have been working toward the view that medicine, in its theory as well as its practice, stabilized class stratification and deflected criticism from socioeconomic conditions. It was a bearer of the dominant liberal ideology which saw the social system in terms of the free interaction of individuals. My argument is that both the behavior of physicians as a marginal middle-class group *and* the theories they produced ought to be seen as part of that ideology. My stronger claim is that the class positions of physicians and patients also contributed to theoretical formulations of illness. Ideologies are stabilizers; the liberal view of free individuals was a stabilizer, in that it was a depoliticized, privatized, individualistic reinterpretation of social structure in terms of character (a potentially biological concept), or personal success and failure (53, pp. 75-76). For Marx, the commodity exchange characteristic of liberal capitalist society replaced all qualitative differences by the single abstract measure of the exchange value. People were reduced to abstract labor power, which was sold as a commodity. From a social point of view everyone was the same, so that the actual social differences between people had to come from natural ones. Thus, *social inequality* was naturalized by an ideology based on *social equality* (9, p. 241):

> Indeed, in so far as the commodity or labour is conceived of only as exchange value . . . then the individuals, the subjects between whom this process goes on, are simply and only conceived of as exchangers. As far as the formal character is concerned, there is absolutely no difference between them, and this is the economic character, the aspect in which they stand towards one another in the exchange relation; it is the indicator of their social function or social relation towards one another. . . . As subjects of exchange, their relation is therefore that of *equality.* . . . And if one individual, say, cheated the other, this would *happen not because of the nature of the social function in which they confront one another*, for this is the *same*, in this they are *equal*; but only because of natural cleverness, persuasiveness etc., in short only the purely individual superiority of one individual over another [italics in original].

From the earlier discussion of marginality, it should not be surprising to find the middle strata in 19th-century Britain espousing the liberal ideology at a time when the bourgeoisie was relaxing such a view (85, p. 46). Again it was the marginal sector which held to an exaggerated—sometimes dated—bourgeois ideology. And it should also come as no surprise to find medicine promoting a similar position. It objectified and universalized the causes of illness—that was science—but simultaneously reflected responsibility back onto the sufferer. Health, vigor, and success went together; so did failure, indolence, and illness (86, 87). This was clear in the hygiene mentality, which implicated abstract features of the environment in disease, and also in the emphasis on refinement, luxury, and relaxed habits. The concrete reality of illness became abstract principles of hygiene for which individuals were ultimately responsible.

The hygienic view stressed self-control (88):

> . . . as self-conquest is the preparatory step, we cannot estimate more than one in a million who would bring *all* the necessary qualifications into the field for obtaining health. . . .[italics in original].[4]

This identification of health with self-discipline was a common form of mediated social control in the 19th century. It went neatly with the various forms of "cultural control" (89, pp. 186-194) (education, religion, friendly societies) by which the bourgeoisie asserted authority over the working class—with the middle strata as vocal spokesmen (89, pp. 163, 166-176). The manners of Victorian politeness were one face; domination was the other (89, pp. 191-193). The former concealed the latter. The issue was the demand for a stable, disciplined work force, internalized as personal responsibility for health and illness. Polite manners established social distance from the working class and set the language in which all social experience was discussed. The medical language of refinement did the same.

The hygiene mentality expressed the insistent reenactment of disciplined social control within the details of everyday life. Indeed, the amenities of privacy and cleanliness advocated by the public health reformers in the 19th century were as much about insinuating self-control, discipline, and regularity into the habits of the emerging industrial work force as they were about the control of disease (90-92).

The principle partly ensured the regimented consciousness necessary to adapt to the arbitrary dictates of alienated life (93, 94). Foucault has analyzed the extension of discipline into the control of the details of movements which made up a previously integrated act. This insertion of control into the interstices of the personal relationship with one's own activity was reproduced in all aspects of daily life, and mirrored in the overt control of people in society. From work discipline to the mechanical model of the body in post-Cartesian philosophy, the image was the same (95). This mentality also redirected the critique of failure away from the socioeconomic conditions and onto the individual. Even food was secondary to washing. Commenting on a paper by Edward Smith, "On the economic value of foods," Edwin Chadwick turned the focus from diet to cleanliness (96). He pointed out that the experience in the Crimea, the work of Aubin on the health of pauper children, and his own experience as a prison medical officer had shown that ventilation and regular washing, not better diet, improved general health. Cleanliness even worked with pigs, which gained one-fifth more weight when regularly and completely washed. In line with a common worry of middle-class writers of the time, Chadwick also pointed out the danger that high wages in urban work led people to substitute tea and bread and butter for oatmeal porridge and milk (96). The aspirations of working people, once again, seem to have been responsible for their plight. If they adopted bourgeois values, such as cleanliness, without aping bourgeois manners, fashions, and foods, they would be healthy. In another paper Edward Smith showed that every working family could eat well if they stuck to certain simple diets, of which he gave several examples (97). The nutritive

---

[4]The quotation continued, ". . . we may venture to trace a modified scale for a comparatively *partial success.*" Pinney (88, pp. 257-258) rejected even that rather austere position, on the grounds that it blurred an absolute distinction between health, achieved by discipline, and sickness, resulting from any deviation from it. Thus, he suspected that the quoted author's position would mislead people into complacency, followed by illness.

value of meals dropped radically if tea or coffee (two drinks which symbolized aspiration and respectability) was added in lieu of other foods.

The same privatizing ideology can be traced in the theoretical structure of 19th-century medicine. This was where the real mediation took place, because it was here that the medical concepts appeared to have autonomous roots. The linking concept which joined the theoretical core of medicine with the more popular hygiene mentality was "constitution." The history of the term shows the increasing emphasis upon the individual as industrialization took hold. Traditionally, it referred to the character of a locality at a certain time, including the people. It was a typology, a physiognomy, comprising the character of the people, the nature of the land and climate, and the prevalent diseases. There was in it a natural bond between the person and his or her environment, and disease was one intrinsic feature of that relationship. But during the 19th century the emphasis shifted away from depicting a total situation onto characterizing the general state of the individual. Constitutional weakness, stressed by an exciting cause, brought about disease (98; 99; 100, p. 731; 101-103).

In one sense constitutional theories of disease could promote a medicine of the whole person. Constitution was an individual character, a product of the uniqueness in health and illness of the person as an integrated totality. In the hands of someone with revolutionary intent, such as Rudolph Virchow in 1848, this natural union between environment and disease through constitution could support severe criticism of a society which made people sick, and a call for reform. Characteristically, Virchow's paper, "The epidemics of 1848," referred not just to disease but to the revolutions (104). Disease and social upheaval were simply two phases in the reaction to a pathological socioeconomic condition. The "money aristocracy," workers as "hands," declining birthrate and prohibition of drink engendered by church authority, indolence and lassitude in the face of what would have provoked an uprising elsewhere, all led to the disastrous typhus epidemic in Silesia. Typhus, on which Virchow was reporting for the Prussian government, and an abortive political revolution went hand in hand (105, pp. 305-307).

Constitution as the theoretical underpinning of medical thought worked in a critical, reformist direction for Virchow. In Britain, constitution generally cut in another, reactionary, way. Indeed, the British medical press did not refer to Virchow's massive report on typhus, in spite of similar outbreaks in Britain and in spite of the swell of interest in public health legislation at the time.

Rosenberg has pointed out how hereditarian ideas, common in 19th-century medicine, could burden a woman with the knowledge that her accumulated experience, before and after childbirth, both mental and physical, was passed on to her child (106, pp. 191-201). Lumbering her children with her own life history (58, pp. 438-439), a mother engendered a debilitated lineage. All constitutional thinking had the same reactionary capability (107):

> The entire mode of living of the individual, his earlier history, his moral character, his habits, his experiences and his conduct . . . can, partly alone, if they are sufficiently pronounced, partly in arbitrary and manifold combinations, effect deviations in constitution.

A person was ultimately responsible for his or her own illness. The same responsibility extended to social class and sex.

Disease was the evidence that a predisposition existed. "The *disordered* condition of the parents' system is brought down to positive *disease* in the offspring. . . ." (108, p. 33, italics in original). The condition of the parents depended upon their habits, as well as on physical determinants, so that the notion of constitution which characterized that overall condition inserted moral values into the natural domain of pathology (108, p. 46):

> The philosophical manner in which the essential nature of all diseases has been studied of late years, has been the means of pointing out that, for the most part, they originate in an unnatural depression of the vital powers. . . . Most of these persons have inherited this unfortunate organization from their parents. . . . Thus the poverty or improvidence of the parents which drives them to seek their dwellings in the worst part of town, acts with a double force upon the offspring; entailing upon them at once ignorance, destitution, and physical and moral degradation.

These predispositions were stable; they could mix with others to produce yet new predispositions. Thus, lineages of disease susceptibility could build up within social groups, so that typologies of predispositions became invisible reproductions of the socioeconomic structure of society.

In this way, cancer and consumption combined to form *lupus*; the rheumatic and consumptive forms engendered *morbus coxae* or hydrocephalus; the scrofulous and syphilitic formed rickets or *molities ossium* (109, 110). Looking at mortality in Alston, Greenhow (111) reported to the General Board of Health that the long lead-mining tradition there had probably engendered a different race, with peculiarities which included the tendency to pulmonary diseases. Chlorosis, a disease in its own right, also predisposed its sufferers to a cluster of other illnesses: phthisis, hysteria, chorea, epilepsy, Basedow's (Graves') disease, endocarditis, ulcer, and cerebral hemorrhage. Indeed, this specific family of diseases distinguished chlorosis in yet another characteristic from anemia (25, pp. 548-554). These examples come from the hard-core medical literature, not from a popularizing fringe.

Thus, constitution as the central presupposition in medical thinking carried the implicit personal responsibility for illness into the hard core of medical theory. The ideological structure of medicine, which concealed the working conditions organized by capitalism, combined with the individualistic ideology of personal responsibility to promote individualism, not only in the marketplace, but also in the sickbed.

If it seems peculiar to speak of medicine doing this kind of ideological work, other examples from health-related areas might make the case more believable. Stedman Jones' impressive study (52) makes it clear that the lower end of London's working class in the second half of the 19th century, the "residuum" as they were called, were caught in an economic dilemma which dictated how and where they lived, ate, and worked. Chronic unemployment and overcrowded housing contributed to the middle-class image of them as almost a separate race of urban degenerates, and it was no accident that theories of biological degeneration blossomed at this time.

The description of the Londoner might even sound like a sympathetic description of the impact of urban life on health, where "the narrow chest, the pale face, the weak eyes and bad teeth of the town-bred child are but too often apparent" (112). If "the less efficient and weaker townsmen [were] thrown out of work" (113) in preference for the sturdy countryman, it only proved the employers' preference for the provincial immigrant, who sustained the vitality of the city. But Stedman Jones argues (52, p. 130):

> What was usually in question was not the debility of the Londoner, but rather his obstinacy and truculence. More often than not, such statements simply expressed the preference of employers for a docile and pliable labour force which they naturally associated with the countryside. In the 1880s, on the other hand, social Darwinism added a cosmic significance to the struggle between the country and the town. Biologism provided a framework for a comprehensive theory of hereditary urban degeneration.

So, in fact, biological degeneration concealed economic exploitation (114).

Wohl (115) has looked into the dramatic accounts of the connection between working mothers and child mortality in the 19th century (60, Ch. 6). He concludes that the working mothers probably contributed to providing a more adequate diet for their families than nonworking mothers, and he also asks why it was that so much attention was given to the supposed deterioration of working-class families because of female work. He notes that, not only was there no evidence to support such a case, but also that contemporary writers ignored the economic necessity for females to work. What they must also have ignored was the capitalist's use of female labor to reduce wages. In this example, the health of urban children, such a focus of 19th-century middle-class concern, absorbed the analytical energy which might have been put into examining the mode and social relations of production; and the responsibility for the poor health of children was deflected onto the personal failure of mothers. We could go on finding examples. The "scientific management" movement of the early 20th century became a scientific study of working efficiency and happiness, and concealed the basic driving force, the extraction of more surplus value from labor. If we are absorbed in the bourgeois conception of the problem, then the study becomes self-explanatory, an elegant science in its own right (8, pp. 60-69; 116).

It is seductive to believe that health is an objective notion shared by all sectors of society. Everyone wants health for everyone. But what I have tried to show historically is that it participates in the conflicts of class in capitalist society (117, 118). Indeed, the sociopolitical context informs the very "recognition" of particular diseases. Naming transfers the locus of pathology from society to the individual (119, 120). With respect to chlorosis and adolescence, my point can be put briefly. Capitalism developed increasingly by calling on youthful female labor. To the extent that the working-class girl was drawn into the labor process, the characteristics of the nonworking girl were exaggerated, first by defining adolescence as a new childlike stage corresponding to the age of intensive laboring in the working class, and then by throwing into ever sharper relief the image of asexual, nonworking, delicate femininity. Chlorosis reinforced this now polarized, dual nature of the youth become an adolescent.

CONCLUSION: MEDICINE AS AN IDEOLOGY

I have been emphasizing the role of medicine as a mediator. Medicine was an ideological system giving the added weight of "naturalized" authority to the bourgeois organization of society. I have tried to show that these values were embodied in the medical theories themselves.

Theories present putatively value-neutral "objects" which seem to relate to each other directly, rather than to mediate social relations. That is their power. In Lukács' formulation (121):

> These unmediated concepts, these "laws" sprout just as inevitably from the soil of capitalism and veil the real relations between objects. They can all be seen as ideas necessarily held by the agents of the capitalist system of production. They are, therefore, objects of knowledge, but the object which is known through them is *not* the capitalist system of production itself, *but the ideology of the ruling class* [emphasis added].

If we look at medicine and at the historical or sociological analyses of medical activity, we see concepts which apparently relate to each other immediately and logically, but which are often a constructed reality which diverts attention from the social formations arising from the system of production—reflections of the dominant ideology which cover the social relations of people. Diseases understood through medical writers are forms of knowledge, but forms which lead to that ideology, and away from the mode and social relations of production.

Having discussed the ideological work of medicine in the broader dimensions of social class and capitalist industrialization, I want briefly to come back to the recent historical literature on women's illnesses in order to place it in this broader historical context. A lot of this literature has been inspired by the feminist interest in the distinctiveness of gender. It has pointed out that a woman, at the mercy of her peculiar biology, was thought to be unable to do the job of a man, or even learn what a man learned, without suffering and burdening her children with disease. Women without sexual desire were suited to help and relieve the sexual tensions of men, but not for employment, education, or sexual autonomy. Authoritative biomedical writers interpreted natural laws in such a way that the social duties expected of women were those commanded by biological necessity. Feminist historians have interpreted a change in any one aspect as raising a threat in others. This implies that the sexual subjugation of women did not just mean sexual submissiveness to the point of annihilating their own sexual desire; it also meant the denial of autonomy to the point of being passive in education, employment, and mature social standing. The conclusion one might draw from this literature is that medical "knowledge" could be misapplied by being turned into an ideology to suit any particular event in the service of the oppression of women, either in the general case (e.g. their biology incapacitates them from higher education), or in the particular encounter between a lady and her physician.

Morantz (122) has addressed herself to this issue by looking at the treatment given to both men and women; she denies that there was any sexually specific sadism in the treatment applied to women. Reinforcing her argument in terms of my social class analysis, I would say that the doctor did not have the option of expressing his anxiety or hostility in the presence of women by misusing his apparently neutral medical knowledge. The continued patronage on which his practice depended would scarcely have allowed him to misuse them in a way inconsistent with dominant values. Although women were being oppressed, we cannot justly conclude that the oppression came from a deliberate misapplication of medical "knowledge" to meet a particular need.

Verbrugge (14) has criticized this literature in the same way, arguing that sexual role divisions should be seen as only one example of hierarchy. She also questions the implicit functionalism which relates medical ideas, personal roles, and social issues together as if they are a self-contained system in which a small number of isolated factors respond to changes in any one of them in such a way as to restore a balance. The orientation is toward an enclosed system to the exclusion of the broader socio-political issues.

Sociological conceptualizing of the social structure of medicine perpetuates a similar exclusion of the socio-political-economic context. Frankenberg (123) points out that functionalist presuppositions prevent us from seeing the possibility of alternative forms of medical organization, such as patient control. For instance, the "sick role" is a doctor's concept (even though made up by sociologists), not a patient's (123, 124). The sociology of medicine uses the concept of the sick role as if it were a value-free description of the patient, but it is really an abstract generalization about the behavior *expected* of a patient in bourgeois society, by which patients are prevented from seeing themselves as a group. For Parsons (125) the notion of the sick role excludes clubbing—forming into a group. Patients by definition are separated individuals.

Such "value-free" theoretical terms, and the underlying framework that supports them, thus fragment historical wholes, so that it becomes plausible to concentrate upon the dynamic relations of elements enclosed within each isolated domain (e.g. scientific management, working mothers and child health, chlorosis and idleness, hysteria and role conflict, the internal history of medical ideas). As the reactions to his book have made clear, this fragmentation in historical writing is what E. P. Thompson flew in the face of by writing of the working class in early-19th-century Britain (126). One side sees organized behavior; the other side sees mobs. One side sees reasonable action in a group; the other side sees irrational turbulence. Class-consciousness flies in the face of the ethic of individualism in historical writing as elsewhere. Similarly, "social control" simultaneously provides a theoretical focus for historical research on social dynamics and suppresses the concrete realities of class struggle organized around production (127).

If we accept uncritically similar bourgeois presuppositions, we will look at doctors and patients as individual actors, behaving or misbehaving, rather than as members of classes, sometimes in conflict with one another, sometimes forming their identities in their relations with one another. We will also miss the fact that medical theories incorporate broader historical aspects such as class behavior, and that medical practitioners behave in accordance with them, not as individuals. Although the idea of role, with its correlative notions of function, stabilization and conflict, is seductive, we should redirect our attention away from the dynamic balance of an enclosed social structure, taken as given, and onto the broader historicized arena.

My purpose in this paper has been to show that we must look at the medicine specific to the development of capitalist society. I have argued that chlorosis characterized adolescence as a new stage in life, one associated with innocence. I have also argued that the middle-class reaction to the working class, accentuated by the marginal middle strata, and the marginality of the doctor, contributed to the perception of chlorosis. Using chlorosis and chronic illness, I also argued that under the putative objectivity of medical concepts lay social relations reinforced by their "naturalized" status. This ideological work of medicine supported class stratification by establishing social distance between the classes, similarly to Foster's "cultural control" (89, pp. 186-189). It also acted more directly to support the capitalist mode of production by deflecting criticism from concrete working conditions onto abstract generalities and onto personal responsibility for illness. In the case of chlorosis, the social distance between classes derived from the capitalist mode of production partly through the construction of adolescence. To concentrate on the stylized innocence of the period between puberty and marriage was inappropriate to the chlorotic working-class girl; this was precisely the point, because it diverted attention from her exploitation. Adolescence meant innocent girlishness—a general concept established by the establishment of the social group itself. But the reality was not innocence, but adulthood; not fashionable habits, but an increasingly demanding work discipline entailing the rationalizing of everyday life; not girlish dependence upon a traditional family, but independent wage earning. In the working class, adolescence meant a pool of labor power; in the aspiration of the middle class, it meant the delineation of those features of the bourgeois ideal. Medicine helped to secure both.

The connection of chlorosis with the mode of production refers to the structural relations in society. It is an example of the mode of production determining the social relations of production. Living those relations rather than standing outside them, the middle-class doctor saw delicate girls with bad habits who ran down their constitutions. They privatized the etiology, so that ultimately the sick individual was responsible. The same applied to groups. In both cases people appeared to be severed from the determinate social relations to which they were actually bound. Ideologies do just that, and in the process they conceptually establish the naturalness of the dominant organization of society. Sharing in that process, medicine reinforced the perception of independent people voluntarily coming together to live and work. Personal irresponsibility and poor habits led to illness. Even in large numbers, their illness did not symbolize the impact of structural features; it meant significant personal failures.

Finally, I am also arguing that chlorosis was constructed partly in support of these ideological uses, and lasted as long as its social meaning lasted. I do not suggest any one-to-one matching of disease to an aspect of society; indeed the complexity of the argument shows the attempt to sketch an approach to the layered and textured mediations involved. The marginality of the physician, the emergence of adolescence, the interdependence of idle and working girls, the concealment of sociogenic illness or illness as protest, and the medicalized formulation of an individualistic bourgeois ideal, were all part of my analysis. Overall, the system of social relations tended to reinforce bourgeois hegemony and medicine gave it a "naturalized" formulation.

Acknowledgment—I would like to thank Jane Caplan, Roger Cooter, Andrew Cunningham, Geof Eley, Kay Flavell, Ludmilla Jordanova, John Pickstone, Roy Porter, Gareth Stedman Jones, Robert Young, and Edward Yoxen for their help.

REFERENCES

1. Tuckett, D., editor. *An Introduction to Medical Sociology.* Tavistock Publications, London, 1976.
2. Woodward, J., and Richards, D., editors. *Health Care and Popular Medicine in Nineteenth Century England: Essays in the Social History of Medicine.* Croom Helm, London, 1977.
3. Grandy, R., editor. *Theories and Observation in Science.* Prentice-Hall, Englewood Cliffs, N.J., 1973.
4. Bloor, D. *Knowledge and Social Imagery.* Routledge and Kegan Paul, London, 1976.
5. Barnes, B. *Scientific Knowledge and Sociological Theory.* Routledge and Kegan Paul, London, 1974.
6. Barnes, B. *Interests and the Growth of Knowledge.* Routledge and Kegan Paul, London, 1977.
7. Young, R. Science *is* social relations. *Radical Science Journal* No. 5: 65-129, 1977.
8. Sohn-Rethel, A. Mental and manual work in Marxism. In *Situating Marx: Evaluations and Departures,* edited by P. Walton and S. Hall, pp. 44-71. Chaucer Publishing Company, London, 1974.
9. Marx, K. *Grundrisse,* translation and foreword by M. Nicolaus. Penguin Books, Harmondsworth, England, 1973.
10. Schmidt, A. *The Concept of Nature in Marx,* translated by B. Fowkes, pp. 124, 227, n. 148. New Left Books, London, 1971.
11. Bourdieu, P. *Symbolic Power,* translated by R. Nice. *Occasional Paper* No. 46, p. 2. Centre for Contemporary Cultural Studies, University of Birmingham, Birmingham, 1977.
12. Hartman, M., and Banner, L., editors. *Clio's Consciousness Raised: New Perspectives on the History of Women.* Harper and Row, New York, 1974.
13. Vicinus, M., editor. *Suffer and be Still.* University of Indiana Press, Bloomington, 1972.
14. Verbrugge, M. Women and medicine in nineteenth-century America. *Signs* 1(4): 957-972, 1976.
15. L'Esperance, J. Doctors and women in nineteenth-century society: Sexuality and role. In *Health Care and Popular Medicine in Nineteenth Century England,* edited by J. Woodward and D. Richards, pp. 105-127. Croom Helm, London, 1977.
16. Smith-Rosenberg, C. Puberty to menopause: The cycle of femininity in nineteenth-century America. In *Clio's Consciousness Raised,* edited by M. Hartman and L. Banner, pp. 23-37. Harper and Row, New York, 1974.
17. Haller, J., and Haller, R. *The Physician and Sexuality in Victorian America.* University of Illinois Press, Urbana, 1974.
18. Smith-Rosenberg, C., and Rosenberg, C. The female animal: Medical and biological views of woman and her role in nineteenth-century America. *Journal of American History* 60(2): 332-356, 1973.
19. Bullough, V., and Voght, M. Women, menstruation and nineteenth-century medicine. *Bull. Hist. Med.* 47(1): 60-82, 1973.
20. Wood, A. The "fashionable diseases": Women's complaints and their treatment in nineteenth-century America. In *Clio's Consciousness Raised,* edited by M. Hartman and L. Banner, pp. 1-37. Harper and Row, New York, 1974.
21. Smith-Rosenberg, C. The hysterical woman: Sex roles and role conflict in nineteenth-century America. *Social Research* 39(4): 652-678, 1972.
22. Hudson, R. The biography of disease: Lessons from chlorosis. *Bull. Hist. Med.* 51(3): 448-463, 1977.
23. Tidy, H. *Synopsis of Medicine,* Ed. 4, p. 611. John Wright and Sons, Bristol, 1925.
24. Chlorose. In *Dictionnaire des dictionnaires de médecine français et étrangers,* edited by A. Fabre, Vol. 2, pp. 483-490. Germer-Baillière, Libraire, Paris, 1840.
25. Immerman, C. Chlorosis. In *Ziemssen's Cyclopaedia of the Practice of Medicine,* edited by A. Buck, Vol. 16, pp. 497-571. Sampson, Low, Marston, Searle, & Rivington, London, 1877.
26. Gusserow, A. Menstruation and dysmenorrhea. In *Clinical Lectures on Subjects Connected with Medicine, Surgery and Obstetrics by Various German Authors,* edited by R. Volkman, Vol. 71, pp. 28-62. New Sydenham Society, London, 1877.

27. Riegel, F. The functions of the stomach in anaemia and chlorosis. In *Nothnagel's Encyclopaedia of Practical Medicine*, translation supervised by A. Stengel, Vol. 4, pp. 816-820. W. B. Saunders, Philadelphia, 1902-1903.
28. Trousseau, A. True and false chlorosis. In his *Lectures on Clinical Medicine Delivered at the Hotel-Dieu, Paris*, translated from the 1858 edition by Sir John Rose Cormack, Vol. 55, pp. 95-117. New Sydenham Society, London, 1872.
29. Crosby, W. Who needs iron? *N. Engl. J. Med.* 297(10): 543-545, 1977.
30. Harris, V. Observations on anaemia. *St. Bartholomew's Hospital Reports* 20: 83-92, 1884.
31. Anaemia. In *Black's Medical Dictionary*, edited by J. Comrie, p. 35. A. and C. Black, London, 1906.
32. Chlorosis. In *Dunglison's Dictionary of Medical Science*, edited by T. Stedman, Ed. 23, p. 237. J. & A. Churchill, London, 1904.
33. Thomson, S. Anaemia. In *Dictionary of Domestic Medicine and Household Surgery*, pp. 22-23, Groombridge and Sons, London, 1852.
34. Hall, M. Chlorosis. In *The Cyclopaedia of Practical Medicine*, edited by J. Forbes, A. Tweedie, and J. Conolley, Vol. 1, pp. 378-379. Sherwood, Gilbert and Piper, and Baldwin and Cradock, London, 1833.
35. Hirsch, A. *Handbook of Geographical and Historical Pathology*, translated from the 2nd German edition by C. Creighton, Vol. 2, pp. 492-501. New Sydenham Society, London, 1885.
36. Hansen-Kolding, A. Die Chlorose im Altertum. *Sudhoffs Archiv für die Geschichte der Medizin* 24: 175-184, 1931.
37. Weissenbach, R. La chlorose est-elle en voie de disparition? et pourquoi? *Le progrès médical* 18: 270-273, May 3, 1924.
38. Campbell, J. Chlorosis; a study of the Guy's Hospital cases during the last thirty years with some remarks on its aetiology and the causes of its diminished frequency. *Guy's Hospital Reports* 73: 247-297, 1923.
39. Lloyd Jones, E. *Chlorosis: The Special Anaemia of Young Women. Its Causes, Pathology and Treatment; Being a Report to the Scientific Grants Committee of the B.M.A.* Baillière Tindall & Cox, London, 1897.
40. Dunbar, H. F. *Emotions and Bodily Change*, pp. 299, 523. Columbia University Press, New York, 1954.
41. Anaemia. In *Black's Medical Dictionary*, edited by J. Comrie, Ed. 8, p. 40. A. and C. Black, London, 1926.
42. Wilkinson, J. Anaemia. In *The British Encyclopaedia of Medical Practice*, edited by Sir H. Rolleston, Vol. 1, p. 450. Butterworth & Company, London, 1936.
43. Sigerist, H. Kultur und Krankheit. *Kyklos* 1: 60-63, 1928.
44. Sagarra, E. *Tradition and Revolution; German Literature and Society 1830-1890*, pp. 75-91. Weidenfeld and Nicolson, London, 1971.
45. Bramsted, E. *Aristocracy and the Middle Class in Germany; Social Types in German Literature, 1830-1900*, Ed. 2, pp. 236-237; 318-319. University of Chicago Press, Chicago, 1964.
46. Thompson, E. *The Making of the English Working Class*, preface. Penguin Books, Harmondsworth, England, 1968.
47. Holloway, S. Medical education in England, 1830-1858: A sociological analysis. *History* 49(167): 299-324, 1964.
48. Jewson, N. Medical knowledge and the patronage system in eighteenth-century England. *Sociology* 8(3): 369-385, 1974.
49. Inkster, I. Marginal men: Aspects of the social role of the medical community in Sheffield, 1790-1850. In *Health Care and Popular Medicine in Nineteenth Century England*, edited by J. Woodward and D. Richards, pp. 128-163. Croom Helm, London, 1977.
50. Gray, R. Religion, culture and social class in late nineteenth and early twentieth century Edinburgh. In *The Lower Middle Class in Britain*, edited by G. Crossick, pp. 134-158. Croom Helm, London, 1977.
51. Donnison, J. *Midwives and Medical Men, a History of Inter-Professional Rivalries and Women's Rights*, pp. 47-50. Schocken Books, New York, 1977.
52. Stedman Jones, G. *Outcast London: Study in the Relationship Between Classes in Victorian Society*, Penguin Books, Harmondsworth, England, 1976.
53. McLeod, H. White collar values and the role of religion. In *The Lower Middle Class in Britain*, edited by G. Crossick, pp. 61-88. Croom Helm, London, 1977.

54. Cominos, P. Late-Victorian sexual respectability and the social system. *International Review of Social History* 8(1): 18-48, 8(2): 216-250, 1963.
55. Roberton, J. *Essays and Notes on the Physiology and Diseases of Women and on Practical Midwifery.* J. Churchill, London, 1851.
56. Laslett, P. Age of menarche in Europe since the eighteenth century. In *The Family in History: Interdisciplinary Essays,* edited by T. Rabb and R. Rotberg, pp. 28-47. Harper and Row, New York, 1973.
57. Medick, H. The proto-industrial family economy: The structural function of household and family during the transition from peasant society to industrial capitalism. *Social History* 1(3): 291-315, 1976.
58. Kern, S. Explosive intimacy: Psychodynamics of the Victorian family. *History of Childhood Quarterly* 1(3): 437-461, 1973-1974.
59. Scott, J., and Tilly, L. Women's work and the family in nineteenth-century Europe. *Comparative Studies in Society and History* 17(1): 36-64, 1975.
60. Anderson, M. *Family Structure in Nineteenth-Century Lancashire,* Ch. 9. Cambridge University Press, Cambridge, 1971.
61. Quincy, J. *Lexicon Physico-Medicum,* Ed. 10, p. 193. T. Longman, London, 1787.
62. Locock, C. Amenorrhaea. In *The Cyclopaedia of Practical Medicine,* edited by J. Forbes, A. Tweedie, and J. Conolley, Vol. 1, pp. 67-71. Sherwood, Gilbert and Piper, and Baldwin and Cradock, 1833.
63. Buchan, W. *Domestic Medicine.* J. Gleave, Manchester, England, 1822.
64. Laycock, T. *A Treatise on the Nervous Diseases of Women,* pp. 140-142. Longman, London, 1840.
65. Gordon, C. Birth of the subject. *Radical Philosophy* No. 17: 15-25, 1977.
66. Kett, J. Adolescence and youth in nineteenth-century America. In *The Family in History,* edited by T. Rabb and R. Rotberg, pp. 95-110. Harper and Row, New York, 1973.
67. Demos, J., and Demos, V. Adolescence in historical perspective. *Journal of Marriage and the Family* 31(4): 632-638, 1969.
68. Roberts, H. The exquisite slave: The role of clothes in the making of the Victorian woman. *Signs* 2(3): 554-569, 1977.
69. Kunzle, D. Dress reform as antifeminism: A response to Helene Roberts's "The exquisite slave: The role of clothes in the making of the Victorian woman." *Signs* 2(3): 570-579, 1977.
70. Clouston, T. Puberty and adolescence medico-psychologically considered. *Edinburgh Medical Journal* 26: 5-17, 1880.
71. Cooter, R. Unspeakable Practices, Natural Acts: Body Pushing, 1832-1851. Unpublished paper, 1978.
72. Fraser, D. *The Evolution of the British Welfare State: A History of Social Policy Since the Industrial Revolution,* pp. 82-87. Macmillan, London, 1973.
73. Mouat, F., and Snell, H. *Hospital Construction and Management,* pp. 12-14. Churchill, London, 1883.
74. Woodward, J. *To Do the Sick No Harm: A Study of the British Voluntary Hospital System to 1875.* Routledge and Kegan Paul, London, 1974.
75. Alexander, S. Women's work in nineteenth-century London; a study of the years 1820-1850. In *The Rights and Wrongs of Women,* edited by J. Mitchell and A. Oakley, pp. 59-111. Penguin Books, Harmondsworth, England, 1976.
76. Ashwell, T. Observations on chlorosis and its complications. *Guy's Hospital Reports* 1: 529-579, 1836.
77. Ord, W. Report on the Sanitary Circumstances of Dressmakers and Other Needlewomen in London. *Sixth Report of the Medical Officer of the Privy Council (1863),* pp. 362-382. Her Majesty's Stationery Office, London, 1864.
78. Marx, K. *Capital,* translation of 3rd German edition by S. Moore and F. Aveling, edited by F. Engels, Vol. 1, pp. 243-244. Lawrence and Wishart, London, 1974.
79. Richardson, B. Work and overwork. *The Social Science Review* 2: 475-481, 1863.
80. Smith, E. Report on the Sanitary Circumstance of Printers in London. *Sixth Report of the Medical Officer of the Privy Council (1863),* pp. 383-415. Her Majesty's Stationery Office, London, 1864.
81. Richardson, B. The diseases of overworked men. *Social Science Review and Journal of the Sciences* new series 1: 1-5, 97-110, 193-202, 289-298, 385-394, 481-496, 1864.
82. Knolty, J. *Darstellung der Verfassung und Einrichtung der Baumwolle-Spinnerei-Fabriken*

in Nieder-Oesterreich, Vienna, 1843. Reviewed in *British and Foreign Medical Review* 18: 147-152, 1844.

83. Ure, A. *The Philosophy of Manufactures*, pp. 384-400. Knight, London, 1835.

84. Engels, F. *The Condition of the Working Class in England (1845)*, authorized English edition, pp. 205-206. Progress Publishers, Moscow, 1973.

85. Crossick, G. The emergence of the lower middle class in Britain. In *The Lower Middle Class in Britain*, edited by G. Crossick, pp. 11-60. Croom Helm, London, 1977.

86. Smiles, S. *Self-Help; With Illustrations of Conduct and Perseverance*, new edition, pp. 317, 319. John Murray, London, 1887.

87. Acton, W. *The Functions and Disorders of the Reproductive System*, pp. 55-69. Lindsay and Blackiston, Philadelphia, 1867. Quoted in Cominos, P., Late-Victorian sexual respectability and the social system, *International Review of Social History* 8(1): 37, 1963.

88. "A Recent Writer on Health." Quoted in Pinney, J., *An Exposure of the Causes of the Present Deteriorated Condition of Health, and Diminished Duration of Life, Compared With That Which is Attainable by Nature . . .*, pp. 256-257, Longman, Rees, Orme, Brown, and Green, London, 1830.

89. Foster, J. *Class Struggle and the Industrial Revolution*. Weidenfeld and Nicolson, London, 1974.

90. Chadwick, E. *Report on the Sanitary Conditions of the Labouring Population of Great Britain (1842)*. Reprinted by Edinburgh University Press, Edinburgh, 1965.

91. Pearson, G. *The Deviant Imagination: Psychiatry, Social Work and Social Change*, pp. 143-176. Macmillan, London, 1975.

92. Schoenwald, R. Training urban man: A hypothesis about the sanitary movement. In *The Victorian City: Images and Realities*, edited by H. Dyos and M. Wolff, Vol. 2, pp. 669-692. Routledge and Kegan Paul, London, 1973.

93. Thompson, E. Time, work-discipline, and industrial capitalism. *Past and Present* No. 38: 56-97, 1967.

94. Harrison, B. *Drink and the Victorians*, pp. 40, 62. Faber and Faber, London, 1971.

95. Foucault, M. *Surveiller et punir*, Section 3. Gallimard, Paris, 1975.

96. Smith, E., and Chadwick, E. (Discussant). On the economic value of foods, having special reference to the dietary of the labouring classes. *Social Science Review and Journal of the Sciences* new series 1: 63-69, 1864.

97. Smith, E. On private and public dietaries. *Social Science Review and Journal of the Sciences* new series 1: 271-276, 1864.

98. Constitution. In *Nysten's Dictionnaire de médecine*, edited by E. Littré and C. Robin, Ed. 10, pp. 319-320. Baillière, Paris, 1855.

99. Galdston, I. The epidemic constitution in historical perspective. *Bull. N.Y. Acad. Med.* 8: 606-619, 1942.

100. Peter, J.-P. Maladès et maladies à la fin du xviiie siècle. *Annales: économies-sociétés-civilisations* 22(4): 711-751, 1967.

101. Greenhow, E. Quoted in Rosen, G., Disease, debility, and death. In *The Victorian City*, edited by H. Dyos and M. Wolff, Vol. 2, pp. 644-645. Routledge and Kegan Paul, London, 1973.

102. Grmek, M. Géographie médicale. *Annales: économies-sociétés-civilisations* 18(6): 1071-1097, 1963.

103. Reynolds, J. Introduction; causes [of disease]. In *A System of Medicine*, edited by J. Reynolds, Vol. 1, pp. 7-11. Macmillan, London, 1866.

104. Virchow, R. Die Epidemien von 1848. *Archiv für pathologische Anatomie, Physiologie und für klinische Medizin* 3: 3-12, 1851.

105. Virchow, R. Mitteilungen über die in Oberschlesien herrschende Typhus-Epidemie. *Archiv für pathologische Anatomie, Physiologie und für klinische Medizin* 2: 143-322, 1849.

106. Rosenberg, C. The bitter fruit: Heredity, disease, and social thought in nineteenth-century America. *Perspectives in American History* 8: 189-235, 1974.

107. Wunderlich, K. *Handbuch der Pathologie und Therapie*, Vol. 1, p. 11. Ebner & Seubert, Stuttgart, 1850. Quoted in Egli, M., *Psychosomatik bei den deutschen Klinikern des 19. Jahrhunderts, Züricher medizingeschlichtliche Abhandlungen*, neue Reihe Nr. 23: p. 37, Juris-Verlag, Zürich, 1964.

108. Strange, W. *An Address to the Middle and Working Classes on the Causes and Prevention of the Excess Sickness and Mortality Prevalent in Large Towns*. Longman (and others), London, 1845.

109. Richardson, B. *The Field of Disease: A Book of Preventive Medicine*, pp. 726-727. Macmillan, London, 1883.

110. Richardson, B. *The Diseases of Modern Life*, pp. 484-486. Macmillan, London, 1876.
111. Greenhow, E. *Papers Relating to the Sanitary State of the People of England . . . General Board of Health (1858), Pioneers of Demography Series*, pp. 63-64. Gregg International Publishers Limited, Westmead, Hampshire, England, 1973.
112. Longstaff, G. Rural depopulation. In *Outcast London*, G. Stedman Jones, p. 128. Penguin Books, Harmondsworth, England, 1976.
113. First report of the Mansion House Conference on the conditions of the unemployed. In *Outcast London*, G. Stedman Jones, pp. 128-129. Penguin Books, Harmondsworth, England, 1976.
114. Weber, G. Degeneration and Progress in Early Nineteenth-Century Social Theory. Paper presented to the conference, New Perspectives in the History of the Life Sciences, 1750-1850, University of Cambridge, March 19-21, 1976.
115. Wohl, A. Working Wives or Healthy Homes: The Late Victorian Controversy. Paper presented to the Society for the Social History of Medicine, University of Cambridge, July 8-10, 1977.
116. Young, R. Who Cares about Objectivity? –And Why? Paper presented in the series Science, Technology and Ideology, Imperial College, University of London, November 2, 1976.
117. *The Political Economy of Health*. A Special Issue of *The Review of Radical Political Economics*, Vol. 9, No. 1, 1977.
118. Navarro, V. *Medicine Under Capitalism*, pp. 92-93, 206-208. N. Watson, New York, 1977.
119. Illich, I. *The Limits to Medicine: Medical Nemesis. The Expropriation of Health*, pp. 168-170. Marion Boyers, London, 1976.
120. Dagognet, F. *Le catalogue de la vie*, p. 9. Presses Universitaires de France, Paris, 1970.
121. Lukács, G. *History and Class Consciousness*, translated by R. Livingston, pp. 13-14. Merlin Press, London, 1971.
122. Morantz, R. The lady and her physician. In *Clio's Consciousness Raised*, edited by M. Hartman and L. Banner, pp. 38-53. Harper and Row, New York, 1974.
123. Frankenberg, R. Functionalism and after? Theory and developments in social science applied to the health field. *Int. J. Health Serv.* 4(3): 411-427, 1974.
124. Waitzkin, H., and Waterman, B. *The Exploitation of Illness in Capitalist Society*, pp. 37-65. Bobbs-Merrill, Indianapolis/New York, 1974.
125. Parsons, T. *The Social System*, pp. 428-479. The Free Press of Glencoe, Glencoe, Ill., 1951.
126. Donnelly, F. Ideology and early English working-class history: Edward Thompson and his critics. *Social History* 1(2): 219-238, 1976.
127. Stedman Jones, G. Class expression *vs.* social control. *History Workshop* No. 4: 163-170, 1977.

CHAPTER 11

Sociobiology: Another Biological Determinism

R. C. Lewontin

The struggle between those who possess social power and those who do not, between "freeman and slave, patrician and plebian, lord and serf, guildmaster and journeyman, in a word, oppressor and oppressed" (1) is a war fought with many and varied weapons. Of highest importance are ideas, weapons in an ideological warfare by which every class struggling to maintain its grip on the world tries to justify its position morally and rationally, while those fighting to overturn the social order produce their own self-justificatory ideology as a counter weapon. If the revolution succeeds, that revolutionary ideology becomes transformed into a weapon of consolidation and conservation whereby yet further revolutionary challenges to the new dominant class can be resisted. Nothing better illustrates the historical progression of such ideological weapons than the revolution that created capitalist society.

The society of Europe before the 17th century (with the exception of certain mercantile Italian republics) was characterized by a static, aristocratic scheme of relations in which both peasants and landowners were bound to each other and to the land and in which change in the social position of individuals was exceedingly rare. Persons were said to owe their position in the world to the grace of God, or to the grace of earthy lords. Even kings ruled "Deo Gratia," and changes in position could occur only by exceptional conferrals or withdrawals of divine or royal grace. But this rigid hierarchy directly obstructed the expansion of both mercantile and manufacturing interests who required access to political and economic power based on their entrepreneurial activities rather than on noble birth.

Moreover, the inalienability of land and the traditional guarantee of access to

Parts of this article have previously appeared in *Biology as a Social Weapon*, edited by Ann Arbor Science for the People (Burgess, Minneapolis, 1977); *Proceedings of the Philosophy of Science Association*, 1976; *The Sciences* 16(2): 6, 1976; and *Behavioral Science* 24: 5-14, 1979.

common land inhibited the rapid expansion of primary production and also maintained a scarcity of labor for manufactories. In Britain, the Acts of Enclosure of the 18th century broke this rigid system, allowing landlords to enclose land for wool production and simultaneously displacing tenants who became the landless industrial work force of the cities. At the same time in France, the old "nobility of the sword" was being challenged by the administrative and legal hierarchy who became the "nobility of the robe" and by the rich commoners of banking and finance. The Bourgeois Revolution was brewing, a revolution that was to break assunder the static feudal-aristocratic bonds and to create instead an entrepreneurial society in which labor and money could more freely adapt to the demands of a rising commercial and industrial middle class. But the Bourgeois Revolution required an ideology justifying the assault on the old order and providing the moral and intellectual underpinnings of the new. This was the ideology of freedom, of individuality, of works as opposed to grace, of equality and the inalienable rights to "life, liberty and the pursuit of happiness." Paine, Jefferson, Diderot, and the Encyclopedists were the ideologues of the revolution and one theme comes through: the old order was characterized by artificial hierarchies and artificial barriers to human desire and ambition; those artificial barriers must be destroyed so that each person may take his or her natural place in society according to desire and ability. This is the origin of the idea of the "equal opportunity society" in which we are now supposed to live.

While the Bourgeois Revolution destroyed those artificial barriers, it seems not to have dispensed with inequality of station. There are still rich and poor, powerful and weak, both within and between nations. How is this to be explained? We might suppose that the inequalities are structural, that the society created by the revolution has inequality built into it and even depends upon that inequality for its operation. But that supposition, if taken seriously, would engender yet another revolution. The alternative is to claim that inequalities reside in properties of individuals rather than in the structure of social relations. This is the claim that our society has produced about as much equality as is humanly possible and that the remaining differences in status and wealth and power are the inevitable manifestations of *natural* inequalities in individual abilities. It is this latter claim that has been incorporated from an early stage into the ideology of the Bourgeois Revolution and which remains the dominant ideology of capitalist societies today. Such a view does not threaten the status quo, but, on the contrary, supports it by telling those who are without power that their position is the inevitable outcome of their own innate deficiencies and that therefore *nothing can be done about it.* A remarkably explicit recent statement of this assertion is that of R. Herrnstein (2), a psychologist and one of the leading ideologues of "natural inequality":

> The privileged classes of the past were probably not much superior biologically to the downtrodden, which is why revolution had a fair chance of success. By removing artificial barriers between classes, society has encouraged the creation of biological barriers. When people can take their natural level in society, the upper classes will, by definition, have greater capacity than the lower.

Here, the entire scheme is laid out. The Bourgeois Revolution succeeded because it was only breaking down artificial barriers, but the remaining inequalities cannot be removed by a further revolution because what is left is the residue of biological differences which are irradicable. We are not told precisely what principle of biology guarantees that biologically "inferior" groups cannot seize power from biologically "superior" ones, but the conceptual and factual errors of such a statement are irrelevant to their function. They are meant to convince us that although we may not live in the best of all *conceivable* worlds, we live in the best of all *possible* worlds.

The ideology of the modern capitalist society is not one of equality of station, but of a natural sorting process aided by universal education in which "intrinsic merit" will be the criterion and source of success. The social program of the state, then, should not be directed toward an "unnatural" equalization of condition, which in any case would be impossible because of its "artificiality," but rather the state should provide the lubricant to ease and promote the movement of individuals into the positions to which their intrinsic natures have predisposed them.

FORMS OF BIOLOGICAL DETERMINISM

The concept that social arrangements are a manifestation of the inner or intrinsic natures of human beings, and are therefore unchangeable, has come to be called *biological determinism.* The degree of rigidity of the determinism varies in different versions of the system, from the notion that biological factors virtually completely determine each individual, to the more subtle idea that human biological nature establishes only "tendencies," natural states toward which human beings will gravitate in the normal course of events. Biological determinism has two complementary facets, both of which are necessary to complete this scheme. First, it is asserted that the *differences* in manifest abilities and power between individuals, classes, sexes, races, and nations result in large part from differences in intrinsic biological properties of individuals. Some of us can paint pictures and others can only paint houses (Jensen) (3); some of us can be doctors but others can only be barbers (Herrnstein) (2). But these facts alone, if they were true, would not in themselves necessarily result in a society of unequal power. After all, there is no reason that differences in ability, whether intrinsic or not, need imply differences in status, wealth, and power. We might build a society in which picture painters and house painters, barbers and surgeons, would be given equal material and psychic rewards. This is the argument of Dobzhansky in *Genetic Diversity and Human Equality* (4). If taken seriously, this argument would deprive our unequal society of the legitimacy offered to it by the argument of biological diversity. To complete its function as a legitimation argument for the present state of the world, biological determinism requires a second facet: the belief in *human nature.* In addition to the biological differences between individuals and groups, it is supposed (5) that there are biological "tendencies" shared by all human beings and their societies, tendencies that result in hierarchically organized societies in which individuals

> compete for the limited resources allocated to their role sector. The best and most entrepreneurial of the role-actors usually gain a disproportionate share of the rewards, while the least successful are displaced to other, less desirable positions.

This description, it must be noted, is not regarded as a historically contingent phenomenon in market societies, but as arising out of the biological nature of the human species. A human society like that envisaged by Dobzhansky, in which genetic differences in ability are not converted into status and wealth differences, would be biologically "unnatural" and therefore either impossible or else could be maintained only under the most rigid totalitarian rule.

The assertion that "human nature" guarantees that the biological differences between individuals and groups will be translated into differences in status, wealth, and power is the other face of biological determinism as a total ideology and represents the consolidation phase of the Bourgeois Revolution. To justify their original ascent to power, the new middle classes had to demand a society in which "intrinsic merit" *could be* rewarded. To maintain their position of power, they claim that intrinsic merit, once free to assert itself, *must be* rewarded. It is all natural and inevitable, so why fight it?

Ideas of human nature appear in a great diversity of social theories and in each one explicitly serve to legitimize political ends. Not even the historicist argument of Marx and Engels (6, 7) was free of an occasional appeal to human nature, in their case to unalienated labor as the essence of human self-realization. Like the claims of the natural inferiority of women, recent arguments about the true nature of man have largely been raised in the realm of the popularization of science. In works by Ardrey (8) and Tiger and Fox (9), for example, it is argued that the human species is naturally territorial, aggressive, male dominant, and so forth, through use of carefully selected observations from ethnography, paleontology, and animal behavior. But this claim has not been restricted to popularizers. Konrad Lorenz, Nobel Prize winner in ethology, has attempted to give human relevance to his observations on lower animals in *On Aggression* (10). He argues that humans lack the built-in controls against intraspecific aggression that characterize other dangerous animals because during most of our evolution we were not predatory carnivores, and therefore some social control of natural human aggression and nastiness must be exercised. More important, the domestication of man has resulted in the loss of natural tendencies to reject from the species "degenerate" types. This rejection must then also be exercised by a social agency. In particular, Lorenz (11) wrote *in 1940 in Germany* during the Nazi extermination campaign:

> The selection for toughness, heroism, social utility ... must be accomplished by some human institution if mankind, in default of selective factors, is not to be ruined by domestication induced degeneracy. The racial ideal as the basis of the state has already accomplished much in this respect.

It is probably a manifestation of the largely unquestioned role of women in our society that the heavy calibre weapons in the hands of the most prestigious biologists and psychologists were, for a long time, not directed against the equality of the sexes. If Terman, Yerkes, Osborne, Agassiz and others felt as threatened by women as they were by blacks, immigrants, and the working class, they did not manifest it in their major pronouncements. Even now, despite the growing women's movement, the number of academics who are willing to publish and legitimize the sexist attitudes they express in private is small, but a few have, and there is some evidence that even the most prestigious are about to enter the fray. The claims of Tiger and Fox (9) for the biological superiority of men were a well-known feature of "pop" ethology a few years ago, and a similar vein of vulgarization of science is contained in Goldberg's *The Inevitability of Patriarchy*, which makes the claim (12, p. 78) that:

> Human biology precludes the possibility of a human social system whose authority structure is not dominated by males, and in which male aggression is not manifested in dominance and attainment of position, of status and power.

We are not told how the discoveries of biology "preclude the possibility" of female equality or domination, but it is clear from the work as a whole that the author believes that "tendencies" inherent in males and females lead ineluctably to a "naturally" asymmetric social system. In addition to males' innately greater aggression, Goldberg maintains (12, p. 204):

> The stereotype that sees the male as more logical than the female is unquestionably correct in observation, and probably correct in its assumption that the qualities observed conform to *innate sexual limitations* analogous to those relevant to physical strength.

The two strains of aggressivity and logic are explicitly drawn together by Eleanor Maccoby (13), who suggests:

> There is good reason to believe that boys are innately more aggressive than girls . . . and if this quality is one which underlies the later growth of analytic thinking, then boys have an advantage which girls will find difficult to overcome.

Like Goldberg, Maccoby brings in fallacious notions of innate tendencies and then converts these tendencies into limitations on groups. The entire typology of "*the* male as more logical than *the* female" is an outmoded 19th-century concept of typical individuals standing for entire groups. What proportion of males manifest a greater logical ability than what proportion of females? What are the "innate" differences in population means? Is the "tendency" manifest simply as a small difference in the average of all males as opposed to the average of all females? If so, why does a difference in average "preclude the possibility" or even make it "difficult to overcome" the dominance of women by men. The intellectual bankruptcy of the vague speculation of male intrinsic superiority immediately appears when any attempt at analysis is made.

The reader should not imagine that the inevitability of male domination is a feature only of the writings of popularizers. The most recent declaration (14) of the biologically inevitable domination of women by men has been made by E. O. Wilson, Professor of Zoology at Harvard and generally regarded as the leading authority on the evolution of animal social behavior:

> In hunter-gatherer societies, men hunt and women stay at home. This strong bias persists in most agricultural and industrial societies and, on that ground alone, appears to have a genetic origin. . . . My own guess is that the genetic bias is intense enough to cause a substantial division of labor even in the most free and most egalitarian of future societies. . . . Even with identical education and equal access to all professions, men are likely to continue to play a disproportionate role in political life, business and science.

The theory that the relation of domination of men over women that characterizes our society has a biological cause and is thus inevitable provides a bridge between theories that differences between groups are genetic and theories that human societies are the result of an innate "human nature."

SOCIOBIOLOGY: THE NEWEST DETERMINISM

The newest wave of human nature determinism has culminated in the publication by E. O. Wilson of *Sociobiology: The New Synthesis* (5), which announces the creation of a new field—sociobiology—and which asserts that such human cultural manifestations as religion, ethics, tribalism, warfare, genocide, cooperation, competition, entrepreneurship, conformity, indoctrinability, and spite (the list is incomplete) are tendencies that are genetically coded in the human genome and established there by natural selection. No evidence at all is presented for a genetic basis of these characteristics, and the arguments for their establishment by natural selection cannot be tested since it postulates hypothetical situations in human prehistory that are uncheckable. For example, homosexuality is asserted to be genetically conditioned (no evidence), it is then asserted that homosexuals leave fewer offspring than heterosexuals (no evidence and a confusion between homosexual *acts* and total homosexuality), but then it is postulated that the "genes" for homosexuality may have been preserved in human prehistory because homosexuals served as helpers to their close relatives (uncheckable story with no ethnographic evidence from present hunters and gatherers to suggest such a phenomenon). The intended use of sociobiology in human social affairs is made crystal clear by its inventor, however. The book begins with the statement (5, p. 4) that

> It may not be too much to say that sociology and the other social sciences, as well as the humanities, are the last branches of biology waiting to be included in the Modern Synthesis. One of the functions of sociobiology, then, is to reformulate the foundations of the social sciences in a way that draws these subjects into the Modern Synthesis.

And it ends with a vision of neurobiologists and sociobiologists as the technocrats of the near future who will provide the necessary knowledge for ethical and political decisions in the planned society (5, p. 574):

> If the decision is taken to mold cultures to fit the requirements of the ecological steady state, some behaviors can be altered experientially without emotional damage or loss in creativity. Others cannot. Uncertainty in the matter means that Skinner's dream of a culture predesigned for happiness will surely have to wait for the new neurobiology. A genetically accurate and hence [sic] completely fair code of ethics must also wait.

Sociobiology is a frankly and explicitly political science whose program is to provide, eventually, the scientific tools of "correct" social organization. Yet the world to be made will be pretty much the aggressive, domination-ridden society we live in now. Why is this? Because (5, p. 575):

> ... we do not know how many of the most valued qualities are linked genetically to more obsolete destructive ones. Cooperativeness toward groupmates might be coupled with aggressivity toward strangers, creativeness with a desire to own and dominate, athletic zeal with a tendency to violent response, and so on. ... If the

planned society–the creation of which seems inevitable in the coming century–were to deliberately steer its members past those stresses and conflicts that once gave the destructive phenotypes their Darwinian edge, the other phenotypes might dwindle with them. In this, the ultimate genetic sense, social control would rob man of his humanity.

Of course it is all put in a hypothetical mode, but the message is clear: the only safe thing to do is to leave things as they are, at least at present. Don't rock the boat until the sociobiologists tell you how.

Sociobiology is an attempt to explain all of animal and human behavior as the product of evolution by natural selection. This includes not only the stereotyped individual and group behavior of lower organisms, but *all* aspects of human social and individual activity that are within the normal human gambit.

Darwin's theory of evolution by natural selection, then, rests on three general principles which are unchallenged in their generality: (a) there is variation in morphology, physiology, and behavior among organisms belonging to the same species–the principle of variation; (b) there is a correlation between parents and offspring in phenotype, so that relatives resemble each other more than do unrelated individuals– the principle of heredity; and (c) some phenotypes leave more offspring than others– the principle of natural selection. These three principles are sufficient to guarantee an evolutionary process. Provided there is variation among objects, that there is some temporal stability in this variation by some mechanism of heritability, and that different sorts of objects leave different numbers of descendants in time, there must be evolutionary change in the composition of the population. So, rocks evolve by natural selection since they vary in hardness, split off rocks of equal hardness, and have different rates of erosion and therefore of survival. Automobiles too evolve by natural selection, as do soft drink containers. The system of explanation is so powerful that it can be applied to almost any situation, and herein lies its weakness. A system of explanation that can potentially be used to explain any observation invites caricature and will be used in a crude and vulgar analogical way by ingenious people. This is what happened to the system of Freudian psychology, which was so all encompassing that it has been used to explain all of history, science, and the arts. So too has the Darwinian theory been vulgarized for the purpose of easy explanation of phenomena. The latest episode in this caricature of Darwinian explanation is the collection of theories, speculations, and observations about animal and human behavior that is called by its adherents "sociobiology."

The general form of sociobiological argument is the following. The behavioral phenotype of a species is described. As for any other aspect of the phenotype, this description cannot be exhaustive, but is framed in terms of those elements that seem significant to the observer. It is then to be demonstrated that this phenotype has been established in the species by natural selection. To do so requires, first, an adaptive story to explain the circumstances that would cause individuals of that phenotype to leave more offspring than individuals of other phenotypes, and, second, an argument that phenotypic differences with respect to the trait are or were heritable. Evolution by natural selection requires genetic differences, or else the differential rate of reproduction of phenotypes can have no effect on population composition in future generations. Each of the three elements of sociobiological theory—description, heritability, and adaptive story—has its own deep methodological problems that have not been faced, or apparently even been considered, by the practitioners of the program.

THE SOCIOBIOLOGICAL ARGUMENT

A Description of Human Nature

The first element in the sociobiological argument is to describe the set of phenotypes under investigation. This is done by making very general and very superficial characterizations of "human nature" by universalizing conventional wisdom. Thus, in Wilson's *Sociobiology* (5) we are told that "men would rather believe than know" and the people are "extraordinarily easy to indoctrinate, indeed they seek it." Xenophobia, domination, entrepreneurship, territoriality, and male dominance are all said to be universals of human behavior and then provided with a biological explanation. The facts of history and of ethnography do not support the universality of these traits, but history is almost completely ignored by sociobiologists and exceptions to these generalizations in the ethnographic record are accounted for by redefinition. For example, it is stated that the exceptions to the "rule" of genocidal warfare are only "temporary aberrations," or that the reason all human societies do not appear to be territorial is that "zoologists have been too narrow in their definition of territoriality." In some cases their claims are directly contradicted by the ethnographic record. For example, present-day "primitive" hunter and gatherer societies do not engage in genocidal warfare, an invention of the modern state, but, on the contrary, engage in a kind of semi-ritual combat in which very few combatants are killed or wounded.

What is immediately striking to the reader of Wilson's *Sociobiology,* or of books by Dawkins (15), Lorenz (10), and others, is the total lack of consideration of the problems of correct description of behavior. While anthropologists have agonized for years over problems of ethnocentrism and, more recently, of sex bias, in the description of human culture, while behaviorist psychologists have concerned themselves with anthropocentrism in studies of rats, and while evolutionary morphologists have questioned the relationship between growth processes and commonly identified units of morphology, sociobiologists seem to have no consciousness of the fundamental problems of the description of behavior. They treat categories like slavery, entrepreneurship, dominance, aggression, tribalism, and territoriality as if they were natural objects of unquestioned status, rather than as historically and ideologically conditioned constructs. Yet any argument about the evolution of entrepreneurship depends critically upon whether it has any existence outside the minds of modern sociologists and historians. There are four forms of error of description committed by sociobiologists, and all require serious study if the field is to become serious science.

Reification. It cannot be assumed that any behavior or institution to which a name can be given necessarily has an existence as a real thing subject to the laws of nature.

Is entrepreneurship a real category for which there are genes and upon which natural selection operates as an entity, or is it an arbitrary construct, historically determined and useful as a way of describing human socioeconomic activity? The same question applies to religion, kinship, altruism, and so on. Any historical view of social thought, as well as any sophisticated comparative ethnography, shows immediately that the categories of description of social institutions are historically contingent. What did "religion" mean to the Greeks (they had no word for it and it did not exist for them as a separate social category), or "revenge" to the Tasaday? Is "violence" real, or is it a social construct without any one-to-one correspondence to an actual physical act (what is "verbal violence" or a "violent exception")? Nothing has a more obfuscating effect on the understanding of society (itself a reification!) than the total confusion between categories of thought and real objects.

Arbitrary Agglomeration. Related to the error of reification is the supposition that the world of phenomena is naturally divided along a given set of suture lines and that this same division applies for all purposes. The problem is serious enough for physical attributes. Is the "hand" an appropriate description for an object that has both genetic and adaptive coherence in evolution? The question is whether it is sensible to talk of the "evolution of the hand" as opposed to, say, the evolution of the fingers, or of the separate parts of the fingers, or of the entire limb. As an example of how the erroneous subdivision of anatomy can give rise to pseudoproblems, let us consider the chin. The chin is the one apparent anatomical exception to the rule that the evolution of the human anatomy has been *neotenic.* That is, the anatomical features of the adult human are much more like those of the fetal ape than the adult ape, so that we may describe human evolution as a trend toward earlier and earlier maturity in embryonic development. But the chin is an exception since it has enlarged during human evolution, while the fetal ape has even less of a chin than its adult form. It turns out, however, that the chin is not in fact an exception because, in an important sense, the chin does not exist. There are two growth fields in the jaw: the *alveolar* containing the teeth and the *mandibular* which is the jaw bone on which the alveolar sits. Both of these show neoteny, in that both are getting smaller in evolution, relative to the rest of the skull, as is the case with the fetal ape. However, the alveolar growth field is regressing faster than the mandibular, so that a protuberance we call the "chin" results. Of course, one might invent a variety of fanciful natural selective stories to explain why the "chin" is getting larger in human evolution, but the truth is rather more prosaic.

What is true of anatomy is even more important for behavior and social organization. Is xenophobia a trait in evolution, as sociobiologists would have us believe? What is the methodological program that will allow us to make a decision? Clearly there are two requirements for an evolutionary trait. There must be genes whose action is nearly entirely concerned with the formation of the trait, so that genetic variation for the trait can occur without important effects on the remainder of the phenotype. Otherwise we cannot isolate the trait for separate evolutionary explanation. Second, the trait must be a unit under natural selection. That is, variation in the described trait must be associated with significant differences in fitness, when the rest of the organism is averaged out. In statistical terms there must be a *marginal* effect of genes on the trait and a *marginal* effect on natural selection. Otherwise the so-called "trait" is an arbitrary unit of description of the organism with no relation to the direct forces of evolution.

False Metaphor. Many of the descriptions of animal behavior are taken metaphorically from human behavior and laid on animals as natural. Human behavior is then seen as a special case of the more general phenomenon "discovered" in animals. The most famous case, antedating sociobiology but incorporated totally into its theory, is that of caste in insects. Caste is a human phenomenon, originally a race or lineage but later a hereditary social group associated with particular trades and social positions. The application of ideas of caste to insects gives legitimacy to the idea that human castes are simply another case of a more generalized phenomenon. But in what sense are insects divided into "castes"? Class structure is an economic and social phenomenon related to and coming out of human historical events and regulating the social and material power of individuals. Castes in India were the outcome of an invasion and conquest of Dravidians by Aryans. High-caste Hindus had a monopoly in social, political, and economic power while untouchables lived at the margin of existence. What has all this to do with ants? Nor does an ant "queen," a totally captive egg-producing machine, force fed by the "workers," bear any resemblance to Elizabeth I or Catherine the Great, or even to the politically powerless Elizabeth II who is nevertheless a multimillionaire. Like caste, slavery is another human institution which bears no important resemblance to its claimed equivalent in insects. Ants do not know commodities, nor capital investment, nor rates of interest, nor slave revolts, nor the anguish of mothers and fathers torn from their children and spouses on auction blocks. But what is true for obvious cases like caste and slavery applies also to "aggression," "warfare," "cooperation," "kinship," "loyalty," "coyness," and a host of other behaviors and institutions that sociobiologists find in animals.

Conflation. Quite different behaviors and institutions are sometimes included under the same rubric as part of the reductionist program of sociobiology. Thus, "aggression" is a term used to explain both antagonistic encounters between individuals in which one attempts to achieve social or physical domination over the other and political aggression as embodied in war. The purpose of this conflation of two quite different phenomena is to derive war from individual aggression and thus explain war reductively as the outcome of the evolved aggressiveness of individuals. Yet war and individual aggression have little to do with each other. War is a calculated political phenomenon undertaken for economic and political gain by a collectivity, and "hostilities" begin without the least "hostility" between individuals. People kill each other in wars for all sorts of reasons, not the least of which is that they are forced to do so against their own wishes by the political power of the state. Similarly, tribalism, a political phenomenon, is confused with individual relationships within communities of linguistically and geographically proximate people. Yet it is now the concensus of anthropologists that tribalism in its modern political meaning has been the enforced product of contact of primitive people with state-organized societies and has been created and exploited for political ends. Conflation is an essential element in socio-biological theory because, without it, the reductionist program fails.

Innateness of Characters

In order for a trait to evolve by natural selection, it is necessary that there be genetic variation in the population for such a trait. Thus, although I might argue that the possession of wings in addition to arms and legs might be advantageous to some vertebrates, none has ever evolved a third pair of appendages, presumably because the genetic variation has never been available. Not only is the qualitative possibility of adaptive evolution constrained by available genetic variation, but the relative rates of evolution of different characters are proportional to the amount of genetic variance for each. These considerations make both retrospective and prospective statements about adaptive evolution extremely uncertain unless there is evidence about genetic variation. For example, it is common in adaptive theory to try to explain life-history patterns (life-history strategies, as they have come to be called by adaptationists) by asserting that the particular pattern of reproductive rates and longevity exhibited by a species has evolved because it is optimal. Codfish lay millions of eggs, each of which has virtually no chance to survive, while the eelpout, *Zoarces,* has very few offspring and bears them alive, rather than laying eggs. Why such a contrast between two marine fish? The adaptationist program attempts to give an answer solely in terms of the relative advantage of increasing egg numbers, as opposed to increasing investment in survival of each egg (see reference 16 for a numerical argument of this kind). But such an argument is illegitimate, for it can only be correct if the available genetic variance for fecundity and maternal care are equal. It may simply have been that codfish ancestors had much more genetic variance for fecundity whereas the ancestral line of *Zoarces* had much more genetic variance for developing a broad pouch. Knowledge of the relative amounts of genetic variance for different traits is essential if evolutionary arguments are to be correct rather than simply plausible.

For prospective studies it is possible, at least in principle, to assay additive genetic variance for different characters in present populations of animals. What is required is that individuals of different degrees of relationship be raised under controlled environmental conditions so that genetic and environmental components of variance can be distinguished. It is not necessary to make controlled matings, provided natural relatives of different degrees, especially parent-offspring, full-sib, and half-sib com-binations, are available. It is essential, however, that genetic similarity not be corre-lated with environmental similarity or else genetic and environmental components of variance will be totally confounded. Unfortunately there is no way in human popula-tions to break the correlation between genetic similarity and environmental similarity, except by randomized adoptions. Such adoptions do not exist as large groups and as a result we have no way of estimating genetic variances in human populations except for single-gene traits in which environmental variation is trivial, e.g. blood groups. The consequence of this methodological difficulty is that we know little or nothing about the genetic variance for any human metric trait—even including height, weight, metabolic rate, and skin color—except that there is clearly some heritable component.

For human psychological traits absolutely nothing is known, because adequate random adoption studies do not exist. It is simply not possible to state whether there is any genetic influence at all on an individual's degree of xenophobia, dominance, entrepreneurship, conformity, indoctrinability, fear of incest, homo- or heterosexuality, or any of the other myriad psychosocial traits with which human sociobiology deals. Although a list of such traits is given by Wilson as having moderate heritability, he appears to have depended on secondary sources for his information. Studies of the heritability of psychosocial traits are virtually all parent-offspring or identical twin correlation studies, neither of which gives estimates of genetic variance unconfounded with environmental variances. Indeed, the highest parent-offspring correlations known are for political party and religious affiliation (17). Nor is there any likelihood that methodologically adequate studies will be made in the foreseeable future.

The problem with retrospective studies is that to argue about the evolution of present-day human populations, it would be necessary to get information about genetic variance in the past. Evidence for genetic variance in the present, even if it were available, would be of little help because evolution by natural selection destroys the genetic variance on which it feeds. It is a fundamental theorem of population genetics that as natural selection proceeds, additive genetic variance is used up and eventually disappears. Thus, if present human populations show no genetic variance for, say, entrepreneurship, it can be claimed by sociobiologists that there used to be such variance but it was used up by selection for the trait. On the other hand, if there were some variance at present, sociobiologists could point to it as evidence for the heritability of entrepreneurial activity. There is no conceivable observation about genetic variance at present that could disprove the contention of past evolution of the trait.

What is so distressing about sociobiological theory is not that adequate estimates of genetic variance are lacking, since that is a problem that plagues all of evolutionary reconstruction, but that the problem is either totally ignored or recognized and glossed over. Genes for conformity, xenophobia, and aggressiveness are simply postulated because they are needed by the theory, not because any evidence for them exists. Especially if characteristics are social rather than individual, the postulation of specific genes is inappropriate.

Sociobiologists sometimes say that they do not really envisage specific genes for warfare or tribalism, but only human genotypes that make these social manifestations possible, given appropriate environmental circumstances. But this argument throws out the baby with the bath water. All manifestations of human culture are the result of the activity of living beings and therefore it follows that everything that has ever been done by our species, individually or collectively, must be biologically possible. But that says nothing except that what has actually happened must have been possible. If sociobiology is to accomplish its program, it must do better than that. It must state what human society cannot do and what it must do and why, or at the very least provide probability statements or descriptions of human norms of reaction for psychosocial traits.

The *norm of reaction* is the basic concept of development genetics (18). The phenotype is the unique result of development of a given genotype in a particular environmental sequence. There is, in general, no one-to-one correspondence between genotype and phenotype, but a function that relates phenotype to the particular combination of genotype and environment. The norm of reaction of a genotype is the enumeration of phenotypes that will arise from various environments. Obviously, the complete norm of reaction of a genotype cannot be specified since that would involve specification of every possible environmental sequence during development. In practice, norms of reaction are determined for specific ranges of particular environmental variables like temperature. There are no generalizations about the shape of norms of reaction and they must be determined experimentally for each genotype and environmental variable. Norms of reaction have not yet been determined even for human anatomical traits, because of the lack of control of human developmental environments. For social traits, the question of what is prohibited by the human genotype becomes a problem of extrapolating social behavior from historical social organizations to unknown future social institutions. Thus, there is no sound scientific basis for statements such as: "Thus, even with identical education and equal access to all professions, men are likely to continue to play a disproportionate role in political life, business and science." (14) Even if domination of women by men were a compositional trait, simply the collection of individual behaviors, it is impossible to say what the manifestation of genotypes relevant to this character—if any—will be in the most egalitarian society.

In summary, both retrospective arguments which attempt to rationalize the current state of a species as adaptive, and prospective arguments which attempt to predict the future evolution or social manifestation of current genotypes, require absolutely that there be information on the kinds of genetic variance available to species and on the norms of reaction of genotypes. The absence of such information, as in humans, makes the adaptive program an exercise in plausible storytelling rather than a science of testable hypotheses.

Adaptive Stories

The easiest part of the adaptive program is the creation of a plausible story explaining why the observed traits of a species are optimal. There are two methods, depending upon the degree of specification of the trait. The first, an experimental one, can be used for extant species where traits and environment are measurable. I will call this method *progressive ad hoc optimization*. A particular aspect of the organisms's life history is isolated as a problem to be solved. By an engineering analysis, the optimal solution is deduced, subject to certain constraints about the nature of the species, and then the species is measured to see whether it has provided the optimal solution. If it has, then a plausible argument is made that the trait examined has in fact arisen as an optimal solution to the posed problem. If, on the other hand, the solution appears not to be optimal, one can try again with a different problem, or what is more usual, a second additional problem is proposed for which the trait must also be optimizing so that the organism is really optimizing both simultaneously. In general, a maximum of a function of N dimensions is not a maximum in each dimension separately. This procedure can be extended until a satisfactory fit is obtained. Often the added problems are not stated quantitatively but added heuristically to rationalize the lack of optimality under the original criterion. Such a progressive *ad hoc* procedure, especially when only one variable is experimentally determined, is guaranteed success, so nothing is tested.

The second method is a nonexperimental, nonquantitative one I call *imaginative reconstruction*. In this method one simply thinks about a species, past or present, and literally inserts a reason why a certain trait should have been favored by natural selection. All of human sociobiological explanation is of this kind. Some such explanations are no doubt correct, but others are not, and, in the absence of experimental falsifiability, there is no way to tell which is which.

The possibility of plausible imaginative reconstruction has been immensely enhanced by Hamilton's (19) principle of extended fitness. Hamilton realized that natural selection could increase the frequency of a trait even if the possession of the trait was at a selective disadvantage, provided the trait increased the fitness of close relatives because close relatives also may carry the gene. So altruists may give up their own reproduction to enhance the reproduction of, say, sibs, and the result would be an increase in the frequency of the altruistic genotypes, if any. A paradigm example of the application of this principle in sociobiology is Wilson's imaginative reconstruction of the evolution of homosexuality (5). It is first postulated that homosexuality is genetic, although there is no evidence on this point and, of course, the manifestation of homosexuality is strongly dependent on history, culture, and class. Second, it is asserted that homosexuals themselves leave fewer offspring than heterosexuals. While this must be true for persons who are exclusively homosexual, there is no information whatever on the reproductive rate of persons engaging in mixed homosexual and heterosexual behavior. Given the two unsubstantiated assumptions of heritability and lower fitness, there is clearly something to be explained since natural selection should have eliminated homosexuality. The answer given is that homosexuals may have devoted their energies to helping their sibs raise children, since they had no children of their own to feed, and thus by the principle of extended fitness increased the frequency of the genes for homosexuality.

The principle of kin selection does not cover every contingency, however. What are we to make of altruistic acts performed toward unrelated individuals? To handle this problem, Trivers (20) has introduced the concept of reciprocal altruism, according to which individuals will benefit from altruistic acts toward others if the recipient remembers the altruistic act and reciprocates at a future time. Genotypes that lead to such reciprocation will be selected for.

By combining arguments of individual advantage, kin selection, and reciprocal altruism, an imaginative reconstruction can be made for any observed behavior. In this way the underlying assumption, that all traits are adaptive, is always confirmed and can never be falsified.

There is one final aspect of sociobiological theory that insulates it from testability. Population genetics makes *quantitative* predictions about the rates of change of genetic composition with time and also provides actual data on the quantitative genetic differences in gene frequencies in present-day human groups. Both kinds of numbers are too small to fit sociobiological theory. Only 100 generations have passed since the Roman Republic, and this time span is far too short for there to have been any major change in gene frequencies. Yet human social institutions have undergone an extraordinary change in those few generations. In a mere 30 generations, Islam rose from nothing to become the greatest culture of the Western World and then declined again into powerlessness. How can one compare the social institutions of the modern British with the political, social, and economic institutions of Roman Britain? Moreover, at least 85 percent of known human genetic variation exists, at present, within any local national population and at least 95 percent within any modern major race. How are we to explain, on a genetic basis, the immense cultural differences between present-day populations? The sociobiologists have the answer. It is the "multiplier effect" (5, pp. 11-13, 596-572), which asserts that an arbitrarily small but unspecified degree of genetic difference will be multiplied up into an arbitrarily large but unspecified degree of cultural difference because culture is such a complex trait. No evidence is given for the existence of such an effect, nor are we told how it would be measured, quantified or specified. This completely free and arbitrary multiplier is the next to the last step in building an air-tight edifice completely impervious to test. The final step is to explain why the multiplier effect has not had a similar role to play in lower animals. It is because of the "threshold effect" (9, p. 573), which guarantees that the multiplier effect will only take hold when the behavior becomes sufficiently complex.

Alternatives to Adaptation

An examination of the dynamical theory of natural selection, of the effects of stochastic variation in gene frequencies, and of the facts of development shows that there are a number of evolutionary forces that are clearly nonadaptive and which may be correct explanations for any number of actual evolutionary events.

First, natural selection does not necessarily lead to adaptation. A mutation which doubles the fecundity of individuals will sweep through a population rapidly. If there has been no change in efficiency of resource utilization, the individuals will leave no more offspring than before but simply lay twice as many eggs, the excess dying because of resource limitation. In what sense are the individuals or the population as a whole better adapted than before? Indeed, if a predator on immature stages is led to switch to the species now that immatures are more plentiful, the population size may actually decrease as a consequence, yet natural selection at all times will favor individuals with higher fecundity.

Second, there are multiple selective peaks when more than a single gene is involved in influencing a character. The existence of multiple peaks means that for a fixed regime of natural selection there are alternative paths of evolution and the particular one taken by a population depends upon chance events. Thus, it is not meaningful to ask for an adaptive explanation of the difference between two species that occupy alternative peaks. For example, there is no adaptive explanation required for the existence of the two-horned rhinoceros in India and the one-horned rhinoceros in Africa. We do not have to explain why two horns are better in the East and one in the West. Rather, they are alternative outcomes of the same general selective process.

Third, the finiteness of real populations results in random changes in gene frequency so that, with a certain probability, genetic combinations with lower reproductive fitness will be fixed in a population. If fitness differences between genotypes are small, there is a very high probability of the loss of favorable genes. This is especially true during times of restriction of population size, which is precisely when environment is likely to be changing and selective pressures for new genotypes most likely to appear. Even in an infinite population, because of Mendelian segregation, a new favorable mutation has a probability of only $2s$ of being incorporated into a population, where s is the selective advantage. Thus, natural selection often fails to establish more fit genotypes.

Fourth, many changes in characters are the result of pleiotropic gene action, rather than the direct result of selection on the character itself. The yellow color of the Malphigian tubules of an insect cannot itself be the subject of natural selection since that color can never be seen by any organism. Rather, it is the pleiotropic consequence of red eye pigment metabolism, which may be adaptive. A special but important case of pleiotropy is the allometric growth of different body parts. In cervine deer, antler size increases more than proportionately to body size (21) so that larger deer have more than proportionately large antlers. It is then unnecessary to give a specifically adaptive reason for the extremely large antlers of large deer. All that is required is that the allometric relation not be specifically maladaptive at the extremes.

Fifth, there is an important random or noise component in development and physiology. The phenotype is not given by the environment and genotype alone, but is also subject to random noise processes at the cellular and molecular levels. In some cases, as for example bristle formation in *Drosophila,* variance from developmental noise may be as great as genetic and environmental variance (22). All individual variation, especially in human social behavior, is not to be explained deterministically and cannot be taken as demanding specifically adaptive stories.

It is undoubtedly true that kin selection has operated in some instances to establish some traits of organisms. It is undoubtedly true that human behavior, like human anatomy, is not impervious to natural selection and that some aspects of human social existence owe their historical manifestations to limitations and initial conditions placed upon them by our evolutionary history. The problem is to create a methodology that will allow a constructive investigation of these questions. Sociobiology is not such a methodology because its chief ambition is total explanatory power over all human social phenomena. It makes itself only into a vulgar caricature of Darwinian explanation in the process of realizing its ambition. Finally, sociobiological theory rests on an erroneous confusion between materialism and reductionism. It is sure that we are material beings and that our social institutions are the products of our material beings, just as thought is the product of a material process. But the content and meaning of human social organization cannot be understood by a total knowledge of biology any more than by a total knowledge of quantum theory. War is not the sum total of individual aggressive feelings, and a society cannot be described if we know the DNA sequence of every individual in it. The naive reductionist program of sociobiology has long been understood to be a fundamental philosophical error. Meaning cannot be found in the movement of molecules.

REFERENCES

1. Marx, K., and Engels, F. *Manifesto of the Communist Party.* International Publishers, New York, 1948.
2. Herrnstein, R. I.Q. *The Atlantic Monthly* 228: 43-64, 1971.
3. Jensen, A. R. How much can we boost IQ and scholastic achievement? *Harvard Educational Review* 39: 1-123, 1969.
4. Dobzhansky, T. *Genetic Diversity and Human Equality.* Basic Books, New York, 1973.
5. Wilson, E. O. *Sociobiology: The New Synthesis.* Harvard University Press, Cambridge, Mass., 1975.
6. Marx, K. *Grundisse.* Dietz, Berlin, 1953.
7. Engels, F. The part played by labor in the transition from ape to man. In *Dialectics of Nature.* Progress Publishers, Moscow, 1934.
8. Ardrey, R. *The Territorial Imperative.* Atheneum, New York, 1966.
9. Tiger, L., and Fox, R. *The Imperial Animal.* Holt-Rinehart and Winston, New York, 1970.
10. Lorenz, K. *On Aggression.* Methuen, London, 1966.
11. Lorenz, K. Durch Domestikation verursachte Störungen arteigenen Verhaltens. *Zeitschrift für angewandte Psychologie und Characterkunde* 59: 56-75, 1940.
12. Goldberg, S. *The Inevitability of Patriarchy.* William Morrow & Co., New York, 1973.
13. Maccoby, E. Woman's intellect. In *The Potential of Women,* edited by S. Farber and H. Wilson. McGraw-Hill, New York, 1963.
14. Wilson, E. O. Human decency is animal. *New York Times Magazine,* October 12, 1975.
15. Dawkins, R. *The Selfish Gene.* Oxford University Press, Oxford, 1976.
16. Lewontin, R. C. Selection for colonizing ability. In *Genetics of Colonizing Species,* edited by H. Baker and G. L. Stebbins, pp. 77-94. Academic Press, New York, 1965.
17. Fuller, J. L., and Thompson, W. R. *Behavior Genetics.* John Wiley and Sons, New York, 1960.
18. Lewontin, R. C. The analysis of variance and the analysis of causes. *Am. J. Hum. Genet.* 26: 400-411, 1974.
19. Hamilton, W.D. The genetical theory of social behavior. *J. Theor. Biol.* 1: 1-52, 1964.
20. Trivers, R. The evolution of reciprocal altruism. *Q. Rev. Biol.* 46: 35-57, 1971.
21. Gould, S. J. Positive allometry of antlers in the "Irish Elk," *Megaloceros giganteus. Nature* 244: 375-376, 1973.
22. Lewontin, R. C. The adaptations of populations to varying environments. *Cold Spring Harbor Symp. Quant. Biol.* 22: 395-408, 1957.

CONTRIBUTORS TO THE VOLUME

CAROL BROWN is associate professor of sociology at the University of Lowell in Lowell, Massachusetts. She previously taught at Queens College, City University of New York, and at the Heller Graduate School for Social Welfare at Brandeis University. Dr. Brown received her Ph.D. in sociology from Columbia University in 1971. She has written articles on allied health manpower and on divorced mothers, her two main research interests.

ELIZABETH COPPOCK is chief of the Systems Unit, Business Survey Method Division, Statistics Canada. She specializes in record linkage methodologies in studying various health-related issues.

ELIZABETH FEE is an assistant professor at the School of Hygiene and Public Health of The Johns Hopkins University, and director of a program on the humanities and public health. She received her Ph.D. from Princeton University in the history and philosophy of science, and has written on the history of women and science, especially in the fields of anthropology and medicine. Her current research interests are in the history of public health; she is writing a history of public health education, and a study of ethical and social values in public health research and practice.

KARL FIGLIO has taught history of medicine at Cambridge University and the University of Michigan, and now lectures in Sociology as Applied to Medicine at the Charing Cross Hospital Medical School and University College, University of London. His interests have included historical and conceptual aspects of brain investigation, metaphor and language in biological thought, history of physiology (especially neuro- and electrophysiology), social history of 19th century medicine (especially the mediation of social forces by medical ideas) and psychoanalysis. Working in a broadly Marxist framework, he has recently been extending the approach taken in this article. He is a member of the *Radical Science Journal* Collective in London.

ANN FLITCRAFT, M.D., a physician at St. Francis Hospital in Hartford, Connecticut, is a founding member of the New Haven Project for Battered Women. She is a research associate in the Department of Surgery at Yale University School of Medicine and co-director of the research project on domestic violence. Dr. Flitcraft has presented testimony on wife abuse to the U.S. Civil Rights Commission, the U.S. House of Representatives Subcommittee on Science and Technology, and the state legislatures of New York and Connecticut.

WILLIAM FRAZIER, M.D., is an associate professor of surgery (plastic), Yale University School of Medicine and the Center for Health Studies, Institution for Social Policy Studies of Yale University. In addition, he is director of the Yale Trauma Program, director of Burn Service and medical director of Emergency Services at Yale-New Haven Hospital. Dr. Frazier is the principal investigator of "Medical Contexts and Sequelae of Domestic Violence."

SHARON D. GARRETT is a doctoral student in public health at the University of California at Los Angeles. Her major interests are medical care organization and finance and she has worked to establish a hospice program for the care of terminally ill patients.

LINDA GORDON is professor of history at the University of Massachusetts in Boston and an editor of the journal *Radical America*. She is the author of *Woman's Body, Woman's Right: A History of Birth Control in America* (Penguin, 1976), *America's Working Women, A Documentary History* (Vintage, 1976) and *Bandit Nationalism: The Origins of the Cossacks* (Suny Press, 1982). She has written many articles on feminism and women's history, and is now completing a study on the history of family violence.

JUDITH L. LADINSKY is an associate professor in the Department of Preventive Medicine, Center for Health Sciences, University of Wisconsin, Madison, Wisconsin. She received her graduate education leading to the Ph.D. at the University of Wisconsin. She spent 7 years in the Department of Gynecology and Obstetrics prior to joining the Department of Preventive Medicine. Her research interests include community medicine, rural health care delivery, and health status and evaluation. She has written numerous articles and two comprehensive health survey monographs.

R. C. LEWONTIN is an evolutionary biologist primarily concerned with the study of genetic variation in human and other populations. He is professor of zoology at the Museum of Comparative Zoology at Harvard University and professor of population sciences at Harvard's School of Public Health. Dr. Lewontin is a member of the Sociobiology Study Group of Science for the People and also of the World Agricultural Research Project, a collective research group studying the political economy of agriculture and agricultural research and teaching on the political economy of agriculture and public health.

A. S. MACPHERSON is chief of the department of community health at the Montreal General Hospital. Following his graduation from the University of Toronto, Dr. Macpherson trained in psychiatry at McGill University. After 8 years on the faculty of medicine at McMaster University, which included the acquisition of an M.Sc. in epidemiology, Dr. Macpherson returned to Montreal to participate in the reform of health services in Quebec.

VICTOR W. MARSHALL was associate professor in sociology at McMaster University, and is now at the University of Toronto, Canada. He received the doctorate in sociology from Princeton University. In addition to his interest in childbirth, his predominant research has been at the other end of the life cycle, and has resulted in several articles and a book on the sociology of aging and dying. Dr. Marshall is involved in collaborative research in evaluating attempts to change health care teams as a mechanism for delivering psychosocial care.

KAREN MESSING (AL-AIDROOS) is a professor at the Université du Québec à Montréal. She teaches university courses in genetics, embryology and biology of women. In addition, she does research and education on reproduction and women's biology at the request of the two major Québec unions, the Confédération des Syndicats Nationaux and the Fédération des Travailleurs du Quebec, under the terms of an agreement between the unions and the university. She is currently doing research on the detection of genetic damage among workers exposed to radiation or solvents. She received her Ph.D. from McGill University.

RONALD RINDFUSS is currently an associate professor in the Department of Sociology at the University of North Carolina at Chapel Hill. His current research centers on the sociology of fertility, in both the United States and Asia. He is co-author of a monograph, *Postwar Fertility Trends and Differentials in the United States.*

EVAN STARK is a research associate at Yale Medical School and the Center for Health Studies at Yale where he helps direct two research projects, one on battering in a medical context and another on the impact of job stress on families. A founding member of the New Haven Project for Battered Women, he is also a member of the East Coast Health Discussion Group and former Chairman of the Socialist Caucus in the American Public Health Association.

INGRID WALDRON is associate professor in the Department of Biology at the University of Pennsylvania. She received her Ph.D. from the University of California at Berkeley in 1967. Her primary current research project is an analysis of two longitudinal data sets to estimate the effects of employment on women's health and the effects of health on whether a woman is employed. Dr. Waldron has also done research on the Type A or coronary-prone behavior pattern, the causes of sex differences in mortality, and the relationship between social and economic characteristics and the levels of blood pressure and serum cholesterol in different societies.

JERRY L. WEAVER is a social science analyst at the Agency for International Development. Dr. Weaver previously served as visiting professor and director of the M.P.A. program at the University of California at Los Angeles. Aside from his interests in development administration and comparative public policies, he has published two books, *Conflict and Control in Health Administration* (1975) and *National Health Policy and the Underserved: Ethnic Minorities, Women and the Elderly* (1976).

KAY WEISS received her Masters of Public Health degree from the University of Texas School of Public Health in 1974. Ms. Weiss' publications include: "The Epidemiology of Vaginal Adenocarcinoma and Adenosis: Current Status," in the *Journal of the American Medical Women's Association,* "Fact Sheet on the Morning-After Pill," in the U.S. Senate Hearings on Quality of Health Care--Human Experimentation, Committee on Labor and Public Welfare, 93rd Congress; and "Afterthoughts on the Morning-After Pill" in *Ms. Magazine,* November 1973.